The Imperiled Economy
BOOK I
Macroeconomics From A Left Perspective

THE IMPERILED ECONOMY

BOOK I

MACROECONOMICS FROM A LEFT PERSPECTIVE

Edited by

Robert Cherry
Christine D'Onofrio
Cigdem Kurdas

Thomas R. Michl
Fred Moseley
Michele I. Naples

The Union for Radical Political Economics
New York

Production Editor: Bill James
Design and Production: Lorraine Press, Salt Lake City, Utah
Cover Art: Linda Briggs

Library of Congress Cataloguing-in-Publication Data

The Imperiled economy.
    Bibliography: p.
    Contents: bk. 1. Macroeconomics from a Left
Perspective.
    1. Macroeconomics.   2. United States — Economic
policy — 1981-   3. Marxian economics. Cherry,
Robert D., 1944-
HB172.5.154   1987   339.5'0973   87-34233

ISBN 0-9333 06-50-4(pbk.)

Published 1987 by The Union for Radical Political Economics URPE
122 West 27th Street, 10th Floor, New York, NY 10001

Printed in the United States of America

Acknowledgements

Several people have helped to make this book a reality. A generous grant from an anonymous donor via the Capp St. Foundation financed the major portion of production costs. Thank you to Michael Jacobs of the URPE National Office, and the URPE Steering Committee for their patient assistance, and to Bill Tabb for his early help in getting this project off the ground. We are grateful to many authors in this book as well as Arlene Geiger, Peter Albin and Raymond Majewski for their comments on various manuscripts. The timely publication of these books would not have been possible without the unstinting efforts of our production editor, Bill James, and of Pat Albers. The advice and assistance offered by Lorraine Press was invaluable. We also thank the authors, who shared the burden of a time-consuming project with tight deadlines. The views presented herein remain those of the authors alone and do not necessarily represent those of the editors or of URPE.

The Editorial Collective

Table of Contents

PART ONE

INTRODUCTION

1

The General Picture

CIGDEM KURDAS

In 1978 the Union for Radical Political Economics published a collection of readings titled *U.S. Capitalism in Crisis*. Since 1978 economic malaise has become chronic and radical analyses of crisis have advanced significantly. This book and its companion volume, *Through the Safety Net,* present a broad selection of recent studies on the nature and causes of the current economic impasse. Like the 1978 book, these are intended for use in undergraduate college courses. To this end various important time series are assembled in a statistical appendix. There is also a general bibliography, containing all references from the essays, at the end of the book.

Capitalist economies worldwide have faltered since the early seventies, and the United States is prominent among the troubled economies. In the 1960s the real value of goods and services produced by industrial nations grew annually by 5 percent. This growth rate fell to below 3.5 percent in the seventies, and going by the experience so far, it is below 2.5 percent for the eighties. All major industrial countries have been experiencing lower growth rates (Council of Economic Advisors 1987:104, 368). We are witnessing an ongoing slow-down that cannot be ascribed to external shocks and isolated incidents; judging by its persistence and spread, the reasons for the slowdown are deep-seated. It has become commonplace to point to the drooping growth rate, to burgeoning debts and bankruptcies, etc. and draw parallels with the 1920s. More and more observers are giving an affirmative answer to the question "Can another Great Depression happen"? Conventional economics still sees nothing but temporary dislocations that will sort themselves out more or less automatically if left alone. This book presents an alternative perspective, one that seeks to understand the logic of capitalistic growth. Looked at from this standpoint, the experience of the last decade becomes part of a historically evolving pattern, rather than the passing disturbance mainstream economists tend to see.[*]

The unemployment situation provides dramatic evidence of structural change in the economy. The highest annual civilian unemployment rate recorded for the sixties is 6.7 percent, the lowest unemployment was 3.5 percent. For the seventies the highest unemployment rate is 8.5 percent, the lowest 4.9 percent. In the eighties the highest civilian unemployment stands at 9.7 percent, and the rate barely went below 6 percent (Council of Economic Advisors 1987:285).[1] Orthodox economics sees this mainly as a result of changes in the composition of the labor force, due for example to the increasing participation of women — an unsubstantiated, indeed highly shaky explanation.[2] Such changes, it is claimed, have raised the "natural rate" of unemployment, so that joblessness at what is defined as "full" employment is higher than it used to be.

---

[*]Editors' Note: As this book was going to press, the financial panic and stock market collapse of October, 1987 was in progress. All the Chapters were completed well before these events, which serves to reinforce and illustrate the works of the authors.

As unemployment rose, real hourly earnings for those who do have jobs fell. Whereas throughout the sixties workers' hourly earnings in real terms had grown consistently year by year, in the seventies they fell in some years and increased at less than 1 percent in other years (Council of Economic Advisors 1987:292). From 1980 to 1986, real hourly earnings fell in four out of a total of seven years. Rounding out the bleak picture of high unemployment and low earnings, poverty became more widespread. The percentage of individuals living below the poverty level had fallen continuously through the sixties. In 1979 it stood at 11.7 percent of total population. By 1983 it had risen to 15.2 percent. It was slightly lower in 1985, but still higher than it had been through the previous decade (Council of Economic Advisors 1987:278). The actual number of people living in poverty, as officially defined, was 35.3 million in 1983, 33.1 million in 1985.

For the United States, the years from 1982 to 1986 have also been marked by a huge trade deficit; an unusual phenomenon for this country. In these four years the deficit went up to $160 billion in 1986. The United States is becoming the world's largest debtor. Felix Rohatyn (1987), the well-known investment banker and market observer, writes: "The Untied States today is headed for a financial and economic crisis," a crisis that will be coming upon a very fragile international finance structure. Less Developed Country debt now stands at more than $1 trillion.

In spite of these developments, mainstream thought by and large takes a complacent view of the economic picture, and preaches the virtues of automatic market forces. Unimpeded adjustments of prices, wages, interest rates and currency values are expected to boost investment, to shrink the trade deficit, and push the economy to full employment. According to this view the problems are due to outside shocks, such as the OPEC oil price hikes, or have been inflicted upon an essentially smooth-functioning market economy by bungling public policy makers. Typically, most of the problems are attributed to the federal budget deficit. The budget deficit, and public debt, have indeed reached unprecedented sizes. But the question, ignored by the mainstream, is whether this is cause or effect. Viewed simply as a political mistake, the deficit appears as an external instigator of economic trouble. Alternatively seen as a response to conflicts and paradoxes inherent in the economic system itself, the deficit is a symptom, and perhaps a short-term solution. Radical economics looks for the internal roots of such phenomena as unemployment, debt, trade and budget deficits, rather than attributing them to exogenous factors.

The question of productivity illustrates the conservative position. Slower Gross National Product growth reflects the slowdown of productivity growth. The Council of Economic Advisors emphasizes that "productivity growth is the main determinant of the economy's long-run capacity to generate increases in real living standards" (Council of Economic Advisors 1987:45). Labor productivity grew at a robust average annual rate of 2.8 percent from 1948 to 1973 in the United States. This rate fell dramatically in the seventies and eighties, it now averages around 1 percent a year. What is behind the decline? In the same *Economic Report of the President* the Council (1987:47) concedes that "a large portion of the decline in productivity growth remains unexplained." Nevertheless, the administration is firm in its belief that a good way to strengthen productivity is to do away with "unnecessary" regulation. Thus, regulations designed to reduce hazards from consumer products, to ensure workplace safety, and others concerned with controlling environmental damage, have been and may continue to be weakened. Again, automatic market mechanisms are supposed to be sufficient to minimize such hazards. Whether or not removing safeguards will help boost productivity and competitiveness is not clear. Another outcome however is: we will be obliged to live in a riskier world. The Occupational Safety & Health Act and the Food & Drug Administration rulings are being attacked, worker compensation for job injuries questioned, pollution control criticized as producing insufficient benefits to meet its costs.[3] Deregulation and other policies made work, consumption, and even breathing more dangerous.

In the past, capitalist economies have emerged from economic crises substantially altered. New structures came into being in response to the conflicts and problems which could not be resolved with existing arrangements. For example, the 1930s Great Depression left in its wake increased state participation in the economy. We are again going through a period of change, the existing institutions are unable to deal with the stalling growth engine. Policies which worked in the fifties and sixties, institutions which used to be bulwarks of a stable, growth-oriented economy are no longer effective. Monetary policy is unreliable (Council of Economic Advisors 1987:63). The bulging federal budget is not flexible enough to be used in pursuing macroeconomic goals. The over-extended banking system is in a precarious state. The number of "problem banks," according to the U.S. Federal Deposit Insurance Corporation, went from 368 in 1977 to 1,140 in 1985 (U.S. Department of Commerce 1987:483). Industrial labor unions, once successful in winning better pay and work conditions, have lost ground. At the international level, there are no effective arrangements to deal with trade imbalances. Policy makers are tottering between free trade ideology and half-hearted protectionism. To complicate matters even further, manufacturing industries are re-locating on a global scale, and moving away from the United States.

Getting back on to a successful growth path may necessitate changes on several fronts, and the contours of the new organizations, policies and relationships are not even clear yet. At any rate, these may very well turn out to foster further accumulation of capital at the expense of the population at large, as in the case of looser environmental safety standards. Our world is being re-made, and not necessarily to our advantage. What we can do is to demand a say in the re-making, and for this we need to understand the causes and nature of the breakdowns in capitalist growth. The essays in this volume point the way to such an understanding. Taken together they help make sense of shifts not only in the economic landscape, but in the political and social environment as well.

Radical explanations of crisis fall into three broad categories. The traditional Marxian explanation focuses on technological change and its impact on profits. By contrast, according to the stagnationist school, restricted aggregate demand is responsible for the dwindling growth rate. Another approach stresses the role of class conflict in the accumulation process; a more recent version of this centers around the idea of social structures of accumulation. Part II, on theories of crisis, contains papers representing all three approaches. The next section then provides empirical perspectives on key variables, including the rate of profit. Part IV, on the international aspects of the crisis, tackles such issues as the world debt and protectionism. Finally, Part V looks at state policies, both fiscal and monetary, and evaluates the conservative measures of the 1980s.

NOTES

1. Total, as opposed to civilian, unemployment is slightly lower.
2. Lawrence H. Summers (1986:339–384) shows that this explanation does not hold up empirically.
3. Chapter 6 of the *Economic Report* (1987) concludes: ''In many cases, government control of risk is neither efficient nor effective. Markets accommodate individual preferences for avoiding risk''... (p. 207).

2

Theories of Unemployment

ROBERT CHERRY

All macroeconomic models assess the ability of capitalism to maintain full employment. Conservative models suggest that the self-regulating properties of labor markets should be relied upon to guarantee full employment. Moreover, these models often imply that well-meaning government policies are likely to have serious long-term negative consequences even when they appear to have some short-run benefits.

Keynesian models have historically provided the theoretical underpinnings for activist macro-policies. All Keynesian models assume that labor markets operate imperfectly and if left to themselves, they would not equilbrate quickly; unemployment would persist. However, there has always been two distinct strains within the Keynesian tradition. One group, sometimes called "prime-pumping" or liberal Keynesians, believe government manipulation of aggregate demand would be sufficient to overcome market imperfections. This group has been very influential in the United States, always providing the chief economic advisors to Democratic presidents. The other group, sometimes labeled post-Keynesians, contend that market rigidities are too widespread to be overcome by simple demand management. These economists contend that government planning, particularly of the distribution of income, is necessary if long-term stable growth is desired. Since the mid-1970s liberal Keynesians have moved closer to the conservative view, possibly in an attempt to maintain their influence within the Democratic Party. This increased differences between the two groups of Keynesians.

This paper will detail the structure of conservative and liberal Keynesian theories of unemployment. It will demonstrate that both viewpoints offer explanations of the labor market which are either inadequate or incorrect. More importantly, both viewpoints rationalize the inability of capitalist economies to provide sufficient jobs for everyone who desires employment. The paper will present alternative radical views which provide a background for subsequent papers in this reader.

CONSERVATIVE VIEWS

Conservatives assume that all markets are self-regulating: prices will adjust quickly to bring about an equilibrium between supply and demand. In the labor market, this implies that if there is deficient demand — involuntary unemployment — wage rates will adjust until demand equals supply. Since there are already sufficient jobs available, neither government fiscal nor monetary policies is capable of reducing this "natural" unemployment rate. Their only impact would be to shift the distribution of employment between private and government-produced goods or between capital and consumer goods. When the supply of, and demand for, jobs equilibriate, there still will be individuals counted by the government as unemployment; economists label this as the "natural" rate of unemployment.

Voluntary Unemployment

Conservatives have developed job search theories to explain why unemployment exists even when there are sufficient jobs for all those seeking employment. Due to a lack of complete information, instantaneous matching of jobs and workers is impossible. As a result, individuals job search before accepting available jobs. These individuals weigh the cost to them of additional unemployment against the expected benefits from further job search. Since these individuals are engaged in active job search, the government counts them as unemployed even though they could have accepted an available job. Conservatives contend that government transfer payments, by lowering the cost of unemployment, increase the length of time individuals will continue to search in the hopes of finding a better job than they have already been offered.

Conservatives contend that the rising national unemployment rate — from 4 percent in the late 1960s to 7 percent by the late 1970s — reflected the growth in the size of the work force comprised of groups (married women and youth) who had weak labor force attachment or found government subsidies (welfare and unemployment insurance) preferrable to continuous employment. Conservatives also contend that general prosperity and the growth of multi-wage earning households has influenced job search behavior.

In the past, when unemployment meant households lost their entire income, many individuals were forced to accept any available job. This was especially true when households had little savings and no access to short-term credit at reasonable rates. In contrast, the growth of multi-wage earning households implies that unemployment will not cause households to lose their income so that individuals can afford to search longer. In addition, households now have more assets and greater access to short-term credit than ever before, making it possible for individuals to maintain living standards without being forced to accept jobs they consider undesirable. From this perspective, a rising "natural" rate reflects prosperity — individuals can "afford" to remain unemployed longer!

According to conservatives, if some groups experience low employment rates or unstable employment, it must reflect their preferences. For example, conservatives suggest that due to personal preferences, black youth have low employment rates. Feldstein and Ellwood (1982) reject the view that black youth employment difficulties reflect an inability to find jobs. They cite data which indicates that few black youth suffer long spells of unemployment. They characterize the small group who do experience long-term difficulties as those without education or proper cultural backgrounds. Indeed, Feldstein and Ellwood contend that within this group, nonemployment reflects their choice to live at home rather than work. Others contend that black youths are unwilling to accept employment because this would cause them to lose welfare and other income transfers.

Feldstein (1973) has also claimed that unemployment among low-wage working adults "cannot be solved by increasing aggregate demand in order to create more jobs. There is no evidence of a shortage of jobs for this group." He stressed that unemployment insurance was a subsidy to idleness, especially for married women with working husbands. He estimated that these women could obtain almost the same net income from unemployment insurance as from working.

Feldstein claimed that not only did unemployment insurance provide an incentive for women to seek unstable employment, it provides an incentive for firms to organize production to serve these preferences. Firms realize that they could pay *lower* wages if they organized production in a discontinuous rather than continuous fashion. From this perspective, the presence of women working at jobs which pay low wages and have unstable working conditions is a result of their preferences rather than their exploitation.

Ineffectiveness of Government Stabilization Policies

Conservatives believe that government stabilization policy can be costly: attempts to lower unemployment rates would generate higher inflation rates and lower savings rates. However, sometimes conservatives admit that the adjustment process to market clearing wages is imperfect. This would seem to indicate that government stabilization policy — temporary macroeconomic stimuli — could be effective at increasing the speed by which the economy reestablishes full employment. However, conservatives reject stabilization policy for a number of reasons.

First, conservatives suggest that the inability of wages to adjust rapidly to market clearing levels often reflects the adverse effects of certain government policies: minimum wage legislation and support of unions. Since these policies limit the ability of wages to be reduced, unemployment in covered labor markets persists when labor demand is deficient. Eventually, workers will shift out of unionized labor markets and markets covered by minimum wage requirements so that the unemployment effects will be mitigated. Wages in the non-unionized and uncovered sectors will decline until these displaced workers are employed. However, since the adjustment process is prolonged, the period of less than full employment would be extended.

Second, conservatives contend that stabilization policies may not be effective. If the stabilization policy chosen is temporary tax cuts then the increases in disposable income would be temporary. According to Milton Friedman's permanent income hypothesis, households will adjust consumer spending only if there is a permanent change in their disposable income so that temporary tax changes would not stimulate spending.

Conservatives also believe government discretionary spending is ineffective. Discretionary spending requires that this would require the gathering of information, a legislative process, and implementation procedures. Thus there would be an extensive time lag between the beginning of a downturn and the implementation of government spending stimuli. Moreover since the projected impact reflects an estimate of the size of the income multiplier, the effects are not known with perfect foresight; the economy could overshoot or undershoot targets. Thus, discretionary fiscal policy may very well have more potential problems than if government relied upon self-regulating mechanisms.

Many of these time lags and information inadequacies would be eliminated if government stabilization policies could follow institutionalized rules rather than require discretionary legislation. Indeed, government unemployment insurance is but one example of *automatic* stabilizers. However, conservatives believe that even automatic stabilizers would be ineffective. Rational expectations models appear to demonstrate that individuals are able to neutralize the anticipated impacts of government spending rules. For example, if the public was aware that in response to an economic downturn federal spending would be increased, they would have already adjusted their spending, investment, and savings decisions to take into account the impact of government stabilization policies. In this case, the fiscal stimuli would not have any further effect on private sector decisions. As a result, government stabilization policy can only be effective if it is hidden from the public; only if the government "fools" the people.

MAINSTREAM LIBERAL VIEWS

Liberal Keynesian economists believe that stabilization policies do not suffer the limitations conservatives stress and that the costs associated with relying upon self-regulating mechanisms are greater than conservatives envision. Liberal Keynesians also believe that various *microeconomic* policies can help reduce long-term employment problems.

Labor Market Adjustments

Liberal Keynesians note that there are substantial impediments to the downward adjustment of wages other than minimum wage legislation or unions. Skill requirements make it difficult for workers to adjust rapidly to changing labor demand. Even if there is an excess demand for certain types of workers and an excess supply of other types of workers, imbalances may not correct due to differences in skills between the two groups. Similarly, if labor demand increases in one area while unemployed workers reside in other areas, imbalances will persist in the absence of government policies. Thus, skill and locational mismatches limit the effectiveness of self-regulating mechanisms.

The usual explanation given for the rapid decline of prices in the presence of excess supply is that suppliers will run sales on unsold merchandise and buyers would seek out the lowest possible price. Liberal Keynesians do not believe this is realistic in many labor markets. They cite cultural factors which limit the degree to which workers can compete among themselves for available jobs. Workers look unfavorably when others attempt to take their jobs away by offering to work at lower wages. Thus even when firms are unconstrained by union or government regulations, "acceptable" behavior codes limit their ability to fire employees in order to hire others at lower wage rates.

Custom also limits the ability of firms to reduce wages of current employees. Workers become accustomed to a certain living standard and will fight fiercely against any attempt to undermine it. Wages also indicate the relative standing of individuals within society so that workers are concerned with the way their salaries compare to other reference groups. Liberal Keynesians suggest that it is extremely difficult to upset wage contours — patterns which describe the wage differentials among workers — even when deficient labor demand for certain groups of workers persists.

Liberal Keynesians also emphasize that firms may have other reasons not to fire workers during periods of excess labor supply. Firms fear that when they would be rehiring during upturns, their most productive laid-off workers may have found other jobs. Thus, for career oriented workers, firms that have the most temporary layoffs will over time have the least productive workers within the industry. As a result, firms will have an economic incentive to maintain employment above production requirements during downturns in order to guarantee the long-term employment of their most skilled workers. Economists characterize this as "labor hoarding."

Firms have additional reasons to favor employment stability even when short-term considerations indicate lay offs and wage reductions. Many firms provide on-the-job training to workers which is costly. During the training period, firms pay workers more than their productive worth but expect to recoup their outlays over the subsequent tenure of trained workers. By maintaining employment despite reduced production requirements, trained workers gain employment security and would be more likely to remain with the firm after obtaining the necessary on-the-job training.

Empirical Disagreements

If only a small wage decline was necessary to generate a substantial increase in labor demand then government should encourage both workers and firms to accept wage declines and temporary layoffs. The modest costs to individual workers and/or firms would be more than compensated for by the increased overall efficiency of labor markets. Indeed, many conservatives believe that labor demand elasticities are large enough to warrant this approach. However, liberal Keynesians (Solow 1980) have little faith in the large elasticity estimates conservatives generate from aggregate production functions. Instead, they emphasize direct labor demand elasticity estimates which are quite low. According to these estimates, workers could eliminate unemployment only by accepting dramatically lower wages — wages which would reduce significantly their yearly income. Even if self-regulating mechanisms generate sufficient jobs, we would be replacing unemployment with increased poverty and dramatically lower living standards.

Liberal Keynesians believe empirical evidence supports the view that individuals form their expectations from past observations rather than by predicting future impacts of anticipated policies. Besides empirical shortcomings, liberal Keynesians believe rational expectations models are inconsistent with optimal information models, rely on ad hoc asymmetric assumptions, and have difficulty incorporating important aspects of the capitalist production process. If individuals form their expectations based upon past observations then they will not be able to quickly adjust to economic fluctuations. Moreover, formal and informal contractual obligations are not easy to adjust in the shortrun so that wage and employment decisions can only respond with contract expirations. Since the private sector can only respond slowly to economic fluctuations, stabilization policies can be effective.

Macro-Policy Limitations

We have seen that liberal Keynesians believe unemployment can persist longer and believe stabilization can be much more effective than conservatives think. While they sometimes use other terms, such as the nonacceleration rate, they too believe microeconomic factors limit the extent to which these policies can permanently reduce unemployment. Even when it appears that aggregate demand stimuli lower unemployment rates below the "natural" rate, liberal Keynesians do not favor such policies. They argue that large long-term costs from increased inflation and budget deficits outweigh any small employment benefits.

Some liberal Keynesians even agree with conservative claims that lower unemployment rates can not be maintained. They claim that as a result of the inability of workers to adjust their wages quickly, if a spending stimuli causes an unanticipated price increase, real wages will decline. As a result, firms expand their production. However, once workers are able to adjust their money wages, production returns to its previous level and the "natural" rate is reestablished. Thus, the spending expansion causes inflation and budget deficits to rise but does not even permanently lower unemployment rates.

Liberal Keynesians reject the notion that government transfer programs and general prosperity have undermined work ethics. However, they believe that skill and locational mismatches have caused the "natural" rate to increase. Liberal Keynesians generally do not believe macro-policies can reduce these mismatches. Instead, they recommend government micro-policies: skill development programs to enable more workers to meet rising entry-level skill requirements and regional planning to eliminate locational imbalances.

CRITIQUES OF MAINSTREAM VIEWS

Mainstream models contend that factors on the supply side — workers' skills, motivation, and locational preferences — are responsible for the "natural" rate of unemployment. Critics contend there are *few* supply-side impediments to reducing unemployment, if the government has the will to do so. Michael Piore (1978) notes: "Never in the post-war period has the government been unsuccessful when it has made an effort to reduce unemployment. On several occasions, unemployment has fallen below the government target." According to Piore, government reluctance to reduce unemployment has been rationalized by claiming that priority must be given to balancing the budget and/or reducing inflation. Thus, critics claim constraints on aggregate demand rather than labor supply are responsible for high unemployment.

Unemployment Problems

Critics contend that mainstream economists underestimate the employment difficulties which exist even when the economy is close to its "natural" rate. They note that official measures ignore discouraged workers and those who are involuntarily part-time employed. If adjustments are made for those who desire but do not have full-time jobs, then the unemployment rate would be substantially higher.

Critics also reject the ease with which some mainstream economists minimize the seriousness of the employment problems women and blacks experience. Feldstein and Ellwood (1982) claim that except for a small group, black youth experience only short spells of unemployment. Unemployment spells are short because most youth do not engage in active job search and drop out of the labor force when not employed. Clark and Summers contend that a more appropriate measure would be the length of time between jobs. They find that the median time for black youth is over six months.

Critics also do not believe skill or locational mismatches have much to do with black employment difficulties. Bennett Harrison (1972) found that the unemployment rate was the same for inner-city and suburban blacks. Thus, locating blacks closer to the suburban employment expansion would have little impact on black unemployment rates. Freeman and Medoff (1982) point out that employment problems are widespread among black youth. They note that in 1978 (when unemployment was 6 percent) over 21 percent of all out-of-school black males, aged 20–24 years old, had no employment in the previous twelve months; up from 13 percent seven years earlier.

Feldstein's (1973) image of women in the labor force — individuals willing to trade-off continuous employment at higher wages for unemployment insurance and lower wage discontinuous employment — makes little sense today. Since 1965, rising female labor force participation rates have been associated with declining female turnover rates; women are more permanent members of the work force. This undermines claims that females seek discontinuous employment. Critics (Lloyd and Neimi 1979) also note that Feldstein, by ignoring potentials for advancement and fringe benefits, grossly underestimates the opportunity costs to married women on unemployment insurance. Finally, European data (Kaufman 1978) indicates that the growth in female labor force participation need not result in higher unemployment rates. Thus, there is little reason to accept natural rate explanations for rising United States unemployment during the 1970s.

Inflation and Budgetary Considerations

Critics believe that the costs of budget deficits and inflation are exaggerated by mainstream economists. Arguments often draw an analogy with private business to demonstrate that persistent deficits are dangerous. This comparison makes sense only if we distinguish between government spending on present consumption from spending on capital goods. We find no problem when a company borrows heavily to finance a worthwhile capital spending project; its revenues would grow fast enough to offset its higher debt servicing costs. We should analyze the government's borrowing in a similar fashion rather than simply assuming that additional debt is bad.

If a deficit was generated by spending on capital goods and capital infrastructure, it would increase the nation's productive capacity and hence the future income potentials of households. In this case, the growth of interest payments — to finance the debt — would be offset by the income growth of households. If this happened then there would be no increase in the debt burden on households even if the government continued to run deficits. Only if the government used funds for present consumption would there be a potential danger; debt would be increasing while earning potentials would be unchanged.

Even if the deficit grows as a result of government spending on present consumption, there is no automatic danger. As long as the deficit is domestically held, it will reflect transfer payment among United States citizens. The rise in tax payments necessary to service the debt will be exactly offset by the rise in interest earnings by government bond holders. Only if the debt is increasingly held by foreigners would a rising debt cause a serious outflow of funds.

Some economists contend that deficits cause spending to increase faster than the ability of society to produce goods. This line of reasoning may make sense if the economy was full, utilizing its productive resources. However, if idle inputs are present then there is no reason why deficits should be associated with inflation. Indeed, even if it would be inflationary this should be avoided only if we believe the costs from rising price levels is significant.

Just as with deficits, critics contend that inflation concerns are based on myths and incomplete analyses. Inflation reflects rising prices. But since GNP accounts indicate that total income must be equal to purchases, total income must rise as rapidly as prices. Theoretically, everyone's income could rise just as fast as the general price level in which case no one would have their real income affected by inflation. It is certainly possible that inflation has distributional impacts; raising some groups' incomes faster than the inflation rate while other groups' income rises at a slower rate. In this case, the *unanticipated* impact of inflation generates winners and losers.

Let us identify these winners and losers. In general, banks have historically lost when there was a rise in inflation rates. They tend to be net creditors and *unanticipated* increases in inflation rates enable debtors to payback loans with cheaper money. For example, the 1979 doubling of oil prices created difficulties for banks. They had negotiated long-term loans at very low fixed rates and now had to pay much higher rates for funds they sought. Not surprisingly, banking interests led the fight against inflation even when it meant reducing aggregate demand and raising unemployment rates. It is unclear that workers had the same interest in fighting inflation.

Many believe that everyone benefits from lower inflation since wage increases are no longer eaten away by higher prices. However, this assumes workers could continue to receive 10–15 percent wage increases while inflation remains low. This impossibility became clear when workers found that declining inflation rates were followed by declining wage increases. Moreover, under the guise of fighting inflation, governments often reduce their subsidies on consumer goods, further reducing workers' real income. Though newspapers applauded the "success" of the Israeli and Argentine governments in stemming inflation, they generally neglected to mention that in both countries the result was a dramatic decline of workers' real incomes; it was the bankers and other creditors who were the beneficiaries.

RADICAL VIEWS

Both post-Keynesian and radical economists believe that concerns for stemming inflation or balancing federal budgets are false and the economic problems faced by those not employed are serious. However, they disagree as to the reason why government officials do not pursue full-employment policies. Post-Keynesians general believe that ideological concerns and capitalist shortsightedness keep politicians and their corporate backers from accepting the benefits from government planning. These economists hope that in the long run these subjective obstacles will be overcome as the benefits from government policies will become compelling. In contrast, radicals believe unemployment persists because it serves the financial and political interests of capitalists.

Radicals contend that the reserve army thesis provides the foundation for explaining the lack of commitment to full-employment policies. This thesis contends that certain subgroups in society benefit from the unemployment of others and will attempt to subvert full-employment policies. Reserve army theories vary as to the nature of benefits (economic versus noneconomic) and as to the subgroups benefitting (economic elites versus high-wage workers).

Michal Kalecki and Michael Piore maintain that the primary function of unemployment is to support political and social stability. Kalecki (1971:140–141) claims that since full employment undermines labor discipline and the social position of management, capitalists accept "unemployment as an integral part of the normal capitalist system." Piore (1978) suggests that government reluctance to pursue full-employment objectives derives from the belief that such policies would create rising expectations among workers. Since these expectations cannot be met, the result would be unrest, which would lead to social and political instability.

Most reserve army theories (Gurley 1971; Boddy and Crotty 1975) emphasize direct economic benefits. Many radicals contend that the principal beneficiaries are capitalists. As a result of unemployment, workers must adapt to the objectives of firms. For those capitalists who employ lower-skilled workers where turnover has little cost, the presence of a reserve army enables them to lower wages. However, even among capitalists who do not directly hire this type of labor, financial benefits accrue. Capitalist can threaten their high-wage workers with replacement; more likely the firm may even pay these workers decent wages but expect them to work long hours and accommodate their lifestyles to the needs of the company. These workers will realize how "lucky" they are to have good jobs and accept the company's perogatives as "normal."

Firms which do not directly employ low-wage labor may also benefit through their purchases from companies that do. Indeed, some companies may shift part of their production to these secondary employers in order to gain the benefits from lower costs without having to employ an exploited work force. Even within high-wage occupations, firms can benefit by being able to set up differential promotion tracks: women and blacks will be in the lower promotion track but will remain "good" workers because their alternatives could be much worse.

While some high-wage workers may be harmed by the reserve army, Herbert Gans and Frances Piven and Robert Cloward believe that many benefit. In summarizing the history of social welfare legislation, Piven and Cloward (1971) note that programs have always been cut back whenever employers claimed that labor shortages would result. Gans (1967) notes that when unemployment rates are low, privileged classes complain about a "servant problem."

Radicals contend that political factors have been responsible for changes in the size of the industrial reserve army. They suggest that after World War II, the Western industrialized nations were able to sustain relatively low unemployment rates due to social contracts between organized labor and the dominant section of big capital. In the United States, organized labor, after purging leftwing elements, agreed to maintain labor discipline and refrain from actions that threaten profitability, management perogatives, and political stability. Big capital agreed to maintain economic growth and low unemployment rates in the unionized sectors.

Increased unemployment during the 1970s reflected a breakdown of these social contracts. Organized labor was unable to fulfill its part of the contract due to its declining influence among workers. Capital was unable to fulfill its part of the contract due to the intensification of foreign competition, which forced a slowdown in the growth rates of real wages. The rising influence of disenfranchised groups of workers and capitalists hastened the breakdown of social contracts. Since the 1950s, women and blacks have demanded a greater share of the economic pie, while medium sized and newer large firms began to compete for a greater share of economic and political power. The growth of international competition has limited the perogatives of United States capitalists still further. Therefore, even if organized labor and big capital desired the maintenance of social contracts, disenfranchised workers and increased competition would have hindered their implementation.

For all of these reasons, capitalist policies during the 1980s have run counter to the liberal Keynesian view. Firms have been willing to "sacrifice" long-term stable relationships in order to cutback on labor costs. Firms have broken unions, demanded givebacks, and replaced high-wage labor with cheap labor in nonunion plants (outsourcing). The government has also undertaken policies to facilitate the lowering of wages: the ability to collect unemployment insurance was limited; welfare guarantees have not kept pace with inflation; and the minimum wage has been frozen at $3.35/hour for seven years. Changes in these policies had certain characteristics which reflected the style of the Reagan Administration. However, radicals stress that these policies began during the Carter years and were supported by the capitalist class in an attempt to improve profitability and reinstitute social acceptance of management perogatives.

CONCLUDING REMARKS

Articles in this book will explore various aspects of the growing problems capitalists faced beginning in the 1970s and the effectiveness of the various strategies undertaken. Many of these articles offer contrasting and sometimes conflicting assessments. However, all begin from the same perspective: capitalism can only be understood as a system which must maintain political and economic control in the hands of capitalists whose interests and objectives are often in conflict with the interests and objectives of working people. All these articles assume that capitalism is incapable of maintaining full employment unless the powers and perogatives of capitalists are severely restrained.

PART TWO

THEORETICAL PERSPECTIVES

3

An Introduction to Radical Theories of Economic Crisis

JAMES N. DEVINE

INTRODUCTION

On April 20, 1987, after several years of alleged economic recovery, a *Business Week*'s "special report" on the United States economy pointed to faltering real growth, falling living standards, widening income inequalities, and the increasing debts of consumers, corporations, and the government. Notable is its title: "Can America Compete"? Gone are the days when the United States could stand aloof from the world economy and enjoy nationally-based prosperity. The world is no longer dominated by the economic might of the United States. Rather, we see intense international competition and uncertainty. In December 1986, looking from another angle, the Third World business magazine *South* warned us to "Stand by for the Crash" as the United States responds to its increasing debt to the rest of the world by cutting its imports and expanding its exports, intensifying and widening the current world depression. To banker Felix Rohatyn (1987:3), the question is, not if "a financial and economic crisis" will occur but "when and how," *despite* some short-term signs of prosperity.

To understand the predicament of the last fifteen years, to go beyond the superficial coverage of the business press, we must first move to a more theoretical level. Radical (or leftist) economists use several theories to analyze the social and economic system, including Marxian, feminist, anti-racist, Keynesian, and institutionalist ideas. But to decipher the quagmire of the 1970s and 1980s, it is Karl Marx who promises insights into "the laws of motion" of capitalism (1967a:10).

This paper surveys both Marxian crisis theory and modern leftist contributions to our understanding of how economic disaster can result from the workings of capitalism. Rather than presenting a rigorous analysis of the impasse of the late 1980s, however, this paper presents some theoretical perspectives. For more down to earth analyses of the current economic bind, see the other articles in this volume.

Before starting with theory, "crisis" must be defined. To Marxists, a crisis is a major and threatening disruption of the growth of a social and economic system, usually generated by that system itself. There are two main types. First, there are short-term or cyclical crises, such as the 1980 and 1981–82 recessions. Second, there are long-term or structural crises — often leading to deep political and social stalemates — such as the Great Depression of the 1930s and the Great Stagflation of the 1970s and its aftermath, the shaky "recovery" of the Reagan years. These will be called "impasses" below.

To analyze both short-term crises and impasses, we start with the abstract and work back to the real world of the late 1980s. This corresponds to a movement from the classical works of Marx to recent research. After a bird's eye view of Marxian crisis theory, our survey turns to the basic process of capitalist growth, the forces leading to its disruption, and the ways in which this trauma can occur.

Marx never presented a complete and unified theory of economic crises and impasses. Instead we see an often productive debate between three main schools of leftist political economy, which is discussed next. Each of the schools presents a distinct view of the forces causing impasses and long-term prosperity. This brings us back to the current quagmire of United States and world capitalism.

Two sections on vital facets of leftist macroeconomics end this survey. First, the monetary and fiscal dimensions of economic crises are discussed, making clear the limits to government macroeconomic policy. Second, the causes of inflation and stagflation are probed. These theories are useful to partisans of all schools and to the skeptical or uncommitted.

MARXIAN CRISIS THEORY: AN OVERVIEW

Marx's view of history and the internal contradictions of economic modes of production are the basis of crisis theory.[1] A "mode of production" combines forces of production and social relations of production. The former consist of the tools, machines, and buildings used in production, plus scientific and technological knowledge and the skills of working people. On the other hand, the production relations are institutions, seen in laws and property rights, organizing production — including a surplus above subsistence needs.[1] For Marx, crises arise because a mode of production generates forces of production that clash with existing relations of production (1973:749).

Crises under capitalism differ from those of other modes of production (ancient slavery, feudalism, and so forth). Feudalism, the system that preceded capitalism in Europe, suffered from agricultural underproduction (i.e., crop failure). Under feudal serfdom, neither the tillers of the soil nor the lords had much incentive to improve agricultural technology. Crises thus arose because food supplies did not grow as fast as the population (Brenner 1976). Capitalism, on the other hand, is an expansive, always-changing, and disruptive system. "All that is solid melts into air" under the onslaught of the capitalist juggernaut.[3] To Marx, capitalism does not stagnate like feudalism, but expands or accumulates too much for its own good.

The possibility of crisis arises first from the use of money, rather than barter, in exchange. This allows purchases and sales to be separated in time and space. Marx thus rejected Say's "law" which claimed that, on average, all which was supplied would be purchased (Marx 1967a:114n). Unlike feudalism, capitalism can suffer from *over*production: no matter how a crisis starts, producers find themselves unable to sell as much as they have produced and still receive the profits they crave. Because capitalism is dominated by production for profit rather than for use, consumers are denied access to useful and even necessary goods when production or sale is unprofitable.

The "anarchy of production," the fact that capitalist growth is unplanned, also encourages crises. For capitalism to grow harmoniously, the different sectors must expand in unison, in proportion. But no "invisible hand" exists to guide capitalists to expand their operations in step. So "disproportionalities" arise among sectors (Marx 1967b: Chaps. 20, 21). This makes crises normal to the capitalist system.

However, Marx argued that both the use of money and the anarchy of production explain only the possibility of crisis, not the actual crisis. Disproportionalities are *results* rather than causes. So deeper analysis is needed. In the *Communist Manifesto,* Marx and Engels blamed crises on "too much civilization, too much means of subsistence, too much industry, too much commerce'' (quoted in Tucker 1978:478). In a word, crises arise from *over-accumulation*: capitalism's failure is based on its previous success. Further, over-accumulation results as capitalism drives itself against barriers of its own creation, not only those imposed by nature. ''The *true barrier* of capitalist production is *capital itself*'' (Marx 1967c:250, his emphasis). This typically creates imbalances that hurt the profitability of production, slowing accumulation. Then disproportionalities arise and spread, causing a general collapse. Production and employment fall drastically.

CAPITALIST ACCUMULATION AND CRISIS

Now we investigate capitalism in more detail, to understand the accumulation process, the rate of profit, and the ways in which accumulation can hurt the profit rate. This gives us some basic ideas on short-term crises and building blocks for the next section.

Marx used the following ''circuit of capital'' diagram to examine a typical capitalist process of spending money to make more money (1967b: Chaps. 1–4):

$$M - C \ (LP, \ RM, \ MP) \ldots P \ldots C' - M + S$$

At the start of this production-realization chain, the capitalist puts out money (M) to buy the commodity inputs for production (C): labor-power (the ability to work, LP), raw materials (RM), and means of production (factories, machinery, and tools, MP). Next, in production (P), labor uses the MP to transform the RM into new commodities (C'), which are then owned by the capitalist. In this phase, some of the capitalist's money is usually tied up for a long time as ''fixed capital,'' as with machinery and factories. The capitalist's goal is to sell the new product C' and to realize not only the initial M but an extra amount (S).

To Marx, the bonus S is surplus value: it is value that workers create beyond that needed to pay for their ability to work (their labor-power). Further, surplus value is the fount of total profit income (industrial and commercial profit, interest, and rent). The S can be positive because workers have no way to earn their livelihood but to work for the capitalists. The ''reserve army'' of unemployed workers usually threatens and competes with employed workers, so that wages are kept low enough to allow the production of S. Surplus value is the basis not only for exalted capitalist living-standards but for accumulation, i.e., expansion of their capital (LP, MP, RM). This increases their capacity to acquire surplus value. It also draws more and more of the world into the capitalist orbit.

Because capitalism is not a simple and peaceful system of small vendors (as seen in mainstream economics), accumulation can be driven to break the production-realization chain. The system suffers from two basic tensions. First, class antagonism wracks the system, since the extraction of surplus value creates enmity between classes, especially in production. Second, competition is a battle, a continual jockeying for position among businesses. No firm can keep a protected position for long. This contest imposes ''coercive laws'' on capitalists, compelling them ''to keep extending [their] capital in order to preserve it'' (Marx 1967a:592). Because of the threat to their survival, accumulation is not voluntary, unless capitalists are willing to abandon their privileges. This can drive them into crises despite all intentions.

The crisis occurs when this forced accumulation produces over-accumulation, breaking the production-realization chain and depressing profit rates. Since profits are the main source of accumulation funds and the profit rate gives capitalists the incentive to invest, profitability's fall eventually means slower accumulation and, thus, a recession.

Before returning to the breaking chain, we examine the profit rate (r).[4] Since capitalists tie up their money for long periods in fixed capital, they care about the ratio of profit income (S) to the fixed capital (K):

$$r = S/K = (S/Y) \ (Y/Z)/(K/Z)$$

where S/Y is the share of profits in total income (Y). This ratio is directly linked to Marx's "rate of surplus-value." Second, Y/Z is the rate of capacity utilization, i.e., the ratio between actual output and income (Y) and what would be produced if capitalists were using all of their fixed capital or capacity (Z). Finally, K/Z is the ratio of the fixed capital to full-capacity output. This is directly related to Marx's "organic composition of capital," measuring the degree to which capitalists use fixed capital.

Following the lead of Weisskopf, Bowles and Gordon's article below, if we bring in the roles of foreign trade and government tax policies, then we conclude that the profit rate can be hurt by not only (1) a falling profit share of income (S/Y), (2) a falling rate of capacity utilization (Y/Z), or (3) a rising fixed capital-to-capacity ratio (K/Z) as indicated by the equation above but also, (4) a falling terms of trade (United States export prices divided by import prices) or, (5) a rising tax burden on profits. All but the last of these fit with Marx's original analysis of breaking links in the circuit of capital.

The first weak link in the production-realization chain is at M − C: capitalism can expand "too much" compared to labor-power supplies, causing wages to rise faster than labor productivity (output per worker) (see Marx 1967a: Chap. 25, sect. 1). This over-accumulation can also affect production (P): the discipline imposed by the reserve army of unemployed workers is sapped so that employed workers lose some of the incentive to labor and to produce surplus value. This "wage squeeze" depresses the rate of surplus value and the income share of profits (S/Y). If the other variables do not change, the profit rate falls. A main proposition is that capitalism cannot tolerate lasting high employment of labor-power. Either a state-planned recession, known as the "political business cycle" (see Kalecki 1943), or slowing accumulation are needed to recreate the reserve army of the unemployed and to boost profitability (Goldstein 1982). Many point to the late 1960s, when official unemployment fell below 4 percent of the labor force, as an example of this kind of wage squeeze on profits (Boddy and Crotty 1975; Armstrong, Glyn and Harrison 1984).

Similarly, in the M − C phase, over-accumulation can occur relative to raw material supplies (Marx 1968:517–519). For example, the drastic oil price hike of 1973 is often blamed on the Organization of Petroleum Exporting Countries (OPEC) or the major oil companies. But many Marxists point to the worldwide surge in energy demand as creating the conditions for the price rise (Armstrong, Glyn and Harrison 1984). This hurt the United States terms of trade, in trade with the rest of the world, and thus, the profit rate (except for oil-producing corporations and nations). This was the "oil crisis."

The second possible snag is in production (P), where class conflict or excessive mechanization can hurt profit rates. The former, the conflict in the capitalist production process, was discussed above. The latter raises the organic composition of capital and K/Z (Marx 1967c: Chap. 13). Unlike other causes of crisis, this one is usually not invoked to explain short-term or cyclical crises. Instead, it is seen as a long-term problem dragging down capitalist accumulation (see below).

After the supply-side links comes the demand side, $C' - M + S$. Total demand for final products may be too weak to allow realization of as much profit as was produced, causing a "realization crisis" (Marx 1967c: Chap. 15). The utilization of capacity (Y/Z) falls, depressing the rate of profit. In classic Marxian thought, these events resulted as accumulation slowed, due to supply-side depression of the profit rate. Many modern leftists, however, see realization problems as a possible cause of the crisis itself: slow growth of wages (relative to productivity) limits consumer demand, causing *underconsumption*.[5] This problem is at the heart of the monopoly/underconsumption theory (see below). Others see underconsumption as contributing to the world collapse of 1929–33 (Devine 1983). Below, Edward Nell presents a view of the current quagmire that involves underconsumption.

At this point, a simple perspective on cyclical crises can be summarized. Accumulation can break each of the links in the production-realization chain. Which link breaks depends on the conditions capitalism encounters, which vary between historical eras. At times realization (demand) conditions allow for high profitability, as in the late 1960s. But then poor production conditions (high wages, low work effort, high K/Z, etc.) make the profit rate too low for steady accumulation. On the other hand, production conditions can be good for profits, encouraging strong accumulation, as when unemployment is high. But under these conditions, realization conditions are poor, blocking growth. Driven by competitive strife, capitalism careens between the two horns of this dilemma, what Marx saw as a contradiction between production and realization (1967c:244–245).[6]

To Marx, crises are restorative, causing the purging of imbalances created by accumulation. Capitalism's internal contradictions "lead to explosions, cataclysms, [and] crises in which by momentaneous suspension of labor and annihilation of a great portion of capital the latter is violently reduced to the point where it can go on" with accumulation (Marx 1973:750).[7] So "permanent crises do not exist" (Marx 1968:497n). Though a downturn restores more "normal" accumulation, the purging is hardly painless to capitalists: many go bankrupt, while financial collapse may occur. Worse, opposition to the system may intensify and crystallize, perhaps to the point of overthrow. Even without the rise of a revolutionary movement, the purging may take a long time. So, though crises may not be permanent, an impasse may last for a long time, as in the Great Depression or the Great Stagflation.

ALTERNATIVE THEORIES OF THE IMPASSE

Turning now to impasses, we must also consider their opposite, long-term prosperity such as that of the 1950s and 1960s. Here modern leftist economists present several distinct major theories, emphasizing different basic tensions driving the system and primary factors lowering the profit rate. Despite this controversy, the main modern radical views of long-term booms and stagnations have similar patterns. Each sees capitalism as suffering from a clash between, (1) an underlying tendency that hurts the profit rate and, (2) counteracting tendencies that can boost it. The former are seen as inherent in capitalism as an economic system, while counter-tendencies are assumed to exist only during a few specific historical eras.[8] The counter-tendencies can swamp the basic drift, causing long-term prosperity. But when the underlying bias wins, profit rates fall over long periods and an impasse results. Below, Fred Moseley, Mark Glick, and Anwar Shaikh provide evidence for the profit rate's fall before the Great Stagflation of the 1970s.

Now we consider each of the main schools, which are named according to the basic tendency emphasized, i.e., the primary factor pulling down the profit rate.[9] It should be noted from the start that there are differences even within schools and that some radical economists (including this author) do not fit in any of the three camps. Still, the three-fold division does give us the broad outlines of the debates within radical economics.

First, the "rising organic composition" school — seen in the articles by David Laibman and Anwar Shaikh below — is closest to Marx in seeing crises as stemming primarily from a clash of the forces and relations of production. The competitive battle pushes capitalists to mechanize production, increasing the organic composition of capital and K/Z. Some authors see high wages as encouraging this result. Given societal limits on rises in the rate of surplus value (and R/Z) and the rate of capacity use, the profit rate falls. A long-term tendency for profit rates to fall leads to increasingly severe crises and class struggles, permanently undermining the system's viability (see, for example, Gillman 1958:Chap. 1).

But the profit rate is not *always* falling. Counteracting forces such as the world-wide expansion of capitalism can boost profit rates for a certain period of time (Marx 1967c:Chap. 14).[10] One author, Ernest Mandel, emphasizes the basic innovations in energy technology to explain the post-World War II affluence and previous long periods of growth (1975:Chap. 4). The impasse after 1970 is seen as a victory of the profit-depressing tendency over the counter-tendencies.

Second, the "social conflict" school — including the article by David Gordon, Tom Weisskopf, and Sam Bowles below — stresses conflict in social relations, in causing impasses, and largely ignores the roles of competition and technical change. They build on the theory of a wage squeeze on profits mentioned in the previous section, but see social conflict as crucial even beyond the realm of worker-capitalist relations. Not only acrimony between social groups within the United States, but also pressure on corporations from the government and international discord, tend to disrupt the system. If unchecked, the conflicts sap profitability and thus, prosperity.

As before, capitalism does not always experience conflict-induced profit squeezes. Rather, "accords" between classes, groups, and nations can temper conflict for long periods of time. Together, these implicit truces form "Social Structures of Accumulation" (SSAs). Weisskopf, Bowles and Gordon argue, below, that prosperity after World War II rested on an SSA consisting of accords between capitalists and workers, between capitalists and citizens, and between the United States and other nations. Eventually the basic conflicts made the SSA obsolete and depressed profit rates.

The third strain of leftist economics is the "monopoly/underconsumption" school, represented by John Bellamy Foster's article below. As Marx had predicted, capitalist accumulation implied the rise of the giant corporation (1967a:624–627). In the monopoly/underconsumption view, this altered the system's laws of motion by curbing competition — and capitalist dynamism. The income distribution tends to shift to help capitalists, raising the rate of surplus value and R/Y. But low wages make consumer demand grow too slowly, which in turn makes companies afraid to accumulate (invest). Thus, demand is too weak to realize the full rise in R/Y. Because of the basic underconsumption tendency, capitalism automatically sinks into stagnation like that of the Great Depression, and stays there.

As with the other views, counteracting forces explain periods of relative prosperity. Wars, military spending, credit expansion, and epoch-making innovations create opportunities for investment and thus stimulate growth. The last counter-tendency refers to the spread of inventions such as the steam engine in the nineteenth century and the internal-combustion engine in the twentieth.[11] When these forces are depleted, stagnation returns.

Criticisms of these three schools focus on the basic tendencies. For the rising organic composition view, many have criticized the theory that K/Z rises enough to actually cause a fall in profit rates, especially since there are so many counter-tendencies. In fact, a rising organic composition encourages productivity to rise, which allows a rise in the rate of surplus value (with real wages constant). Critics of the social conflict school doubt that conflict always disrupts capitalism: divisions in the United States working class are rampant, while capitalists often compete with each other. Sometimes workers and capitalists ally with each other, for example, for special benefits from the government. Second, are there no other laws of motion of the system besides conflict? The monopoly/underconsumption view has also been subject to strong criticisms. Much doubt concerns the emphasis on monopoly, especially in a period of intense international competition such as the 1980s, and the presumed reversal of capitalism's dynamism. Second, is it reasonable to assume that the working class is *always* so weak that wages fall behind productivity?

Next, because these three views are so abstract, they are incomplete: important elements of the current impasse seem to have been missed or played down. For example, the differences between the current impasse and previous long-term crises (or between long prosperities) might be forgotten if we stay so theoretical.[12] One key historical difference between the post-World War II era and before was the United States international predominance in manufacturing. The power of United States industry can be seen as allowing the domestic accords posited by the social conflict school — or as counter-acting the basic tendencies seen by the other two camps. If so, then *deindustrialization,* the relative obsolescence of United States industry and intensifying competition from abroad, must have played a role in the resurrection of fundamental tendencies toward impasse. Even if one rejects the three basic tendencies, deindustrialization is crucial.[13] The *Business Week* emphasis on boosting productivity reflects the problem of deindus-trialization. Further, the growing movement of capital to more profitable climes — or at least the *threat* of capital flight — destabilized the domestic economy, as argued by Bluestone and Harrison (1982). The re-emergence of intense international competition also unhinged the international Bretton Woods system.[14] Finally, we have to probe the role of the intensifying debt crisis of the underdeveloped nations, as in Art MacEwan and Cheryl Payer's articles below.

Going further from the abstract to our own experiences, we must bring in the diverse impacts of the impasse on different groups within the working class. For example, how has the impasse affected ethnic minorities? Is the ''feminization of poverty'' partly the result of the economic quagmire? Have some industries and regions been exempted from the more general mess? These issues are discussed in the accompanying volume, *Through the Safety Net*.

Despite the differences between the schools and the criticisms above, leftist economists do agree the recovery from the current impasse is far from automatic: the resurrection of tendencies promoting prosperity seems unlikely. Many predict the continuation of the current malaise for decades. Alternatively, the crisis could intensify as the world debt crisis, international rivalry and protectionism, and the plight of primary producers, stimulate economic and financial collapse.

To understand this last possibility, we must consider important aspects of the current mess, the roles of money, the government, inflation, and stagflation.

THE ROLE OF MONEY AND THE GOVERNMENT

In all the theories above, the profit rate's fall implies over-production, recession, or even long-term stagnation. On the other hand, Keynesian economics promises that monetary policy and the government's fiscal policy can prevent or at least moderate crises and impasses. All leftist economists are skeptical of this claim. Again we emphasize the work of recent authors, and play down the work of Marx himself, who wrote about a very different monetary and governmental environment. For more discussion of Marx's view of money and crisis, see James Crotty's article below.

Consider monetary issues first. The flow of M is clearly important since it appears twice in the production-realization chain. M need not be hard cash; in fact, most of it is credit (loans), allowing capitalists to spend beyond their current incomes. Leftist economists typically differ from the mainstream in seeing credit supplies as being mostly outside of the control of a central bank such as the Federal Reserve.[15] As textbooks emphasize, the banking system "creates credit" through lending. This is also true of other financial institutions, such as mutual funds. It is becoming increasingly clear that this credit creation is not predictable or regular. Being profit-seekers, financiers actively compete to loan. They then seek ways to finance their credit-creation by borrowing. Two methods stand out: the issuance of new kinds of IOUs to sell to the public (for example, Certificates of Deposit) and the use of international credit markets (such as the Eurocurrency market). All of this encourages rapid change in financial institutions, which may easily get out of the central bank's control. Nowadays, the Fed has the ability to cause only large changes in credit supplies, causing extreme pressure on the viability of the banking system, depression, or severe inflation. It is unable to "fine-tune" money supply growth (as suggested by Milton Friedman and the monetarists) to keep it on some pre-determined path.

The credit system is affected by the dynamics of accumulation. With profit rates sliding, how can industrial capitalists pay for the accumulation needed to survive the competitive battle? They increasingly turn to borrowing to pay for accumulation: Robert Pollin's article below argues that excessive corporate debt in the 1980s resulted from the long-term fall in profit rates. The banking system is glad to provide (at a price, indicated by interest rates and so forth). Because capitalists need not cut back on accumulation, growing debt puts off the onset of the crisis and downturn. But credit later can intensify a downturn: debts eventually have to be paid off out of profits, which is difficult with profit rates falling. Greater accumulation of debts to help paying for past ones makes the financial system more fragile (prone to collapse). Given excessive indebtedness, a recession can be amplified by a financial panic, involving a scramble for hard cash to pay the interest and principal on the loans. Massive bankruptcies of industrial companies and runs on the financial institutions can make the recession more profound, as in the early 1930s.

Though recent experience in the United States has been milder than at the onset of the Great Depression, each of the business cycle peaks after the early 1960s, has coincided with a financial crisis as seen in Henry Martin's article below. Worse, the problem seems to be intensifying. This is the problem referred to by Felix Rohatyn at the start of this essay.

Not all financial crises result from low profit rates.[16] Financial bubbles and panics have arisen on occasion because "Wall Street" speculation about future profitability often has little connection with the real world of capitalist production. If the production-realization process is itself ready for a fall, financial panics can hurt "real" accumulation, as with the stock market crash of 1929.

If government monetary policy is weak, what about fiscal policy? Keynesian use of government deficits to steer the economy started with the early 1960s and climaxed with Reagan's record-breaking deficits. Though such policies clearly affect aggregate demand, capacity utilization, and thus profit rates, they have severe shortcomings. Keynesian policies cannot abolish the underlying crisis tendencies of capitalism; they allow greater surplus-value realization but typically do not promote surplus value production. They thus cannot erase the wage-squeeze or rises in the organic composition of capital. Even in the monopoly/underconsumption view, stabilization requires steadily increasing deficits.

Further, leftist economists point to the long-term negative results of the government policies involved. For example, because it does not compete with capitalist investments, Keynesianism is most likely to be based on military spending. Indeed, military Keynesianism is key to the dubious Reagan "recovery." Any resulting prosperity, however, is purchased at the cost of waste, inflation, or even war.

Second, state demand management become increasingly difficult in an international system of competing nation-states with capital that can easily move to more profitable locales. The limited "success" of Keynesian policies in the 1960s arose because of the United States dominance in the world at the time. In the 1980s, large United States government deficits often helped foreign economies more than domestic producers. Sectors such as the farmers and other exporting industries fell behind. United States policy-makers now try to promote domestic stability by begging foreign countries (especially West Germany and Japan) to engage in appropriate policies!

Both fiscal and monetary policies are shaped and limited by capitalist laws of motion. Because of class discord, the state's efforts to promote profitable accumulation can increase popular disenchantment with business leaders and mainstream politicians.[17] Second, competition among capitalists affects state policies: different fractions of the capitalist class press their goals through political action committees and lobbyists, often clashing with each other and with the long-term needs of the capitalist system. These so-called "special interests" sometimes ally with unorganized segments of the working class and even unions to drum up support for everything from pork-barrel programs to protectionism.

The personal goals of politicians play a role in determining the timing of booms and recessions. The current system of presidential election and the popularity of falling unemployment rates make it likely that booms will occur before elections and recessions soon after (see Tufte 1978). This helps explain the economic booms of 1972, 1976, and 1984. Sometimes, however, the threat of upcoming elections may evoke contractionary policies, as in 1980. All of this suggests that the Keynesian ideal of abolishing crises through fiscal policy will never be reached.

The shaky prosperity of recent years has been based almost entirely on large government deficits rather than in the buoyancy of the economy. Deficits have meant a growing government debt, while interest on this debt has become increasingly important in the budget. Since government IOUs are largely owned by the rich, the recent trend toward increasing inequality between the incomes of the rich and poor has intensified. Moreover, much of the borrowing was from abroad, so that the United States now owes more to the rest of the world than vice-versa — for the first time since World War I. As noted at the start of this paper, *South* magazine and many others fear the effects on the world economy as the United States pushes exports and cuts imports to pay for its foreign debt.

INFLATION AND STAGFLATION

"Inflation" is a sustained increase in most prices in the economy. The modern leftist view of inflation can be understood by examining first demand and then supply. Despite this familiar framework, leftist economists reject the mainstream view of inflation as easy to abolish. (For more on inflation, see David Kotz's article below.)

On the demand side, the hard-to-control expansion of credit discussed above sets the stage for inflation (see Lipietz 1985). Credit allows capitalists and other borrowers to buy more goods and services than is justified by their incomes — or by current output. Corporate, government, and consumer borrowing causes inflation if commodity production does not expand quickly to serve demand. Modifying the old saw, "too much credit chasing too few goods" implies inflation.

Why, then, are there too few goods? This gets us to the supply side. One option is that too few resources (LP, MP, and RM) are available to allow the increase in production as demand increases. Low unemployment also undermines workers' incentive to produce output. In sum, we should expect inflation to be higher at lower unemployment rates, as in the late 1960s. This is the familiar "Phillips curve" seen in textbooks.

But as everybody knows from the experience of the 1970s, it is quite possible to have both high inflation and unemployment at the same time. In the 1980s, we see that though inflation eased, it continued *despite extremely high unemployment*. That is, how can we have "stagflation," a combination of acute unemployment and serious inflation (*stag*nation + in*flation*)? There is clearly some cause for inflation beyond "too few goods."

An obvious culprit besides low unemployment is "supply shocks." As is so often mentioned, the oil companies and OPEC raised oil prices dramatically in 1973–74 and 1979 (encouraged by high world demand for raw materials). These events clearly boosted inflation in those years, since oil is such an important raw material. But this view does not explain why the resulting inflation was more than just a one-shot increase in prices. Nor does it explain why ridding the economy of inflation has been such a long and painful process.

To answer these questions, we must examine the kind of inflation that has become "built into" the normal workings of a capitalist economy. This is "structural inflation" that persists even in the face of severe unemployment.[15] Structural inflation results from the conflicts between groups, among them labor, capitalists, middle-class groups, and OPEC, over the production and distribution of the product. Each group tries to win a larger share of the pie by restricting output and hiking prices. But since so many sectors are raising prices, no one can win for long. This implies that they must continue to jockey to improve or protect their incomes, or to make up for losses in their piece of the pie (see Rosenberg and Weisskopf 1981).[16] Once this multi-sided conflict over the production and distribution of the product starts, it is hard to stop without a drastic recession (as in 1980–82) or good luck (the falling or low oil prices of recent years).

What starts the structural inflation rolling? Lasting Phillips-curve inflation and large supply shocks are likely suspects: both the high employment in the late 1960s and the 1973–74 oil shock can be seen as helping to start the stubborn inflation of the 1970s. But leftist economists point to deeper causes, seeing spiraling structural inflation as part of the general economic malaise of the 1970s. Those who emphasize the role of monopoly argue that recessions, far from automatically dampening inflation, encourage corporations to raise prices: falling demand hurts capacity utilization and profit rates, so corporations hike prices to restore profit rates. (Below, David Kotz presents this view.) Those emphasizing the long-term fall in the rate of profit see that fall as encouraging inflation: raising prices seems at first to boost profitability, but since it does not do so in reality, capitalists end up futilely increasing prices without solving the conundrum of low profit rates (Devine 1986). Third, the social conflict school argues that a breakdown in the SSA unleashed structural inflation, while political stalemate prevented the deep recession needed to abolish the inflation (Bowles, Gordon and Weisskopf 1983:116–119).

The last two decades have been labeled the Great Stagflation because increasing structural inflation has made state policies less able to maintain full employment, even as officially defined. Longer and deeper recessions have been needed to tame inflation (even when the United States has been lucky with oil prices). It also pushes government policy-makers and mainstream economists to weaken full-employment targets to cover up policy failures: while many talked of 4 percent official unemployment as "full employment" in the 1960s, now 6 percent or even 7 percent is targeted.[17] It is leftist economists' contention that this lowering of goals and these policy failures are reflections of the basic flaws of capitalism as a system that lead to the impasse.

ACKNOWLEDGEMENTS

I have relied on an article by Roger Alcaly (1978). See that article for further discussion. Thanks to Fred Moseley, Cigdem Kurdas, and Anwar Shaikh for their comments on an earlier draft. Of course, all sins, both venial and mortal, are mine alone.

NOTES

1. While other institutions and historically-specific events contribute to the actual form or timing of a crisis, their roles depend crucially on these contradictions.

2. Definitions come from Edwards, Reich and Weisskopf (1978:39–40). For two of Marx's exposition of these ideas, see Marx and Engels "The German Ideology" and Marx's "Preface" to "A Contribution to the Critique of Political Economy" in, Tucker (1978:146–200 and 3–6).

3. See the *Communist Manifesto* in Tucker (1978:475–477).

4. Here I ignore the difference between value and price categories. As Foley (1982) and others make clear, prices and Marxian values are connected at the level of the economy as a whole. The main difference involves the treatment of unproductive labor (labor that does not produce surplus value), a subject beyond the scope of this essay.

5. Underconsumption must be distinguished from over-production, which can occur not only due to low consumer demand but to inadequate demand of other sorts.

6. See Devine (1983, 1987) for development of these ideas. In the former article, I point to a case where production and realization conditions for profitable accumulation are both met for a few years (specifically, the 1920s). In this case, the economy is subject to increasing fluctuations.

7. Also, "crises are always but momentary and forcible solutions of the existing contradictions. They are violent eruptions which for a time restore the disturbed equilibrium" (Marx 1967c:249).

8. This is a mirror-image of the mainstream view that sees a contest between, (1) the underlying movement of capitalism toward harmony and stable growth with full employment and, (2) the counteracting exogenous shocks leading to disequilibrium. In some Marxian theories, however, the counter-tendencies raising the profit rate result from the basic tendency.

9. A fourth school is not discussed here because it is not represented below. The "regulation" school, centered in France, sees capitalist mass production as needing a stable mass consumer market in order to avoid a realization crisis such as that of 1929–33. A social system of "Fordist regulation" allows wage incomes to rise with production to avoid such a collapse. See, for example, Lipietz (1987).

10. Anwar Shaikh has argued that instead of raising the *rate* of profit, counter-acting tendencies only raise the total amount of profit.

11. The emphasis on epoch-making innovations by Mandel of the rising organic composition school and Baran and Sweezy (1966) of the monopoly/underconsumption school is akin to Joseph Schumpeter's (1939) conservative theory of long waves.

12. In their article below, Gordon, Weisskopf and Bowles do acknowledge that crises do not always arise from the capitalist class being "too weak" (as they allege took place in the 1960s). A general realization crises can result when the capitalist class is "too strong," as in the 1920s. See Devine (1983, 1987) for a different version of this idea.

13. See Brenner (1986). Cohen and Zysman (1987) argue the importance of manufacturing to national prosperity.

14. See Parboni (1981) and Cohen and Rogers (1983).

15. Marx wrote at the time of the gold standard. Nonetheless, he agreed with the Banking school of his time, which saw the money supply as hard to control. Crotty's article below suggests that modern leftists share many assumptions of the post-Keynesian school when it comes to monetary issues. For recent summaries of the latter literature suggesting that money and credit supplies are endogenous, see Sherman and Evans (1984 Chap. 17) and Lavoie (1984:771–797).

16. Note that Engels referred to crises that arise autonomously in the credit system (in Marx 1967c:236n). Minsky (1982) and post-Keynesians see fragility as mostly arising from within finance itself.

17. James O'Connor's *The Fiscal Crisis of the State* (1973) emphasizes the contradiction between promoting accumulation and the legitimation of the system.

18. Here I am following Eckstein (1981) who saw the inflation rate as the sum of three components: Phillips-curve inflation, supply-shock inflation, and core or structural inflation.

19. This theory assumes that many organizations have some power, like a monopoly, to set prices. Clearly, there are some groups who lose due to inflation, including those on fixed incomes or without bargaining power (that is, the poor).

20. However, some, such as Krashevski (1986) stick to "old fashioned" definitions of full employment.

4

Technical Change and the Contradictions of Capitalism

DAVID LAIBMAN

INTRODUCTION: THE ISSUES

Capitalist society exists *in history;* it is a social organism with a "lifeline," in the palm-reading sense; a path of development from infancy and youth, through maturity, to old age, and eventual replacement by higher forms of social organization. A central task of Marxist theory is therefore to determine the nature of capitalism's historical limits; its aging process, the way its contradictions mature and deepen.

All societies begin with a set of production activities, in which people interact with nature to extract their means of existence. Development of the *productive forces* — the power to draw upon and transform the natural environment — is a crucial part of a society's maturation path. In tracing the lifeline of capitalist society, then, technical change — transformation of the labor process, from the industrial revolution and the rise of "machinofacture" to the present-day electronics revolution — plays a prominent role. Marxists have sought to understand the forces propelling changes in production techniques; their social character and impact, both in the workplace and in society at large; and their general trend of development. The relation of technical change to the class structure of society is surely of major importance here; as is its relation to the *rate of profit* — the most general indicator of the efficiency of the capitalist economy in its own terms — since this is the root of long-term, or general, crisis.

This chapter is not a systematic introduction to these concepts in the classical Marxist texts; to develop Marx's argument in its own terms would mean a lengthy presentation of his special vocabulary and definitions, which will not be attempted here. Nor will I present a survey of contemporary Marxist theories and their criticism. Rather, I hope to discuss the main issues informally, and in language which is as self-evident and accessible as possible. I have kept the text clear of references; a bibliographical appendix covers the main source literature.

HISTORY, SOCIETY, AND TECHNICAL CHANGE

That capitalists urgently and continually revolutionize techniques of production is hardly a matter of dispute. Somewhat more controversial are Marx's claims concerning "concentration and centralization" of capital (fewer and larger units of capital, as small fish get eaten by the big ones), and polarization in the class structure (the middle strata are depleted and the working class recruited).

There have been several attempts to portray the evolution of capitalist societies in terms of stages, drawn from historical experience. The most common of these posits a transition from a liberal stage to a late-capitalist, or state-monopoly-capitalist, stage. Some recent work has elaborated on the concept of stages, by designating periods in the relation between classes as "social structures of accumulation." We must ask, however, whether the stages conception amounts to more than a descriptive account of historical events. How many stages are there? Is there a progressive sequence of stages, and if so, on what is it based? These questions point to one issue: the stages as segments of the lifeline of a single social system; capitalism. To show that the stages share a common *process of development,* we must identify aspects of capitalist accumulation that are *not unique to each stage.* Put simply, I believe that one unifying thread is capitalism's unique shaping of technical change.

Technology, and technical change, mirror the society which produces them; they are not the result of some neutral, pre-existing "nature" or "march of science." The question, however, remains: have we been able to present technical change in a capitalist economy as a dynamic process, with a determinate direction? Is it enough to refer merely to rising labor productivity? Arguments can indeed be made that rising productivity, and factors that eventually cause the growth rate of productivity to decline, are important elements in the theory of capitalist crisis. To do justice to this line of thought, however, we need to grasp not just productivity growth, but also changes in the structure of production; the relation of investment in physical capital to the quantity of labor in production. The concept of a *bias* of technical change,[1] stemming from the choice of technical changes by individual capitalists pursuing their goals within a specifically capitalist framework, has important implications for long-term crisis — the length of capitalism's lifeline.

THE BIAS OF TECHNICAL CHANGE: THE CLASSICAL ARGUMENT

To set the stage for the discussion to follow, we will need a few simple definitions. We want to think about an industrial capitalist economy, in which fixed capital is the most prominent part of a capitalist's investment; for the sake of simplicity, then, we ignore raw materials and the part of fixed capital that depreciates in each period. Production is represented by a stock of fixed capital (the non-human inputs, machinery, plant, etc.), a flow of current labor, and a flow of output. ("Flows" are measured by a period of time, per year, per week, etc.) The usual problems arise when we try to think about how these stocks and flows are measured; imagine either an all-purpose commodity with a straight-forward natural unit of measurement, or some sort of "constant dollar" index.

The argument proceeds in terms of two concepts, each of which is a relation between a flow and the stock of fixed capital. We define the *output ratio* as the ratio of *output* to fixed capital, or output per unit of fixed capital.[2] Output is divided between the two classes, workers and capitalists (we ignore intermediate strata, government, etc. for present purposes); it is therefore wages plus profits. Our second major concept is the *rate of profit,* defined as the ratio of *profit* to fixed capital, or profit per unit of fixed capital. Notice that, if wages were zero, output and profits would be the same. The output ratio is therefore the maximum possible rate of profit.

We can now locate the classical argument: in a capitalist economy, the *output ratio has an inherent tendency to fall.* Why? Begin with casual observation: in the eighteenth century, a score or so of workers may have worked together in a "manufactory," with simple tools inherited from the artisan tradition, and a minimum of machinery and equipment. By contrast, the nineteenth century may be represented by the steam-driven machinery of England's textile industry, with thousands of workers in factories, and fixed capital playing an important role. Finally, consider the present, with enormous aggregations of fixed capital in modern automated, computer-managed production. In their drive to accumulate capital, capitalists have enormously enhanced the role of the fixed capital stock in production.

Marx's argument is buttressed by observations concerning class conflict, and in particular the use of machinery as a weapon against workers in the class struggle. Machines do not demand higher wages in a tight labor market, nor go on strike, nor demand coffee breaks, changes in work rules, etc. Moreover, the combined efforts of capitalists to replace workers with machines may cause the pool of unemployed workers to swell, and this may have the desired (from the capitalist viewpoint) effect of driving down the wages of the employed.

The implications of a tendency for the output ratio to fall can now be outlined. If the *maximum* rate of profit is falling, sooner or later the *actual* rate, lying between a floor of zero and a collapsing ceiling, must also turn downward. (The only way this could be postponed is by a rise in the *share of profits in output,* which might temporarily offset the fall in output per unit of capital.) If the rate of profit, in turn, is falling, then the rate of growth sooner or later must turn downward. This is why capitalism's contradictions might get worse over time; why its lifeline is finite in length.[3] In many ways, the rate of profit has long seemed to be the central concept, being simultaneously the capitalists' own strategic target and the main indicator of the power of capital to do what it must do to survive — namely, expand. Marx's "law of the falling tendency of the rate of profit," therefore, has figured prominently in discussions of long-term crisis.

THE COUNTER-CRITIQUE

Attentive readers may already have seen some holes in the foregoing argument. We will now examine them, beginning with the falling output ratio.

We can see more clearly what is happening here if we write this ratio in a slightly fuller form:

$$\frac{\text{output}}{\text{capital}} = \frac{\text{output/labor}}{\text{capital/labor}}$$

In this form we can see that the output ratio is a ratio of ratios, with output per unit of labor, or *labor productivity,* in the numerator, and fixed capital per unit of labor in the denominator. Clearly, the output ratio will fall if, and only if, productivity (which is clearly rising) rises *more slowly* than the physical capital/labor ratio (which is also clearly rising). The capital/labor ratio is an index of the degree of mechanization, and Marx's arguments concerning the use of mechanization as a weapon against workers certainly supports the view that it rises over time, as does the casual evidence referred to above. The question, however, is whether the capital/labor ratio rises more rapidly than productivity, in general. Productivity is also stimulated by the capitalist search for higher profits and for weapons to fight each other with, as well as for use as the "battering ram" breaking down barriers to capitalist penetration around the world. There seems to be no reason why the denominator should necessarily rise more rapidly than the numerator; the whole trend is therefore called into question.

However, even if we assume that new techniques have come into existence with a lower output ratio than those in common use — and that workers are able to resist a rise in the profit share, so that no offset takes place — a further, and seemingly devastating, question must be answered: Why would capitalists, who are perpetually in search of higher profit rates, willingly introduce techniques which result in a lowered rate of profit? And, assuming they have done so out of the inability to read the situation correctly, once they discover that profit rates have fallen with the introduction of the new technique, won't they go back to the old techniques, which yielded higher rates of return? This question seems to put an end, once and for all, to speculation about any long-term tendency of the profit rate to fall stemming from technical change. Moreover, it focuses attention on an important requirement for any theory tracing a connection between technical change and a falling rate of profit (or between anything and anything else, for that matter); it must be based clearly on the assumption of rational behavior on the part of individual capitalists.

Some contemporary Marxist economists, notably Nobuo Okishio, have called attention to the relationship between individual and crowd in capitalist competition, which provides an answer to the question: How can the rate of profit which matters for the choice of technique differ from the one which eventually materializes?

To understand the Okishio Theorem, imagine a capitalist economy composed of numerous sectors, each sector producing one sort of good. Conditions are competitive, in the sense that capitalists can move their capital freely from one sector to another; therefore, the rate of profit has come to be the same in every sector, and prices of inputs and outputs have adjusted accordingly. Now focus on one sector, and notice that it is composed of many individual firms. Finally, consider just one of those firms, the place where decisions about technical change are made.

An engineer runs into the firm's head office with blueprints for a new technique. The question is, should the firm adopt it? It involves different inputs of machinery and raw materials, and different amounts of some sorts of materials (we ignore for the present the fact that new techniques usually mean entirely new *types* of inputs and outputs).

The firm will "cost up" the new technique: find the relationship between expected revenue from sale of the good and the cost of producing it, and therefore the expected rate of profit. And it does this assuming that it is the *innovator* of this new method, installing it first, before any competitors, either already in the industry or potentially in it, have had a chance to copy it. In these conditions, since the firm is one of many producing the good, the prices of inputs and outputs will not be affected by the firm's decision. The firm is therefore calculating a very special "innovator's" rate of profit, and it will not decide to install the new technique unless this special rate of profit is higher than the prevailing one.

Now suppose the innovator's profit rate is indeed higher. The firm knows quite well that, once word gets around, its competitors will not sit still and let it lap up these special profits forever. When everyone gets into the act, all sorts of things start to happen. Prices of inputs and outputs in the industry are affected (the market notices large changes of this kind); presumably, many capitals enter the industry, since it has a higher-than-average rate of profit, and the price of the good produced by this industry will fall. All of these price changes upset the delicate balance of input and output prices in all industries (not just the one where the madness began!). The final outcome must be a readjustment of all prices, so that eventually a new balance emerges, in which all industries are once again earning the same rate of profit. Like the old man in Hemingway's *Old Man and the Sea*, the innovating firm does not get to keep the results of its innovation, but must share it with greedy competitors. Notice that this innovation will occur even if the firm where it began is able to anticipate this sharing-out process: the sharing will not be instantaneous, and in the meantime the firm will get those high innovator's profits; if it does not, its competitors will! (Here the Hemingway analogy breaks down; the old man had to get his catch to shore before he could enjoy it.)

Now we come to the key question: Is the new, balanced profit rate higher than, lower than, or the same as, the original one? To answer this question, Okishio makes a crucial assumption: through all the turmoil of the transition brought about by the change in technique in the one industry, the real wages of the workers have remained constant. And on this assumption, the Okishio Theorem can be stated: if the new technique yielded innovator's profits higher than the old balanced rate, then the new balanced rate must also be higher.

In summary: First, Marx never backed up his assertion that the output ratio would fall. Second, he never clearly answered the question: Why would capitalists ever willingly lower the profit rate? And third, even when we introduce the innovator/rebalancing dynamics, the result is that rational capitalists will never act so as to bring about a falling rate of profit.[4] Whatever criticisms we may have of approaches to crisis theory that rely on *ad hoc* stages, or that explain falling profits as resulting from class struggle (but how are the strengths of the conflicting classes to be explained?), or from shortfalls of demand (and no one has yet produced a satisfactory long-term version of this approach, in my view), we still seem to be at a dead end in attempting to relate long-term trends to capitalism-specific peculiarities of technical change.

A THEORY OF ENDOGENOUS, AND MAYBE BIASED, TECHNICAL CHANGE

In the Okishio approach, although a new technique is subjected to a sophisticated innovator's analysis, it still seems simply to fall from the sky, rather than being "endogenous"; conditioned by the capitalist social structure.

Imagine a firm in an industry in a competitive capitalist economy, in which there has emerged a uniform rate of profit of 10 percent. The firm is also, of course, earning exactly 10 percent, on a capital stock of 200. We assume the output ratio is 50 percent, so the production process generates an output of 100, of which 20 (10 percent of 200) is profits, and the remaining 80 goes to wages. (This profit share of 20 percent is undoubtedly unrealistically low; the numbers, however, have been chosen for easy calculation, not for correspondence with the real world.)

As before, an engineer runs in with a new technique and messes everything up. She/he proposes raising output by 10 percent, to 110; but this can only be done if mechanization increases the capital stock by 20 percent, to 240. From the standpoint of the innovator, the wage remains 80; it is determined by general conditions in the industry and the economy, and will not be affected by this particular innovation. That leaves 30 (110–80) for profits, forming an innovator's profit rate of 30/240, or 12.5 percent. This is two-and-one-half percentage points above the norm! We again assume that, in the intensely competitive conditions which prevail, the firm will have no choice but to install the new technique: those temporary innovator's profits are the key to growth and survival. Notice that this will be done even though the output ratio falls to 110/240, or about 46 percent.

The new technique now spreads to the industry as a whole. Here the beginning of wisdom is that technical change disrupts all existing norms: work rules, output norms for piece rates, managerial hierarchies, wage scales, all must be re-established, either through negotiation, or by means of more informal methods of class conflict. In our simple example, the only item which can be treated explicitly is wage scales. Productivity has gone up by 10 percent. The question is, what will happen to wages?

One answer, of course, is that given by Okishio: nothing. If the wage stays constant at 80, the rate of profit will remain 12.5 percent after the new technique is introduced; this illustrates Okishio's proposition that the rate of profit can not fall as a result of technical change. Notice, however, that in this case, in which capitalists reap all the benefits of technical change, the *profit share has risen,* from 20 percent to about 27 percent.

But this is not the only possible answer. First, in competitive conditions, the price of the product may fall as productivity rises. With given *money* wages, this would mean a rise in *real* wages; in fact, they would rise by the same percentage as productivity, 10 percent. Indeed, if we think of the profit share of output as the most appropriate measure of the balance of class forces in the conflict between labor and capital, then — assuming that the technical change has not altered this balance significantly — the profit *share* will remain constant. In this case, wages will rise by 10 percent, to 88. Profits will then be 110–88, or 22. The profit share is the same as before the innovation, 22/110, or 20 percent; the profit *rate*, however, has now *fallen* to 22/240, or 9.1666 percent. It should be clear that, with a falling output ratio and a constant profit share, the profit rate must fall. Remember also that the firm *must* innovate, and the imitators *must* imitate, even if their experience suggests that real wages will eventually catch up with productivity. Anticipating the fall in the profit rate from 10 percent to 9⅙ percent, capitalists will still have no choice but to proceed with the new technique.

Of course, the eventual effect on the rate of profit depends not only on the nature of the new technique, but also on the social, class process set in motion by the technical change. It should be emphasized, however, that this is just as true of the constant-real-wage case as it is of the constant-relative-shares case. For the real wage to remain constant in the face of rising productivity and profits, the capitalists must have gone on a rampage! You will imagine, and I think correctly, that the actual situation may well lie somewhere between the two extremes. What emerges as a general rule *in the case of a falling output ratio* is that *either* the profit share must rise *or* the profit rate must fall, *or* both. If a falling *rate* of profit affects the capitalist lifeline in one way, and a rising *share* or profit affects it in another, then we may focus on the most important issue: why did the new technique involve a falling output ratio? This is the underlying source of the critical tendency, and we are still simply postulating this change, rather than explaining it. After all, if the new technique had shown a constant or rising output ratio, then a constant or rising profit rate would have been compatible with a constant or falling profit share. It is the existence and superiority of new techniques which lower the output ratio that must be established.

But before turning to that issue, consider the question, raised above, concerning reversibility of technical change. If the profit rate has fallen — as in our constant-shares case — why then will capitalists not revert to the old technique? Consider what would happen if some hapless (and no doubt soon to be extinct) capitalist were to return to a capital stock of 200 and an output of 100, after the new technique has been generalized, and wages have risen to 88. That would leave a profit of 12, for a profit rate of 12/200 or 6 percent! This is in fact the rate that would accrue to any firms which failed to make the original transition between techniques, showing why firms will *jump* to install new techniques that lower their rate of profit from 10 percent to 9⅙ percent! If a falling-rate-of-profit process is in place, then it is not reversible.

The question remains: why were we allowed to assume that the new technique had a lower output ratio than the old one? The answer is that we weren't — necessarily! But to see what is involved, let's assume that our engineer does not simply discover a single new technique in the laboratory, but rather can propose research on a range of new techniques, with different increases in mechanization and productivity.

The engineer can bring about productivity increases, but not, of course, infinite ones. Each time you ask her/him to add (say) another five percentage points to the increase in productivity, the "cost" in terms of additional capital stocks will be greater. For example: to achieve an initial 5 percent rise in productivity, it may only be necessary to increase the capital stock by 4 percent. (This would mean a rising output ratio.) But adding another five percentage points in productivity (a 10 percent rise overall) will require a further *16* percentage points of capital-stock increase, for a total of 20 percent. (This is the case used in the example above.) It might even be possible, within a "short period" time frame, to raise productivity by still another 5 points, to 15 percent; but this, according to our assumptions, might require a 30-point additional increase in the capital stock (a 50 percent overall rise). The terms of this trade-off will undoubtedly reflect capitalist social structures as much as any kind of "pure" natural or technological factors.

The situation can be summed up as follows:

new technique	change in output	change in capital stock	innovator's profit rate	new balanced profit rate
A	5%	4%	12.019%	10.096%
B	10%	20%	12.500%	9.166%
C	15%	50%	11.666%	7.666%

If techniques A, B and C were indeed the only choices available, it would clearly be most beneficial from a social standpoint to adopt technique A, since it yields a higher return than the prevailing 10 percent — although, to be sure, not by much! (There is much more to the complex issue of social criteria for choice of technique, but we will not pursue the matter here.) The choice for the individual capitalist is equally clear, and different: it is technique B, with the highest innovator's rate of 12.5 percent. The figures for the new balanced profit rate assume a constant profit share of 20 percent and technique B, as we have seen before, produces a fall in that rate to 9.1666 percent.

How likely is it that the technique which yields the highest innovator's profit rate (B in the example) is also one which lowers the output ratio? Is it possible that a technique like A might be the one that looks best to the innovating capitalist? It is hard to give a precise answer, without developing a more formal model (see the bibliographical appendix). But we can do one more little experiment. Suppose the profit share had been 30 percent instead of 20 percent; this makes the original profit rate 15 percent instead of 10 percent. Now if we re-examine techniques A and B, we will find that the innovator's profit rate in A is 16.827 percent, compared with 16.666 percent for B; and that the new balanced rate is 15.144 percent for A, compared with 13.75 percent for B. So the technique that raises the output ratio (technique A) also has the highest innovator's profit rate *and* the highest actual rate; the divergence between private and social interest that resulted in the falling profit rate tendency is eliminated. We can conclude that a high wage share (low profit share) is conducive to the falling-profit-rate tendency, and vice versa. For a given income distribution, however, the matter turns on the extent to which productivity increases can be obtained without mechanizing, and the rate at which diminishing returns to mechanization set in. The less the resources a society can devote to fundamental science, and the more *slowly* diminishing returns set in (owing perhaps to an engineering culture based on a long-established search for high innovator's profits), the more likely it is that the path of technical change will be biased, in the sense of showing a falling output ratio. While this issue needs much more study, it points in (what I think is) the right direction: the relation between capitalist economic structures in general and the institutions concerned with the actual production of technical change — the funding of scientific research and the setting of priorities for it, the types of signals received by the engineering community, the time horizon of competitive capitalists and its effect on the rate of dissemination of new techniques; etc., etc.

CONCLUSION: TECHNICAL CHANGE AND CRISIS

We are really just at the beginning of the story. Suppose we have a presumption that capitalist economies exhibit a long-term bias toward a falling output ratio. That, of course, is itself an example of the fettering of progress by a system of social organization, since a rising output ratio, if anything, would be desirable. But the falling output ratio has another important implication, which we have already explored: it implies that at least one of two great macro tendencies — falling rate of profit; rising profit share (rate of exploitation) — must be operative. The falling rate of profit implies an eventually falling rate of growth, with attendant crises of finance, technological shake-out, expectations, competition with socialist planned economies, and much else that needs to be spelled out. The rising profit share, in turn, is associated with pervasive problems of effective demand: with a falling relative wage, the base of total demand is narrowed, and under these circumstances it will be increasingly difficult for investment demand, which must ultimately be based on anticipation of strong demand for consumer goods, to take up the slack.

It should be noted that, if the profit share rises over time (as in fact happens in a full model of capitalist growth based on the theory of technical change described in this paper, as well as in at least some versions of capitalist reality), the bias toward a falling output ratio will weaken over time, and the economy may tend toward steady growth at a low but no-longer-falling profit rate. The importance of the falling profit rate tendency, then, depends on whether the system will run up against a minimum-profit-rate barrier while biased technical change is still operative. Elaboration of a theory of this "financial" barrier, and of the related "stagnation" barrier (a maximum profit share) is beyond the scope of this paper; it would amount to a precise statement of the conditions in which the cyclical crises associated with a falling profit rate and a rising profit share, respectively, become permanent and "nonreproductive." Contact with the barriers, in turn, should be seen as the basis of the need for *structural transformation*, perhaps transition to a new regime or "social structure" of accumulation. The crisis of the 1930s surely propelled a transition of this kind, to a new stage in which the state takes on a new direct role: it helps raise the maximum profit share (the stagnation barrier) by evolving, under pressure from workers, new institutional forms of support (the "social wage"); and lower the minimum profit rate (the financial barrier) by means of subsidies to research and development, guarantees in financial markets, allowing the private sector to exploit nationalized industries through its terms of trade with those industries, etc. Government spending and taxation nevertheless lower the *after-tax* profit rate, constituting a second source of intensifying contradiction, along with biased technical change.

It is tempting to think of the current crisis as a crisis of this new regime of accumulation, with the new barriers again threatening to become effective. This approach places our thinking about the present complex situation of late capitalist society into continuity with Marx's falling-rate-of-profit approach, without making the latter into a fetish or ignoring the obvious difficulties with its earlier formulations.

The theory of biased technical change therefore serves as a "unified field theory" bringing together the several strands in traditional Marxist theorizing about crisis. It establishes the relevance, if not necessarily the ever-present reality, of a falling-profit-rate tendency, but does this without excluding analysis of problems of demand and realization of profits, nor of the changing balance of class power in the labor (and other) markets. Finally, to the extent that a path of technical change can be defined, and in a way that is relevant for crisis theory, the foundation is laid for a unified vision of the stages through which capitalist accumulation passes.

This is one element, but I believe a necessary one, in the continuing study of capitalism's lifeline. It helps us to look at the system's palm, so to speak, and see more than wrinkles, (working-class) calluses, and (capitalist) diamond rings.

APPENDIX
AN INTRODUCTORY BIBLIOGRAPHY

History, Society and Technical Change. For the classical twentieth-century Marxist theory of stages, see Pevzner (1984), Fairley (1980), and, with variations, Baran and Sweezy (1966). For samples of the more recent "social structures of accumulation" approach; Gordon, Edwards and Reich (1981), Edwards, Reich and Weisskopf (1986, esp. Chap. 2). The classical text for the social determination of technical change is, of course, Marx (1967, especially Chap. 10, "Machinery and Modern Industry," and Chaps. 24 and 25, on the trend in the "organic composition of capital"). For more recent discussions, see Braverman (1974) and Levidow and Young (1981).

The Bias of Technical Change: The Classical Argument. In addition to *Capital*, Vol. I, cited just above, the source discussion for this section is Marx (1967, Vol. III, Part III). Arguments which defend and develop the classical theory, although not necessarily in the same way as I have done in the text, will be found in Fine and Harris (1979), Mage (1963), Rosdolsky (1977: Chap. 26); Shaikh (1978) and Weeks (1982).

The Counter-Critique. Critical works on the Marxian theory are legion; I will mention Sweezy (1942), Robinson (1942), Gottheil (1966: Chap. 8), Blaug (1968), Steedman (1977), and van Parijs (1980). For the original statement of the Okishio theorem, Okishio (1961) and for elaborations and extensions, Roemer (1978). On demand-oriented crises originating in a rising profit share, Baran and Sweezy (1966), Foster (1982). The "class struggle" centered view of crisis may be represented by Glyn and Sutcliffe (1972) and Itoh (1978).

A Theory of Endogenous, and Maybe Biased, Technical Change. Since this section contains my own approach, I may be permitted to cite a few papers in which these ideas are developed more fully; Laibman (1977; 1981; 1982; 1983; forthcoming).

NOTES

1. By "bias," I mean a systematic (non-random) change in the proportion of input to output. A "capital-using" bias is equivalent to a fall in the output ratio, defined immediately below.

2. Some readers may wish to link the argument of this paper to those which are expressed in terms of traditional Marxist categories. To start them off, I will note that the output ratio $= Y/K$, where Y is output, and K is the capital stock. This, in turn, is equal to $L/(L/Y)K$. L/Y may be thought of as the value of a unit of output, where value is measured in terms of labor time. $(L/Y)K$ is therefore the value (in labor time) of the capital stock. The ratio Y/K, then, is formally identical to $(v+s)/C$, where $v+s$ is the flow of current labor time, in standard Marxian notation, and C is the stock of constant capital (also in terms of labor time). For reasons which I develop elsewhere, I believe Marx's organic composition of capital is best represented by the formula $C/(v+s)$. My output ratio is thus the reciprocal of Marx's organic composition of capital, and my discussion of the trend in the output ratio parallels the traditional formulation in terms of the organic composition of capital.

3. This passage may be clearer to some readers if rendered in symbols. The rate of profit is $P/K = (P/Y)(Y/K)$. If P/Y were $= 1$, then clearly $P/K = Y/K$. If Y/K falls, then P/K falls, unless P/Y rises in an offsetting manner. Now the growth rate of the capital stock may be written as investment over the capital stock: I/K. $I/K = (I/P)(P/K)$. From this, we read off that the rate of growth will fall if the rate of profit falls, unless the share of investment (accumulation) in profit rises sufficiently to offset that fall.

4. Criticisms of the Okishio Theorem have focused on the fact that his argument is conducted in terms of transitions between equilibria, and that "equilibrium" in any sense is a violation of Marx's conception of capitalism. There have also been efforts to replace the innovator's, or "transitional," rate of profit with some other target; or to argue that capitalists have systematically distorted expectations. I believe that these counter-arguments do not hit their mark. Equilibrium conditions are used as analytical tools by all great economists, including Marx, and this has nothing to do with the idealization known as "perfectly competitive equilibrium" in neoclassical economics. Also, and for reasons that cannot be fully elaborated here, I believe that the rate of profit, and for purposes of technical change-choices the innovator's rate of profit, remain the most basic and important measure of the power of capital, and the target of capitalist activity, as the business literature widely attests. Finally, the theory of capitalist crisis would only be weakened by allowing it to rest on any view other than one of rationality of expectations, in the sense that capitalists, sizing up their interests from the standpoint of the unique and historically transient position which they occupy in the class structure, are able to draw conclusions from past experience and act accordingly. The interested reader may follow up the arguments on all sides as cited in the bibliographical appendix to this paper.

5

Power, Accumulation, and Crisis: The Rise and Demise of the Postwar Social Structure of Accumulation

DAVID M. GORDON, THOMAS E. WEISSKOPF, and SAMUEL BOWLES*

INTRODUCTION

Crisis may occur in capitalist economies because the capitalist class is "too strong" or because it is "too weak."[1]

When the capitalist class is "too strong" it shifts the income distribution in its favor, reducing the ratio of working class consumption to national income and rendering the economy prone to crises of underconsumption or — in more contemporary Keynesian terms — a failure of aggregate demand. When the capitalist class is "too weak," the working class or other claimants on income reduce the rate of exploitation, squeezing the profit rate and reducing the level of investment (perhaps by inducing investors to seek greener pastures elsewhere).

Karl Marx referred to the first as a crisis in the realization of surplus value and the second as a crisis in the production of surplus value. They may also be characterized (respectively) as "demand-side" and "supply-side" crises. The result in each case is ultimately the same — a decline in the rate of profit, a reduction in the level of investment, a stalled accumulation process, and a stagnation or decline in the rate of growth of both demand and output. Thus what begins as a crisis in surplus-value production, for example, sooner or later turns into a crisis in surplus-value realization.

Some United States historians have argued that the Great Depression of the 1930s was a demand-side crisis, brought about in part by the political and economic defeats of the working class in the post-World War I era. The most recent crisis of the United States economy, in contrast, appears to have originated as a supply-side crisis brought about by the erosion of the hegemony of the United States capitalist class in the world economic system and by effective challenges to capitalist prerogatives mounted by workers and citizens during the 1960s and early 1970s. Once and only after these mounting barriers to surplus-value production had initially reduced corporate profitability, both stagnating investment and political efforts to roll back these challenges resulted in demand-side problems as well, further reinforcing the dynamic of crisis (Bowles, Gordon and Weisskopf 1983, 1986).

We elaborate this Marxian "supply-side" interpretation in this essay, arguing that the stagflation of the last nearly two decades in the United States can best be viewed as a general crisis of the legitimacy and stability of the postwar capitalist system, one which

---

*The authors' names are ordered randomly.

challenged not only the wealth of capital but its power as well. We build upon two complementary perspectives to elaborate this argument.

The first pursues the general approach to economic crisis which we call ''challenges to capitalist control'' (Weisskopf, Bowles and Gordon 1985). The second erects a bridge between this general approach and more concrete analysis of specific crises: We argue that understanding capitalist crisis requires building on general institutional concepts such as class and the capitalist mode of production to construct more historically-specific institutional concepts encompassed by the concept of a ''social structure of accumulation'' (SSA).[2] Combining these two perspectives, we believe, provides the most promising foundation for understanding the recent crisis of the United States economy.

We develop our argument here in four principal sections. We first elaborate the two cornerstones of our interpretation and use them for an analysis of the rise and demise of the postwar capitalist system in the United States. We then apply this analysis to a review of the contradictions of conservative economics in the 1980s. We further compare this kind of interpretation with alternative macroeconomic perspectives. We close with a brief review of the political implications of this analysis.

CHALLENGES TO CAPITALIST CONTROL OF THE SOCIAL STRUCTURE OF ACCUMULATION

Our analysis builds on an intrinsic proposition of the Marxian approach to macroeconomic dynamics. The pace of the economy is driven by the rate of capital accumulation while capital accumulation in turn is fundamentally conditioned by the level and stability of capitalist profitability. As profits go, in short, so goes the economy. In order to analyze crisis, therefore, it is essential first to determine the sources of declining profitability and then from there to trace through the connections from profitability to accumulation to economic growth.

Figure 1 expresses part of this connection, graphing the time pattern of the relationship between the rate of corporate profit and the rate of net capital accumulation from 1951 to 1985.[3] Profitability fell first after the mid-1960s and accumulation soon followed, at a lag of roughly two years. While no graph can ever establish causal linkages, the relationship depicted in Figure 1 is certainly consistent with general Marxian expectations.

Power and Profits

We turn then to the corporate rate of profit as a fundamental underlying determinant of accumulation and growth. Profits are not a payment to a scarce productive input.[4] Nor can the capitalist class as a whole make profits from its dealings with itself, for as Marx stressed in the early chapters of *Capital* (1967), the buying and selling of commodities is a zero-sum game for the buyers and sellers as a group: the gains of those who buy cheap and sell dear are necessarily offset by the losses of those who sell cheap and buy dear.

Profits are made possible, rather, by the power of the capitalist class over other economic actors which it confronts. Capitalists can indeed make profits through their economic relations with economic actors outside the capitalist class. When workers sell their labor power cheap and buy their wage goods dear, for example, a profit may be made. The capitalist class of a given economy may make profits, similarly, through its

Figure 1
The Rate of Profit
and the Rate of Accumulation

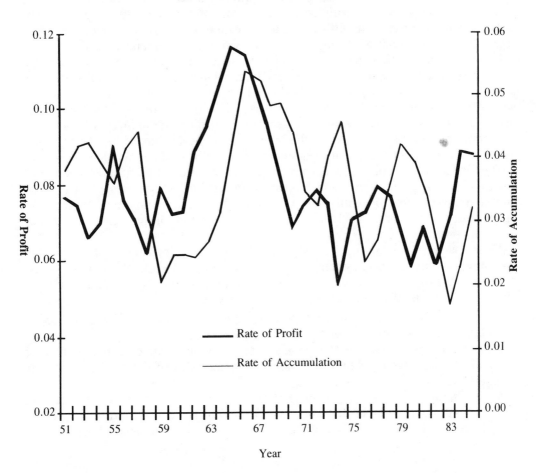

exchange with other buyers and sellers outside that economy, given favorable prices of exports and imports.

While some of the relationships between a national capitalist class and other economic actors are market exchanges, many are not. First of all, the worker who sells labor power cheap and buys wage goods dear will not contribute to profits unless the worker's employer also succeeds in getting the worker to work hard and well enough to produce a net output greater than the wage. And while the extraction of labor from the worker is influenced by wages, prices, and other market phenomena, it is proximately effected through an authority relationship at the workplace itself. Second, and similarly, while the international terms of trade depend on import and export prices, the determination of these prices involves the exercise of diplomatic, military and other pressures quite different in character from marketplace exchange.

A third relationship affecting the profit rate — that between the capitalist class and the state — also reflects the exercise of power: The alignment of forces in the formation of state policy may affect the after-tax profit rate directly through the effective tax rate on profits, and it may affect the profit rate as well through state policies affecting the supply of labor, the rate of capacity utilization, the direction of technical change, and many aspects of capital's relations with workers and with foreign buyers and sellers.

It may be illuminating, then, to consider profits as the spoils of a three-front war fought by capital in its dealings with workers, foreign buyers and sellers, and the state (or indirectly with the citizenry). Capital's ability to fight effectively on these three fronts will further be affected by the intensity of inter-capitalist competition, determining how tightly and cohesively its troops are organized for battle. The military analogies are deliberate; they are intended to stress the essentially political nature of the profit rate and the strategic nature of the social interactions involved in its determination.

The fundamentally political character of the determination of profits does not imply, however, that we cannot analyze the impact of this kind of political struggle with some precision. It is possible to identify quite clearly the channels through which the condition of this three-front war is likely to have direct impact on an aggregate measure of corporate profitability.

These channels can be highlighted with a relatively simple model of a capitalist economy in an open world system (Bowles, Gordon and Weisskopf 1986:137–9 and Appendix A). In such a model, it can be shown that the economy-wide average net after-tax profit rate of capitalists depends on six specific factors:

1. The *real wage rate*, or the cost of hiring an hour of labor power as a productive input: the lower the real wage, the higher the rate of profit.
2. The *intensity of labor,* or the amount of labor services extracted from an hour of labor power purchased for production: the higher the intensity of labor, the higher the profitability.
3. The *terms of trade*, or the relative cost (in domestic products) of acquiring foreign-produced inputs for production: the more favorable the terms of trade, the lower will be the costs of acquiring foreign-produced inputs and the higher will be the rate of profit.
4. The *input-output coefficients of production*, or the amount of output which can be produced with one unit of any given factor input: the larger the amount of output which can be produced with given inputs, the higher will be the rate of profit.
5. The *rate of capacity utilization*, or the ratio of productive capital used in production to the stock of capital actually owned: the higher the utilization rate, the less waste of owned capital will take place and the higher will be the rate of profit.
6. The *profit tax rate*, or the percentage of before-tax profits which are taxed by the government: the higher this tax rate, the lower will be profitability.

It is reasonably obvious, given our introductory remarks, that at least the first three factors and the last in this list clearly and directly reflect power relationships. The greater the power of capital over labor, other things being equal, the lower will be the real wage rate and/or the higher will be the intensity of labor. The more dominating domestic capital is in its relationships with foreign buyers and sellers, similarly, the more favorable will be the terms of trade. And the more effectively capital wages battle with citizens through the state, finally, the lower will be the corporate tax rate.

It takes only a little more investigation to ascertain the power relationships which might affect the other items in the list. Power relationships between capital and the citizenry, mediated by the state, may profoundly affect the kinds of subsidies and R&D which influence the direction of technical change and therefore the input-output coefficients. State relations will also directly determine the corporate-profit tax rate. And it may be the case, as we have argued for the specific case of the United States after World War II, that power relations between capital and labor are likely to affect the level of utilization in the aggregate economy.

The intensity of inter-capitalist rivalry, influenced by the relative power of capitalist firms, is also likely to affect several of the profit-rate determinants: for example, moderated competition will make it easier for firms to pass on rising costs through higher prices, thus lowering real wages, while the global market power of United States firms will help sustain relatively favorable terms of trade.

If one could adequately chart the course of the power relationships affecting these variables, in short, one could make considerable progress toward understanding the sources of movements in the rate of profit and the pace of capital accumulation. Where to turn in that mapping exercise?[5]

Social Structures of Accumulation

We believe that the perspective afforded by the concept of a social structure of accumulation (SSA) provides an invaluable guide for this kind of analytic project.

The SSA model begins with the basic Marxian proposition outlined above: Profitability conditions the pace of accumulation which in turn substantially regulates the rate of economic growth.

But the accumulation of capital through capitalist production cannot be analyzed as if it takes place either in a vacuum or in chaos. Capitalists cannot and will not invest in production unless they are able to make reasonably determinate calculations about their expected rate of return. And the socioeconomic environment external to the individual firm will profoundly affect those expectations. *Without a stable and favorable external environment*, capitalist investment in production will not proceed.

The specific set of institutions which make up this external environment has been called the "social structure of accumulation." Its specific elements include the institutions whose structure and stability are necessary for capital accumulation to take place, such as the state of labor-management relations and the stability of the financial system. It is at least theoretically plausible that such an SSA will alternatively stimulate and constrain the pace of capital accumulation. If the constituent institutions of the social structure of accumulation are favorable to capital and working smoothly without challenge, capitalists are likely to feel enthusiastic and secure about the prospects for investing in the expansion of productive capacity. But if the social structure of accumulation begins to become shaky, if class conflict or past capital accumulation have pressed the institutions to their limits and they begin to lose their legitimacy, capitalists will be more disposed to put their money to other uses — consumption, financial investments, or assets abroad.

It is not simply a problem, moreover, of achieving a sufficiently high and stable rate of profit. For the profit rate can be *too* high. If wage income is relatively low and capitalists do not spend enough out of their relatively high profits on investment, there may not be enough effective demand to absorb the products of capitalist production. If inventories of unsold goods then pile up, capitalists will eventually cut back on production unless the state can continuously make up the difference.

The functions of the constituent institutions of a given social structure of accumulation, in short, are both daunting and fundamental. Their health and vitality substantially determine *both* whether or not capitalists expect the profit rate to settle stably at a sufficiently attractive level to justify investment over alternative uses *and* whether or not the right balance is achieved between profitability and effective demand.

There is good reason, moreover, for believing that capitalism has experienced successive *stages* in its institutional capacity to achieve these daunting tasks.[6] The history of at least the United States economy over the past 150 years suggests a clear historical rhythm of alternating expansion and contraction over roughly 50-year swings. In each of the two previous instances of crisis — in the 1890s and the 1930s — basic changes in economic and political institutions proved necessary before a return to prosperity was possible. The paths to this economic restructuring were tangled with thickets of competing political interests, and it took years to clear the way for a decisive political resolution. This path-clearing appears to have required, in the more formal language of this section, the construction of a new SSA before accumulation could revive.

The Crisis of the Postwar SSA in the United States

We have elsewhere provided a historical account of the rise and demise of the postwar social structure of accumulation in the United States, describing its initial consolidation and its ultimate erosion under increasingly effective challenges to capitalist control (Bowles, Gordon and Weisskopf 1983: Chap. 4).

Our basic argument is that the postwar SSA rested upon four principal buttresses of United States capitalist power, each of which involved a particular set of institutionalized power relations allowing United States corporations to achieve predominant control over potential challengers in the immediate postwar period. We refer to these four institutional axes as the *capital-labor accord, Pax Americana,* the *capital-citizen accord,* and the *moderation of inter-capitalist rivalry,* respectively.[7] They remained relatively solid into the 1960s, but the success of the SSA in promoting economic growth proved ultimately contradictory. Workers, foreign suppliers of raw materials, and domestic citizens began to question and to resist the previously established structures of power. The growing strength of other capitalist nations, as well as the success of anti-capitalist movements in the Third World, further challenged the power of United States capital. Increased competition both domestically and internationally reduced capitalists' ability to protect their profitability from these incursions. The postwar capitalist system consequently began to erode; corporate capitalists found it increasingly difficult to control the terms of their interaction with the other major actors on the economic scene.

We briefly review each of these four power axes on its own institutional terms.

The Capital-Labor Accord. The first set of institutions governed relations between capital and labor in the United States after the late 1940s. This accord involved an explicit and implicit *quid pro quo*, assuring management control over enterprise decision-making (with union submission and cooperation) in exchange for the promise to workers of real compensation rising along with labor productivity, improved working conditions, and greater job security — in short, a share in capitalist prosperity. The accord also consolidated the relative advantages of the unionized over the non-unionized part of the workforce and contributed to an intensification of labor segmentation along job, gender, and racial lines (Gordon, Edwards and Reich 1982). The accord was administered, on capital's side, by an increasingly bureaucratic and hierarchical system of labor management. This system of bureaucratic control was backed up by an expanding army of management cadres devoted to supervision and discipline.

The capital-labor accord worked for a while. But it appears that the effectiveness of corporate control over labor was beginning to decline after the mid-1960s. Workers were not staging a political revolt against the capitalist system, to be sure, but, from the mid-1960s through at least the mid-1970s, many were becoming increasingly restive with bureaucratic control and many were beginning to experience — and undoubtedly to appreciate — much greater protection from insistent corporate discipline as the cost to workers of losing their jobs began to decline.[8] Corporate profits were bound to suffer.

Pax Americana. The second buttress of United States capitalist power was the postwar structure of international economic institutions and political relations that assured the United States a dominant role in the world capitalist economy. *Pax Americana* provided favorable terms for United States capitalists in their interaction with foreign suppliers of both wage goods and intermediate goods and with foreign buyers of United States produced goods. Equally important, the increasingly open world economy gave United States capital the mobility it needed to make its threats of plant closings credible in bargaining with United States workers and citizens over wages, working conditions and tax rates.

Though the United States-dominated world system conferred significant advantages on United States capital in its relations with United States workers, it affected profitability in the domestic economy most directly through its impact on the terms on which the United States could obtain goods and services from abroad. This is reflected in the United States terms of trade. The better this relative price, the more favorable the terms on which United States firms can obtain imported inputs. As one might have expected from the extent of United States power for the first couple of decades after World War II, the United States terms of trade improved substantially for a time.

But after roughly the mid-1960s, United States corporations faced growing international challenges:

— Challenges from the Third World began to undermine United States international domination in the mid-1960s. The failure of the 1961 Bay of Pigs invasion and especially the long and humiliating failure to stem the revolutionary tide in South Vietnam marked a significant and escalating erosion of the United States government's capacity to "keep the world safe" for private enterprise.

— Another significant challenge in the world economy came from exporters of raw materials, primarily in Third World nations. By the early 1970s, the economic bargaining power of some of the Third World raw-material-exporting nations increased substantially; OPEC, the cartel of oil-exporting nations, was the most visible and important example.

These international challenges combined to diminish United States international power and, with it, the ability of United States corporations to profit from their powerful leverage over foreign buyers and sellers.

The Capital-Citizen Accord. The postwar SSA also included a set of political arrangements which regulated the inherent conflict between capitalists' quest for profits and people's demands for economic security and for the social accountability of business. An expanded role for the state in providing for citizens' needs was suitably circumscribed by the capitalist principle of profitability as the ultimate criterion guiding public policy.

By the mid-1960s, support for business was now being challenged. Beginning with occupational health-and-safety campaigns, a wide variety of movements emerged to challenge the hallowed identity of private greed and public virtue. With striking speed, these movements led to new government regulations affecting traffic safety, occupational health and safety, environmental protection, consumer product safety, and nuclear power generation.

In many cases these challenges arose from a wider appreciation of the importance of values like environmental protection. But in many cases, as well, they resulted much more simply from defensive and protective reactions against the rising and increasingly serious hazards of life in the postwar regime. Faced with these spreading hazards, people had no choice but to react. United States capital was able to reap substantial advantages from the corporate-citizen accord for two decades. But the contradictions of the postwar capitalist system eventually blew up in the collective capitalist face.

The Moderation of Inter-Capitalist Rivalry. For a substantial period after World War II, United States corporations were able to enjoy the fruits of substantially attenuated inter-capitalist competition. Most strikingly, the wartime devastation of the Japanese and the leading European economies left United States capitalists in the enviable position of unrivalled kings of the mountain, able effectively to dominate corporations from other advanced capitalist countries. Perhaps equally important, the rapid pace of accumulation in the domestic economy tended to provide ample room for growth for most large United States corporations within their own industries, reducing the likelihood of inter-industry merger bids or capital entry.

After the mid-1960s, however, this comfortable cushion of moderated competition began to turn into a bed of thorns. In both the international and domestic economies, intensifying competition began substantially to reduce United States capitalists' ability to maintain stability in their own ranks and deal effectively with external challengers.

— One challenge came from the increasingly intensive competition waged by corporations in Europe and Japan. Having recovered from the devastation of World War II, these corporations were able to cut into United States corporate shares of international export markets and to provide increasingly stiff import competition in the United States.

— As growth and accumulation in the United States economy slowed, further, inter-capitalist competition intensified on the domestic terrain as well (Shepherd 1982). From the merger wave of the late 1960s through the junk bond buyouts of the 1980s, firms were forced more and more to protect their rear flanks from takeovers all the while they were fighting forward battles with workers, foreign buyers and sellers, and citizens. As domestic rates of profit plunged in many industries, as well, corporations often chose to switch rather than to fight, lifting their capital out of their home industries and seeking to penetrate others; this exposed many corporations to increased exposure to market rivalry with domestic as well as foreign invaders.

Whatever the source of the challenges, United States corporations were more and more pressed after the mid-1960s by increasingly intense inter-capitalist rivalry. Their ability to organize their own ranks for battle and to pass on through higher prices the costs of their three-front war was substantially undercut.

Basic Foundations

We now have in place the essential elements for an interpretation of the stagnation of the United States economy since the mid-1960s. To recapitulate, the basic argument proceeds in four steps:

1. Long-term accumulation in a capitalist economy is fundamentally profit-led. In order to understand the pace of investment and growth, one must apprehend the determinants of capitalist profitability.

2. The rate of profit in a capitalist economy is directly affected by the power relations mediating capitalists' interactions with workers, foreign buyers and sellers, and the citizenry. The battlefield conditions in this three-front war, mediated by the degree of cohesiveness within the capitalist ranks, can potentially influence all of the major factors determining the corporate rate of profit.

3. Capitalist power and the pace of accumulation are shaped in capitalist economies by the constituent institutions of a given social structure of accumulation. When those institutions are in place and stably effecting capitalist domination, capital accumulation can proceed at a vigorous pace. When the viability of those institutions begins to erode, profitability is likely to suffer and stagnation is likely to follow.

Table 1
The Rise and Demise of the Postwar Social Structure of Accumulation

Phase	Capital-Labor Accord	Pax Americana	Capital-Citizen Accord	Inter-Capitalist Rivalry
Boom: 1948– 1966	Cost of job loss rises Workers' resistance down	U.S. Military dominance Terms of trade improve	Government support for accumulation; profits main state priority	Corporations insulated from domestic & foreign competition
Erosion: 1966– 1973	Cost of job loss plunges Workers' resistance spreads	Military power challenged Terms of trade hold steady	Citizen movements take hold	Foreign competition & domestic mergers begin to affect corporations
Stalemate: 1973– 1979	Stagnant economy creates stalemate between capital and labor	OPEC, declining $ result in sharp deterioration in U.S. terms of trade	Citizen movements effect new fetters on business	Pressure of foreign competition & domestic rivalry intensifies

4. This approach appears to apply closely to the case of the postwar capitalist system in the United States. United States corporations achieved considerable power through the construction of a new SSA after World War II, enjoying substantial leverage through their domination of the capital-labor accord, Pax Americana, and the capital-citizen accord as well as through the moderation of intercapitalist rivalry. As challenges to capitalist control developed along all four of those institutional axes in the 1960s, United States corporations watched their power erode and, consequently, their profitability decline. Table 1 provides a brief glimpse of the dynamics of SSA consolidation and erosion in the United States economy from 1948 through 1979.[9] Table 2 then summarizes the linkages flowing from the four institutional power dimensions highlighted by this historical outline to the determinants of the profit rate outlined in the first sub-section on "Power and Profits." These linkages make possible a complete analysis of the connections running from the SSA through the profit rate to accumulation and growth.[10]

Table 2
Linkages Between the Postwar SSA and Components of the Profit Rate

While there is no simple (one-to-one) correspondence between each of the dimensions of capitalist power and the determinants of the profit rate, we list here the four main dimensions of capitalist power in the postwar SSA of the United States, and the primary variables through which these power relations affected the profit rate:

Labor Accord	real wage rate, labor intensity, capacity utilization
Pax Americana	terms of trade, profit tax rate
Citizen Accord	input-output coefficients, profit tax rate, capacity utilization
Capitalist Rivalry	real wage rate, terms of trade, capacity utilization

THE CONTRADICTIONS OF CONSERVATIVE ECONOMICS

That analysis extends through the 1970s. Building on that base, we can interpret the "conservative economics" reigning during the 1980s in large part as a consistent effort to restore corporate profitability by rolling back effective challenges to United States capitalist power: by raising the cost of job loss, improving the terms of trade, more vigorously flexing United States military power, reducing the intensity of government regulation, and dramatically reducing capital's share of the total government tax burden. As any observer could easily report, and as the underlying data for our quantitative indicators of the SSA also clearly confirm, the Reagan Administration made substantial progress on all of these fronts. Did it succeed in reviving the net after-tax rate of profit?

The average net after-tax rate of profit during the business cycle from 1974 to 1979 was 5.5 percent. The average net after-tax rate of profit during the not-quite-completed business cycle from 1980 through 1985 was 5.7 percent.[11] The average rate of profit in the 1960–66 cycle, by contrast, was 8.0 percent. For all of the triumphs of business interests in Washington and throughout the economy in the 1980s, the profit rate did not significantly rebound.

This appears to pose a puzzle. Conservative economics sought to roll back challenges to capital's power and succeeded in obtaining much more favorable values for many of the indicators along our four SSA power dimensions than had earlier prevailed. And yet, actual profitability did not improve.

The basic solution to this puzzle, we believe, lies in the inherent contradictions of conservative macroeconomic policy. Conservative economics relied heavily on the monetarist policies initiated in 1979 by Paul Volcker of the Fed and intensified when the Reagan Administration came to power in 1981. These policies resulted in extremely low rates of capacity utilization during the three-year recession from 1980 to 1982. Another consequence of this policy was a highly inflated value for the dollar; the resultant improvement in the United States terms of trade was similarly contradictory, in that it reduced the competitiveness of United States products on the world market and thus exacerbated the decline in capacity utilization. In sum, conservative economics won the battle for capitalist power but had apparently not yet won the war for corporate profitability, by the mid-1980s, because of the high cost of the battlefield victories imposed by the terms of the postwar SSA.

ALTERNATIVE EXPLANATIONS OF STAGNATION

Since other contributions to this volume elaborate a variety of alternative accounts of the stagnation of the United States economy over the past nearly two decades, we pause only briefly here to highlight some of the central differences between the account outlined in this essay and other possible explanations of the recent crisis.

Mainstream Accounts

It is common among mainstream economists to attribute the stagnation of the United States economy to a variety of "exogenous" shocks such as the oil-price jolts of 1973 and 1979 or to macroeconomic mismanagement (for presentation and critique of these views, see Bowles, Gordon and Weisskopf 1983: Chap. 3). We find, however, that these analyses are substantially incomplete and miss much of what happened in the United States economy during the rise and demise of the postwar capitalist system. Our empirical explorations suggest three principal shortcomings of conventional mainstream accounts.

— Many mainstream accounts date the crisis from the oil-price shock of 1973, but almost every salient economic indicator suggests that it began much earlier — in the mid-1960s (Bowles, Gordon and Weisskopf 1983: Chap. 2).

— Most mainstream accounts of productivity growth, profitability, and investment ignore the sorts of social determinations of macroeconomic performance which our emphasis on "challenges to capital" highlights. In a series of detailed comparisons, we find that attention to these social determinations uniformly improves our ability to explain movements in productivity growth, profitability and investment (in addition to previously cited work, see also Weisskopf, Bowles and Gordon 1983).

— Far from resulting from "exogenous shocks," the crisis of the United States economy appears to flow from the internal evolution of the postwar capitalist system. In each of our econometric investigations, we find no evidence of "structural change" in the models, suggesting that the same factors which help account for the boom also help account for the subsequent crisis.

An "Over-Investment" Crisis?

Some Marxist economists stress the importance of capitalists' collectively "irrational" decisions to "over-invest," leading to a decline in profitability from a rising organic composition of capital (see the essay in this volume by David Laibman). It is certainly true that the ratio of capital to output increased fairly steadily during the period of crisis and that, in this nominal respect, this focus on capitalist "over-investment" is potentially fruitful.

But our own analyses suggest that this kind of explanation of the postwar crisis is incomplete at best: Once one accounts for the influence of the SSA power dimensions on corporate profitability, there is no further explanatory power to be gained from adding a term to account for movements in the capital intensity of production. It does not appear, in other words, that this "over-investment" perspective offers much additional empirical insight beyond that afforded by the approach outlined here.[12]

An "Underconsumption" Crisis?

Some Marxist and post-Keynesian economists highlight problems of "underconsumption" or "effective demand" as underlying causes of the crisis of the United States economy (see the essays in this volume by John Bellamy Foster and by Edward J. Nell). These interpretations would suggest that the rate of growth of demand turned down before the rate of profit and the pace of investment, not after their inflection points; and, according to at least some accounts, that these problems of underconsumption resulted from a shift in the income distribution toward capital as a result of capital's being ''too strong.'' We find two main problems with the empirical usefulness of this approach (see Weisskopf, Bowles and Gordon 1985:266–272):

— All of the available evidence seems to suggest that the rate of profit declined substantially *before* the downturn in the rate of growth of output or consumption.

— Despite many common assertions about the rising power of monopolies, we find that there was neither an increase in monopolistic competition nor a decisive shift in the income distribution away from labor toward capital just before or during the initial years of the crisis. Indeed, as we noted earlier, available evidence suggests that there was an intensification of inter-capitalist competition during precisely this period.

POLITICAL IMPLICATIONS

Capitalism is a contradictory system of power relationships that evolves in large measure through the continuing but changing forms of class struggle, international conflict and other tensions to which its structure gives rise.

To analyze the latest capitalist economic crisis we have built upon a theoretical approach to the analysis of a capitalist system which focuses on its imbedded power relations and its historically contingent and inherently contradictory social structure of accumulation. We have argued that the initial decline of corporate profitability in the postwar period can be explained by a corresponding decline in the power of the United States capitalist class to deal with growing challenges from the domestic working class, the domestic citizenry, and foreign suppliers and buyers — challenges which themselves arose out of the dynamics of the postwar boom. In the last decade, in a political climate influenced by high levels of unemployment, United States capital has scored major political victories over all those groups whose challenges form the heart of our analysis of the origins of the economic crisis. But the challengers were turned back at a very high cost in economic stagnation associated with the major recessions of 1974–75 and 1980–82. Profitability has remained, on average, at a relatively low level. We attribute this outcome to the inherent contradictions of conservative macroeconomic policy under the prevailing postwar SSA.

To achieve a true victory on behalf of capital, conservative economics would have needed to alter the underlying relationship between the rate of capacity utilization and the SSA power dimensions. If it were possible to enhance capitalist power without having to depress capacity utilization to such a significant extent, this would permit much higher levels of profitability to be attained over an extended period of time and would amount eventually to a genuine alteration of the postwar SSA.

Is there any evidence that this has yet been accomplished? At the time of completion of this article, it is still too early to draw a final conclusion on the consequences of conservative economics. First, because the current business cycle did not reach its peak in 1985, our comparison of 1974–79 with 1980–85 is subject to revision. Second, and ultimately more important, it is possible that a trade-off between capacity utilization and some of the SSA variables more favorable to capital will prove to have emerged after another few years. The verdict will become far clearer when we see how heavy a dose of macroeconomic restraint will be required to keep the latest economic recovery from eroding the significant gains that capital had achieved through the monetarist ''cold bath'' of the early 1980s.

From a broader historical perspective, periods of economic crisis have always been periods of political conflict and institutional innovation. The nature of the political conflicts and the likely outcomes can differ radically, however, depending not only on the political organization of the contending parties and the ideological environment, but also on the nature of the economic crisis itself.

If, for example, the crisis results from the capitalist class being too strong and the demand for goods and services being insufficient as a result, a politically attractive opportunity arises for the left. In this case the short-run and the long-run interests of the working class appear to coincide: a weakening of the capitalist class will help both to end the crisis and also to increase the economic strength with which the working class can carry on the long struggle for a socialist alternative. Thus the Keynesian and social democratic policies which emerged as the dominant programs for the labor movement following the Great Depression promised to redistribute income to labor, farmers, and other non-capitalist groups and thereby stimulate demand for goods and services and end the crisis.

No such happy coincidence of short-term material interests and longer-term radical objectives is associated with the type of supply-side crisis which results initially when the capitalist class is ''too weak.'' The most obvious exit from the crisis is that pointed to by the right: strengthen the capitalist class, restore profits and rekindle the capitalist accumulation process. In the absence of basic institutional change, any success the left may have in obstructing the restoration of unchallenged capitalist hegemony, or in further eroding capitalist power, will merely deepen the crisis. This may perhaps lay the groundwork for a more radical change, but its immediate impact on people will be a worsening of economic distress and insecurity— hardly the kind of promise upon which mass mobilizations can build.

This does not mean, of course, that there are no options for progressive forces in the face of a supply-side crisis. But it does mean that these options must be considerably more radical than those capable of resolving a demand-side crisis. If many during the Great Depression advocated a democratic and egalitarian resolution of the crisis through a redistribution of *purchasing power*, as a means of achieving a higher level of demand, an exit from today's crisis favorable to progressive forces requires the redistribution of *power itself*.

What, then, are the political implications of our analysis? If we are right that profits are central to the vitality of the United States economy as long as it remains capitalist, and that it was rising challenges from non-capitalist forces that caused the initial decline in profitability and the high costs of keeping people down that perpetuated the profitability problem, how can we confront those who contend that economic recovery hinges on capital's ability to control its challengers firmly and efficiently? How can we derive a progressive political strategy — a strategy designed to foster more popular control, more democracy, more socialism — from an analysis that seems to blame progressive political forces for the economic crisis?

Two brief observations may be in order.

First, the fact that successful challenges initiated the crisis in no way assures that beating back the challenges will be an effective way to boost profits and restore the growth process. This point has been well illustrated by the high cost of United States capital's recent efforts to regain the upper hand after their setbacks in the initial stages of the current economic crisis. It is still quite unclear whether capital has yet amassed the political and economic leverage to accomplish what would amount to the construction of a new capitalist social structure of accumulation.

Second, and more important, there is a flaw in the reasoning that would seek to repress challengers as a basis for economic recovery: it presumes that there is no alternative to capitalism, and that the best we can hope for is therefore the restoration of a more efficient system of capitalist exploitation. But we believe that there *is* a socialist democratic alternative — one that offers both an alternative strategy and an alternative vision of the future.

Our analysis points to a political program based on a critique of the legitimacy of capitalist power and to an economic program highlighting the gains to be made from reducing the waste inherent in the imposition and maintenance of capitalist control. By showing that exploitation is fundamentally costly, and that its reduction is compatible with — if not necessary for — a return to economic security and opportunity, we can potentially undermine a major source of capitalist legitimacy and strength. By highlighting the problem of political power, moreover, our analysis points to popular control in both the state and the economy — that is, socialist democracy — as a progressive political alternative. Rather than legitimizing a repressive *status quo*, our theory of the crisis and declining profitability seems to us to dramatize the effectiveness of popular power and therefore to underscore its potential for social transformation.

NOTES

1. We place these terms in quotation marks to suggest their relativity: "too strong" and "too weak" refer solely to the conditions for the smooth reproduction of the capitalist accumulation process, not to some other standard of political or moral desirability or behavior.
2. The concept of the social structure of accumulation was introduced in David M. Gordon (1978), and further developed and applied in Gordon (1980); and Gordon, Richard Edwards and Michael Reich (1982). This perspective is very closely related to a framework developed more or less independently in France known as the "regulation approach"; this approach builds upon the concept of a "regime of accumulation" or, alternatively, a "system of regulation." See, for example, Michel Aglietta (1979) and Alain Lipietz (1986).
3. The "rate of accumulation" is defined for the purposes of this discussion as the rate of change of the net capital stock; this measure is thus equivalent to the ratio of net investment to the lagged (net) capital stock and is highly correlated with the ratio of net investment to GNP.
4. Contrary to the distributional theory of neoclassical economics, neither profits nor wages represents the return to a scarce factor of production; capital is not a productive input (though machines are), while labor is not scarce but rather almost always in excess supply.
5. It may be useful to conclude this section on "challenges to capitalist control" by relating it to a more traditional formulation within Marxian economics called "profit squeeze" theories of crisis (see the introduction to this section by Jim Devine for a review of this traditional account.) The two explanations share in common the perspective that crisis may occur because capitalists are "too weak." Ours expands upon the traditional formulation in three respects: First, we stress that

power relationships may affect more components of the rate of profit than the profit share, as the list in this section indicates. Second, we place a greater stress on the centrality of power relationships in the determination of the basic conditions of profitability, an emphasis which has been somewhat more implicit in traditional profit-squeeze accounts. Third, we recognize that attempts to restore capitalist power — for example, through restrictive monetary and fiscal policy — may replenish the reserve army of labor but fail to restore the profit rate as a result of their negative effects on capacity utilization.

6. This involves a more formal argument about the connection between the SSA and long economic swings. See the references in footnote 2 above.

7. In our earlier work we had neglected the dimension here labeled the "moderation of inter-capitalist rivalry"; we introduce it in this essay in order to help overcome some inadequacies in earlier formulations.

   We should also stress for the purposes of clarification that we consider these four particular institutional axes to apply concretely *only* to the postwar United States; we do not intend a more general argument that any social structure of accumulation at any time can most usefully be characterized by this specific institutional configuration.

8. This analysis builds heavily on the concept of the cost of job loss. For details on definition and measurement, see the essay by Juliet B. Schor in this volume.

9. This table is based on quantitative indicators defined and presented in Bowles, Gordon and Weisskopf (1986: Section 4) and some subsequent unpublished empirical work.

10. In other work we have traced the last link in this connection — from profitability to accumulation and growth. For that analysis we refer to that component of profitability which reflects the influence of underlying SSA institutional factors as the "underlying rate of profit"; we hypothesize that investment flows are especially sensitive to movements in this component of profitability. See Gordon, Weisskopf and Bowles (1986).

11. At the time of writing we could not compute a precise estimate of the rate of profit for 1986 because of the unavailability of data on the net capital stock. A rough estimate of the rate of profit for 1986 suggests that it declined from its 1985 level (from .073 to roughly .072). As a result, although another year of "recovery" improved the cycle average over that for 1980–85, there was still insufficient improvement to warrant the conclusion that corporate profitability had reco-vered. Based on our very approximate estimate for 1986, the estimated cycle average for 1980–86 was 6.0 percent; the difference between this value and the mean for 1974–79 was not statistically significant.

12. This exercise is presented in an unpublished appendix to Bowles, Gordon and Weisskopf (1986), available from the authors. The reverse conclusion does not hold: if the variables representing our approach are added to an equation modelling the "over-investment" perspec-tive, the explanatory power of that equation increases substantially.

6

What Is Stagnation?

JOHN BELLAMY FOSTER

INTRODUCTION

For a majority of mainstream and radical economists, the answer to the question "What is Stagnation"? is fairly simple and straightforward and devoid of any real theoretical significance in and of itself. Either it is seen as a period of longer and deeper than average recessions, or it stands for a long-cycle downturn, which will be followed more or less automatically, after some 25 years duration, by a long-cycle upturn. However, in the case of most of those thinkers on the left who continue to emphasize the primacy of demand-side constraints on the accumulation process in "the present as history," the search for an answer to the above question is nothing less than an attempt to address the central contradiction of the mature monopoly capitalist system.

The purpose of this article is to uncover the complex historical logic through which the phenomenon of stagnation is manifested in modern capitalism, as explained in the work of such radical demand-side theorists as Michal Kalecki, Josef Steindl, Paul Baran, Paul Sweezy and Harry Magdoff. Beginning with the reasons why a condition of stagnation (the main traits of which are widening underemployment, stop-and-start investment and slow growth) has come to represent the normal trend-line of the modern economy around which the recurrent fluctuations of the business cycle occur, the analysis will then shift to a consideration of the various self-limiting forces that sparked the expansionary wave of the 1960s; and how a waning of these forces, or of their positive effects, has led in the 1970s and 1980s to a resurfacing of stagnation and a doubling-over of economic contradictions. The seriousness of the multi-layered crisis that emerges from such a conception of political economic evolution, will then be contrasted, in the conclusion, to the relative complacency engendered by the dominant supply-side strategy for the renewal of American capitalism.

THE STAGNATION PROBLEM

What might be thought of as constituting the logical starting point for all work on the problem of economic stagnation is a recognition of the fact that there is nothing natural or automatic about the fulfillment of a long-run rate of growth that guarantees full capacity production under advanced capitalism. As the conservative economist Joseph Schumpeter wrote in *Capitalism, Socialism and Democracy* (1942): "The power of the business process itself to produce that result [full employment] has, however, been called into question by many economists. . . . We will refer to them by a term that has gained some currency, Stagnationists" (Schumpeter 1947:329).

In utilizing this label for all of those that had lost faith in the ability of "the business process itself" to generate full employment, Schumpeter had in mind such notable theorists as John Maynard Keynes and Alvin Hansen, Keynes's leading interpreter in the

United States (Schumpeter 1951:283–284). Faced with the Great Depression of the 1930s, Hansen's first reaction, like that of most liberal economists during the first eight years of stagnation (prior to 1937), was to trace the problem to such alleged supply-side causes as the high, inflexible wage rates that were thought to have been institutionalized in the economy during the New Era of the 1920s, and which supposedly prevented a smooth adjustment once the downturn had set in (Stoneman 1979:44–50; Foster 1983). But this initial interpretation, was to be summarily discarded in Hansen's case, as in numerous others, when the United States was suddenly struck by the sharp downturn of 1937, which occurred well before the economy had fully recovered from the conditions of depression, and which led to a rapid rise in unemployment from 14 percent in 1937 to 19 percent in 1938. Confronted with this failure of the economy to achieve a full recovery, and relying on the analytical framework introduced by Keynes, Hansen advanced, in such works as *Full Recovery or Stagnation?* (1938), the idea that the capital-rich society of the twentieth century was afflicted by growing difficulties in absorbing potential net savings. Not only was there a "rising propensity to save" among the wealthier elements; but it was also true that such previous inducements to "spontaneous" (as opposed to income-induced) investment as a rapid rate of population growth, a seemingly endless open frontier, and technological innovations of a heavily capital-absorbing character, all of which had underwritten nineteenth century industrialization in the United States, had either come to an end or could be expected to be of diminishing influence as stimulating forces in the foreseeable future.[1] All of which suggested that the economy was likely to move "sidewise" rather than forward if left entirely to its own devices (Hansen 1955:549).

In opposition to this perspective, Schumpeter, Hansen's greatest antagonist in the debate of the late 1930s, attributed stagnation — to the extent that it was something more than a "normal" downturn in the presumed 50 year Kondratieff cycle — not to any failure of capitalism's supposed natural tendency to generate full employment, but rather to the interference of anti-business interests, notably Roosevelt's New Deal (Schumpeter 1939:1011–1050; Magdoff and Sweezy 1987:31). It was only the intrusions of the state within the economic domain which, according to this view, kept a full recovery from taking place "of itself" (Schumpeter 1934:20).

The appearance of the Second World War in Europe and Asia and the rapid rise in United States war production, however, soon transformed the nature of the economic debate, with GNP rising by 70 percent in just six years in response to war-generated demand; and in the prosperity that greeted the United States in the aftermath of the war stagnation was for a time forgotten (Heilbroner 1980:160). It was not until the appearance of what the orthodox economist Paul Samuelson was to call "the Eisenhower stagnation" of 1954–60, following the Korean War, that the issue was temporarily raised again in a major way (Walker and Vatter 1986:325). Pointing then to the statement by Schumpeter quoted above, Hansen was to remark: "I fully accept Schumpeter's definition of stagnationists in *Capitalism, Socialism and Democracy*... I like this definition because it stresses in a precise way the essential issue which is as follows: Can the economy *automatically* produce full employment? Can *automatic* forces alone, under modern conditions, be relied upon to the degree that was possible in the expansionist nineteenth century"? (Hansen 1955:557). The answer was obviously "No"! "We can at no time facilely expect," Hansen had written in *Full Recovery or Stagnation?*, "that a recovery will just automatically complete itself. There is never any assurance that business will surely carry on to a full measure of prosperity. For 'carrying on' means that new investment shall be developed" (Hansen 1938:283).

At the root of the problem was the fact that in an advanced capitalist economy, characterized by a high savings potential and abundant productive capacity, investment tended to be cut off (as far as the normal income generation process was concerned) well before a full employment level of production was reached. For in the contradictory world of capitalism investment produces additional demand in the short-run but new productive capacity after just a few years. And under conditions of a widening underemployment gap (or overall slack demand) the danger to capital of finding itself with too much excess capacity often has the effect of shutting off potential net investment before it can actually be generated, creating a vicious circle of stagnation instead of the virtuous circle of rapid growth predicted in most textbooks. As the Marxist economist Michal Kalecki—often credited with having discovered the essentials of Keynes's *General Theory* before Keynes himself, in essays published in Poland — wrote in the closing sentences of his *Essays in the Theory of Economic Fluctuations* (1939), "The tragedy of investment is that it causes crisis because it is useful. Doubtless many people will consider this theory paradoxical. But it is not the theory which is paradoxical, but its subject — the capitalist economy" (Kalecki 1939:149).

Indeed, what was largely "paradoxical" from a liberal economic standpoint — which, insofar as it rested on neoclassical foundations, had little room for concepts of class or monopoly within its core analytical framework — could be much more easily comprehended by a Marxist theorist like Kalecki, who took as his starting point the class composition of both output and demand. Relying on the simple model of the capitalist economy embedded in Marx's reproduction schemes, Kalecki emphasized that the demand for capital goods is equal to reinvested gross profits, while the demand for wage goods (the great bulk of the consumption goods sector) equals total wages (workers' savings being considered so marginal as to be safely disregarded in the analysis).[2] Rapid accumulation requires a much faster growth in the former than in the latter, but this eventually generates inordinate productive capacity in relation to effective demand, as the gap between the capacity to produce and the capacity to consume widens — although the degree to which this contradiction actually surfaces depends on the relative autonomy of investment from final consumption characteristic of any particular phase of capitalist development (Kalecki 1968).

To elaborate the point somewhat differently, any continual plowing back of profits into new investment would mean that the means of production (Department 1 in the Marxian reproduction schemes, the demand for which comes largely out of gross profits) would expand very much faster than articles of consumption (or Department 2, the demand for which comes mainly from wages). This, in fact, is the basic pattern of every accumulation boom. But it is a self-annihilating process. Sooner or later (depending on historical conditions determining the degree to which the investment process is self-sustaining) the means of production are built up to such a prodigious extent that a social disproportionality develops been the capacity to produce and the corresponding demand. A crisis of overaccumulation rooted in overexploitation then occurs.

Under these circumstances, in which investment (or new capital formation) is inhibited by capital stock already in existence, capitalist expansion becomes increasingly dependent on what Hansen termed "spontaneous" or non-income induced sources of demand. Reversing the traditional assumption of rapid growth under capitalism, Kalecki contended—in a critique of the early Russian Marxist Michael Tugan-Baranovski, who had denied the existence of a problem of final demand — "that an expanded reproduction will take place if there exist factors that simply do not permit the system to remain in the state of simple reproduction [or stationary state]...." (Kalecki 1967:154). Or as he explained in his *Theory of Economic Dynamics:* "Our analysis shows... that long-run development is not inherent in the capitalist economy. Thus specific 'development factors' are required to sustain a long-run upward movement" (Kalecki 1965:161).

Hence, in the absence of "external" factors such as a clustering of technological innovations of a capital absorbing character, or massive government spending on a wartime scale, a well-developed capitalist economy was likely to sink into a pattern of slow growth and rising unemployment and excess capacity, with capital formation fluctuating around the level of zero net investment. Moreover, as a consequence of the steady rise in what Kalecki termed "the degree of monopoly" (reflected in widening profit margins and growing concentration and centralization of capital) "the retardation in the increase in capital and output" would tend to become more severe (Kalecki 1965:161).[3]

The argument with respect to the effect of growing monopolization on the accumulation process was to be carried forward by Josef Steindl, one of Kalecki's colleagues at the Oxford Institute of Statistics during the Second World War, whose major work on the subject was published in 1952 under the title *Maturity and Stagnation in American Capitalism.* For Steindl: "The decrease in the rate of growth of capital in the mature [monopolistic] economy and the concomitant decrease in the rate of profit tend to bring about a decline in the share of profits in incomes, and a decline in the share of capitalists' savings in profits" (Steindl 1976:1945). To account for this situation, the traditional Marxian conception of realization crisis (or a crisis associated with insufficient effective demand) needed a new interpretation, focusing in particular on the significance of excess capacity. Describing the essence of this new approach, first in Kaleckian and then in classical Marxist terms, he wrote:

> If we think of it, the tendency for the capitalists' share of the product to increase does, after all, exist *potentially.* It is a consequence of the growth of oligopoly. The expression of this tendency can only be an *increase in gross profit margins.* That means that the actual share of *net* incomes of capitalists need not increase at all. The increased gross margins may be compensated by a reduced degree of utilization so that there is not a shift of actual income from wages to profits, but a shift of potential income of workers to wastage in excess capacity.
>
> This could be very easily represented in Marxist terms. We should have to say that as a consequence of the rise of oligopoly, the rate of *surplus value produced* tends to increase: the rate of exploitation rises. But as Marx explained, producing surplus value does not necessarily mean realising it, and the realisation depends on the existence of a sufficient market. We should now say that surplus value can be realised only to the extent to which there is a corresponding amount of investment and capitalists' consumption. If this amount does not increase, then the rise in the rate of surplus value *produced* will not lead to any increase in surplus value *realised,* but only to excess capacity" (Steindl 1976:245).

As Steindl went on to remark, the "gross profit margin," or the mark-up on cost price in Kaleckian theory, might be "tentatively" identified with "surplus value produced"

(Steindl 1976:245-246). The theory then states that although the rate of surplus value, and the value rate of profit at the level of production, are increasing, net realized profit rates may actually be stagnant (or even in decline, along with investment), as reflected in rising amounts of excess capacity. Moreover, the logic of the argument is such that it is precisely because monopoly capital seeks to maintain its high gross margins (and excessive rates of surplus value), in the face of downturns in demand, by reducing its utilization rate rather than its prices, that a chronic condition of secular stagnation emerges, since the degree of capacity utilization is itself the main determinant of investment demand. At one and the same time monopoly capital promotes excess capacity in order to maintain its gross profit margins (rate of surplus value), and demonstrates an enormous "fear" of additional, unplanned excess capacity—causing it to cut back on the level of investment whenever the operating rate falls below a certain point.[4] With the resulting stagnation of normal investment demand, a widening under-employment gap becomes a characteristic feature of the modern economy.

The radical implications of Steindl's book, together with the fact that it appeared in the middle of the Korean War boom, virtually guaranteed that his work would be ignored by mainstream economists the vast majority of whom — although momentarily dismayed by the cyclical downturn of the Eisenhower years — were eager to stand at the forefront of what the rebellious sociologist C. Wright Mills was to dub, "The Great American Celebration."[5] "The ghost of Thomas Carlyle," Paul Samuelson wrote in 1964, "should be relieved to know that economics, after all, has not been a dismal science. It has been the cheerful, but impatient science of growth" (Samuelson 1964:730).

It was in this overall climate of Cold War elation that Paul Baran and Paul Sweezy, inspired by the contributions of Kalecki and Steindl (as well as Marx, Veblen, Keynes and Hansen), began to collaborate on a study — published in 1966, two years after Baran's death, under the title *Monopoly Capital* — designed to demonstrate that stagnation was still the main specter haunting the United States economy. According to this theory, Marx's "law of the tendency of the rate of profit to fall" associated with accumulation in the nineteenth century era of free competition, had been replaced, with the emergence of the more restrictive competitive environment of monopoly capitalism at the beginning of the twentieth century, by a "law of the tendency of the surplus to rise" (defining surplus as "the gap, at any given level of production, between output and socially necessary costs of production").[6] Under these circumstances, the critical economic problem became one of surplus absorption. "In general," the authors pointed out, "surplus can be absorbed in three ways: (1) it can be consumed, (2) it can be invested, and (3) it can be wasted" (Baran and Sweezy 1966:79). Capitalist consumption, however, represented a declining proportion of capitalist demand as income grew; which meant that "the investment-seeking share of surplus" tended to rise. But investment itself was hindered by the fact that it created new productive capacity, which could not be expanded for long periods of time without a proportional expansion in final, wage-based demand. And although there was always some possibility of new "epoch-making innovations" arising that could help propel investment forward, all such innovations — resembling the steam engine, the railroad and the automobile in their overall effect — were few and far between. Nor was a vigorous public works campaign (that is a massive program of state employment in the areas of productive consumption and investment) likely to arise to alleviate the problem as long as the logic of the system held sway. Since to think otherwise was to deny the modalities of political power in an advanced capitalist society, where vested interests within the ruling class tended to block any state activities that competed with or diminished the role of the market. Hence, Baran and Sweezy concluded that the system had a powerful tendency to stagnation, largely counteracted thus far through the promotion of economic waste by means of "the sales effort" (including its penetration into the production process) and military expenditures, and through the expansion of the financial sector. All such "protective reactions of the system" were, however, subject to a kind of law of diminishing returns, and could be expected to lead to a doubling-over of contradictions in the not too distant future (Baran and Sweezy 1966:72, 79; Sweezy 1972:42; Magdoff and Sweezy 1981:182; Foster 1986: 221–224).

The changes wrought in the nature and logic of the system, according to Baran and Sweezy's analysis, occurred at the secondary level of the competition of capitals and the distribution of surplus product, and did not alter the more fundamental tendencies within the system uncovered by Marx, connected with the production of surplus value and the growing predominance of its relative form (that is the shift to ever more intensive forms of production). In fact, the growth of Taylorism or scientific management in the early decades of the twentieth century — the theoretical basis of which, as Harry Braverman demonstrated in *Labor and Monopoly Capital* (1974), was already provided by Marx's analysis of the labor process in Volume I of *Capital* — was viewed, from the standpoint of the overall monopoly capital argument, as the key element in a complex historical transition. Indeed, it was the shift to ever greater cost-cutting at the point of production, together with the effectual banning of price competition in concentrated industries, which both raised the rate of surplus value and "skewed its distribution toward the larger units of capital" — thereby generating the chronic pattern of realization crisis (or widening effective demand gap) that has characterized the modern era (Sweezy 1981:63–65, 68–70, 1987:15–16; Foster 1984a:65–-67).

THE REGIME OF CAPITAL

The distinctive characteristics of the foregoing perspective can be brought out more clearly by taking a short detour and making a number of comparisons with recent fashionable trends emanating from French political economy. Like radical stagnation theorists, writers in the new French "regulation school" derive many of their insights from the "realization crisis" strand of Marxian political economy; and therefore emphasize the constraints placed on the selling of commodities, and on the realization of the surplus value (or profits) embodied in these commodities, due to the limits of effective demand. The central categories of this school of thought find their clearest expression in the work of Alain Lipietz, who has written in his book *Mirages and Miracles* (1987) that:

> One of the great contradictions of this mode of production relates to its 'commodity' side. Although capitalists can organize production in their factories down to the last detail and can, given their habits and their calculations, establish there an 'iron law of proportionality,' in their dealings with the rest of society they behave like any other gambler: their products may or may not find a buyer at a price which makes production profitable (this is the famous realization problem). Yet it works... except, of course, when there is a crisis. In order to understand how it works we have to produce new concepts. A number of French research workers have proposed the concepts of 'regime of accumulation' and 'mode of regulation' (Lipietz 1987:14).

The first of these concepts is nothing other than Marx's reproduction schemes (the input-output or departmental matrix established by the class composition of social output and demand) placed in a very long-run institutional context. Or as Lipietz himself explains it: "A regime of accumulation can be defined in terms of a *schema of reproduction* which describes how social labor is allocated over a period of time and how products are distributed between different departments of production [that is, the capital goods department and the consumption goods department] over the same period" (Lipietz 1987:32–33).

In terms of historical stages, the regulation school contends that two broad "regimes of accumulation" can be distinguished, corresponding generally to the traditional Marxist stages of competitive and monopoly capitalism, but defined in terms of the predominance in the first of extensive reproduction geared to the building-up of the means of production, and in the second of intensive reproduction dependent on the growth of mass consumption (Lipietz 1987:33).

Moreover, to understand how a particular regime of accumulation is actually "realized" in any particular phase of history it is necessary, according to this perspective, to introduce the secondary and more concrete category of a "mode of regulation," consisting of "institutional forms, procedures and habits." The mode of regulation that "reproduced" the extensive regime of the nineteenth century is labeled "competitive regulation," and "was characterized... by price movements that were highly responsive to demand." In contrast, the mode of regulation that was eventually to uphold the intensive regime of accumulation — once the Great Depression made it clear that competitive regulation was no longer adequate for the realization of the system at this stage — is referred to by Lipietz as "monopolistic regulation." This "new *'monopolistic'* mode of regulation," he contends, "incorporated both productivity rises and the corresponding rise in popular consumption into the determination of wages and nominal prices *a priori....* [T]his regime is now known as 'Fordism' " (Lipietz 1987:34–36). The present crisis is then a crisis of "Fordism," or of a mode of regulation that relies on high wages and mass consumption, underwritten by high productivity.

Despite the occasional insights that it provides, this approach, when viewed from the quite different perspective of stagnation theory, has at least one very serious and perhaps fatal shortcoming. What appears to be missing is any concrete consideration of the problem of investment or capital accumulation as such. Indeed, the entire emphasis of the theory, insofar as it focuses on the so-called "Fordist" dynamic, is rather on consumption; and instead of tracing the problem of expanded reproduction to the tendency of investment to stagnate (due to overexploitation, overcapacity, and the lack of external stimuli like new capital-absorbing technologies and markets), the failures of the system in the present stage are thought to be reducible to the limits of "overconsumption" (Davis 1986:206–221). But as Kalecki said: "The workers spend what they get; the capitalists get what they spend" (Robinson 1966:ix). Thus, the realization problem has to be seen mainly in relation to problems associated with investment out of profits rather than wage-based consumption. Without a clear understanding of the historical problem of investment — which in the monopoly capitalist era cannot simply be seen as a reflex of movements in the profit rate — what remains is a largely impressionistic account of the evolution of the system that dresses up, but does not otherwise significantly alter, the ruling class' own interpretation. Nothing therefore is easier for Lipietz than simply to infer, in conformity with the dominant supply-side ideology, that, "the present crisis in intensive accumulation is a crisis in *profitability*, whereas the crisis of the 1930s was a crisis of overproduction" (Lipietz 1987:43). Or as he has stated elsewhere: "I agree with Weisskopf, Bowles and Gordon [1985] that the present crisis occurred because the capitalist class was 'too weak' rather than 'too strong' " (Lipietz 1986:13).[7]

From the standpoint of stagnation theory, such an assessment is of course wrong. Thus, among the numerous conceptual errors associated with this kind of supply-side interpretation of the present crisis (shared by the regulation school and profit squeeze theorists alike), the following are particularly notable: (1) the confusion of *ex post* wage and profit shares in national income accounts with the *ex ante* rate of exploitation at the level of production; (2) the pretense that aggregate productivity statistics for the whole economy are concrete indicators of conditions on the factory floor, without regard to such factors as the utilization of capital stock; and (3) the failure to adopt a theoretical framework that distinguishes between productive and unproductive labor (and between profits and surplus value) (see Foster 1984a:68–70; Szymanski 1984).

Still, all of the foregoing is less important than the fact that this type of assessment simply misses the point. For the secular tendencies of advanced monopoly capitalism in the United States cannot be concretely accounted for by a purported "overconsumption" and underexploitation squeeze on profits — even when an ill-defined long cycle is brought in to bolster the argument — but only in terms of the long-run stagnation of investment resulting from the constant tendency of the system to produce a relative overaccumulation of capital. As long as the laws of motion of monopoly capitalism remain supreme, there will be a tendency to generate a larger "investment-seeking surplus" at a full employment level of output than the system can profitably absorb. Hence, there is no escaping the fact that the inner logic of capitalism promotes the kind of disproportionalities associated with a capitalist class that is "too strong" and a working class that is "too weak." "The very necessity of *general political action*," Marx once observed, "affords the proof that in its merely economic action capital is the stronger side" (Marx 1935:59).

THE END OF PROSPERITY

The reasons for the extraordinary rise and fall of the economic prosperity that characterized the immediate post-Second World War period, cannot therefore be found in any simple phenomenon of "Fordist overconsumption" (or Keynesian "overemployment" and "underexploitation"). Rather, it is necessary to take a closer look at the historical conditions affecting long-term capital formation, in a system where the ruling class, in its purely economic action, is ultimately the stronger side.

The factors or combination of factors that in the course of capitalist history have usually been associated with long waves of sustained growth have generally consisted of: (1) the generation and adoption of epoch-making innovations that induce heavy capital investment, new forms of infrastructural development, the spread of population into new locations, etc.; (2) expansion of military spending in preparation for war; (3) the rebuilding of the industrial base in the aftermath of war; (4) a period of relatively smooth expansion of the credit and debt structure (normally preceded by earlier debt-deflations — that is massive depreciation of financial assets); (5) the dominance of a single hegemonic power within the world capitalist economy; and (6) development of new markets in the periphery of the world economy (Magdoff 1982:3).

Such conditions allow for the absorption of surplus to a degree that is, in the longer run, unsustainable. Each of these factors came into play to some extent in the long wave expansion of the immediate post-Second World War era. The 1950s saw the second great wave in the automobilization of America, which has to be understood as including the building of the interstate highway system, as well as the expansion of the auto, glass, rubber and steel industries; the conditions of which were partly provided by the enormous growth of consumer liquidity that had accumulated during the war, allowing for a vast growth in the consumer credit system. Ever greedy for customers, the automobile industry became the model for a pattern of expansion based on a constantly augmented ''sales effort,'' in which the costs of selling goods became inextricably connected with the costs of production. Other technologies originally generated by war demand such as the jet aircraft also created new markets for investment. The rebuilding of the war-torn economies of Europe and Japan, which received an enormous boost from the remilitarization of the United States economy in connection with the Korean War, as well as from the the extension of the mass use of automobiles to these countries, boosted the overall expansion. The two regional wars fought by the United States in Korea and Indochina produced record peaks in the economy in those years, as well as the longest business cycle expansion (106 months) from February 1961 to December 1969 that the twentieth century United States economy has experienced. The same years also saw a steady building up of the financial sector of the economy (banks, other financial institutions, real estate and insurance), which rose as a percent of goods production from 21 percent in 1950 to 33 percent in 1970 and 40 percent in 1985 (Magdoff and Sweezy 1987: 23). The rise of the United States to a position of hegemony in the world capitalist economy was accompanied by a straddling of the globe by United States military bases, a flow of economic aid to Europe through the Marshall Plan, and the sending of aid subsequently to client states throughout the world. The trade and monetary regimes associated with the General Agreement of Tariffs and Trade (GATT), the International Monetary Fund (IMF) and the World Bank — all backed up by United States hegemony — resulted in a much freer circulation of capital around the globe, as well as the setting up of rules for disciplining Third World states. Multinational corporations — constituting increasingly important mechanisms of imperialism — soon girded the globe (Magdoff 1982:3-5).

What is important to understand is that all of these factors were either self-limiting in character, or could be expected to result in the doubling-over of economic contradictions in the not too distant future (or sometimes both). The wave of automobilization, as well as the demand associated with the spread of the commercial aircraft industry, had essentially petered out by the mid-1960s, entering a phase of simple reproduction. American ingenuity in building sales costs and other unproductive (or unreproductive) expenditures into the price of vehicles and other products, undoubtedly made United States companies more vulnerable over the long run to foreign competition. The rebuilding of the war-devastated economies in Europe and Japan was eventually completed, resulting in a slowing down in the growth rate of these countries. The use of American military power to combat revolutions around the globe came up against the reality of what Gabriel Kolko has called ''the perpetual crisis of American foreign policy'' and the inevitable defeat in Vietnam (Kolko 1984:348–398). Concentration of the economy on military output was to be of diminishing effectiveness in terms of its employment effects due to the high technology character of such spending; resulted in a prohibitive growth in the federal deficit; and increasingly appeared to carry long-term costs associated with the structuring of output toward non-reproductive luxury goods (Baran and Sweezy 1966:213–217; Foster 1984b:339–345). The growth of the debt economy resulted in added fragility in an economy increasingly characterized by stagflation (stagnation plus inflation), credit crunches, rising interest rates, and a growing federal deficit. The revival of competitor nations in Europe and Japan, as well as the expansion of productive capacity in certain key Third World countries, undermined United States hegemony and weakened the world economy, as international surplus capacity emerged in industry after industry. The spread of multinational corporations resulted in a greater concentration of surplus in the core states and undermined employment in those states. The hypertrophy of the world financial structure — not unrelated to the spread of multinational banking — meanwhile created a global debt crisis that threatened to destabilize both core and periphery.

Some theorists, confronted with this decline in the secular growth trend of the advanced capitalist economies since the mid- or late-1960s, have argued, following Schumpeter and others, that it is nothing more than the down phase in a 50 year Kondratieff cycle, that will be automatically succeeded by a 25 year expansionary phase beginning "in about 1990" (Wallerstein 1982:40). Yet, while the existence of long *waves* in a general sense cannot be denied, the existence of long *cycles,* in the sense that they generate, like other business cycles, their own "forces of reversal" has never been demonstrated. More specifically, while long wave expansions are based on *self-limiting* factors that spur investment and allow it to overcome powerful tendencies toward stagnation *for a time,* there is nothing in the nature of a long wave downturn that will *automatically* generate an upturn in the secular trend. As Paul Sweezy has written: "It was the Second World War that brought the stagnation of the 1930s to an end. We still do not know what will bring the stagnation of the 1970s and 1980s to an end — or what kind of end it will be" (Magdoff and Sweezy 1987:37–38).

THE SCOURGE OF SUPPLY-SIDE THEORY

It is an all but settled maxim of the dominant economic policy makers today that the current weakness of the United States economy can be attributed to supply-side factors: mainly high wages, low labor productivity, and excessive state spending. The solution, which the Reagan Administration has religiously followed, is to break unions, increase unemployment, force down wages, cut back on state spending that benefits those at the bottom of society, and reform the tax system to redistribute income from the poor to the rich. The result has been continued stagnation, with unemployment averaging almost 7 percent and capacity utilization standing at about 79 percent in 1986, 4 years into the recovery phase of the business cycle.

The gap between prevailing economic wisdom and concrete reality is nowhere more apparent than at the point of production. One of the most frequently heard justifications for what Lord Nicholas Kaldor has called "the scourge" of monetarist and supply-side economics has to do with the alleged decline in productivity on the factory floor (Kaldor 1986:64–70). But as liberal economist Lester Thurow of the Massachusetts Institute of Technology points out:

> If... one looks carefully at the .5 percent per year rate of growth of nonfarm business productivity between 1978 and 1985, one discovers some interesting facts. During those years American business firms reduced their blue-collar payrolls by 1.9 million workers, or 6

percent, while increasing the business G.N.P. by 18 percent [after correction for inflation]. If one produces 18 percent more while reducing inputs by 6 percent, one has achieved a 24 percent increase in productivity. Divide that number by seven years; the calculation shows that the blue-collar workers of America on the factory floor were generating a rate of growth of productivity in excess of 3 percent per year — world class (Thurow 1986:26).

Indeed, insofar as there is "a problem" in generating a high rate of productivity, it lies not at the point of production, but in the proliferation of unproductive employment (white collar positions devoted to management, sales and finance, and the growth of the service sector) and the rise of excess capacity itself (which depresses productivity as overhead costs rise as a proportion of total output). Such facts should warn one of the dangers of uncritically accepting the supply-side case despite its omnipresence in policy circles. They also suggest that the main contradictions of monopoly capitalism lie not on the cost or supply-side but in the utilization of potential surplus product.[8] Indeed, the countervailing factors that in the past have helped to stabilize "the regime of accumulation" — factors like a growing "sales effort," inflation, deficits, financial expansion, ever greater reliance on military spending, etc. — are increasingly associated with a doubling-over of economic contradictions and the emergence of a society that is more and more irrational, when judged in terms of either demand *or* supply (Wolff 1987).

In any case: "From the social point of view, the central problem is not cutting costs or raising productivity, but how and where to allocate resources in order to eliminate poverty and to improve the quality of life on the job and at home" (Magdoff and Sweezy 1981:177). Socialists need to struggle against the scourge of supply-side theory not because it is bad economics — which it undoubtedly is — but because it conflicts with basic social needs that can be met only in a transformed social order.

NOTES

1. It is worth noting in this connection that somewhere between 40 and 50 percent of all private capital formation in the United States in the last two decades of the nineteenth century may have been accounted for by the railroad alone (Baran and Sweezy 1966:221).

2. Aside from the fact that workers are often by necessity long-term dis-savers, Kalecki's assumption (based on Marx) that workers' savings are nonexistent, is more than reasonable in this context, since any marginal savings out of wages would only make the realization problem worse, while not otherwise altering the general case. For a portrayal of "the class composition of social output and demand" embodied in Marx's reproduction schemes, see the input-output table for simple reproduction provided in Foster (1984b:340–342).

3. The significance attributed to the increasing concentration and centralization of capital by such theorists as Kalecki, Josef Steindl, Paul Baran and Paul Sweezy, has been subjected to harsh criticism by numerous liberal and even some left-wing analysts. Thus in a recent critique of this perspective (directed in particular at the late Al Szymanski) Samuel Bowles, David Gordon and Thomas Weisskopf use data from Table 896 of the *Statistical Abstract of the United States 1982–83,* to argue that "one does not find much of an increase" in the percentage share of manufacturing assets owned by the 100 largest manufacturing firms between 1960, when the figure is 46.4 percent, and 1980, when it is 46.7 percent. However, what these authors do not tell their readers, is that the second line of the Table shows a *sizable increase* in the percentage share of manufacturing assets held by the 200 largest manufacturing firms from 56.3 percent in 1960 to 59.7 percent in 1980 (and 60 percent in 1981) (see Weisskopf, Bowles and Gordon 1985:268; Szymanski 1984).

4. "Studies have shown that capital spending plans accelerate when operating [capacity utilization] rates move significantly above the 80 percent level and decelerate when they dip below it" (*Business Week*, August 3, 1981:12). For data and analysis on capacity utilization and business investment in the United States economy from 1920 to 1975 see Foster (1984c).

5. The one mainstream theorist who stood as an exception to this general failure to acknowledge the importance of Steindl's book was Alvin Hansen. As he summarized the main thrust of Steindl's argument: "The trend toward oligopoly raised profit margins. This development tended to produce excess capacity. Excess capacity — a decline in the rate of utilization of capital stock — led to a falling off in the rate of growth of capital. This is the essence of stagnation as Steindl sees it" (Hansen 1955:550).

6. For works by theorists who give a central place to "the law of the tendency of the rate of profit to fall" even under the conditions of advanced capitalism, see the essays by David Laibman and Anwar Shaikh in this volume.

7. For the views of Samuel Bowles, David Gordon and Thomas Weisskopf see their essay in this volume.

8. Data compiled by Peter Bernstein (1983: 24) shows a significant upward drift in the capacity/capital stock ratio in manufacturing from 1948 to the mid-1970s, suggesting that a shift to capital-saving innovations (as Hansen once contended) is a major factor in the reemergence of stagnation in the 1970s and 1980s.

7

The Role of Money and Finance in Marx's Crisis Theory

JIM CROTTY

INTRODUCTION

There is a striking paradox that confronts the reader of the Marxian crisis theory literature written in English. On the one hand, it is evident that monetary and financial problems have been and continue to be at the very center of the recurring economic crises that have afflicted most capitalist economies in the past fifteen to twenty years. These economies have experienced secularly rising debt burdens, roller-coaster inflation, domestic credit crunches and recurring waves of bankruptcy. Simultaneously, the international financial system that guided the general prosperity of the 1950s and 1960s has broken down, giving way to a decade of unpredictable, gyrating exchange rates. International debt crises of suffocating magnitude ensnare most of the Third World and a good deal of the Second as well.

On the other hand, until recently the Marxian crisis theory literature has had little to say about monetary and financial aspects of capitalist macrodynamics.[1] Issues of money, credit, financial intermediation, inflation and the institutional structure of domestic and international financial regimes have been relatively neglected as debate raged around impediments to accumulation in the sphere of production. Yet a well-developed, rich monetary and financial theory is essential to the construction of a Marxian theory of accumulation and crisis adequate to comprehend the complex and threatening events of the current era.[2]

In the body of this paper I will argue for the importance of money, credit and financial intermediation in a Marxist theory of accumulation and crisis.[3] My major objective is to demonstrate that the relative neglect of money and finance in the Marxian literature is inconsistent with Marx's own emphasis on these aspects of accumulation and crisis and to show that the de facto dismissal of the centrality of money and finance in much of this literature is based on a basic misunderstanding of Marx's analytical methodology.

THE LOGIC OF MARX'S CRISIS THEORY: AN OVERVIEW

Modern Marxian crisis theorists typically take as the starting point of their analysis a thorough study of the laws of capitalist *production*. Only when they have accomplished this task do they turn their attention to the sphere of *circulation*, the sphere that incorporates monetary and financial phenomena. And their analysis of circulation is, in most cases, conducted more or less in passing.

Worse yet, in treating circulation as subsidiary to production, such theorists mistakenly assume that they are reproducing the methodology Marx used in *Capital*. Contrary to the interpretation implicit in much of the traditional literature, however, I read Marx as building his theory of capitalism's laws of motion on the fundamental methodological assumption that circulation and production constitute a unified whole and that aspects of production have no *a priori* logical priority over aspects of circulation in the analysis of accumulation and crisis.

The logic of exposition used by Marx in *Capital* reflects this assumption. Part One of Volume One, entitled "Commodities and Money," contains an analysis, conducted at a high level of abstraction, of the commodity exchange economy or simple commodity production (hereafter SCP). Here Marx abstracts from the specifics of production or class relations to the maximum feasible extent and analyzes those economic laws shared by *all* economic systems in which production and distribution are organized through the exchange of commodities on competitive markets. The theory of capitalism proper does not begin until Chapter Four, after the presentation of an extensive analysis of the general properties of the commodity exchange economy. Most important, the analysis of capitalist production relations that occupies much of the remainder of *Capital* assumes and is conditioned by the previously theorized model of commodity exchange. The complete theory of the capitalist mode of production then is the contradictory unity of capitalist commodity exchange and capitalist production, or of circulation and production.

In Part One of Volume One Marx presents an analysis of the crisis potential of the advanced (nonbarter) commodity exchange economy, an analysis that takes place almost entirely in the sphere of circulation. In this analysis of SCP Marx constructs a key concept that he elsewhere refers to as "abstract forms of crisis." Basing his analysis of the crisis "possibilities" in SCP on the functions of money and the natural evolution of contracts and credit in commodity exchange, Marx shows that any economic system organized through commodity exchange is structurally vulnerable to disequilibrium and crisis. And the degree and character of the instability of SCP and of capitalism depends upon the relative importance and particular institutional underpinnings of the various functions performed by money in each different mode of economic organization. Thus, before Marx even begins his analysis of specifically capitalist production relations he has established that the theory of money and credit and the theory of crisis are intimately intertwined.

In the remaining sections of this paper I further develop these ideas. I begin with a discussion of Marx's theory of the crisis potential of simple commodity circulation.

SIMPLE COMMODITY PRODUCTION
AND ABSTRACT FORMS OF CRISIS

Perhaps the best statement by Marx on the role of monetary and financial phenomena in his theory of capitalist crisis can be found in Chapter 17 of *Theories of Surplus Value*. In this chapter Marx introduces a concept that is central to his development of the methodology of crisis theory and central to my argument about the key role played by monetary and financial behavior in his theory: the concept of an *abstract form* or model *of crisis*. Marx uses these models to demonstrate that a commodity exchange economy has crisis potential independently of its specific production relations.

In Chapter Three of Volume One of *Capital,* Marx discusses five different functions performed by money in SCP: as measure of value, means of circulation, store of value or hoard, means of payment of debt contracts and as means of international payments settlement or world money. In Chapter 17, Marx differentiates his abstract forms of SCP on the basis of the functions of money that each form incorporates. He concentrates on two such abstract forms of crisis. The first explicitly incorporates money as means of circulation and implicitly considers money as measure of value and as store of value. The second, more complete or "more concrete" abstract form incorporates money as means of payment of debt. In both Chapter Three of Volume One of *Capital* and Chapter 17 of *Theories of Surplus Value* Marx uses his analysis of the functions of money in SCP to attack Say's Law and to demonstrate that commodity exchange economies contain the "formal possibilities of crisis." Moreover, the more important the advanced functions of money in the economy, the more crisis-prone the economy becomes.

Both chapters present these same basic arguments; nevertheless, they are complements. The analysis in *Capital* presents a richer, more detailed discussion of the various functions of money, while in Chapter 17 Marx is much more explicit about the analytical method he is using to develop his theory of capitalist crisis.

The First Abstract Form of Crisis: Money as Means of Circulation

In Part One of Volume One Marx compares two logically distinct forms of non-capitalist commodity exchange: barter and simple commodity production. In direct barter, C-C, products are exchanged for products without the intermediation of money. Marx's concept of barter reflects a simple, uncomplicated way of economic life, one implicitly assumed to take place within limited geographic boundaries.

As such, C-C holds no interest for Marx insofar as his task is to develop a crisis theory. In barter, the individual act of commodity exchange is a complete act; C-C represents simultaneous purchase and sale because each transactor makes a sale through the same act by which she/he purchases.

When we proceed to SCP, however, money as means of circulation ruptures the simultaneity of purchase and sale. C-M-C consists of two logically distinct phases, C-M and M-C. C-M may represent the final stage of exchange for the money holder, but it only represents the starting point for the commodity owner who has exchanged the product for money. This transactor must now go on to attempt to complete the exchange cycle through a third party. The third agent, of course, must find a fourth, who desires to engage in a C-M transaction with the third agent. And so on.

SCP is thus qualitatively different from barter in that it separates the acts of purchase and sale in *time* and *space* and inevitably draws vast numbers of producers into a complex, interlocked *system* of social relations of production and exchange. Since each individual agent's sale of a commodity is dependent upon the successful sales and purchases by innumerable others the entire society of commodity producers is drawn together in a network of mutual interdependence, a system in which rupture at any point can lead to disruption everywhere, a system beyond anyone's control. And the creation of this system, the breaking through the boundaries and limitations of barter, is accomplished by and through money. Because it is the medium of circulation, money becomes the medium of social cohesion, the tie that binds the fortunes of economic agents one to another.

Money introduces the passage of *time* into the model. In turn, the separation of purchase and sale, or the passage of time while money is suspended between acts of circulation, implicitly introduces two new related monetary concepts into Marx's analysis: money as an asset, "hoard" or store of wealth, and the "velocity" of money or its speed of circulation. Money as hoard is a component of the first form of crisis.

Marx's argument clearly implies that the velocity of money as a medium of circulation may slow down. Money can be held rather than spent for some variable period of time. A significant increase in the demand to hold money as a store of value implies a general decline in the demand for commodities or a problem of overproduction. The idea that velocity can slow down is intimately related to Marx's assertion that there can be a general excess supply of commodities — a crisis of reproduction — in SCP. For example:

> At a given moment, the supply of all commodities can be greater than the demand for all commodities, since the demand for the *general commodity*, money, exchange value, is greater than the demand for all particular commodities... (Marx 1968:504–505).

Chapter Three thus contains Marx's basic argument that it is the intervention of money into direct commodity circulation that creates the potential for crises. In Chapter 17 of *Theories of Surplus Value* Marx presents the same basic analysis, but the language he uses makes it harder to misunderstand the theoretical status of the abstract forms of crisis in SCP and their centrality in his theory of *capitalist* crisis. To quote from Chapter 17:

> Crisis results from the impossibility to sell... The difficulty of converting the commodity into money, of selling it, arises from the fact that the commodity must be turned into money but the money need not be immediately turned into commodity, and therefore *sale* and *purchase* can be separated. We have said that this form contains the possibility of crisis, that is to say, the possibility that elements which are correlated, which are inseparable, are separated... (Marx 1968:509).

The SCP model theorized only through the function of money as means of circulation thus represents a "form" within which crisis is possible. Having established this point, Marx immediately tells us that a theory of a form with crisis potential is not yet a theory of crises, an explanation of why capitalist crises *must* take place:

> The *general possibility* of crisis is the formal metamorphosis of capital itself, the separation in time and space, of purchase and sale. But this is never the *cause* of the crisis. For it is nothing but the *most general form of crisis*, i.e., the crisis in its *most generalized expression*. But it cannot be said that the *abstract form of crisis* is the *cause of crisis*. If one asks what its cause, one wants to know why *its abstract form*, the form of its possibility, turns from possibility to actuality (Marx 1968:515).

And if one does want to know why crisis "turns from possibility to actuality," one must shift the focus of the analysis from circulation to production or from SCP to capitalist production relations. What one should *not* do is forget that the abstract forms of crisis constitute the framework within which the analysis of production takes place, a framework which is itself transformed in that analysis.

Even this framework is incomplete, however. The completion of the abstract framework for crisis in SCP requires the integration of the remaining functions of money in the model.

The Second Abstract Form of Crisis: Money as Means of Payment or the Contract Economy

In Chapter 17, Marx introduces money as means of payment of debt in the theory of SCP. This is the key analytical step required to demonstrate that money, commercial credit and financial intermediation play a central role in Marx's crisis theory. With his analysis of money as means of payment in SCP, Marx introduces the concepts of contracts and credit, extends the degree of systematic interdependence of economic agents, substantially alters the impact of time and the role of history in the model, theorizes the monetary crisis and lays the foundation for the financial crisis, and introduces the essential notion of a contractually rigid or financially fragile reproduction process. Clearly, the significance of money as means of payment for Marx's crisis theory is more profound than most of the modern Marxian crisis literature acknowledges.

Contracts, Marx tells us, develop naturally out of the evolution of the circulation process. Contractual arrangements to buy or sell commodities at a future date arise initially out of regularly repeated transactions between the same buyers and sellers. The circulation of commodities thus "gives rise to private, legally enforcible contracts among commodity owners" (Marx 1970:40).

It is with commercial or trade credit contracts, however, that money first acts as a means of *deferred* payment: credit creates a gap of profound theoretical significance between the time when money acts as a means of circulation and the time when money acts as means of payment. The addition of the function of money as means of payment to the SCP form extends the separation in time between purchase and final sale involved in commodity circulation and makes the process more complex: instead of two separate acts required to complete circulation we now have three: C-D, C-M, and M-D; where D stands for a debt contract. Agent A sells a commodity to agent B on credit; a credit contract, D, alienates her/his product. Agent B, the borrower, now must resell this commodity (or one produced using it as input) to agent C in order to obtain the money needed as means of deferred payment to fulfill the contract with A.

The time of circulation is extended because the same commodity must be sold twice: once to B and once to C. The circulation process has also become more complex because agent A now depends *directly* on the behavior and circumstances of two other agents to complete the conversion of the commodity into money.

The concept of a *contractual commitment* adds a whole new dimension to the theory of the crisis potential of SCP. The problem of crisis in the first abstract form of crisis is essentially one of unpredictability. Since purchase and sale, supply and demand are "independent," no agent can be sure that the labor embodied in her/his commodities will be exchangeable for an equal amount of the socially necessary labor time of others. Moreover, there is no mechanism to assure that any deviation from equilibrium will be immediately self-correcting. The agents in the first abstract form of SCP, in other words, are subject to the anarchy of an economy not under their control. Nevertheless, there is a high potential degree of resilience or flexibility here because there are few transmission mechanisms to infect one cycle of reproduction with the problems of previous cycles.

With contracts all this changes. In the second form of crisis in SCP the reproduction process must drag its history with it as burden and constraint. Once future commitments are embedded in the system through contracts, a price vector which would have cleared commodity markets in the absence of contracts may not produce coherence: only prices that enable most of the contracts to be fulfilled can avoid crisis. *Contracts and credit create a variable degree of rigidity or fragility in the reproduction process.*[4]

Two central elements are involved in Marx's stress on the significance of money as means of payment. First, agents undertake contractual commitments at one point in time to exchange money (or commodities) at a specific time in the future. These contracts are based on expectations of the prices that will prevail at the relevant future date. If relative prices or the absolute price level change in an unexpected way between the time the contract was written and the end-point of the contract, one of the contracting agents — the debtor in a credit contract — may not be able to fulfill the contractual commitment. Of course, there is no way that agents can know what future price structures will be like: the future — especially in anarchic, market-organized economies — is in principle unknowable.

Second, the contract economy develops a complex interdependent *system* of interlocked commitments drawing most agents into its web. The contract economy, in other words, can evolve into a very rigid, fragile condition in which relatively minor unforeseen events can disrupt reproduction through a snowballing, falling-dominoe process of contractual failures, bankruptcies and their after-effects. The emergence of contractual commitments means that it may not be sufficient for crisis avoidance for agents to be able to sell their commodities or even to sell them at the right price: they must sell at the required price *within a restricted time period*.

Finally, Marx links the second form of crisis potential to the particular aspect of crisis known as a money crisis or monetary crisis, that phase in the development of an economic downturn in which agents are *forced* to sell commodities to raise the money required to meet contractual commitments. The money crisis is characterized by a collapse in commodity prices and a "fleeing" to the money-form. When financial intermediation is fully integrated in the model, the money crisis includes falling prices for financial assets and rising interest rates, increasing inability to obtain credit at any price, and a flight from all risky assets, a flight that itself causes assets previously thought of as safe to become classified as risky.

> These are the formal *possibilities* of crisis. The form mentioned first is possible without the latter — that is to say, crises are possible without credit, without money functioning as a means of payment. But the second form is not possible *without the first* — that is to say, without the separation between purchase and sale. But in the latter case, the crisis occurs not only because the commodity is unsaleable, but because it is not saleable within a *particular period of time*, and the crisis arises and derives its character not only from the unsaleability of the commodity, but from the *nonfulfillment of a whole series of payments* which depend on the sale of this particular commodity within this particular period of time. This is the *characteristic form of money crisis*.

> If the *crisis* appears, therefore, because purchase and sale become separated, it becomes a money crisis, as soon as money has developed as *means of payment,* and this *second form* of crisis follows as a matter of course, when the *first occurs* (Marx 1968:514).

It is impossible to miss in this quotation the crucial role the contract economy plays in Marx's crisis theory. Price instability, disappointed expectations and random loss of wealth are possible in the first form of crisis, but it is the contractual rigidities of money as means of payment that convert this simple anarchy into a serious potential for economic collapse.

Historically, the rigidification of the economic system through a pervasive, interlocking system of contractual obligations is an accomplishment of capitalism. But in Marx's analytic method, the general crisis or money crisis is an abstract theoretical attribute of commodity-exchange-in-general, or of SCP, and is thus theorized prior to the analysis of capitalist social relations.

Thus, the step Marx takes when he introduces money as means of payment into SCP is a major step in the development of his crisis theory. Contracts, especially credit contracts, link reproduction cycles together, making reproduction in one period depend on reproduction cycles that took place many periods past: *reproduction is now hostage to its own history*. Time takes on a qualitatively greater significance in the analysis and the concept of increasing fragility or rigidity in the reproduction process now plays a potentially dominating role in crisis theory. Thus, Marx's analysis become more inherently and fundamentally historical: history and historic time step centerstage into the spotlight of Marx's crisis theory.

I conclude this section by returning to a fundamental point raised earlier. For Marx, an abstract form has no content, crisis potential is not the same as crisis cause, and a crisis framework is not yet a theory of crisis. To make a crisis theory out of crisis potential, it is necessary to integrate an analysis of the crisis tendencies of capitalist production relations with the abstract forms of crisis of SCP.

MOVING FROM SIMPLE COMMODITY PRODUCTION TO CAPITALISM

Marx constructs a four step argument to move from the abstract forms of crisis to a theory of capitalist crisis. First, he argues that his analysis of the crisis potential of SCP must be incorporated in capitalist crisis theory because capitalism is a commodity exchange mode of production. Second, he argues that the historical development of a complex contract-credit system and the rise of capitalism are simultaneous and symbiotic. Third, he analyses those aspects of capitalist production relations that cause the rate of profit to alternately rise and fall over time, creating the unstable growth patterns characteristic of capitalist economies. Fourth, he integrates these tendencies or laws of capitalist production relations into the analysis of abstract crisis forms to generate a unified theory of the capitalist reproduction process. Because of space limitations I move directly to a consideration of the fourth step in Marx's argument.

THE UNITY OF CIRCULATION AND PRODUCTION

Perhaps the simplest way to summarize Marx's view of the role of financial phenomena in the accumulation process is as follows: credit is an important and often dominating accelerator and destabilizer of accumulation. The contract-credit system feeds the accumulation process in the upswing, driving it at a pace it could not possibly otherwise attain, while it simultaneously gives to accumulation the fragile, rigid character I have stressed: it creates what Marx calls an "over-sensitivity" in the process.[5]

A full treatment of Marx's analysis of the relationship between commercial credit and financial intermediation and capitalism's laws of motion in either the short or long run is well beyond the scope of this paper. However, I would like to highlight some conclusions of that analysis which reinforce my main theme concerning the crucial importance of money, contracts, credit and financial intermediation in Marx's crisis theory.

Overheating the Expansion
Marx's theory of accumulation and crisis centers on the rate of profit. An expansion requires the existence of an "attractive" rate of profit. Moreover, a profit rate considered to be attractive by the capitalist class of any particular historical period will, if maintained for some period of time, generate confident expectations that satisfactorily profitable

conditions will continue to prevail for the foreseeable future. This confidence, in turn, will lead industrial capitalists not only to reinvest retained earnings but to seek external funding as well. The same climate of confidence will induce financial intermediaries to expand credit aggressively; credit will be made available at moderate rates of interest. Vigorous capital investment will initially increase profits; in turn, sustained high profits will serve to increase confidence and improve the business climate.[6] Assessments of the risk involved in real or financial investment will diminish with each profitable period that passes, leading to the use of greater debt leverage all around. Enterprises will seek additional debt as long as the interest rate remains sufficiently below the expected rate of profit. In the rose-colored perspective of the expansion, not only do profit expectations become more bouyant, the required margin of safety between the expected profit rate and the rate of interest narrows as well.

In short, what might have been a moderate expansion in the absence of cheap and available credit may become a runaway boom when superheated by the credit system. Of course, *it must be emphasized that in Marx's theory the high profit of the expansion is attainable only because the underlying production relations make it possible*. But it is the credit and financial system that accelerates the forward motion of the system, thereby helping transform boom-induced confidence into euphoria. It is the capitalist credit system according to Marx that is "the principal lever of overproduction and excessive speculation in commerce" (Marx 1981:572). "Banking and credit," he tells us "become the most powerful means for driving capitalist production beyond its own barriers and one of the most effective vehicles for crisis and swindling" (Marx 1981:742).

The Crisis and Contraction

The over-heated expansion erupts into crisis when two conditions hold. First, combining his analysis of the abstract forms of crisis with the analysis of the role of credit and financial intermediation in capitalist accumulation, Marx theorizes the increasing fragility of the contract-credit system in the mature expansion. As the expansion over-heats, the ability to fulfill contractual obligations will be increasingly threatened by any significant decline in the rate of profit. Second, Marx's analysis of the laws of motion of capitalist production relations generates the multicausal tendencies of the rate of profit to fall at some point in every expansion. *The integration of these two phenomena is Marx's theory of crisis.* Neither one theorized in isolation from the other adequately reflects Marx's understanding of the unity and contradiction of circulation and production in capitalism.

The critical step in the integration of production and circulation in crisis theory is the recognition that the *trend or average rate of profit in any historical period is the center of gravity around which the contract-credit system develops*. As accumulation proceeds the trend profit rate acts as a magnet attracting the rate of interest. In the early expansion the rate of profit rises while the interest rate remains stable, opening up a gap between them which fuels the investment boom. As the profit rate peaks, however, the interest rate rises to narrow that gap; the interest rate is both pulled-up by the strong demand for loanable funds by businesses and pushed up by the increasing illiquidity of the economy. As the expansion matures, the interest rate creeps up on the profit rate. In other words, according to Marx the gap between profit and interest rates rises dramatically in the early-to-mid-expansion and declines thereafter (see Marx 1981:619–620).

Thus, a web of financial and other contractual commitments will be woven ever tighter around the profit rate as long as it does not fall, or as long as reductions in it are seen as temporary deviations around a stable or rising long-term trend. Of central importance, the margin of safety separating profit flows from required interest payments and principal repayments tends to decline as the expansion matures. "[I]t is precisely the development of the credit and banking system which... seeks to press all money capital into the service of production... that makes the entire [economic] organism *oversensitive*" (Marx 1981:706; emphasis added).

With reproduction in this "oversensitive" or fragile condition, either of two developments can trigger a crisis and subsequent collapse. On the one hand, a semi-autonomous monetary and financial crisis can produce a sharp drop in the availability of credit and an equally sharp rise in its cost. This can be enough to rupture an accumulation process so dependent upon credit. As Marx noted:

> In a system of production where the entire interconnection of reproduction rests on credit, a crisis must evidently break out if credit is suddenly withdrawn and only cash payment is accepted, in the form of a violent scramble for means of payment (1981:621).

On the other hand, with the contract-credit system in a fragile condition any substantial decline in the rate of profit may bring on a crisis. It is at this point of the analysis that the problems in the sphere of production emphasized in the traditional crisis theory literature become most important. When the tendency for the rate of profit to fall theorized by Marx finally takes hold, the contract-credit system may rupture. The tighter the contractual web, the quicker the rupture. The system of interlocking commitments may be more or less sensitive, more or less robust, more or less fragile; the profit rate therefore has some variable degree of downward flexibility it can experience before contract-credit structures are threatened. *But the condition of the contract-credit system establishes a floor below which the profit rate cannot fall in any particular period without triggering a general crisis.*

Should the profit rate fall too fast or too far, contractual obligations cannot be fulfilled, the credit system comes under duress, confidence shatters, interest rates soar, risk-aversion rises dramatically and the forced sale of real and financial assets caused by a desperate effort to obtain money as a means of payment sends commodity and financial asset prices into a tailspin. *The crisis is triggered or caused by the union of a falling rate of profit and an oversensitive contract-credit system.*

At the end of his treatment of the "Law of the Tendency of the Rate of Profit to Fall" in Part Three of Volume Three of *Capital* Marx links the rupture of the contract-credit network directly to the falling profit rate in forceful and colorful language. When the profit rate falls:

> . . . since certain price relationships are assumed in the reproduction process, and govern it, this process is thrown into stagnation and confusion by the general fall in prices. This disturbance and stagnation paralyses the function of money as a means of payment, which is given along with the development of capital and depends on... presupposed price relations. The chain of payment obligations at specific dates is broken in a hundred places, and this is still further intensified by an accompanying breakdown of the credit system, which had developed alongside capital. All this therefore leads to violent and acute crises, sudden forcible devaluations, an actual stagnation and disruption in the reproduction process and hence to an actual decline in reproduction (Marx 1981:363).

I cannot present here a complete discussion of the various ways in which a fragile contract-credit system can generate a crisis in the face of a falling profit rate. However, it should be clear that a massive wave of bankruptcies need not take place for a sharp downturn to occur. The mere existence of the potential for financial crisis will induce risk-averse business behavior as soon as the *threat* of bankruptcy makes itself clear. The fall in the profit rate will shatter the rosy expectations of industrial and financial capitalists; their confidence will turn into caution or perhaps even fear. Interest rates will continue to rise even as the profit rate falls due to distress borrowing by those firms whose cash-flow has turned negative, and to the forced sale of financial assets by those individuals and firms that unexpectedly need cash to meet contractual commitments they had thought they could finance from projected income-flows that failed to materialize. The commitment of future expected cash-flows required by long-term investment projects will now make them appear too risky to undertake. Real investment *will* decline; it could collapse. The decline of investment will drag overall economic activity down with it; the rate of profit will fall even further. The drive for liquidity will accelerate. And so on. Although the ensuing economic downturn may actually ruin or bankrupt only a modest subset of the most exposed firms, it will be enough to make corporate and bank executives cautious, if not frightened: stagnation follows.

On the other hand, *if* a major fall in the profit rate occurs within a very complex, highly rigid, very fragile matrix of contractual commitments built up over an extended period of time, a major economic collapse, general or universal crisis, or massive depression is likely to result. *The condition of the contract-credit structure is a prime codeterminant of the depth and duration of the economic downturn in Marx's crisis theory. It is the severity of the decline in the profit rate in combination with the condition of the contract matrix that dictates the dynamics of the crisis, downturn and stagnation.*

CONCLUSION

In summary, I have argued that the theory of money, contracts, commercial credit and financial intermediation is of central importance in Marx's theory of accumulation and crisis; it is neither subsidiary to, a "mere reflection" of, nor less important than the theory of production proper.

Several critics of Marx's crisis theory have argued that, paradoxically, it has no theory of the crisis itself. They claim that Marx presented no answer to such questions as: Why doesn't the decline in the profit rate cause a lower rate of balanced growth rather than a crisis?; Where is the analytical mechanism that connects a decline in the profit rate to a recession or depression?

The traditional crisis theory literature either fails to answer these questions or gives a different answer than the one Marx gave. The reason for this, I believe, is that this literature does not understand Marx's methodology as I have explained it in this paper. Marx begins *not* with production, but with circulation or exchange. Only after an extensive discussion of the crisis potential of SCP has been conducted are the crisis tendencies of capitalist production relations analyzed. We know before entering an analysis of the sphere of production that "certain price relationships are assumed in the reproduction process, and govern it." We know that money as means of payment — the contract-credit system — "which is given along with the development of capital . . . depends on those presupposed price relationships." If the presupposed price relationships unravel, if the average profit rate declines, the "chain of payment obligations at specific dates is broken in a hundred places, and this is still further intensified by an accompanying breakdown of the credit system... All this leads to violent and acute crises.. and hence an actual decline in reproduction."

This is *Marx's* answer to the question of why a decline in the rate of profit leads to a crisis rather than a mere slowing down in the rate of accumulation. The integration of his analysis of capitalist commodity circulation, of the contract-credit system, with traditional theories of the tendency of the rate of profit to decline at some point in every expansion changes the essential condition for crisis-avoidance. From the analysis of production relations alone, a non-negative profit rate may be all that is required, but with the production sector integrated with the contract-credit system, the economy must maintain the "normal," "usual" or expected profit rate to avert a crisis. This is the language Marx himself uses:

> In [simple] reproduction, just as in the accumulation of capital, it is not only a question of replacing *the same* quantity of use-values of which capital consists, on the former scale or on an enlarged scale [in the case of accumulation], but of replacing the *value* of the capital advanced along with the *usual* rate of profit [surplus value] (1968:494; emphasis on the word "usual" added).

Similarly, in the section of Chapter 17 entitled "On the Forms of Crisis" Marx states:

> The rate of profit falls.... The fixed charges — interest, rent — which were based on the anticipation of a *constant* rate of profit and exploitation of labour, remain the same and in part *cannot be paid*. Hence crisis. Crisis of labour and crisis of capital. This is therefore a disturbance in the reproduction process.... (1968:516).

Here, then, is the integration of the crisis potential of capitalist commodity-exchange and the crisis tendencies of capitalist production relations. The contract-credit system, through a multiplicity of transmission mechanisms that I have only touched on in this paper can accelerate accumulation and extend its life, but it also creates a crisis trigger that detonates when accumulation falters. Marx's analysis of the sphere of production explains why the profit rate must eventually fall, but it is his analysis of the abstract forms of crisis that explains why and when a falling-but-positive profit rate generates a crisis. On the one hand, the abstract from has no content; it does not explain why and when a crisis will erupt. On the other hand, a tendency for the rate of profit to decline does not explain why and when a crisis will erupt. Together, as the contradictory unity of production and circulation, they provide both form and content for crisis theory.

There is, of course, a lesson to be learned from this exercise in rethinking Marx's method of analysis of economic crises. Marxists who continue to neglect financial phenomena in their own analysis of the current crisis in the United States and world economy have only themselves to blame for their mistake. Marx got it right — money and finance belong at the center of crisis theory.

ACKNOWLEDGEMENTS

A more extensive treatment of the issues addressed in this paper can be found in James Crotty, "The Centrality of Money, Credit and Financial Intermediation in Marx's Crisis Theory," in S. Resnick and R. Wolff, editors, *Rethinking Marxism*. New York: Autonomedia, 1985, pp. 45–82.

NOTES

1. For a sample of recent writings on the theory of money and finance in the Marxist tradition see the works by Suzanne de Brunhoff, Duncan Foley, David Harvey, Peter Kenway, Robert Pollin and Martin Wolfson listed in the General Bibliography.

2. It is interesting to note that the work of Keynes and a number of economists substantially influenced by him stands in contrast to Marxian theories of accumulation and crisis on this point. Whereas the Marxian tradition has an underdeveloped theory of money and finance but a rich literature devoted to the sphere of production, the Keynesians have produced interesting and important work on monetary and financial aspects of capitalist instability while almost totally neglecting production relations, the labor process, and the class structure. The writings of Hyman Minsky are especially important in this regard. See for example, Minsky (1975, 1982 and 1986). Charles Kindleberger's work is also relevant here, see Kindleberger (1973, 1978 and 1982).

3. Marx uses the term "crisis" to refer to several different types of ruptures in the capitalist growth process: a generalized inability to sell commodities at prices that adequately reflect their values; a regularly repeated phase of the business cycle; a "flight" from financial assets other than money; and a collapse of accumulation of such severity that the reproduction of capitalist social relations themselves is threatened. I follow Marx here and hope that the specific meaning of the word crisis will be made clear by the context within which the term is used.

4. My discussion to this point stresses the vulnerability or crisis-prone nature of an economy with a complex contract-credit network. It should be understood, however, that the introduction of money as means of payment, and, later, financial intermediation has both positive and negative effects on accumulation. Contracts and credit help resolve or eliminate impediments to realization and circulation of commodities even as they heighten the crisis potential of the system. The impressive growth of the capitalist world system and of its constituent national economies could not have occurred in the absence of the development of complex financial intermediation: financial intermediation is both a necessary condition for the successful reproduction of the capitalist economy as well as a major impediment to it. In other words, it has a contradictory relation to accumulation.

5. This discussion will deal with the general categories of accumulation, crisis and collapse; I will abstract as far as possible from the important distinction between business cycles, on the one hand, and long-swings, structural or institutional change and the periodization of the history of capitalist social formations on the other. I merely note that the study of the institutional structure of (domestic and international) financial intermediation must be an integral component of a Marxian theory of structural change in capitalism. See, for example, Marx's emphasis on financial intermediation and the centralization of capital in his discussion of accumulation.

6. I abstract here from an analysis of the various ways in which a period of recession or depression helps to create conditions in the sphere of production and the sphere of circulation that contribute to the rising rate of profit in the subsequent expansion. My discussion in the text takes for granted the appropriate cyclical behavior of nonfinancial determinants of the profit rate.

8

Radical Theories of Inflation

DAVID M. KOTZ

POSTWAR INFLATION AND THE INADEQUACY OF CONVENTIONAL THEORIES

Conventional macroeconomics offers two versions of inflation theory, one Keynesian and one Monetarist. The textbook Keynesian demand-pull theory holds that in the macroeconomy as a whole, as in the case of the market for apples or oranges, excess demand is the cause of price increases.

The Keynesian demand-pull theory requires, however, one further condition before a continuing inflation will occur: full employment. A central idea of Keynesian economics is that demand determines the level of real output. When demand exceeds supply below full employment, the excess demand is assumed to cause firms to hire unemployed workers and produce more output, rather than simply raising prices.

Below full employment, excess demand may cause temporary inflation, but once output has risen to equal the level of demand, no further price increases should occur.[1] After full employment is reached, excess aggregate demand cannot call forth more real output in the short run, but instead brings inflation, which continues as long as demand remains greater than real output.[2]

The Monetarist theory of inflation holds that an increase in nominal aggregate demand can occur if, and only if, the supply of money increases. While the underlying mechanism of inflation is demand-pull, for Monetarism the ultimate cause of the excess demand, and hence of the inflation, is the excessive growth of money.

Prior to the 1970s significant inflations in the United States occurred under three sets of circumstances: wartime, rapid economic expansions, and periods of social and political breakdown. Such inflationary episodes are easily explained by either the Keynesian or the Monetarist theories. But in the period 1970–82, double digit inflation coexisted with peacetime economic stagnation. In 1970–82 the inflation rate for producer prices averaged 8.1 percent per year, while the civilian unemployment rate averaged a historically high 6.7 percent and the manufacturing capacity utilization rate averaged a low 79.8 percent. Such inflation amidst stagnation is not readily explained based on the mainstream inflation theories.[3]

Mainstream economists have nevertheless sought to explain this inflation in terms of their theory. Adding in the inflationary impact of the 1970s oil price boosts does not do it. A leading Keynesian, William Nordhaus (1980), found that the 1973–74 oil shock could account for only 11 percent of the increased inflation during 1973–79 in the advanced capitalist countries. Apparently something other than oil price increases was creating a powerful, underlying inflationary impetus in that period. It required three years of severely depressed conditions, in 1980-82, to finally douse the inflation.

This experience has led non-mainstream economists to propose alternative inflation mechanisms, which might more readily explain the 1970–82 inflation. Most such theories fall under the heading either of conflict theory or mark-up pricing theory.

ALTERNATIVE THEORIES OF INFLATION

The Keynesian and Monetarist inflation theories have two important elements in common. For both, inflation is essentially a demand driven phenomenon. For the Keynesian view, excess spending pulls up prices. Monetarism has essentially the same mechanism, except that Monetarists insist that an increase in aggregate nominal spending is possible only if the money supply increases. The second common element, which underlies the first, is the assumption that individual actors cannot raise the price of whatever they sell, unless there is excess demand for that product. This assumption is central to the mainstream conception of how markets operate.

The most influential radical inflation theories reject, explicitly or implicitly, the view that prices rise only in response to excess demand. It is assumed that key economic actors have the power to raise the price of what they sell, under certain conditions, even in the absence of excess demand. It is claimed that such an exercise of power can generate an aggregate, ongoing inflation. Such phenomena as confict among groups and classes, monopoly power, and rule-based rather than maximizing behavior, play a role in the various non-mainstream inflation theories.

Conflict Theories

Conflict theories regard inflation as the result of struggles among economic groups over income shares (Rowthorn 1977; Rapping 1979; Rosenberg and Weisskopf 1981). In such theories it is assumed that capitalists, workers, and other economic groups each have a target real income. The target may be conceived of as a particular level of real income, a particular share of the total income, or a particular rate of growth of real income. In addition to capital and labor, such models sometimes include welfare recipients, the state, and the foreign sector as competing claimants on real income.

If the total claims for real income by all the groups is not greater than the actual real output produced, then price stability is possible. But if total claims exceed real output available, inflation results. The mechanism can be explained most easily for a two-group model, with only capital and labor.

First, we make the simplifying assumption, to be relaxed shortly, that labor has full power to set the nominal wage level each year and that capital has full power to determine the price level. We further assume that labor sets the wage at the beginning of each year on the assumption that prices will not change, and that capital sets the price after labor sets the wage. Thus, labor will set the wage at the level intended to achieve a predetermined real income level, and capital will set the price to achieve a predetermined real profit level. If the sum of labor's and capital's target real income levels equals the actual real output, then these two decisions are consistent with one another.

If in the next period the sum of labor's and capital's target income grows by an amount equal to the growth of real output, then capital will not raise the price level, because labor's wage increase will leave exactly the amount of real income left over for profits that capital had sought, at current prices. However, if labor and capital together attempt to increase their real incomes by more than the increase in real output, capital must raise the price level to achieve its real income goal. This will cause labor's real income to fall below its target, and a wage-price spiral will follow.

The conflict theory can be illustrated by the following simple model. With only two classes, total net income equals wage income plus profit income:

$$PY = wL + PR \tag{1}$$

where P = price level, Y = aggregate real net income, w = the nominal wage rate per unit of labor, L = the quantity of labor hired, and R = aggregate real profits. Rearranging equation (1), we obtain:

$$P = w/\{A(1 - S)\} \tag{2}$$

where,

A = average productivity of labor (Y/L)
S = profit share of income (R/Y).

Equation (2) is commonly used to show that if nominal wages rise at the same rate as labor productivity, then price stability is consistent with unchanged shares for wages and profits. Interpreted as an illustration of the conflict theory, equation (2) shows that if labor seeks to increase its share of total income, by raising nominal wages faster than the average productivity of labor is rising, then if capital tries simultaneously to maintain the profit share of income, it must raise the price level. Similarly, if capital tries to raise the share of profits, while nominal wages rise in step with labor productivity, it can do so only by raising the price level.

This model can be made more realistic by allowing labor to build some expectation of inflation into its target nominal wage level. In that case, labor's expected rate of inflation becomes a base inflation rate for that period; any excess of total real income demands over total real income available will lead to inflation above the expected rate.

One can also allow for limits on the power of labor to achieve its target nominal income and capital to achieve its target price level. Labor's power to set nominal wages is limited both by pressure from the reserve army of unemployed workers and by the resistance of capital. Capital's pricing power is limited mainly by competitive pressures, since it is assumed that consumers are not an effective force against price increases. Then one can distinguish among three variables: the target real income level of each group; the target levels of nominal wages and prices derived from each group's real income targets plus each group's assumptions about future inflation; and the extent to which the actual nominal wage/price that is set falls short of the nominal targets. The determinants of each variable for each group can then be explored.

Such a conflict model can be used to explain particular real-world inflation experiences. The Phillips curve tradeoff between unemployment and inflation can thus be explained by noting that, when the unemployment rate falls, labor's power to set wages is enhanced, which increases the rate of wage growth, and all else equal, the rate of inflation.

The conflict theory can also be used to explain the inflation amidst stagnation of the 1970–82 period. A major determinant of both labor's and capital's target real income is assumed to be past experience of real income growth. During 1950–70, both labor and capital experienced rapid real income growth, permitted by the rapid growth of total real income in that period. In 1970–82 total real income grew much more slowly, as capitalism entered a period of severe economic difficulties: the real gross domestic product of the nonfinancial corporate business sector grew at 2.5 percent per year in the latter period, compared to 4.3 percent per year in the former period. However, advocates of this theory assert, the real income targets of labor and capital in the 1970s had been formed during the preceding twenty prosperous years. Thus, capital and labor began to battle each other, raising prices and wages in a vain attempt to maintain past growth rates of real income.

Notice that neither demand nor money growth has entered directly into this analysis. But they do play a role in the background. Radicals argue that in the 1970s powerful depressive forces were operating in the United States (and world capitalist) economy. By maintaining fiscal and monetary policy at sufficiently stimulative levels, a full collapse of the economy was averted in the 1970s, and capital and labor retained the power to continue their conflict over income. When monetary policy turned sharply restrictive in 1979, the economy slipped into a deep recession lasting for three years. That was enough to break the back of the conflict inflation. It did so by driving the unemployment rate so high that labor lost virtually all of its power to set nominal wages. Real wages fell sharply after 1978, dropping by 11.2 percent between 1978 and 1982, and by 1982 the cycle of conflict had been decisively broken.

The conflict theory of inflation has its weaknesses. Perhaps the biggest is the claim that capital seeks some fixed target level of profits. Both Marxian and neoclassical economics have traditionally held that capitalists always seek the maximum possible profits, and there are significant theoretical and empirical grounds for believing this view. While workers are not subject to a competitive process that compels income maximization on pain of eventual extinction, capitalists are. If raising prices in a stagnant period will raise profits, should that not have been the case before the stagnant period? Why did the capitalists content themselves with profits less than what they might have obtained, before the stagnant period set in?

Markup Pricing Theories

While conflict theories of inflation have been developed mainly by radical economists, markup pricing theories of inflation have been proposed by a varied group of radical, post-Keynesian, and institutionalist economists. This second set of inflation theories argues that inflation can arise from the price-setting mechanism that characterizes contemporary capitalism. According to this theory, prices are not set by supply and demand but by the application of a fixed markup to the cost of production. Under certain conditions, such markup pricing behavior can lead to inflation, according to this view.

There is a large literature on this subject. The theories fall into two main subgroups. The first subgroup, developed mainly by radical and institutionalist economists, stresses the role of monopoly power in determining price markup behavior. Writers in this category include Sherman (1983) and Blair (1974). Such theories begin by noting that many empirical studies of price setting by price leaders in concentrated industries find that some kind of markup pricing system is used. Sherman argues that such behavior, while inconsistent with short-run profit maximization, is nevertheless a means to gain maximum growth and profits over the long run. By contrast, Blair asserts that such firms do not seek maximum profits in any sense but rather aim for a customary level of profits.

Advocates of this view argue that markup pricing explains the puzzling phenomenon of inflation, rather than deflation, amidst recession. With demand falling short of supply when a recession begins, prices should fall, and they do in competitive industries, according to this view. However, in concentrated industries, declining demand means reduced output, which raises average total costs as fixed costs are spread over a smaller number of units of output. With average costs rising, firms follow their markup pricing rule and raise the price. On the macro level, such perverse behavior by the sizeable concentrated sector of the economy creates inflation during the recession.

Critics of this view argue that large firms do not apply markup rules in such a rigid manner. They suggest that the reason for using markup rules is to follow long-run considerations rather than trying to adjust prices every time the supply/demand situation changes. The consequence of setting prices in the manner described by Sherman or Blair would be a tendency for concentrated industry prices to rise in recessions and fall in expansions; this would exacerbate swings in output by the firms over the business cycle, which would appear to be contrary to good long-run planning. It is also not clear why firms should wait until a recession to raise prices, since they presumably had such power before the recession struck.

This version of markup pricing does not offer a ready explanation of the persistent inflation of 1970–82. Growing monopoly power might have led firms to gradually raise their markup over time, causing steadily rising prices; but there is no evidence of a significant increase in industrial concentration over that period.

The second main subgroup of markup pricing inflation theories, developed mainly by post-Keynesian economists, presents markup pricing as a macro level phenomenon that is not necessarily linked specifically to concentrated industries. Writers in this category include Weintraub (1978) and Peterson (1984).

The basic relationship of this version of markup pricing inflation theory can be derived from equation (2), which was used above to illustrate the conflict theory. We define,

$$k = 1/(1-S). \tag{3}$$

Substituting k into equation (2) yields,

$$P = kw/A. \tag{4}$$

Equation (4) is known as the wage-cost-markup equation. The variable k is the markup, which is regarded as constant. The grounds for this assumption is the widely cited empirical finding that the profit (and the wage) share of total income has remained constant over the past century.

Equation (4) is an identity, but it is turned into a theory of inflation by adding the assumption that causation flows from the right side of the equation to the left. That is, it is assumed that movements in the nominal wage rate, relative to labor productivity, determine the path of the price level. Weintraub (1978) regards labor productivity growth as constant over the long run. Hence, the inflation rate is determined by the rate of growth of nominal wages. The latter is assumed to be the outcome of a complex process of bargaining between labor and capital. If that process produces a growth rate in wages that exceeds the growth rate of labor productivity, then inflation results.

The inflation amidst stagnation during 1970–82 can be explained based on this version of markup pricing inflation theory. The stagnation of the 1970s included as one of its

aspects a significant slowdown in labor productivity growth: during 1970–82 it grew at
0.9 percent per year, compared to a 2.2 percent annual growth rate during 1950–70. If
nominal wage growth did not slow down, this productivity growth slowdown would
cause inflation.

The most common critique of this wage cost markup theory centers on the direction of
causation. Critics suggest that the causation may be the reverse of what is claimed: rising
prices lead to rising wages, as workers seek to defend their living standards. Post-
Keynesians have made some attempt to provide empirical support for their view of the
causal relations; for example, Shannon and Wallace (1985) offer econometric evidence
that wage changes cause price changes and not vice versa. But it has not been possible to
settle this debate decisively based on the empirical evidence.

I have proposed an inflation theory that combines elements of conflict and markup
theories of inflation (Kotz 1982). In this theory, the monopoly sector of capital sets prices
by a markup over costs, with the size of the markup determined by the need to prevent
new entry into monopoly sector industries. In a long period of stagnation, entry into
monopoly sector industries become more difficult. Hence, monopoly capitalists increase
their markups to take advantage of the increased difficulty of entry. This then leads to a
process of conflict inflation, as competitive capital and the working class both raise the
price of what they sell in response to the initial monopoly capital price boost, and
monopoly capital responds in turn to their responses. It is claimed that this process can
account for the inflation amidst stagnation of 1970–82. Unlike other markup pricing
theories, this one shows why markup pricing is a profit maximizing strategy for the long
run.

It is noteworthy that equation (2), which was developed to illustrate the conflict theory
of inflation, is essentially the same equation as equation (4), which is the basis of the
markup theory. The conflict theory and the markup theory appear different, but under-
neath they have a similar structure. Both view price setting as potentially a means to
achieve a certain real income target. The monopoly version of the markup theory takes
wages as given, and focuses on big capital's strategic manipulation of prices to achieve
desired profit results. The wage cost markup version of the markup theory takes the profit
share as given, and focuses on labor's manipulation of nominal wages to achieve its
desired real income. The conflict theory is a generalization of the two. For conflict
theory, neither profits nor wages are taken as given; both are regarded as subject to
manipulation to achieve a desired real income result. Inflation then results, not from the
actions of one group alone, but from the conflict among groups generated by such
behavior.[4]

For all of the above non-mainstream theories of inflation, fiscal and monetary policy
must be sufficiently expansionary to permit the inflation process to continue. Sharply
contractionary fiscal or monetary policy, by severely curtailing aggregate demand,
would severely depress the economy and break the power of whichever group or groups
were causing the inflation. Thus, if the fiscal and monetary policymakers fear to bring on
a severe depression, they are forced to accommodate the inflation. But such policies are
not, in a meaningful sense, the cause of the inflation, the impetus for which arises
elsewhere.

Other radical theories of inflation have been developed that fall outside the conflict and
markup approaches. Sweezy and Magdoff (1975) stress the role of debt expansion in the

inflationary process. DeVroey (1984) suggests that widespread bad debts can generate monetary expansion and inflation. Naples (1985) contends that the profit rate equalization process of Marxian value theory can lead to chronic inflation.

POLICY IMPLICATIONS

Both the conflict and markup pricing theories of inflation imply that the price mechanism of modern capitalism generates problems at the macro level. The power of capitalists and/or workers, and possible other groups as well, to pursue real income goals by raising the price of whatever they sell, can lead to inflation. The obvious policy implication is the need for some kind of social intervention in the price-setting process, to prevent such unrestrained exercise of power from leading to inflation.

Contractionary fiscal and monetary policy may be thought of as such a social intervention, in that it creates economic conditions in which the power to raise prices is undermined. But that policy is a blunt instrument for this purpose, and it imposes a large cost in lost output, high unemployment, and reduced wages and profits.

Non-mainstream economists have proposed various forms of incomes policies as a more direct method to restrain conflict or markup pricing inflation. It is argued that an incomes policy, through which the government directly restrains the growth of prices and/or wages, permits the pursuit of a sufficiently expansionary fiscal and monetary policy to achieve a low level of unemployment, high rate of capacity use, and rapid growth of real output.[5]

One possible type of incomes policy is wage-price controls, through which the government promulgates mandatory guidelines for price and wage increases, backed up by legal sanctions. Post-Keynesians have proposed an alternative to this approach known as a Tax-based Incomes Policy, or TIP. The original major proposal of a TIP was made by Wallich and Weintraub (1971).

The most common TIP proposal is based on the wage cost markup theory, embodied in equation (4). To achieve price stability, the government should set a target rate of nominal wage growth equal to the long-run rate of labor productivity growth. Any corporation that allowed its workers' wage rates to rise faster than that target would have to pay a surcharge on its corporate income tax. If the threat of a surcharge were completely successful in deterring over-guideline wage increases, then according to the wage-cost-markup theory, no inflation should occur. According to this view, no guidelines are necessary for prices, since restraining wage growth is sufficient to prevent price increases.

Advocates of such a TIP argue that it is superior to mandatory controls because, in addition to avoiding the creation of a large enforcement bureaucracy, it also allows the market mechanism to work. The relative prices of various products would remain free to move in response to changes in supply and demand. Advocates of this TIP also claim it is evenhanded, because it threatens tax surcharges for capital and demands wage restraint from labor.

Critics charge that, far from being evenhanded, TIP would line up capital and the state against labor. Critics are not so sure that capital's share of income must remain forever constant, and an effective TIP might enable capital to raise its share by preventing labor from defending its real income in the face of inflation.

Another problem with TIP is that productivity growth has not maintained the magical 3 percent annual rate over the long run that economists used to believe it would. There is no predictable long-run productivity growth rate, which makes it difficult to choose the correct guideline for wage growth. In any event, the TIP plan for wage guidelines without price guidelines is anathema to organized labor and is probably politically unfeasible.[6]

Radical economists have proposed a TIP that would be based on guidelines for price increases rather than wage increases (Bowles, Gordon and Weisskopf 1984). Under this proposal, any corporation which raised prices by more than 2 percent per year would be assessed a special excise tax equal to half of the excess price increase. There would be some flexibility to accommodate unusually rapid cost increases, and the revenue generated by the special excise tax would be applied to subsidize industries with large externally-based cost increases.

Bowles, Gordon and Weisskopf argue that their proposed system would effectively restrain inflation while providing strong stimulus to increase labor productivity, since profits could not be increased by means of large price increases. They also contend that it would avert the need for an unduly large enforcement bureaucracy, and by avoiding mandatory controls on prices, would allow the market mechanism to operate to some extent.

Critics question whether such a TIP on prices would be effective in restraining inflation. Firms facing significantly inelastic demand conditions would still come out ahead from a price increase, even after paying the excise tax penalty. In fact, if one follows the logic of the conflict theory advocated by Bowles et al., a firm with a great deal of pricing power might raise prices by a larger amount due to the tax, in order to reach the target after-tax profit goal.

The problems faced by any form of TIP suggest that mandatory price controls might be a reasonable alternative. They were very effective during World War II, when inflation was kept under 3 percent a year during 1943–45 despite unemployment rates under 2 percent and shortages of many goods. And real GNP rose rapidly during the war years despite the price controls.

But the wartime experience also points out that mandatory price controls work well only when combined with serious planning of the economy, which was also a part of the wartime economic management system. Most radical economists argue that the inflation problems of modern capitalism are a symptom of the failure of the price mechanism. Mandatory price controls may be needed to overcome the inflation produced by this faulty price mechanism, but price controls alone are insufficient. If the price mechanism is to be at least partly superceded by public controls, then the price mechanism cannot be depended on to direct the allocation of resources. Thus, price controls lead to the demand for significant public planning of resource allocation.

NOTES

1. Similarly, when aggregate demand is falling in a recession, deflation should occur until the recession bottoms out.
2. The textbook Keynesian theory sometimes distinguishes between "demand" inflation and "supply" (or "cost-push") inflation. The latter type of inflation is said to occur when production costs rise, due to increases in the price of labor, raw materials, or other important inputs. The

increased cost of production reduces the quantity of output that firms will supply at current prices. As output declines below the level of demand, a temporary inflation occurs, with the price level rising until a new equilibrium is achieved. Note that the mechanism of such "cost-push" inflation is still excess demand relative to output.

3. Furthermore, the failure of deflation to occur in business cycle recessions since World War II, in contrast to prewar experience, is also apparently in conflict with the mainstream demand-pull theory.

4. Both conflict and markup theories may appear to bear some resemblance to the Keynesian cost-push inflation theory discussed above. But there is an essential difference. The textbook Keynesian theory allows cost increases to produce price increases only by means of the resulting shortage of supply relative to demand. Thus, such "cost-push" inflation is the result of traditional market forces. By contrast, both the conflict and markup theories assume firms have the power to raise prices in the absence of any shortage of supply relative to demand.

5. Radical economists normally combine an incomes policy with a range of other policy measures and structural reforms, believing that incomes policies and expansionary macropolicy alone are insufficient.

6. Other post-Keynesians have proposed alternative versions of TIP, some of which include price guidelines as well as wage guidelines, while others proposed tax subsidies in place of tax penalties.

9

Transformational Growth and Stagnation

EDWARD NELL

Can a capitalist economy continue growing in the absence of structural change? Can it grow like a balloon, keeping its proportions intact, with no new products and processes? The answer is no. The capitalist system has two and only two long-run options, enforced by competition — transformational growth or stagnation. Moreover, a major phase of transformational growth is drawing to a close, so that the system's tendency to stagnate is more apparent than ever.

Total demand is the sum of consumption, investment, government spending and net exports. Investment, besides being a component of demand, expands productive capacity; demand has to increase at the same rate as potential production. Otherwise underutilization and excess capacity will discourage further accumulation of capital and lead to stagnation. I will consider the future growth possibilities of these two key variables; consumption and investment. This paper seeks to provide a historical explanation of the forces behind consumption and investment, which is missing in existing work on stagnation (see Baran and Sweezy 1966; Steindl 1976; and the piece by Bellamy Foster in this volume).

Basically, competition tends to increase both productivity and saving, thus reducing the need for investment. Competition puts continuous pressure on business to cut costs and produce more efficiently. This increases productive potential. But competition also requires corporate business to hold down wages and salaries and to pay out dividend and profit incomes in gingerly fashion. So worker consumption is held back by the slow growth of wages and capitalist consumption by the witholding of profit income by corporations. Productive capacity thus tends to expand faster than consumption — which means that investment has little reason to grow unless there are major pressures transforming the way people live. Let's examine this more closely.

As income per household increases the character of consumption changes. At low levels of income households spend a higher percentage of income on necessities, food, clothing and shelter, but as income rises the spending on such items rises less than in proportion, and new items enter the budget, for example, education, entertainment and travel.[1] The reasons are easy to see. The basic necessities have to be purchased in order to maintain a life style that will permit the earning of an income and the raising of a family. These necessities fit together to make the life style; a certain kind of house will have a certain size of kitchen, with such-and-such equipment. This does not altogether determine, but it limits and predisposes the pattern of food purchases and resulting diet. To change the diet in certain ways would mean buying new kitchen equipment, and learning new cooking skills, not just buying new or different foods. But a new kitchen would very likely mean a new house, that is, a major domestic investment and a new life style. And that could very well require a major change in social status. So long as social positions remain unchanged, a rise in income will lead only to minor changes in basic and established patterns of spending, and the additional income will go on new products or on non-basics like luxuries and entertainment. Adapting this to the aggregate, if the social structure is given, a rise in income will lead to greater *discretionary* spending.

We can go further. Given the distribution of income, — this is an important qualification — a critical or watershed level of income can be found for any category of consumer good above which the proportion of additional income spent on the good or service will decline. That is, if income is growing, spending will not grow in pace for those goods whose watershed level is at or below the current level of income. Such markets, e.g. consumer durables, are "growth-saturated." So long as the income distribution is fixed they do not grow as fast as the economy as a whole; hence a point will be reached at which growth has to begin to decelerate, as more and more goods reach their watershed levels. New products alone will not change this, if the new products are merely improved versions of existing ones, enabling established activities to be performed a little better. A transformation is required that will change the income distribution so as to create new markets. (Other social parameters may be equally important, e.g., the urban-rural division, the pattern of marriage and family formation, the degree of education and literacy. A change in the urban-rural division might bring a flood of new workers to the cities, creating new markets for urban consumer goods.)

Suppose an economy were growing on a steady path; per capita incomes would be rising, but after a time, when income reached the critical level for some category of consumer goods, demand for them would grow more slowly than income. But might not demand for some "higher" good or service increase, and so take up the slack? If it did, of course, a slump could be avoided. But such a change is not steady growth, it is part of what we call a transformation. Nor would it take place automatically, at the required rate. Production of the new good will have to be expanded, and the new consumers will have to learn its use. If the growth slowdown in the necessities is pronounced while the expansion in the "higher" goods is still tentative the result will be a tendency to slump.

To overcome the tendency to stagnation the system requires the infusion of new products and new processes, for then competition will force their adoption — if only for firms to protect their market positions. Adopting a new process or adding a new product means investing, and when a new technological principle catches on this will take place on a grand scale. So growth requires transformation, and it is the transformation that will ensure that markets will expand. Without transformative pressures, attempts to keep the economy growing fast enough will run into greater and greater difficulty.

THE NATURE OF TRANSFORMATIONAL GROWTH

New products and new processes normally arise because a new principle has been developed and, in a variety of contexts, is generating new ways of doing things.

By a "new principle" is meant a new way of accomplishing some general social purpose, like the provision of power or facilitating communications or transport. The basic social purposes, of course, are the provisioning of the population with food, clothing, shelter, transport, education, and so on. New principles will usually be formulated initially in quite general terms, so that how and where one is to be applied may, in the early stages, be quite unclear. Experiments will be tried in many different areas, wherever the new principle seems to offer a prospect for improvement. An example is the internal combustion engine, which unlike earlier engines, permits rapid acceleration and deceleration. This characteristic made possible not only the automotive industry with all its related sectors, but revolutionized agricultural production with the tractor and further led to propeller-driven ships and airplanes. As the uses of the new principle are explored new products and new processes both will become available — indeed, the distinction itself is not always valid, for many new processes depend on the use of new products. And many new products, in turn, are only made possible by new processes. The tractor was a new product, but it made new farming processes possible; petroleum cracking was a new process, which created petrochemicals and plastics. By generating both new products and new processes, a new principle thereby displaces both labor and resources from a variety of older ways of doing things.

However, the new products and processes do not simply displace older ways of doing things; think of the impact of the automobile on American culture and the American way of life. When transport was by horse and buggy, or by foot, the farmer went to town once a week, the worker lived walking distance from the factory. No longer. There is a new social landscape. From drive-in movies to drive-in banking, in suburbs and along freeways, the mores of everything from courtship to commerce have been radically transformed, and not always for the better.

So the application of a new principle tends to generate an interlocked set of new products and processes, which create new activities, which in turn combine to create new forms of social life. For the original principle applied to a social objective or function — transportation, in the case of the automobile, power supply and light, in the case of electricity — which itself was interlocked with other social objectives or functions, so that when the mode of achieving one is radically changed, the others must be adapted in various ways, to take advantage of the opportunities created by the improvements. The result is the development of new industries, and the modification of old ones. With the development of the tractor, capable not only of pulling heavy loads but of running machinery off the engine's power drive, farming becomes mechanized. Not only is the horse displaced, the skills of the mechanic displace those of the harness-maker, the groom, and the wheelwright and carriage-maker. The character of rural life changes.

Transformational growth tends to be expansive. The more new products and new processes change the system, rendering old factories and skills worthless, the more they create new opportunities and new jobs. For everything destroyed has to be replaced, and the means of production for these new products and processes will have to be redesigned and rebuilt. Blacksmith shops and bicycle shops must be re-equipped to repair motor vehicles. So investment will be stimulated. New jobs will require new skills, so there will have to be training programs. Training programs in turn require teachers. The new factories will have to be located appropriately, and this will lead to construction. Roads will have to be built to service the new factories and suburbs; shopping centers will spring up. Construction and road building requires earth-moving equipment; this will draw again on the principles of the internal combustion engine, and will in its turn generate factories and jobs. All these changes will bring new groups into prosperity, displacing others, and generating new market patterns.

A warning, however: in the absence of specific governmental planning, there is no reason to expect that the expansion generated by the investment to meet the demand for new products and process will just offset or re-absorb the displaced labor and resources resulting from the introduction of these new products and processes. Even if the old dogs can be taught new tricks no one may find it worthwhile to do so. In any case, why should new jobs come on line at the same time and in the same places that older workers with now obsolete skills are being forced out? The traditional reply will be that the price mechanism will ensure it — the displaced labor and supplies, being desperate and therefore cheap, will quickly be snatched up by the expanding new sectors. But the traditional theory is simple-minded: the displaced factors are cheap but investment in new products and processes must be guided by long-term considerations, not by momentary advantages. The displaced labor and equipment will not be suitable, being specific to the old technology. Cheapness is no bargain when the quality is wrong.

THE DIRECTION OF INNOVATION: FROM HOUSEHOLD TO INDUSTRY

Transformational growth is not random; it normally proceeds in a certain *direction*. In the early stages of capitalism the basic provisioning for social existence — food, clothing, shelter, transport, education — was still carried out within the household or domestic economy, by the methods of the traditional crafts. The family household was the unit that raised and socialized the new generation. The pattern of control over these activities was defined by the kinship system, which determined the inheritance of property and therefore of the power to make decisions about investment, location, production, employment and training.[2]

Growth in nineteenth-century America began from a largely rural and small town system of family farms and family firms operating traditional crafts, which expanded by adding new regions. This was gradually transformed into modern corporate industry and corporate farming, operating large-scale scientific industrial methods, marketing on a mass basis, and controlled by a professional career management, largely independent of the kinship system. A kinship-based class and property system has thus been (partially) transformed into an educational-and-career based income hierarchy. (Class and property, of course, provide a head-start in education and career.) Activities and control were shifted from the kinship-oriented domestic economy to the bureaucratically controlled industrial system, creating new markets in the process. It is this pattern of development that has created the long term pressure for technological change and investment.

These developments could be expected to change the nature of rural and small-town life, and to enlarge the cities and the manufacturing sector at the expense of the former. And this has indeed been the pattern of the past century. But at a certain point a new pattern began to become evident: just as crafts gave way to industrial mass production, drawing on massive sources of power and economies of scale, so the latter is giving way to automated and computerized systems of production, drawing on accumulated information. The industrial economy substitutes energy for the skills of the craftsman; the computerized economy substitutes information and control of complex operations for the energy and scale economies of the industrial system. In the first movement, factory work expands at the expense of agriculture and the crafts; in the second, office and white-collar work expand at the expense of manufacturing. In the first, classes are transformed into hierarchies and the Night Watchman State turns into the Welfare State; in the second, capital is institutionalized and sets out to dominate the state. Schematically, the Craft Economy gives way to Modern Industry, as capital develops an appropriate technology, and this in turn, yields to the Information Economy, as capital develops appropriate controls and institutional forms.

In the craft economy, artisans make products to the specification of their customers. By contrast, modern industry is mass production; its standardized product is turned out for everyone. "You can have any color you want," said Henry Ford, "as long as it is black." Of course, industry did not remain that standardized. Alfred Sloan and GM succeeded Ford as the dominant force in modern American industry. GM's products were differentiated to appeal to different groups, while model changes and built-in obsolescence insured strong replacement demand. But the basic hardware of the product was still standardized and costs were still kept down by long product lines. The information economy of the 1980s makes it possible to produce according to customer specifications while keeping advantages of long production lines. This is because computerized equipment can instantaneously adjust the specifications of successive products on the production line. Such flexibility duplicates advanced workers' skills and the result is the destruction of skilled jobs, replacing them with unskilled and semi-skilled ones. So, high wage jobs are displaced, and low-wage jobs are created, while productivity is enhanced. If this remains the pattern, the information economy will reinforce the tendency to stagnation.

THE TRANSFORMATION DRAWS TO AN END

The falling off of consumer growth in the advanced countries, coupled with the rapid rise in the growth rate of world trade, and especially with the emergence of fast-growing consumer markets in the NDC's, has created pressure for the export of both capital and jobs. The effect tends to be stagnation and plant-closings at home, and the development of dualism and dependency abroad. Nor will this trend be easily reversed: for the era of transformational growth seems to be ending in the advanced countries. It is not a matter of a "shortage" of new inventions or new technology; in fact we are in an era of almost unprecedented technological innovation, coupled, paradoxically, with stagnation in investment. Let us look at this paradox from the vantage point of what that been argued so far.

The creation of new consumer markets has largely taken place by destroying the traditional activities and organization of the family. The production system that directly supported everyday life, even as recently as a century ago, was largely organized through the household. More than half the population still worked the land, and another third lived in small towns. These households grew much of their own food, put up preserves every autumn, cooked whatever they ate, made their own bread, cookies, cakes, etc., mended their own clothes (and made many of them), made soaps and candles, grew or collected herbs for medicinal purposes, mended and often made furniture, and repaired and sometimes even built the houses they lived in. Of course, the basic consumer goods and most means of production were produced in factories, managed by capital, even then. Shoes and leather goods, for example, cloth, most basic clothing, patent medicines, building materials, staple foodstuffs, oil and kerosene, lamps, household furniture, stoves, kitchen utensils and all luxury goods, all were produced for profit and marketed on what was already becoming a national basis. But the household was not a "final consumer"; the household produced. Indeed, members of the household were skilled in many serious crafts—sewing, woodworking, cooking and preserving, carpentry, herbal medicine, and many others. But besides craft work many activities now routinely conducted outside the home went on within it. For example, birth and death and serious illness were largely handled in the family, with the assistance of outside specialists, to be sure, but the basic work was done in the home. Moreover, the family did much of the educating of the children and virtually all of the caring for the aged and infirm.

Of course, not every family possessed all the skills or performed all these activities. Some households would specialize and exchange would take place, either barter within the framework of the extended family, or monetary exchange within the local community — perhaps more commonly, both. However, such local specialization and exchange still remained fundamentally within the sphere of the household. Even though money might change hands, the activities were neither industrial in their technology nor capitalist in their organization.

Much more could be said about the production activities of the pre-modern, non-urban household. It is important to realize the extent to which the circumstances of the everyday lives of our grandparents or great-grandparents were something they largely created themselves, through the exercise of craft skills in the home. By contrast, we buy the circumstances of our lives in the shopping center and from the real estate developer, together with service contracts, should anything go wrong, as it certainly will. A glance over the very partial list of crafts skills and activities mentioned above is enough to reveal a central, and often overlooked, feature of our economic development over the past century. Every one of these domestic crafts and household skills has been replaced by a major industry, dominated by one or more giant, multinational firms. The household has been depleted, and has lost the power to control or shape its everyday circumstances (a loss actively resisted by the "do-it-yourself" movement, and by the counterculture), while the market has expanded. The growth of capital has taken place at the expense of the household.

Of course, it can be immediately protested that this is a distorted and perverse way of describing a well-known phenomenon — the freeing of both men and women from onerous toil. Progress, indeed, should be measured by the replacement of old fashioned, even primitive, ways of doing things with modern technologically superior mass produc-tion. We can buy bread cheaper than we could make it; perhaps homemade bread is better than the supermarkets', but the same could hardly be said about homemade clothes or furniture or soaps or cosmetics or medicines. (*Hand*made clothes or furniture — that is, made by skilled craftsmen — may be better than mass-produced ones, but the modern crafts have themselves been transformed by industrial technology, and use its tools and materials.) The reasons for these developments are simple: the new products are fre-quently better, always cheaper, and moving production out of the household has provided a vast increase in leisure time.

There is no reason to deny this, and the only critisism of this view is that it is seriously incomplete. True, the new products are cheaper, frequently better, and their introduction lightens the burden of daily work. But this is not simply the onward march of progress; along with growth there is destruction. Basic activities have all been moved out of the home and traditional skills have been lost. The market and the state, between them, have taken over most of the functions previously performed by the family. Small wonder, then, that the extended family has ceased to be a significant feature of modern life, and even the nuclear family shows signs of disintegration. Apart from the conceiving of children and caring for them while they are quite young, the family system is no longer the central agency responsible for the reproduction of the material and social circumstances of everyday life. The development of the economy — and of the state — has been a process of taking over these functions, producing the goods and services required on an industrial scale, by new and more powerful processes, and then marketing them commercially, with the state providing the infrastructure to make this possible. That, for better or worse, has been the process of transformational growth.

And, evidently, it has come to an end. Given the distribution of income, and in the absence of a major attempt to create new incomes for the poor, there is nothing left to transform. The funeral business developed in the 1950s, nursing homes in the 1960s, the birthing business began before World War II, and had fully taken over by the end of the 1950s. The traditional crafts had long since perished, and the internal combustion engine drove people off the land and into the cities and suburbs. This last process went on during the 1950s, but slowed to a trickle by the late 1960s, and even reversed itself a few years during the 1970s. For the well-to-do and for the middle classes, probably for the top three-fifths of the income distribution, the transformation is more or less complete, and what we are now seeing is the slow disintegration of an institution — marriage, the family and kinship system — which no longer has social functions commensurate with its ideological and mythic status.

Transformational growth of the kind we have known over the past century, seems more or less over, at least in the absence of a major attempt to create new incomes for the poor. The shift of production from the household to industry, together with the destruction of traditional crafts, has largely been completed in the advanced West. Among sections of the urban poor, and among most of the rural poor there is still a ways to go. But, of course, *the process is only beginning in the newly industrializing world*. Thus the flight of capital abroad is entirely appropriate.

In the United States the progressive deskilling of many jobs has made them ripe for taking over and automating. And the development of computers has enormously enlarged the potential scope of automation. But this kind of investment alone is not likely to produce a boom, since it displaces high-skill, highly paid jobs, while creating jobs of low skill and low pay. So, on balance, it is likely to intensify the unemployment problem. We have arrived at what seems to be the end of one era, but the shape of the next is not yet clear. What will the next transformation consist of?

PUBLIC VS. PRIVATE GOODS

At low levels of income, households will chiefly be concerned with meeting basic material needs — food, clothing, shelter, transport. These will be largely private goods in the economist's sense, although some transport may be collective. But as income increases the household will increasingly try to introduce "higher" — more distinctly human — levels of activity into their consumption pattern. For example, education, entertainment, and communication, all of which are essentially collective, all rise as a percentage of household budgets, as we consider higher income levels. By "private goods" (or services) we mean something produced for consumption by a family or individual which can be bought and consumed without regard to whether anyone else is also concurrently consuming that object. Hamburgers, easy chairs, eye glasses, men's shirts, car washes, and haircuts are all goods the consumption of which by any one consumer is wholly independent of the coordinated consumption of that good by others. Hamburgers and easy chairs, of course, would not be produced unless there were a large enough market. But the actual act of consumption does not have to be coordinated; I can eat a hamburger today even if nobody else does. However, everyone in the group has to turn up at the same room, having done the same reading, for the seminar to take place. The telephone call won't be complete unless the party being called answers; more generally, no one would install a telephone unless they expected many others to do so at the same time. Of course, many ostensibly "private" goods have a hidden public aspect. Automobiles are private — but they depend on highways which are public. Moreover, if everyone goes driving at once, there is a traffic jam; one party's successful consumption depends on others *not* acting at the same time.

Economists define private goods by the exclusion principle — one person's consumption of a particular item precludes another's — and the payments principle — whoever pays for the good decides who shall consume it. When either or both of these are violated — you and I can both cross the bridge at the same time; if you pay your taxes and the bridge is built, I can take a free ride — the normal neoclassical analysis of optimality will not hold. But our interest here is quite different; optimality is not the issue, so we are free to take a different perspective. Instead of non-exclusiveness, our interest turns on collective consuming — goods at least some of whose uses require, in principle, to be consumed publicly, that is, in an act or acts coordinated with at least some other agents. The basic household needs — food, clothing, and shelter — are predominately private, whereas the "higher" needs are predominately public. Hence, as affluence increases, demand will tend to shift towards public goods. Production, and therefore investment, has to shift accordingly.

The production and consumption of public goods, by their nature, normally requires coordination by a public agency, usually the state. So the tendency for the share of the state in GNP to rise all over the affluent world appears to be well-grounded in the nature of things, and not easily reversible. However, it would be a mistake to think that private capital will readily accept this, and indeed, its refusal to do so has had a profound impact on the character of our everyday lives.

In order to earn private profit on collective consumption capital has to *privatize* the consumption of inherently public goods and services. This, of course, distorts the distribution of the public good, but it often affects the nature of the good as well. The commercialization of the media of communication is a good example. Copyrights and patents provide another example. Nothing is so obviously a public good as an idea or a work of art. Yet both have been reduced to the status of commodities, from the sale of which money is to be made. The effect, of course, is to exclude people who cannot afford the price from the benefits, and consequently to inhibit not only their consumption but also (especially in the case of education) their development. And this, in turn, limits the possibilities for still others, who might have learned or profited from interacting with them. In short, privatizing public goods — limiting access to them to those who can pay fees — both distorts the goods themselves and limits the development of citizens.

This may be true, but why should it be a problem for capital? If the point is to explain the difficulties in reestablishing prosperity, why does it matter if privatization distorts? Because the process creates barriers both to the increase of productivity and to the development of markets. If education is limited, then, for example, so is the market for computers. Privatization creates negative externalities. But with markets for normal goods maturing, capital must either move abroad or invade the domain of public goods, if it is to find markets. The next transformation requires the development of more public services and goods, but if this is to be done by private enterprise, it will also mean their commercialization. And this will raise barriers to the future accumulation of capital.

PUBLIC GOODS AND INVESTMENT

Consider an innovation in the design or nature of a private good. When the previous good was produced in the household or in the craft economy, the displacement creates leisure time and the development of the market leads to an investment boom. There may be adjustment problems, but the overall effect is to stimulate activity. It is not so clear when an industrially produced good is displaced. The electric can opener displaces the mechanical can opener, and thereby devalues the capital invested in the production of the older product, while generating investment in the production of the new. The effect could be a reduction in total employment, and indeed in total activity, for the new product could perform the job well enough to reduce the total spending required to have the function performed to the degree wanted by households. An innovation may save on labor in two senses; it may require less labor to produce, and also less household labor to use. And it may require fewer total resources to produce, while still getting the job done. On the other hand the new product might be both better — performing the function faster or more accurately or to a higher degree — and more expensive, so generating more investment and (though not necessarily) more employment than it displaces. In short, a new private good may lead to a reduction in activity and employment if it is simply cheaper than the good it displaces. Of course, being cheaper, it may appeal to a wider market, so the displacement effect could be swamped by the scale effect. And this can be expected if the product is still in the expansive phase of development. But if the good's development is already mature, so that it is already being marketed in all social classes, an innovation which simply cheapens the good will reduce activity. Ideally, this should be counted a benefit, since it means that labor and resources are now free to engage in the production of other things. But on the individual level, no company likes to see its revenue decline, while on the aggregate level, less spending means less activity. Released resources are left idle. What could and should be a social benefit tends to become a disaster, if left to the mercy of the free market.

A new public good, or a new good with public aspects, will be adopted not simply because it is cheaper or does the same job better, but because it makes possible new aspects of life. A new public good can therefore create new demand even if it displaces other industrial goods, as air travel displaced the ocean liners. But the shift from private to public is likely to be accompanied by a rising information and service content in marketed goods. Cars become smaller but smarter; less steel and more electronics is needed. The demands placed on the manufacturing sector are quantitatively less and qualitatively different. It is not always necessary to scrap old and build new factories; it may be enough to renovate and refashion. The creation of productive capacity, in other words, may be undertaken not by adding more, but by improving and reorganizing what is at hand. This is the significance of computerization and the development of the information economy. However desirable these innovations may be both in terms of cost and in terms of saving the environment, they will not set off a boom in the manufacturing sector.

New public goods are likely to be information-intensive; privatization is likely to create negative externalities; technical innovation can displace investment demand; and the great market development of the industrial economy seems to have drawn to a close. The ending of traditional transformational growth may have left the system without a reliable means of counteracting its inherent tendencies to stagnation.

NOTES

1. See Pasinetti (1981) for a discussion of Engel curves, which show for each class of commodities the proportion of household income that will be spent on it at each level of income.
2. Suggestive arguments along these lines can be found in Lefebvre (1971), who relates the development of market-centered consumption to the development of bureucracy, and in Diamond (1979).

PART THREE

EMPIRICAL PERSPECTIVES

10

Marxian Crisis Theory and the Postwar U.S. Economy

FRED MOSELEY

INTRODUCTION

The most important conclusion of Marx's theory of capitalism is that the rate of profit would tend to decline over time as a result of technological change. According to Marx's theory, the rate of profit varies directly with the rate of surplus value and inversely with the composition of capital. Marx argued that both the composition of capital and the rate of surplus value would tend to increase as a result of technological change, thus having offsetting effects on the rate of profit (Marx 1977:Parts 4 and 7). However, Marx argued further that the composition of capital would increase at a faster rate than the rate of surplus value, so that the net effect of technological change would be a decline in the rate of profit (Marx 1982:Part 3). Thus, according to Marx's theory, competition forces capitalists to introduce new technology in an attempt to raise or maintain their individual rates of profit, but these very attempts have the unintended aggregate consequence of reducing the rate of profit for the economy as a whole.

The main purpose of this paper is to subject these important conclusions of Marx's theory to an empirical test. Annual estimates of the three key Marxian ratios are derived for the postwar United States economy in order to determine whether or not these ratios changed in the directions predicted by Marx's theory.

There has been much theoretical controversy over whether or not Marx conclusively proved that the rate of profit must fall as a result of technological change.[1] This paper will not enter into this long and continuing debate. Instead, this paper is concerned solely with the empirical question of whether or not the actual trends of the three Marxian ratios were in the directions which Marx at least expected and asserted, if not conclusively proved.

There have been two other empirical studies of the Marxian ratios for the postwar United States economy, one by Weisskopf and the other by Wolff. According to both of these studies, the rate of profit declined, as predicted by Marx's theory, but for a different reason than given by Marx's theory: because the rate of surplus value declined rather than because the composition of capital increased.

However, I argue that Weisskopf's and Wolff's estimates do not provide a reliable empirical test of Marx's theory because these estimates are derived from data categories which differ in significant respects from the variables in Marx's theory. The most important discrepancy between Marx's concepts and these estimates is that the latter do not take into account Marx's distinction between *productive capital and unproductive capital*. The first section of this paper briefly reviews this important distinction in Marx's theory. The second section presents my estimates of the Marxian variables and compares my estimates with Weisskopf's and Wolff's estimates. The main conclusion of this comparison is that if Marx's distinction between productive capital and unproductive capital is taken into account, then the trends of the composition of capital and the rate of surplus value are in the opposite directions of the trends of Weisskopf's and Wolff's estimates. The final section compares the Marxian rate of profit with the conventional rate of profit and presents a Marxian explanation of the decline in the conventional rate of profit in the postwar United States economy.

1. PRODUCTIVE CAPITAL AND UNPRODUCTIVE CAPITAL

The three Marxian ratios are defined in terms of three fundamental variables: constant capital, variable capital and surplus value. The *composition of capital* (CC) is defined as the ratio of the accumulated stock of constant capital (C) to the annual flow to variable capital (V); i.e. $CC = C/V$.[2] The *rate of surplus value* (RS) is defined as the ratio of the annual flow of surplus value (S) to the annual flow of variable capital; i.e. $RS = S/V$. And the *rate of profit* (RP) is defined as the ratio of the annual flow of surplus value to the accumulated stock of constant capital; i.e. $RP = S/C$.[3]

The most important conceptual issue involved in the precise definition of these three fundamental variables and thus in the estimation of the three Marxian ratios is whether the concepts of constant capital and variable capital include all the capital invested in capitalist enterprises, or instead include only the capital invested in production activities.[4] I argue that Marx's concepts of constant capital and variable capital include only the capital invested in *production activities,* where "production" is defined fairly broadly to include such activities as transportation and storage, but specifically does not include the following two types of activities within capitalist enterprises:

1. *Circulation activites,* or activities related to the exchange of commodities, including such activities as sales, purchasing, accounting, advertising, debt/credit relations, financial analysis, legal counsel, etc.,

2. *Supervision activities,* or activities related to the control of the labor of production workers, including such activities as management, supervision, record-keeping, etc.

This distinction between production and non-production activities within capitalist enterprises is based on Marx's theory of value and surplus value. Marx assumed that the value of commodities is determined by the quantity of abstract labor required to *produce* these commodities, not including the labor required to perform the functions of circulation and supervision (Marx 1977:Chap. 1). From this fundamental premise, it follows that the past labor contained in the means of production consumed in the production of commodities adds to the value of the commodities produced, and the current labor employed in the production of commodities both adds to the value of the commodities and produces surplus value (Marx 1977:Chap. 7). Since, according to this theory, the capital invested in the material and labor inputs to capitalist production results in the production of value and surplus value, Marx referred to this capital as "productive capital."

However, according to Marx's theory, the (past and current) labor required to perform the non-production functions of circulation and supervision, although entirely necessary within the capitalist mode of production, nonetheless does not add to the value of the commodities produced and hence does not result in the production of surplus value. Circulation labor does not add to the value of commodities because the exchange process is assumed to be the exchange of equivalent values; no additional value is created in the exchange of equivalent values. Instead, a given amount of value is transformed from commodities to money, or vice versa (Marx 1977:Chap. 5; Marx 1981:Part 1, especially

Chapt. 6; Marx 1982:Chap. 17). Similarly, supervisory labor does not add to the value of commodities because this labor is not technically necessary for production, but is instead necessary because of the antagonistic relation between capitalists and workers over the intensity of the labor of workers (Marx 1977:448–451; 1982:382–390; 1968:Vol. 3:353–361, 494–506).[5]

Capital must of course be invested in both materials and labor in order to carry out the unproductive functions of circulation and supervision, but, according to Marx's theory, this capital nonetheless does not result in the production of value and surplus value. For this reason, Marx referred to the capital invested in these unproductive functions as "unproductive capital." Since this unproductive capital produces no value, it cannot be recovered out of value which it produces. Instead, according to Marx's theory, this unproductive capital is recovered, together with a profit, out of the surplus value produced by productive labor employed in capitalist production (Marx 1982:Chap. 17).

Marx's concepts of productive capital and unproductive capital are parallel to his more widely discussed concepts of productive labor and unproductive labor. Productive labor is labor employed in capitalist production which produces value and surplus value. Unproductive labor is labor employed in the unproductive functions of circulation and supervision within capitalist enterprises (Rubin 1972; Gough 1972; Braverman 1974; Moseley 1983; Leadbeater 1985).[6]

It follows from these definitions of productive capital and unproductive capital that the concepts of constant capital and variable capital refer only to productive capital. The distinction between constant capital and variable capital was derived by Marx from the different roles performed by the means of production and labor power utilized within capitalist production in the production of value and surplus value. The means of production transfer their value to the value of the products; hence the capital used to purchase these means of production is called constant capital. On the other hand, the labor utilized within capitalist production produces additional value greater than its cost which is the source of surplus value; hence the capital used to purchase this labor power is called variable capital.

This distinction obviously does not apply to the capital which is not exchanged for the inputs to production. The value of the means of circulation and the means of supervision is not transferred to the value of the products; hence the capital used to purchase these materials does not function as constant capital. Similarly, the labor utilized in circulation and supervision does not produce value or surplus value; hence the capital used to purchase this labor power does not function as variable capital.

Weisskopf and Wolff do not take into account Marx's distinction between productive capital and unproductive capital in their empirical studies of Marxian crisis theory. In later works, they both justify this interpretation by noting that their primary aim was not to derive precise estimates of Marx's variables, but was instead to explain the changes in the conventional rate of profit, because this rate of profit is a more direct determinant of capital investment. However, both studies are presented, at least in part, as empirical tests of the predictions of Marx's theory (i.e. rising composition of capital and falling rate of profit) and have been widely interpreted in this way. For this purpose, one should take into account Marx's distinction between productive capital and unproductive capital. Furthermore, even if one's primary aim is to explain the conventional rate of profit, that in itself is no reason to ignore Marx's distinction between productive capital and unproductive capital. The trend in the conventional rate of profit can be analyzed in terms of Marx's variables, including the concepts of productive capital and unproductive capital. Such an analysis of the conventional rate of profit will be presented in Section 3 below.

2. ESTIMATES OF THE MARXIAN RATIOS

Estimates of constant capital, variable capital, and surplus value in the United States were derived for each year from 1947 to 1982, based on the definitions of these variables given above.[7] The data sources and methods used to derive these estimates are described briefly in the Appendix and more fully in the references cited therein.

From these estimates of the fundamental variables, estimates of the three Marxian ratios were calculated for each year of the study. These estimates show the following trends.

The composition of capital increased 62 percent over the period of study, from 3.46 in 1947 to 5.59 in 1982, as predicted by Marx's theory. Measured in terms of five-year averages, the composition of capital increased 46 percent over this period, from an average of 3.62 in 1947–51 to an average of 5.29 in 1978–82.[8]

The rate of surplus value increased 35 percent over this period, from 1.40 in 1947 to 1.89 in 1982, again as predicted by Marx's theory. In terms of five-year averages, the rate of surplus value increased 23 percent from 1.42 in 1947–51 to 1.75 in 1978–82.

Since the increase in the composition of capital was significantly greater than the increase in the rate of surplus value, the rate of profit declined 17 percent over this period, from 0.40 in 1947 to 0.34 in 1982. Measured in terms of five-year averages, the rate of profit declined 15 percent, from 0.39 in 1947–51 to 0.33 in 1978–82. Thus Marx's theory of the falling rate of profit is supported by the evidence of the postwar United States economy.[9]

These estimates will now be compared with Weisskopf's and Wolff's estimates of the Marxian variables for the postwar United States economy, discussed in the introduction. The main difference between my estimates and these other two sets of estimates is that my estimates of the composition of capital and the rate of surplus value have roughly the opposite trends as these other two estimates. For the composition of capital, Wolff's estimates declined 8 percent (from 1947 to 1976) and Weisskopf's estimates showed essentially no trend (from 1949 to 1975). By contrast, my estimates of the composition of capital increased significantly, 41 percent over Wolff's period and 39 percent over Weisskopf's period (see Figure 1). Even more strikingly, both Wolff's and Weisskopf's estimates of the rate of surplus value declined significantly (22 percent and 28 percent, respectively), whereas my estimates of the rate of surplus value increased significantly, 20 percent over Wolff's period and 15 percent over Weisskopf's period (see Figure 2). These divergent trends in the composition of capital and the rate of surplus value had roughly offsetting effects on the trend in the rate of profit, so that all three estimates of the rate of profit show a significant declining trend, with the decline in my estimates slightly less than the decline in the other estimates.

Thus my estimates suggest an entirely different cause of the decline in the rate of profit than is suggested by Weisskopf's and Wolff's estimates. These latter estimates suggest that the cause of the decline in the rate of profit was a decline in the rate of surplus value,

Figure 1
Estimates of the Composition of Capital

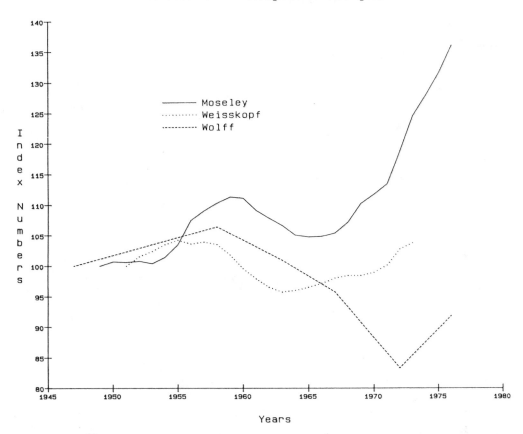

contrary to Marx's prediction. By contrast, my estimates suggest that the cause of the decline in the rate of profit was an increase in the composition (greater than the increase in the rate of surplus value), consistent with Marx's prediction.

These divergent trends in the estimates of the composition of capital and the rate of surplus value are due almost entirely to the different treatments of Marx's distinction between productive capital and unproductive capital discussed above. This issue accounts for 68 percent of the difference between the trends of Weisskopf's and my estimates of the composition of capital, and for 65 percent of the difference between the trends of our estimates of the rate of surplus value. Similarly, this issue accounts for 44 percent of the difference between the trends of Wolff's and my estimates of the composition of capital and for 85 percent of the difference between the trends of our estimates of the rate of surplus value.[10]

Thus the conclusion one reaches concerning the trends of the composition of capital and the rate of surplus value and thus concerning the cause of the decline in the rate of profit in the postwar United States economy depends almost entirely on one's interpretation of the appropriate treatment of Marx's distinction between productive capital and

Figure 2
Estimates of the Rate of Surplus Value

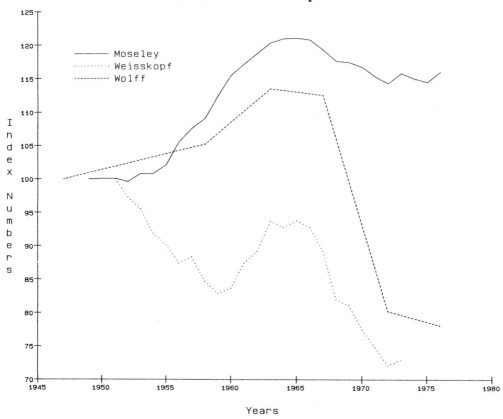

Years

unproductive capital. If this distinction is taken into account, as I have argued it should be in an empirical test of Marx's theory, then the decline in the rate of profit in the postwar United States economy was caused by an increase in the composition of capital, not by a decrease in the rate of surplus value.

3. CONVENTIONAL RATE OF PROFIT

The above analysis has been concerned with the rate of profit as Marx defined it. Weisskopf and Wolff argue that in an analysis of the current economic crisis, one should focus instead on the rate of profit as conventionally defined, since the conventional rate of profit is a more direct determinant of investment spending. The major differences between the two concepts of the rate of profit are the following:

Profit (P), the numerator in the conventional ratio, differs from surplus value (S), the numerator in the Marxian ratio, primarily in that surplus value includes the annual flow of unproductive capital (U_f) (mainly the wages of non-production workers, but also the depreciation of non-production buildings and equipment and the costs of materials) and profit does not include these unproductive costs. Algebraically:

$$P = S - U_f \qquad (1)$$

Similarly, with respect to the denominators in the two ratios, the conventional concept of capital (K), differs from the Marxian concept of constant capital (C) primarily in that the stock of capital invested in non-production structures and equipment (U_s) is included in the conventional concept and not included in the Marxian concepts. Algebraically:

$$K = C + U_s \tag{2}$$

Combining equations (1) and (2), we obtain the following Marxian equation for the conventional rate of profit (CRP):

$$CRP = \frac{P}{K} = \frac{S - U_f}{C + U_s} \tag{3}$$

Finally, dividing all terms on the right-hand side of the above equation, the annual flow of variable capital, we obtain:

$$CRP = \frac{S/V - U_f/V}{C/V + U_s/V} = \frac{RS - UF}{CC + US} \tag{4}$$

From equation (4) we can see that, according to this Marxian analytical framework, the conventional rate of profit depends not only on the composition of capital and the rate of surplus value (the determinants of the Marxian rate of profit), but also on the two ratios of unproductive capital to variable capital ($UF = U_f/V$ and $US = U_s/V$). More precisely, the conventional rate of profit varies inversely with these two ratios of unproductive capital to variable capital.

In the postwar United States economy, the conventional rate of profit declined even more than the Marxian rate of profit. The before-tax conventional rate of profit in the Business sector declined 44 percent, from 0.25 in 1947 to 0.14 in 1982. This significant decline in the conventional rate of profit would seem to be an important cause of the decline in capital investment over the last decade and hence of the current economic crisis.

According to the Marxian analytical framework outlined above, the causes of this significant decline in the conventional rate of profit were an increase in the composition of capital and increases in both ratios of unproductive capital to variable capital (UF and US). Estimates of these latter two ratios were derived for each year of my period of study. These estimates show that the ratio of the flow of unproductive capital to variable capital (UF) increased a very significant 114 percent over this period, from 0.54 in 1947 to 1.14 in 1982, and that the ratio of the stock of unproductive capital to variable capital (US) increased an even greater 160 percent over this period, from 0.42 in 1947 to 1.10 in 1982. Of these causes, the increase in the ratio of the flow of unproductive capital to variable capital (UF) contributed the most to the decline in the conventional rate of profit.[11]

This conclusion raises the further question: what were the underlying causes of the very significant increases in the ratios of unproductive capital to variable capital, especially the ratio UF? The most important direct cause of the increase in this latter ratio was a roughly proportional increase in the ratio of unproductive labor (UL) to productive labor (PL) in the postwar United States economy. Estimates of the ratio UL/PL were also derived for each year of my period of study (for a description of the sources and methods used to derive these estimates, see Moseley 1985a). According to these estimates, the number of unproductive workers (i.e. workers employed in circulation and supervision activities) increased by 180 percent over the postwar period, while the number of productive workers increased only 40 percent, thus resulting in a 103 percent increase in the ratio UL/PL.

CONCLUSION

A full discussion of the implications of this Marxian explanation of the decline in the conventional rate of profit is beyond the scope of this paper, but a few tentative remarks will be made in closing. If this Marxian explanation is valid, then it suggests that it will be very difficult to increase the conventional rate of profit in the future and thus for the economy to fully recover from the current crisis. For this explanation implies that in order to increase the rate of profit, the composition of capital must be reduced and/or the ratios of unproductive capital to variable capital must be reduced. The primary mechanism through which the composition of capital could be reduced (and has been reduced in depressions of the past) is through the widespread bankruptcies of capitalist enterprises, which results in the devaluation of the capital invested in buildings and equipment. Less is known about how the ratios of unproductive capital to variable capital might be reduced, but it would seem that the most important means would be in some way to reduce the number of unproductive workers employed in capitalist enterprises. However, the mechanism through which such a reduction in unproductive workers might take place is not clear. To the extent that these unproductive workers perform necessary functions within capitalist enterprises, it may prove to be difficult to reduce their numbers. And if such a reduction were accomplished, the rate of unemployment would increase correspondingly. Thus the analysis presented here suggests that the most likely scenario for the United States economy over the next decade or so is a continuation, and perhaps a worsening, of the current economic crisis.

APPENDIX

DATA SOURCES AND METHODS

1. *Constant Capital* (stock): The sum of fixed capital and circulating capital. *Fixed capital:* the current value of buildings and equipment used for production activities. Estimates are derived from BEA data for "net private nonresidential fixed capital" (current cost), excluding various types of buildings and equipment used for circulation and supervision activities (e.g. office, computing, and accounting machines; furniture and fixtures; commercial buildings; etc). *Circulating capital:* the current value of inventories. Estimates are derived from NIPA data for "business inventories." Detailed description in Moseley (1985b).
2. *Variable Capital* (annual flow): The total compensation (including supplements and benefits) of production workers. Estimates are derived from NIPA data for "total employee compensation" in the Business sector of the economy, excluding the compensation of non-production workers. The percentage of total employee compensation within each of the eight major industry classifications that was paid to production workers is estimated using data from various sources, primarily the Censuses of Manufacturing, Mining, and Construction, which provides data for the

wages of "production workers," and the BLS *Employment and Earnings* (Establishment Survey), which provides data for the numbers of "production workers" in the Manufacturing, Mining, and Construction industries and for the number of "non-supervisory employees" in the other industries. Detailed description in Moseley (1985a).

3. *Surplus Value* (annual flow): The difference between new-value and variable capital. Estimates of *new-value* (or "value added") are derived from NIPA data for the "net product" of the Business sector, excluding "imputations" which do not correspond to goods and services actually sold on the market (80 percent of which is the value of the "housing services" of owner-occupied homes). Detailed description in Moseley (1985a).

ACKNOWLEDGEMENTS

I gratefully acknowledge very helpful comments on an earlier draft of this paper by Tom Michl and Ahmed Tonak. All errors of course remain my own.

NOTES

1. See Fine and Harris (1979:Chap. 4) for a review of the issues involved in this debate. Also see David Laibman's paper in the first section of this book.

2. Marx's concept of the composition of capital actually refers to three distinct but related ratios: the technical, value, and organic compositions of capital. Strictly speaking, Marx's theory of the falling rate of profit is presented in terms of the organic composition of capital. However, for the purpose of simplification, the composition of capital in this paper refers to the value composition, as defined in the text. The trends in the value and organic compositions will usually be in the same direction, though with different percentage rates of change. Estimates of both ratios will be presented below.

3. Since the stock of variable capital is negligibly small, it is ignored in the denominator of the rate of profit for purposes of simplification.

4. Other conceptual issues involved in the estimation of the Marxian ratios include: (1) whether the Marxian variables should be estimated in terms of current prices or in terms of labor-hours; (2) whether the Marxian variables refer only to capitalist production or also refer to various forms of non-capitalist production in the contemporary economy (mainly government production, but also household and non-profit institution production); and (3) whether the taxes on wages should be considered a part of variable capital or surplus value. Briefly stated, I argue that; (1) the Marxian variables should be estimated in terms of prices; (2) the Marxian variables refer only to capitalist production; and (3) the taxes on wages are a part of variable capital. Weisskopf adopts essentially the same interpretation on all these other issues and Wolff adopts the opposite interpretation on all these other issues. These issues are discussed in a longer version of this paper available upon request from the author.

5. Marx acknowledged that some part of the labor of managers and supervisors is technically necessary for production to the extent that they perform the functions of planning and coordinating production activities. This part of the labor of managers and supervisors Marx considered to be productive labor which produces value and surplus value. However, Marx argued that only a small percentage of the labor of managers and supervisors is devoted to these productive functions and that most of their labor is devoted instead to the unproductive function of controlling the labor of production workers. Marx pointed to the examples of cooperative factories in England, which had largely eliminated managers and supervisors, to demonstrate how little of their labor is actually necessary for production (see references cited in the text).

6. Marx also used the concept of unproductive labor in the broader sense to include labor employed in non-capitalist production, or "labor employed by revenue" (Marx 1968:Vol. 1, Chap. 4 and Addendum 12). Adam Smith used the concepts of unproductive labor to refer only to labor employed in non-capitalist production, not to labor employed in non-production activities within capitalist enterprises. In this paper, the term unproductive labor refers only to the latter category of labor within capitalist enterprises employed in unproductive activities.

7. My estimates end in 1982 because some of the data required to derive estimates of variable capital come from the Censuses of Manufacturing, Mining, and Construction which are conducted only every 5 years. The next Censuses are being conducted this year (1987), but the data from them will not be available for two or three years from now.

8. Following a commonly accepted definition of the *organic* composition of capital as the ratio of constant capital to the sum of variable capital and surplus value, this ratio increased 27 percent over this period, from 1.53 in 1947 to 1.94 in 1982, consistent with the most rigorous formulation of Marx's theory. In terms of five-year averages, the organic composition of capital increased an equivalent 27 percent, from 1.52 in 1947–51 to 1.93 in 1978–82.

9. These estimates were further adjusted to take into account the effects of different rates of capacity utilization, using a method adopted from Feldstein and Summers (1977), and using the Federal Reserve Board measure of the capacity utilization rate. These adjusted estimates show: (1) a smaller increase in the composition of capital from 1947 to 1982 (52 percent) than in the unadjusted estimates; (2) an almost equal increase in the rate of surplus value (33 percent); and thus (3) a smaller decline in the rate of profit (7 percent). For the five-year averages, the adjusted estimates show almost exactly the same percentage changes as the unadjusted estimates (48 percent increase in the composition of capital, 22 percent increase in the rate of surplus value, and 16 percent decline in the rate of profit).

10. The method used to calculate these percentages is adopted from Denison (1969), which reconciles Denison's estimates of inputs and output in the United States economy (1950–62) with Jorgenson and Griliches' estimates of these variables. Further details on this reconciliation of my estimates with Weisskopf's and Wolff's estimates are available upon request from the author.

11. The method used to estimate the contribution of each of the Marxian determinants to the total change in the conventional rate of profit is adopted from Wolff (1986:97–99). The results of this analysis show that the contributions of each of the determinants to the total change in the conventional rate of profit (-0.112) were as follows: the ratio UF (-0.160), the composition of capital (-0.059), the ratio US (-0.019), and the rate of surplus value (0.126).

11

The Falling Rate of Profit and the Economic Crisis in the U.S.

ANWAR SHAIKH

INTRODUCTION

The developed capitalist world entered a crisis phase in the early 1970s. It came a bit earlier in the countries with the relatively less developed capitals, such as England; and it came a bit later in those with relatively advanced capitals, such as West Germany. The United States was just in the middle. And Japan was of course the last to feel the effects of the crisis.

It is the argument of this paper that this worldwide crisis is basically caused by a long-term decline in profit rates in most advanced capitalist countries, due to a mechanism which is built-in to capitalist growth itself. The economic and financial crisis of United States capitalism is primarily due to this same general fall in the profit rate, and only secondarily to any slippage of United States productivity relative to that of its most advanced competitors such as Japan and West Germany. In what follows I will show how and why the profit motive leads to periodic and devastating general crises. Then I will present and analyze the empirical evidence, primarily for the United States. Lastly, I will try and draw out some of the implications of all this for ongoing struggles in the United States.

PROFIT AND TECHNICAL CHANGE

Profit is the veritable bottom line of the whole capitalist system. And in order to get as much profit as possible, individual firms must constantly struggle on two fronts: against workers, in the labor process; and against other capitalists, in the battle for sales.

In the labor process, the productivity of labor is determined by two things: the nature of the technology being used, and the length and intensity of the work effort being extracted from labor. Productivity can therefore be raised by ''improving'' the technology (improvements being defined by the point of view of capitalists) and/or by intensifying the work effort. Firms constantly push workers to work harder. Productivity schemes, piecework, and threats are all part of this pressure. But there are limits to how far the work effort can be pushed. Therefore, in the long run it is the development of new methods of production which becomes the critical factor underlying a secular rise in the productivity of labor.

On the other front, in the battle over sales, firms must also use every available method and trick. Advertising, whether true or false, works just fine. So does bribery, espionage, and even a little industrial sabotage every now and then. However, in the end it is the cost of the product which emerges as the crucial variable. The lower the price for a product of a given quality, the better the chances of success (higher quality for a given price is the same as selling a given quality for a lower price). It comes as no surprise, therefore, that businesses are continually preoccupied with the idea of lowering costs.

Increasing the productivity of labor to get the most out of the labor process and reducing unit costs to get the most out of the market is how the profit motive is put into practice. The drive to raise productivity leads above all to the *mechanization of production*. Machines replace workers, materialized labor replaces living labor. More fixed capital is required per worker. But if mechanization is to be successful as a weapon against other capitalists, it must also reduce unit costs. And once again, it is fixed capital which comes to the rescue. Larger scale plant and equipment tie up greater amounts of fixed capital per unit product in the initial investment, which is precisely what makes it possible for them to achieve lower operating costs per unit product. Higher fixed costs are traded off in return for lower variable costs — as long as the overall costs per unit output are reduced. This is the *capitalization of production*.

Once a new, lower cost method of production becomes feasible, then the whole investment picture changes. The first few firms to adopt the new method are in a position to lower their selling prices, undersell their competitors, and expand their own shares of the market. All firms thus face a round of falling prices (relative to the trend of the price level, which has other determinants as well). Under such circumstances, the firms with the lowest unit costs have the greatest chance of survival precisely because price reductions damage the anticipated profit rates of the higher cost methods more than those of the lower cost ones. A firm with unit costs of $100 is much more vulnerable than a firm with unit costs of $80, since a drop of price from $120 to $100 could wipe out the former while still leaving the latter with a healthy profit. While profit rates as a whole might fall, those of the lower cost firms *would rise relative to all others* because they would fall proportionately less (their elasticity with respect to price would be smaller, other things being equal). Indeed, the new lower cost producers could always drive prices down to the point where their own profit rates were the highest ones in the market. This means that the very existence of a cheaper method of production would change the investment picture in such a way as to make its expected rate of return the highest now available. Since capitalist investment is motivated by the highest expected rate of return, competition among capitals would enforce the adoption of the lowest cost production methods.

But there is a catch here. It can be shown that while more heavily capitalized methods of production may benefit individual capitalists by lowering their unit costs of production, they nonetheless also tend to lower the average rate of profit for the economy as a whole. Thus the same factor which fuels the competitive struggle among individual capitalists also produces a *slow but steady downward drift in the economy wide average rate of profit* (Shaikh 1978b, 1987; Nakatani 1979).

It is important to emphasize here that this built-in tendency towards a falling rate of profit is not generated by rising real wages. Insofar as workers are successful in their struggles for higher wages, they may *accelerate* the fall in the rate of profit. But this effect is limited because rising real wages are generally constrained by the growth of productivity. No firm can sustain rising unit labor costs (real wages rising faster than productivity) for any length of time without risking extinction. Thus, whereas class struggles over the length and intensity of the working day and over wages are vital in determining the exact level of real wages and the rate of profit, they operate within limits regulated by the built-in tendencies of the system. These tendencies are the result of the class relation itself, of capitalist production as a characteristic form of exploitation, and of the systematic mechanization and capitalization of production to which it gives rise. Class struggles which aim to overthrow them must therefore take on the system itself.

Lastly, note that the process described above depends on two essential elements: the competition of capitals, which enforces the adoption of methods with lower unit cost of production; and the capitalization of production, in which lower unit variable costs are generally achieved at the expense of higher unit fixed costs. It is interesting to note that these processes are so familiar to the business world that they have come to represent the standard pattern of technical change not only in empirical studies (Pratten 1971:306–307) but also in some management textbooks (Weston and Brigham 1982:145–147). Yet academic writings tend to present a very different picture. Most neo-Ricardian and neo-Marxian authors, like their neoclassical colleagues, implicitly or explicitly analyze capitalist competition and technical change within the profoundly ideological framework of "perfect competition." This framework is constructed in such a way as to rule out the kinds of aggressive, price-cutting competitive behavior described above. Not surprisingly, within the harmonious world of perfect competition a secularly falling rate of profit *can only be caused by workers* through some combination of excessive wage demands (wage squeeze) and reduced effort (productivity slowdown). While it is understandable that neoclassical economists would adopt a framework which is tailored to portray capitalism in the most favorable of lights, it is far less understandable when some radicals insist on doing the very same thing (Roemer 1979; Steedman, Armstrong and Glyn 1980; Laibman 1982).

THE FALLING RATE OF PROFIT, CYCLES, AND CRISES

Capitalist growth is a turbulent and erratic process in which demand and supply constantly fluctuate around various inner tendencies. It is therefore important to separate out the different levels operating in this process. This means distinguishing between partial crises, business cycles and general crises. First of all, the anarchy and turbulence inherent in capitalist reproduction give rise to all sorts of disturbances and partial crises due to specific events such as crop failures, monetary disruptions, stock market panics, etc. Secondly, below the surface of these erratic disturbances are a series of more rhythmic fluctuations which are called business cycles. Research points to at least three distinct patterns which exist up to the present time: a short (3–4 year) inventory investment cycle which is referred to as "the business cycle"; a medium (7–11 year) fixed capital equipment cycle which is what the term business cycle referred to in the nineteenth and early twentieth centuries; and a longer (15–25 year) fixed capital structures cycle. Finally, underlying all of the above disruptions and cycles is a long (45–60 year) rhythm in which accumulation first accelerates, then decelerates, and finally stagnates (van Duijn 1983: Chap. 1). It is in this last stagnant phase that the system tends toward general economic crises: extended periods of stagnation, stagflation (stagnant accumulation with inflation) and/or depression, with attendant social and political problems (Mandel 1975: Chap. 4).

The theory of the falling rate of profit addresses itself to this long rhythm of accumulation and its associated general crises. Capitalism runs on profit. As capitalists invest, they add to their aggregate capital stock. With a constant rate of profit, the total amount of profit would grow correspondingly. But when the rate of profit is falling, profit grows more slowly than the capital stock. What is more, a secular fall in the rate of profit progressively undermines the incentive to invest and thus slows down the rate of growth of the capital stock itself. It can be shown that both of these effects of a falling rate of profit serve to undermine the growth of total profits. An initially accelerating mass of profit thus begins to decelerate until at some point it stagnates or even declines. And when total profits are stagnant, the capitalist class as a whole finds itself in the position of having invested in additional capital without getting any additional profit. This means that a portion of its capital stock is really redundant.[1] If the situation persists, as it would if it was the result of a long-term decline in the rate of profit, then investment is cut back, excess capacity becomes widespread, and workers are laid off in droves. This is an all too familiar picture.

Once the crisis breaks out, the whole scenario changes. Inventories pile up and profits fall, often quite sharply. Firms increase their borrowing to tide them over the bad times, and this drives up interest rates — which only makes matters worse for firms, though of course it makes banks happy. On the other hand, as businesses start to fail, they default on their debts, and this puts the banks into jeopardy. The rising tide of business bankruptcies begins to trigger bank failures. Interest rates reverse themselves and begin to fall. The stock market index slides downward.

For workers, matters are even worse. Layoffs and business failures give rise to widespread unemployment and increasing hardship as savings and unemployment benefits run out in the face of a persistent lack of jobs. On the other hand, those workers who do still have jobs come under severe pressure to make major concessions on wages and working conditions in order to save their jobs. In all of this, it is of course the ones on the bottom — nonwhites, women, teenagers, the non-unionized — who usually get hit the hardest.

The above patterns are common to all depressions. They always produce great social turmoil and precipitate broad institutional changes. But in the past these patterns have played themselves out in two different ways: the long decline and steady attrition of what was originally known as the Great Depression of 1873–1893; and the sharp collapse and widespread devastation of the subsequent Great Depression of 1929–1941. The current phase seems to resemble the former — so far. But the enormous overhang of debt which has papered over this crisis always contains the threat of the latter.

THE EMPIRICAL EVIDENCE ON THE FALLING RATE OF PROFIT

The theory of the falling rate of profit requires us to empirically separate out structural patterns from various cyclical or conjunctural fluctuations. Since the latter fluctuations generally show up as variations in capacity utilization, we must adjust stock-flow ratios such as the rate of profit and the capital-output ratio for short, medium and long-run changes in capacity utilization. This is a fairly standard procedure, provided one has an adequate measure of capacity utilization. The problem is that most available measures tend to focus on short-run fluctuations, so that adjustments which use them fail to remove the effects of longer term fluctuations in capacity utilization. This problem applies to survey measures of operating rates (BEA, Census, and Rinfret Associates), to the Federal Reserve Board measure (which gets its trend of capacity from survey data on operating rates) and to peak to peak measures (Shnader 1984; Rost 1983). The sole exception occurs with the capacity utilization index initially developed by Foss and subsequently improved by others (Christensen and Jorgenson 1969). This index is based upon the utilization rates of the electric motors which drive capital equipment, and therefore picks up not only short run but also medium and long-term fluctuations in capacity utilization. Unfortunately, the data series needed to construct this index was discontinued in 1963. But it turns out that the McGraw-Hill survey data on expansion investment and on annual additions to capacity can be used to construct a new measure of capacity utilization. A strong independent check of the validity of this new measure is provided by the fact that it is remarkably similar to the Foss electric motor utilization index over the period of their overlap from 1947–1963. Moreover, when put alongside the widely used Federal Reserve Board index of capacity utilization, even though all three measures behave alike in the short run, the Federal Reserve Board index diverges considerably from the other two in the long run (see Figure 5 in Appendix B). This bears out my comments on the deficiencies of conventional measures for long-run analysis. Appendix B outlines the construction of the new capacity utilization index, and a more detailed paper on the subject is available from the author upon request.

The four figures below show that the basic predictions of the theory of the falling rate of profit are borne out by the data for the postwar period (1947–1985). All data sources and methods are described in Appendix A.

Figure 1 shows that, adjusting for fluctuations in capacity utilization, the ratio of capital to production-worker wages (the value composition of capital K/Wp*) rises by

Figure 1
Capital Intensity
Adj for Changes in Capacity Utilization

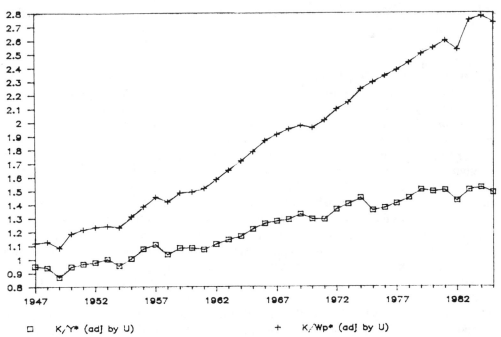

□   K/Y* (adj by U)   +   K/Wp* (adj by U)

Figure 2
Productivity and Real Wages
(Natural Log's)

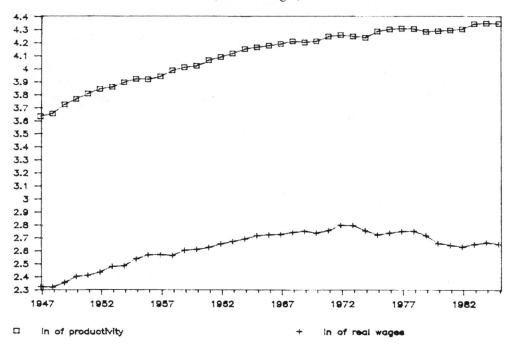

□   ln of productivity   +   ln of real wages

103 percent, while the capital-output ratio K/Y* rises by 56 percent. Figure 2 shows that productivity y rises faster than real wages rwp, just as the theory anticipates. From a Marxist point of view, the ratio of y to rwp is an index of the rate of exploitation of workers, and this index *rises* 46 percent in 38 years.

Figure 3 shows that the profit rate adjusted for variations in capacity utilization falls by almost 53 percent over the postwar period. Since the ratio of profits to production worker wages actually rises slightly over this period (from .40 in 1947 to .46 in 1985), *the fall in the rate of profit is entirely explained by the rise in fixed capital relative to production worker wages (i.e. by the rise in the value composition of capital).* This is an absolutely central result. The unadjusted (actual) profit rate is also depicted, and one can see that it oscillates around the adjusted (potential) rate. This too is an expectation of the theory. Taken together, Figures 1–3 provide strong empirical support for the basic Marxian analysis of the structural tendencies of capitalist accumulation (Shaikh 1987). Finally, Figure 4 addresses the connection between a secularly falling rate of profit and a general economic crisis. It will be recalled that according to theoretical expectations, a falling rate of profit leads to an eventual stagnation in the total amount of profit, which in turn signals the beginning of the crisis phase. The top series in Figure 4 shows that the total amount of real pre-tax corporate profits peaks between 1966–1968, and then starts to fluctuate ever more sharply around a basically stagnant trend (post-tax profits behave in roughly the same way). This would imply that the United States entered a crisis phase around 1967 (the dividing line shown in the graph). It is particularly striking that the

Figure 3
Profit Rates

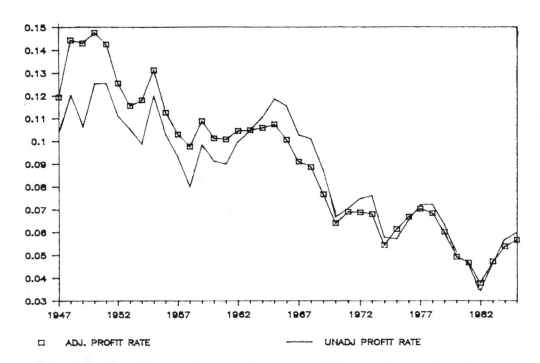

☐   ADJ. PROFIT RATE   ────── UNADJ PROFIT RATE

second series in Figure 4, which represents the real stock market index, *also* stagnates around the same time (actually a bit earlier, as befitting its role in attempting to forecast profitability), and then starts falling steadily. From its early peak in 1965 to its low in 1982, the stock market index fell *over 56 percent in real terms, which is about the same as it fell in the worst part of the previous Great Depression.* It is a sobering fact that the current Dow Jones would have to stand at 3000 in order to simply catch up to 1965 in real terms.

The preceding analysis leads us to expect a qualitative change in the behavior of the system after 1967. And the data amply confirms this. In the first phase from 1947–1967, the system grows at a healthy pace: unemployment averages 4.8 percent, real wages per production worker grow by almost 50 percent, and the average annual federal budget deficit is a mere $1.7 billion. By way of contrast, during the second phase from 1968–1985, unemployment rises sharply to a peak of almost 10 percent in 1982 and then ends up hovering around the historically high level of 7.5 percent, real wages actually *fall* by 8.5 percent over the whole period, so that by 1985 they have fallen back to the levels of 23 years earlier, and the average federal budget deficit explodes to $70 billion (an increase of over *forty-fold* over the average in the first period).

Figures 2–4 also enable us to briefly address three alternate explanations of the present economic crisis.[2] The first of these is the *underconsumption/stagnation* approach (Sweezy 1981) which argues that the crisis originates in a deficiency of demand which leads to falling capacity utilization, falling profits, slowed growth, and eventual crisis. If

Figure 4
Real Profits & Stock Market Index

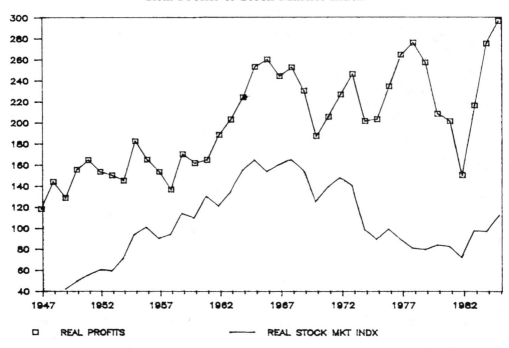

this theory is correct, adjusting the rate of profit for capacity utilization should produce a stable or even rising rate of profit. But the data show just the opposite. The adjusted rate of profit falls strongly throughout the postwar period (Figure 3), even in the boom phase from 1947–1967 when demand is strong and capacity utilization is rising (Appendix B, Figure 5). Indeed, once these critical facts are recognized, it becomes possible to see that the fall-off in demand and hence in capacity utilization occurs in the crisis phase itself, as a consequence of the falling rate of profit (rather than as its cause).

The second explanation is called the *wage squeeze* approach, which traces the crisis back to some combination of excessive growth in real wages (Glyn and Sutcliffe 1972) and a slowdown in productivity growth due to a reduction in worker effort in the late 1960s (Bowles, Gordon and Weisskopf 1983). From the latter point of view, the root of the problem can be found in a supposed upsurge of worker resistance and alienation in the late 1960s, buttressed by the greater security afforded by high employment and a benign Welfare State. But this notion loses all of its force once we recognize that the slowdown in productivity originates directly in a slowdown in the rate of capital accumulation, which in turn has its roots in the already noted decline in profitability. Capital accumulation means the introduction of new, more modern methods of production with correspondingly higher levels of productivity, so that when the former slows down the latter does so also. In fact, the rate of growth of fixed capital peaks in 1966, and then begins to decline thereafter (Kopcke 1982). This suggests that the observed slowdown in productivity growth is an effect, not a basic cause, of the onset of the crisis. It should be noted, incidentally, that the sharp rise in unemployment from 1968–1973 and the parallel slowdown in real wage growth cast serious doubt on any story that roots the whole problem in the putative strength and security of workers in this same period (Bowles, Gordon and Weisskopf 1983).

The third explanation relies on the damaging effects of *foreign competition*, particularly one notion that the gains made by Japan and Germany cause United States profitability to decline which in turn eventually triggers a worldwide decline (Brenner 1986). But this argument confuses secondary factors with primary ones. First of all, such international competition cannot explain the persistent decline in the United States rate of profit over the whole postwar period. Secondly, over the 1965–78 period for which there exists comparable data for all three countries, and during which competition is supposedly the most intense, the Japanese rate of profit declines somewhat *more* (− 33 percent) than the United States (− 30 percent), while the German declines somewhat *less* (− 19 percent) (OECD 1982). This hardly supports the notion that the evolution of profit rates is primarily explained by the competitive positions of these countries.

There are many other subsidiary facts which reinforce the basic argument made in this paper. The current wave of bankruptcies is at an epidemic level, and it is accelerating. In the throes of the recession of 1982, there were *36 business bankruptcies every hour of the business day* in the first quarter of the year, and the annual business failure rate had climbed to 89. Since then it has climbed even higher, to 114 by 1985, a level which is surpassed only by the worst two years of the Great Depression. Workers suffer the most here, because in 80 percent of bankruptcies the jobs are lost altogether. And of course, throughout all of this the Reagan government has been actively dismantling the social support system, rather than trying to strengthen it. What is more, as businesses fail, so do banks. In recent years, the problem has shifted to the farm sector, and from there to the farm banks themselves. All in all, the situation has become so dangerous that it has become increasingly commonplace to see business press headlines such as, "Under Major Banks, Land Mines" (*New York Times*, Jan. 11, 1985) and "Scenario for Disaster"? (*Financial World,* Nov. 26, 1985, p. 12). Virtually the same pattern can be found in Europe, where business and bank failures have also begun to approach the historic highs only seen before in the Great Depression. Worst of all, because of the international scope of the modern banking system, the fate of hundreds of American and foreign banks is directly tied to that of dozens of debt-ridden Third World nations. Whole nations, most notably Mexico, the Phillipines, Argentina and Brazil, are already over the edge of bankruptcy. A default by any one of them could trigger a whole round of such defaults, which in turn could easily lead to the collapse of the world-wide banking system. The nine largest United States banks alone have over *$76 billion* tied up in loans to Third World countries, many of whom are not even able to pay the interest, let alone the principal, on their debts.

SUMMARY AND CONCLUSIONS

The Great Depression of 1873 (the original "Great Depression") lasted 20 years. This was a period of great social turmoil and of great restructuring of the capitalist system. It was marked by widespread concentration and centralization of capital, and culminated in the age of imperialism. The Great Depression of 1929 lasted 10–12 years. It too was a period of great social change and turmoil. It culminated in a bloody and devastating world war. And now the profit motive which dominates this system has once again brought us to the brink of another devastating collapse. So far the state has managed to stave off such a collapse by propping up the credit and banking system and by occasionally pumping up the economy. It has therefore succeeded in *stretching out* the crisis, transforming potential collapse and deflation (as in the 1930s) into stagnation.

A crisis is not only a period of great distress but also one of great possibility. One way or another, the capitalist system will be changed. The current corporate strategy is clearly attempting to place the burden of the crisis on the backs of working people and to restructure the system so as to greatly increase profitability. As the crisis drags on, the attempts to divide the working class continue to mount: the employed against the employed, men against women, black against white, and unions against environmental and anti-nuclear forces.

We do not have to submit to this. Once we recognize that the problem stems from the very nature of the profit motive, from capital itself, then we can attempt to go beyond the automatic defense of liberal Keynesian policies and prescriptions, beyond the myth of an all powerful state which can somehow save us from the devastation of a crisis, and beyond individual or local defensive struggles. This means attempting to rebuild the broad ties which were forged among working people in the last Great Depression; attempting to join our separate struggles for jobs, for civil rights for women and non-whites, for the preservation of the environment, and for the struggle against imperialism; and above all, attempting to create a social system which is regulated by the needs of people instead of by profit. It is clear in many parts of the capitalist world that the current world crisis is an objectively revolutionary situation. We need to bring the message home. Either we fight to make socialism possible, or we submit to corporate rule. This is, in the end, an issue of class struggle.

APPENDIX A

MAIN DATA SOURCES AND METHODS

The data covers the nonagricultural and nonresidential sector. I leave out agriculture because there is no data available on production workers in agriculture, and I leave out the residential business sector because it includes a very large fictitious component (national accounts treat homeowners as residential businesses renting out their homes to themselves).

Figure 1: K/Y^*, K/Wp^*, where K = fixed nonresidential, nonagricultural capital stock (bill \$), from the Office of Business Economics (OBE), Department of Commerce, for 1947–1980, extended to 1985 by regressing the OBE series on the corresponding Bureau of Economic Analysis (BEA) series (R squared = .99938) and using the BEA data to extrapolate. U = a new capacity utilization index described in the text and in Appendix B, graphed in Figure 5 below. Y^* = Y/U, where Y = current-\$ nonresidential, nonagricultural GDP, calculated as GDP — Farm — Gross Housing Product in *National Income and Product Accounts of the U.S., 1929–1982, (NIPA)* Table 1.7, lines 2,7 and Table 1.23, line 7. Updates to 1985 are from various *Survey of Current Business (SCB)*. Wp^* = Wp/U, where Wp = $wp \times Lp$, wp = the annual wage of production workers, *Economic Report of the President, (ERP)* 1986, Table B.39, Col 1, multiplied by 52 (weeks), and Lp = no. of production workers in mining, constr., manuf., transp./ utilities, and services, *Employment and Training Report of the President*, 1986, Table C-2.

Figure 2: y, rwp, where y = productivity = real nonagricultural, nonresidential output per production worker = (Y/pgnp)/Lp, pgnp = implicit price deflator for GNP, *SCB*, Feb. 1986, Table 5, p. 22, and rwp = annual real wage of production workers, *ERP*, Table B39, Col 2.

Figure 3: r*, r where r* = r/U = adjusted (potential) rate of profit, and r = P/K = unadjusted (actual) rate of profit, where P = Corporate Profits with IVA and CCA, *NIPA*, Table 6.18A-B, line 1, for 1947–82, and various *SCB's* for subsequent years. This profit data does not come in sufficient detail to allow us to exclude the agricultural and residential sectors, but related data in Table 6.19A indicate that altogether these sectors probably account for less than 3 percent of total profits.

Figure 4: Real Profit = P/pgdpi, Real Stock Market Index = ST/pgdpi where pgdpi = implicit price deflator for gross private domestic investment, 1982 = 100, *SCB*, Feb. 1986, Table 5, p. 22, and ST = Standard and Poors Composite index, *ERP*, Table B91.

Additional statistics discussed in the text are: business failure rates, *Historical Statistics of the U.S.: Colonial Times to 1970*, Series V23, p. 912, and *ERP*, Table 92; the unemployment rate, *ERP*, Table B35, all civilian workers; federal government budget surpluses and deficits, *ERP*, Table B73, Col 3; comparable profit rates for Japan, Germany, and the United States are gross operating surplus over gross capital stock, both in current-$, from *National Accounts, 1963–1980*, Vol II, Annex III, OECD, July 1982.

APPENDIX B

CAPACITY UTILIZATION INDEXES

My index of capacity utilization is created by dividing the Federal Reserve Board (FRB) index of industrial production by an index of industrial capacity. This is the procedure which also underlies the widely used Federal Reserve Board index of capacity utilization (FRBCU). The difference arises from the fact that our index of capacity is based on a new use of annual McGraw-Hill (MH) survey data on business plans. I wish to particularly thank Ken Kline of DRI for making the original questionaires and data available to me.

Among other things, the MH survey provides two widely used series: the annual additions to capacity in manufacturing (DCAP), and the annual proportion of gross investment (E) which goes towards the expansion of capacity (as opposed to its replacement). Up to now, these two series have been used independently. By combining them, I have been able to correct for a major deficiency in the existing MH capacity index. This latter index is created by simply cumulating the annual additions to capacity to arrive at an index of the level of capacity, *on the assumption* that the survey responses on additions to capacity refer to *net*, not gross, additions. But it soon became clear that the resulting capacity index had a strong upward bias because firms seemed to interpret the survey question in terms of *gross* additions to capacity (which is hardly surprising since all the prior questions on the survey form refer to gross additions to capital stock, i.e. to gross investment) (Rost 1983). In order to address the above ambiguity in the survey response, I assume that of the total additions to capacity (DCAP), a yet unknown fraction p represents gross additions (GDCAP = pDCAP) and rest net (NDCAP = (1-p)DCAP). The gross additions were multiplied by the capacity expansion proportion of gross investment (E), in order to convert gross into net, and then added to the previously assumed net additions (NDCAP). The result is a new measure of net additions to capacity NDCAP* = p(DCAP)E + (1-p)DCAP, which can then be cumulated to create the new index of capacity upon which my capacity utilization index is based.

It is worth noting that the existing MH and the FRB procedures implicitly assume that $p = 0$ (all additions are net), while Rost of the FRB's Division of Research and Statistics concludes that $p = 1$ (all additions are gross) (Rost 1983:520). I estimate p by finding the particular value that makes my measure correspond most closely to the Foss electric motor utilization index (described earlier in the text, and recalculated by me) over the period of their overlap from 1950–1962. This is done by means of a nonlinear least squares estimation procedure, with p constrained to be $0 < p < 1$. Interestingly, the optimal value turns out to be $p = 1$, just as Rost suggests. Calculations are available from the author upon request.

Figure 5
Capacity Utilization Measures

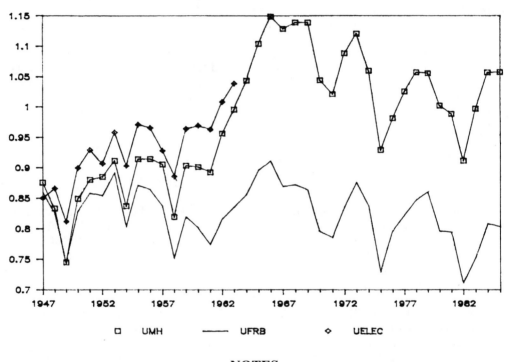

NOTES

1. The above description corresponds to the highest level of abstraction. Once we introduce the rate of interest into the analysis, then total industrial profit can be separated into two components: the amount equivalent to interest which could be earned on the total capital invested; and the amount of profit above that, which Marx calls profit-of-enterprise. At this more concrete level of analysis, the critical point comes when the mass of profit-of-enterprise stagnates — i.e. when the incremental rate of return on capital equals the interest rate.
2. For more detailed discussions of underconsumption/stagnation and wage squeeze theories of the crisis, see Shaikh (1978a, 1986).

12

The Current Crisis in Light of the Great Depression

MARK GLICK

INTRODUCTION

One distinguishing feature of current Marxian analysis of crisis and stagnation, as opposed to orthodox economic approaches, is its emphasis on basic structural tendencies as opposed to policy mistakes. This has also been the case concerning their different approaches to the current crisis. By most measures, the 1970s and 1980s must be considered periods of subnormal economic performance. While the 1970s were years of uncontrolled inflation coupled with frequent recessions, the 1980s have been a decade of slow growth. The growth of GNP recorded in the 1980s was only one-third of the average rate of growth of the 1950s and 1960s. Recently, a number of Marxists have focused their explanation of this situation on the decline in profitability in the United States economy. Empirical evidence of declining aggregate profitability has made this type of Marxist analysis increasingly popular (Moseley 1986; Pollin 1986; Wolff 1986; Bowles, Gordon and Weisskopf 1986). This paper focuses on two aspects of the Marxian falling rate of profit approach to crisis.[1] First, it will attempt to provide an explanation for the fall which fits the empirical data. Secondly, it will address the issue of whether any evidence exists to support the claim that declines in profitability result from recurring patterns or ''laws of motion'' rather than historically specific events. In attempting to answer each of these questions I will focus on a comparison of the current situation with the economic events leading up to the Great Depression. Throughout, I will draw on previous research with Gerard Dumenil and only present new evidence when needed.

THE THEORETICAL FRAMEWORK: THE TENDENCY FOR THE RATE OF PROFIT TO FALL

Modern Marxist views concerning the law of the tendency for the rate of profit to fall can only be understood by initial reference to Okishio's famous paper in 1961 (Okishio 1961). Okishio showed that if real wages were held constant and if capitalists chose the best technology available from the point of view of profitability, then the rate of profit could not decrease, even after the new equilibrium general rate of profit was established. The logic of Okishio's proof was so compelling that advocates of the falling rate of profit view were forced to challenge one of Okishio's assumptions as a starting point for any analysis of a macroeconomic decline in profitability. One type of reply to Okishio has been to focus on the Okishian choice of technology and to argue that it is not consistent with actual capitalist competition (Shaikh 1978). But in my opinion, this approach raises other theoretical problems (Giussani 1986), and has also not been shown to be consistent with existing evidence on capitalist rilvary from the industrial organization field and the management literature.[2] A second response has been to accept the role of rising real wages in the process which causes the rate of profit to decline. One such approach was developed by Dumenil and provided the framework for our previous investigations (Dumenil, Glick and Rangel 1985; see also Foley 1986).

Every falling rate of profit theory must not only make an assumption concerning distribution (constant or rising real wages), but must also provide an analysis of the effects of new technologies. The thesis concerning technological change advanced here is that new technologies are chosen which raise the rate of profit, and that their introduction is, in general, induced by rising costs, usually labor costs. *However, the new technologies cannot compensate for these rising costs which induce them.* Increased productivity of labor must be paid for by an increased advance of fixed capital — an increased capital output ratio, or in Marx's terms, an increased organic composition of capital. The fact that rising wages cause the rate of profit to fall is trivial. However, the fact that technological change cannot compensate for this rise, is an important Marxian hypothesis concerning the historical evolution of technological change. Thus, increases in real wages usher in periods of technological change which only partially compensate for increased costs, a combination which results in a lower rate of profit compared with the rate of profit which prevailed prior to the change in distribution. In response, capitalists often attempt to adjust to this downward pressure on profitability through counter-tendencies (often concentrated in specific periods). One important such counter-tendency in the history of United States capitalism has been the more intensive use of fixed capital (Foss 1984).

Although it is usually accepted that Marx himself allowed for the possibility that wages can accelerate mechanization (see Marx 1976:515), it is sometimes contended that he did not consider changes in distribution when deriving his famous "law." Although it is impossible to locate one definitive statement in Marx, he does leave us scattered evidence that he did not consider the tendency for the rate of profit to fall in an environment of constant real wages or a given wage bundle. Instead, beginning with his discussion of relative surplus value in Vol. I, Marx argued that workers usually obtain some benefit from higher productivity through class struggle:

> The amount of this fall [of nominal wages] depends on the relative weight thrown into the scales by the pressure of capital on the one side, and the resistance of the worker on the other (Marx 1976:659).

Further evidence, as many have pointed out, can be found in his discussion of the tendency for the rate of profit to fall, where Marx assumes a constant rate of surplus value (Laibman 1982; Foley 1986). Such an assumption *implies* a rising real wage when productivity increases.

> A gradual fall in the general rate of profit, given that the rate of surplus value, or the level of exploitation of labor by capital, remains the same (Marx 1982:318).

As the discussion unfolds, however, the assumption of a constant rate of surplus value is lifted: "the tendential fall in the rate of profit is linked with a tendential rise in the rate of surplus value" (Marx 1982:347). Even though Marx eventually links the falling rate of profit to a rising rate of surplus value, he never goes so far as to discuss in a detailed way a constant real wage (a maximum increase in the rate of surplus value) as a condition compatible with the tendency of the rate of profit to fall.

As opposed to Marxists, mainstream economists have treated Marx's contention about the rate of profit with comtempt, largely because the Marxian assumption about the character of technological change runs counter to their beliefs. The common understanding among orthodox economists has been that innovations are inherently attractive, yielding new and improved products for consumers and raising profitability for producers (Kamien and Schwartz 1975; Gold 1976:4). Unfortunately, these beliefs have not stood up to empirical tests. Although empirical research on the impact of technological change has been scanty, important grounds exist to question the position that technological change is a panacea for profitability (see, e.g. Gold 1976:13–15). Despite evidence to the contrary, this mainstream assumption about modern technology has remained firmly ingrained, and has left the mainstream of the profession baffled by declining secular profitability.

TWO PERIODS OF DECLINE IN THE RATE OF PROFIT IN THE U.S. ECONOMY

In order to empirically study the actual causes and effects of a decline in the rate of profit, it is first necessary to accurately identify the periods in United States history which have displayed a clear downward tendency. In a previous paper (Dumenil, Glick and Rangel 1986) we traced, using the available studies and data concerning the rate of profit, the profile of the rate of profit from 1900 to 1985 in the United States.

Figure 1
The Pre-Tax Rate of Profit: Gross Replacement Cost Capital
U.S. Total Economy, 1929–1983

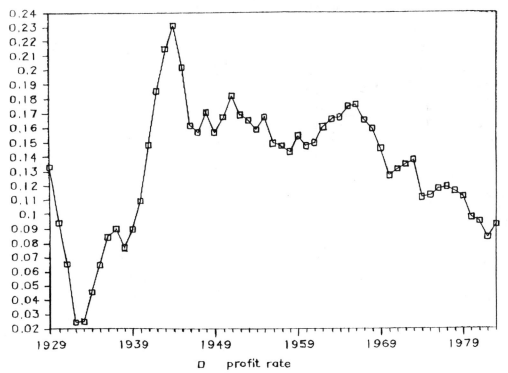

□   profit rate

Source: Department of Commerce (1985), Musgrave (1986).

This profile was constructed from two segments. For the period 1929 to 1985, fairly reliable data exist from the National Income and Product Accounts and the Bureau of Economic Analysis. Although recent revisions show that these data must be used cautiously, they are the best available source of information on the rate of profit. Nevertheless, profit rate data for this period do raise a number of difficult issues. For example, which sector of the economy should be considered? What definition of the rate of profit should be used? What adjustments to the rate of profit should be made? These questions were addressed in (Dumenil, Glick and Rangel 1986), and can not be answered here. Our basic finding in that paper was that a general profile of profitability exists, which appears to be common to the corporate sector and total economy, for pre-corporate tax measures of profitability. Figure 1 displays a representative rate of profit for the total economy from 1929 to 1985.

From 1929, the rate of profit declines into the Depression bottoming out in 1932–1933. After 1933, a recovery begins which peaks during the Second World War. Following the war, the well-known pattern of the rate of profit is displayed. First there is a fall into the 1958 recession, then a rise to a new peak in 1966. After 1966, there is a plunge downward into the 1970s from which the rate of profit never recovers. If the Depression and the war are considered exceptional and temporary phenomenon, there appears to be a flat trend with a major decline following 1966.[3] Since the decline occurs

Figure 2
The Rate of Profit: Replacement Cost Capital
Total U.S. Economy, 1899–1929

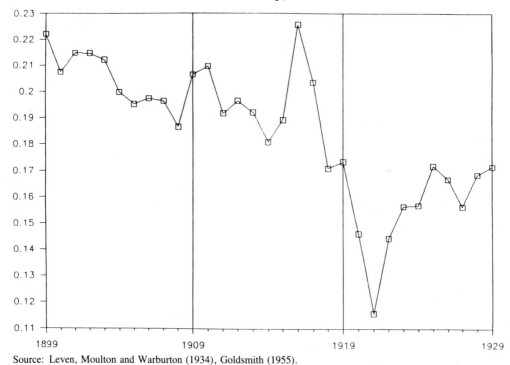

Source: Leven, Moulton and Warburton (1934), Goldsmith (1955).

after 1966, it is easy to understand why many Marxists in the 1960s claimed that the falling rate of profit was obsolete (Baran and Sweezy 1966).

Before 1929 it is more difficult to find reliable data.[4] We believe that the most reliable data can be found in Leven, Moulton and Warburton (1934) and Goldsmith (1955). Figure 2 constructs the aggregate rate of profit for the United States economy from these two sources.[5]

Figure 2 shows that the level of profitability at the turn of the century was higher than any subsequent year before the Depression (with the exception of World War I). Until 1915, the rate of profit decreases. There is an increase during World War I which is due to the prosperity in agriculture. However, after the war there is a dramatic decline from which the rate of profit never again recovers. Thus, counter to popular prejudice, the 1920s was a decade of profit rate stagnation, not one of exceptional profitability. This profile of the rate of profit is in concert with almost all previous studies of the rate of profit for this period.[6]

In order to assess the pattern of profitability over the entire twentieth century in the United States it is necessary to find an accurate linking of the pre- and post-1929 data series. We confronted this issue in depth in Dumenil, Glick and Rangel (1986), by comparing all of the available data series which include both pre-1929 years and the post World War II years. We found almost unanimous agreement that 1929 should be placed about at the level of the middle 1950s[7]. If the linkage is performed in this manner, we are left with the distinct impression that the long-run rate of profit in the United States displays two downward steps (beginning in 1919 and 1966), with an unusual recovery during World War II.[8]

At the beginning of this paper I raised the issue of whether the falling rate of profit is a recurring pattern or a historically specific phenomenon. Research into this question, in my opinion, should naturally begin with the study of these two downward steps in the history of United States profitability just identified.[9] The following two sections consider each of these periods of decline in turn.

THE GREAT DEPRESSION: THE FIRST STEP DOWNWARD

Unlike the current crisis, it is almost gospel among Marxists that the roots of the Great Depression lie in the development of a situation of insufficient demand in the late 1920s. Baran and Sweezy introduced this approach to American Marxists in their book, *Monopoly Capital* (Baran and Sweezy 1966). They argued that underconsumptionist stagnation was inherent in the United States economy even before the Depression. The tendency, however, remained latent until the summer of 1929 due to World War I and the demand created by the automobile. Sidney Coontz, in the same year, published an account of the Depression based on the overproduction of consumer goods relative to demand (Coontz 1966). The latest version of the lack of demand origin of the crash has been developed by the Monopoly Regulation School in France (Aglietta 1979). In fact, the roots of the underconsumption conception of the Depression are much deeper than these modern accounts, originating in the orthodoxy of the Third International. The degree of commitment to this approach among Marxists is actually surprising given the lack of supporting evidence. As Figure 2 illustrates, the degree of profitability was relatively low, not high, in the 1920s, and, more importantly, other economic variables which might reflect insufficient demand do not indicate the existence of an underconsumption situation. In particular, neither consumption nor utilization of capacity show signs of weakness in the late 1920s (for details, see Dumenil, Glick and Rangel 1987). A closer examination of profitability and the determinants of profitability during this period should have pointed Marxists toward a different avenue of research — one within the falling rate of profit framework.

The first downward step in profitability following World War I appears to closely follow the scenario outlined in the first section. This can be illustrated by reference to Figures 3 and 4 which decompose the rate of profit in Figure 2 in the following way:

$$p/k = p/y \cdot y/k$$

where p = profit, k = stock of capital, and y is total income.

Figure 3
The Share of Profit in National Income
Total U.S. Economy, 1899–1929

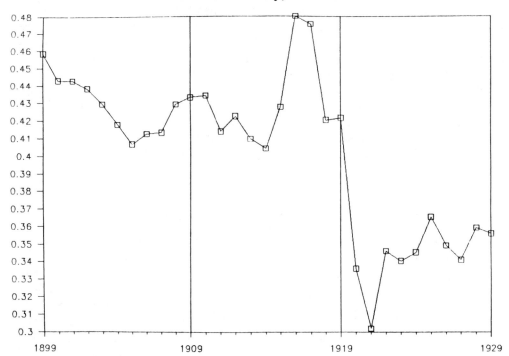

Source: Leven, Moulton and Warburton (1934).

Figure 3 shows that the decline in the rate of profit following World War I primarily reflected changes in distribution. In a previous paper (Dumenil, Glick and Rangel 1987) we traced this change in distribution to a well documented and dramatic increase in real wages which occurred at the end of the war, and was related to the inability to reduce money wages in a period of strong deflation. This increase resulted in a wave of technological change (well known in the 1920s) which was induced by the rise in labor

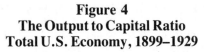

Figure 4
The Output to Capital Ratio
Total U.S. Economy, 1899–1929

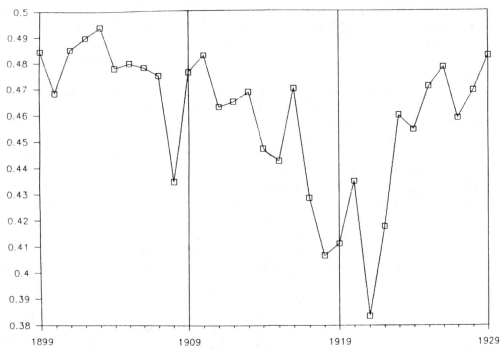

Source: Leven, Moulton and Warburton (1934); Goldsmith (1955).

costs. As evidence, one might consult the survey research project concerning innovation initiated at the N.B.E.R. in the 1920s, whose results were published by Harry Jerome (Jerome 1934). The study included macro evidence of innovation, as well as onsite inspections and interviews. The major finding was that a continual process of technological innovation could be identified since the turn of the century, but that this process was accelerated after 1922. One of the frequently cited reasons for the acceleration was high labor costs:

> Mechanization reached 'a somewhat unusual speed in the twenties...' because of 'high wages, restrictive immigration, relatively low prices for capital goods and an abundant and easy credit market' (Jerome 1934:21–22).

Other early empirical studies also confirmed this result (see Dumenil, Glick and Rangel 1987).

Figure 4 shows that, as a result of the innovation, the output to capital ratio increased in the 1920s, partially compensating for the change in distribution. Despite this progress, the downward tendency in the rate of profit was not offset.

Thus, the facts behind the first downward step in the rate of profit appear to fit well with the hypothesized theory of the rate of profit based on changes in distribution and induced technological change.

THE CURRENT CRISIS: THE SECOND STEP DOWNWARD

There have been a number of attempts to explain the recent decline in the rate of profit following 1966 (see references in Dumenil, Glick and Rangel 1987). The traditional explanation which simply associates the rate of profit with a rising organic composition is very difficult to establish. The rate of profit begins to decline in 1966, while the organic composition rises most strongly in the late 1960s and early 1970s, not in the early sixties, as expected by the orthodox view. Less orthodox radicals have proposed other explanations, including associating the decline with intensified class struggles and international events (Bowles, Gordon and Weisskopf 1986). Again, little evidence can be found that the decline in profitability was caused by either rising real wages or falling productivity (see e.g., evidence in Weisskopf 1985).

In an earlier paper we argued that the current decline can be explained by the same Marxist explanation of the tendency of the rate of profit to fall as occurred prior to the Depression, but we emphasized that the second step downward occurred in an international setting (Dumenil, Glick and Rangel 1985). The details of the argument are set out in our previous article, only the outline of which, with new evidence, will be presented here.

For the current decline in the rate of profit to be described as a "law of motion" it is necessary to link it to a recurring pattern. The fall in the rate of profit in the early 1920s was a result of rising labor costs and the wave of technological change which these new costs induced. The second decline, at first sight, does not appear to fit this scenario. Real wages in the post World War II United States economy do not display any period of exceptional increase capable of explaining the specifically concentrated decline in the profit rate in the second half of the 1960s. Although the trend is determined by wages and technological change, in our opinion, the huge fluctuations (the rise in the early 1960s, the fall in the late 1960s) are related to international competition.

The link between the United States movements in the rate of profit and international competition is evident from the fact that there is an international trade-off in profitability between the United States and Japan during the 1960s (Dumenil, Glick and Rangel 1984:159). In the early 1960s when the profit rate in the United States was soaring, Japan's profit rate was declining. But, when in 1966 the United States rate of return began to decline, the Japanese rate of profit made a dramatic upturn. We argued that this trade-off was the combined effect of the catch-up of Japan and Europe and important fluctuations in the rates of exchange between currencies which impacted on capacity utilization. These phenomena were evident, not only through unit cost data for both countries, but from a comparison of their relative growths in productivity as well. Until 1966, United States and Japanese productivity growth was about equal. However, after 1966, Japanese productivity grew at a far faster pace (Dumenil, Glick and Rangel 1985:148). However, if a fall in sales because of this competition was the only reason for the profit rate decline, the adjustment for capacity utilization would have stemmed the fall. As Bosworth shows, such an adjustment did not take out the decline (Bosworth 1982:281). In fact, the major statistical reason for the initial decline is neither a fall in sales, nor a rise in capital costs, but a decline in profit margins (Nordhaus 1974). We hypothesized that the inability to maintain the previous profit margins on the part of United States firms was due to a decreasing trend in profitability on a world scale, made acute in the United States in this period by exceptional pressure on prices from the threat of foreign competition.

Since the publication of the 1985 article, I have sought microeconomic evidence which might help establish our hypothesized relationships. If competition with Japan is part of the explanation for the decline in United States profitability, and since competition occurs in individual product markets, an industry level analysis should be illuminating. Unfortunately, although industry profit rate data for 2-digit industries is available for both the United States and Japan, it is not available for the crucial decade of the 1960s. However, trade data for United States industries is available and can be helpful. Using the share of imports in the domestic market as a proxy for import penetration, it can be shown that, in almost every industry, a close relationship exists between profitability and foreign competition.[10]

The notion that the post-1966 decline in the rate of profit in the United States is related to international competition seems to indicate that it is a historically specific phenomenon. *Nevertheless, I would argue the contrary position.* The post-1966 decline in profitability follows the same pattern of events as the post-1919 decline except that there are international linkages. To see why, we must consider the evolution of wages in Germany and Japan.

Figure 5
Real Wages in the United States, Japan, and Germany

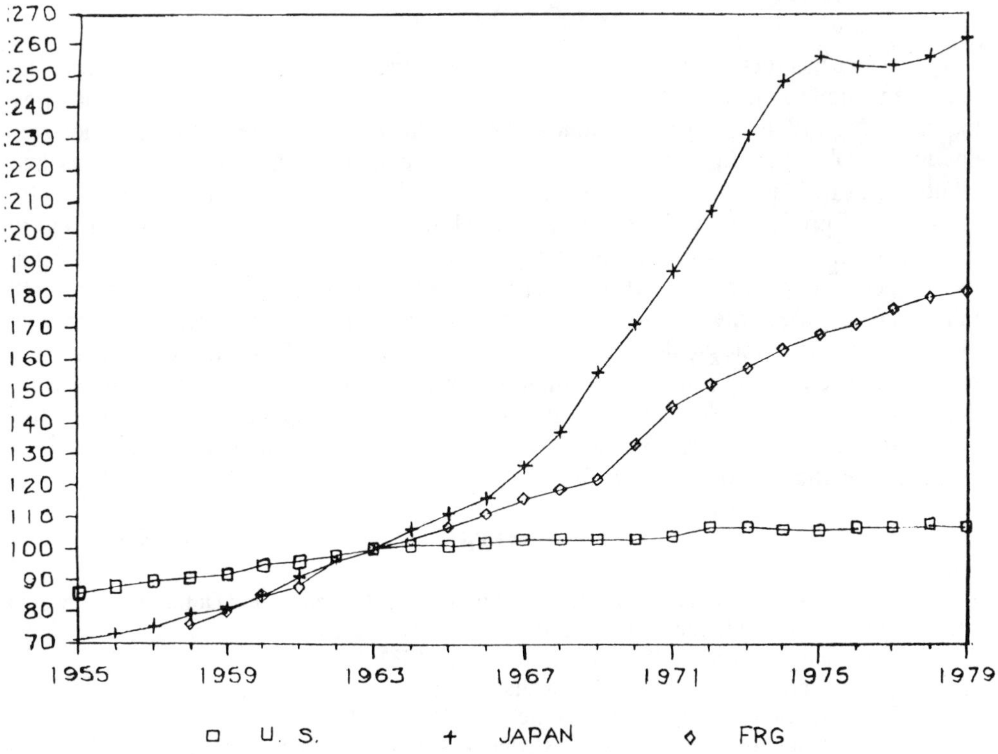

Source: O.E.C.D.

Figure 5 shows that, although United States wages rise at a slow even ascent throughout the postwar period, Japanese and German wages are rising sharply. In Japan in particular, the rise in labor costs is exceptional. It can therefore be hypothesized that a pattern of events similar, in a different context, to that which we identified for the 1920s occurred in most advanced countries, and that rising wages played an important role. This change in distribution was less important in the United States, but the technological catch-up of competitors put progressively more pressure on United States enterprises. Thus, in spite of the effects of world competition, evidence does exist to support the claim that a recurring pattern, a ''law of motion'' can be detected in both downward steps in profitability identified earlier.

The implications of the above, if valid, are important for an analysis of the present economic situation in the United States. After almost a decade of stagnating real wages and high levels of unemployment, aggregate profitability has still not been restored to its previous pre-1966 levels. Since profitability is the foundation of capitalist production, we should not expect a return to economic prosperity without a costly and fundamental metamorphosis: increased government intervention to reduce the risk of investment, the reorganization of the labor process, the intensification of imperialist domination, etc. It appears that without important changes, the present low levels of profitability cannot sustain even short periods of stable growth. Whether such transformations necessitate a dramatic economic rupture like the collapse of 1929 is an open question.

CONCLUSION

This paper has focused on the issue of the historical evidence concerning Marx's law of the tendency for the rate of profit to fall. It has been shown that the long-term profile of the rate of profit in the United States (1900–1984) has displayed two distinct steps downward. A recurring pattern which might be called a ''law of motion'' has been identified as the causal pattern of events during each period of decline. The first decline in the rate of profit occurred after World War I and was a result of rising wages and the inability of the technological change they induced to offset the cost increases. During the second period of decline after 1966, international competition was the trigger behind the fall, but intensified international competition in the United States was linked to wage increases and technological change in Japan and Europe. Thus, a similar pattern of events occurred through an international transmission. Finally, it has been argued that this view, which stresses the historical importance of induced technological innovation and its limited ability to restore profitability, is consistent with Marx's analysis of the tendency for the rate of profit to fall.

NOTES

1. This paper is part of a larger research project with Gerard Dumenil and Dominque Levy at the CEPREMAP, Paris, and Hans Ehrbar at the University of Utah.
2. See, for example, Porter (1980) and Zeithaml and Fry (1984).
3. Using this data, 1929 is slightly lower than' usual.
4. For further discussion see Dumenil, Glick and Rangel (1987).
5. For a full account of how this data was constructed see the appendix to Dumenil, Glick and Rangel (1987).
6. For references see Dumenil, Glick and Rangel (1987).

7. Thus, Figure 1 places 1929 at an abnormally low point.

8. This recovery will be the subject of a forthcoming paper. It is possible that it is only an artifact of data bias.

9. Prior to 1900 data is not available. The decline in the rate of profit during the Depression is a result of a crisis, not a cause of the crisis. In addition, profit rate data from other countries are only available for the post-World War II period and often strongly related to international develop-ments.

10. Regression results will be published in a forthcoming paper. For a similar study of the United Kingdom, see (Turner 1980).

13

Financial Instability in the U.S. Economy

HENRY MARTIN

INTRODUCTION

In 1984 the effective failure of the Continental Illinois National Bank shocked the financial system both here and abroad, and initiated a financial crisis; the crisis threatened to set off a chain reaction of failures and bankruptcies, and a cumulative downward spiral of output and employment. Other financial disturbances have occurred regularly in the United States in the period since 1966 (and also in the nineteenth and early twentieth centuries). Yet equally as significant as this period of financial instability was the earlier postwar period (1945–65), an unprecedented period of financial stability. Thus the purpose of this paper is threefold: (1) to discuss briefly the forces responsible for financial crises in the later postwar period, (2) to determine why these crises did not occur in the earlier period, and (3) to understand how a period of stability in the earlier period was transformed into a period of instability in the later period.

The thesis presented here is that the conditions for financial crises to occur are created as the result of the interaction of two factors: (1) business-cycle developments that are endogenous to the normal workings of a capitalist economy, and (2) the specific institutional structure of the financial system that has evolved historically. Once these conditions are created, surprise events can initiate the crisis itself.

The first section of the paper will discuss the cyclical forces in the economy and financial system that helped create the conditions for financial crises to occur in the United States since 1966. The second section will describe the institutional structure of the financial system in the early postwar period, and explain why financial crises did not occur during that period. The final section will trace the process of erosion of this structure and the resulting increase in financial instability.

CYCLICAL FORCES LEADING TO FINANCIAL CRISIS

A financial crisis has occurred near the peak of every business-cycle expansion since 1966 (if the growth recession of 1966–67 is included in the business-cycle chronology). In each of these expansions, developments have occurred which have increased the vulnerability of the financial system significantly as the peak of the expansion approached. This vulnerability, in the context of the long-term conditions in the financial system (discussed below), set the stage for surprise events to initiate a financial crisis.[1] It is necessary, then, to specify those developments.

During the course of each business-cycle expansion, corporations took on increasing amounts of debt. The increased reliance upon credit led to a deterioration in the financial strength of corporate balance sheets: debt increased in relation to equity, the maturity of that debt shortened, and liquidity declined. As the peak of the expansion neared, profits began to fall as well.

The decline in corporate profitability called into question the continued viability of the economic expansion. Due to declining profits, corporations found it increasingly more difficult to meet their escalating debt service requirements. Also, because current profits are an important barometer of the direction of future profits, and because these expected profits play a central role in the demand for investment, the decline in profits increased the reluctance of business corporations to undertake new investment projects.

On the other hand, corporations had a need to finance current investment expenditures that had been committed in the past; the abandonment of these projects would mean losses and possible loss of market share. However, corporations were less able to finance these projects out of internal funds because of the decline in profits. Thus although the demand for funds to finance new projects was beginning to slow down, corporations had an increasingly inelastic demand for external funds for what might be called "necessitous" borrowing — to meet debt repayment schedules and to finish partly completed investment projects.

The corporations turned to the banks and other suppliers of credit to meet the demand for funds. The banks were reluctant to extend new loans partly because they were experiencing increasingly severe losses on the loans that they already had outstanding. In addition, their reserves were being restrained by a monetary policy which typically became relatively tight near the peak of the expansion.

Most banks were forced to gradually restrict their credit. However, the larger banks were able to meet the loan demands of their best customers primarily because of their better access to the market for "purchased" funds (large certificates of deposit, Eurodollar borrowings, commercial paper, etc.). These funds are expensive, uninsured, and extremely volatile. Nonetheless, the explosive growth of loan commitments in recent years bears testimony to the willingness of the banks to attempt to meet corporate loan demands. It also indicates the priority that corporations put on a guaranteed supply of funds in a time of need. (Some corporations with sufficiently good credit ratings were also able to borrow directly in the commercial paper market.)

Although the necessitous borrowing needs of the large corporations were accommodated, the situation in the financial system was quite delicate and unstable. At the peak of each business-cycle expansion, an unexpected event occurred which disrupted these financing patterns or shocked the confidence of market participants. These surprise events led to a sudden limitation in the supply of credit and initiated the financial crisis.

In the crises considered in the postwar period, there were two types of surprise events. The first was an institutional constraint imposed by government authorities, whose purpose was to limit the continued expansion of credit by the banks. In 1966, Regulation Q interest-rate ceilings were kept in place, and in March 1980 explicit credit controls were instituted.

The second type of surprise event was either a default or failure (or the threat of one) which shocked investor and/or depositor confidence. For example, in 1970 it was the Penn Central bankruptcy; in 1974 the threatened failures of Franklin National Bank and the Real Estate Investment Trusts (REITs); and in recent years the failures of Drysdale, Penn Square, and Continental, the threatened default of Mexico, etc.[2]

There are two important points which should be stressed regarding the process leading towards financial crises. The first is that the crisis occurs because the forms of credit that serve as near-money during normal times no longer do so when confidence is jolted and normal financing patterns are interrupted by the surprise events. In that case, only money—hard cash—will do. In the context of this abrupt restriction of credit, a financial crisis can be defined simply as a sudden, intense demand for money.

The second point is that the financial crisis is an integral part of the endogenous developments that occur in the economic and financial systems as the expansion phase of the business cycle nears its peak. The inability of income—profits—to continue to keep pace with the rapid increase in debt means that the further expansion of the debt structure becomes increasingly threatened. The timing of the interruption of the debt-creation process by the surprise event is of course unpredictable, but at the same time the existence of such an event should best be understood as itself an endogenous reaction to the pressures building in the financial system as the expansion proceeds.

In the later postwar period, actions by the authorities to control excessive credit creation near the peak of the business-cycle expansion — even over and above tight monetary and fiscal policy—have often become necessary. Because large banks have been relatively successful in continuing the expansion of credit despite tight monetary policy, such policy responses have become fairly predictable reactions to the given conditions. Likewise, the sudden bankruptcies and defaults that have been discussed above have occurred primarily because the financial system at that point in the business cycle had become exceedingly fragile.[3] The primary question has been which will occur first—the institutional constraint or the surprise default—to interrupt the supply of credit and initiate the financial crisis.

Before moving on, it would be useful to mention the ways in which the financial crises in the postwar period have been resolved. In almost all instances the Federal Reserve Board has acted in its role as a lender of last resort to make money available to all those who were so desperately seeking it. For the most part these actions of the Federal Reserve calmed fears and eased the immediate crisis. Less restrictive monetary and fiscal policies were then employed to restore the profitability of the corporate sector, ease the pressures on the financial system, and move the economy, at least temporarily, away from crisis.

THE POSTWAR FINANCIAL SYSTEM

As a result of the trauma of the Great Depression, and due to developments during the Depression and World War II, the financial system in the United States was profoundly affected. A financial environment was created that protected financial institutions from adversity. It was supported by three pillars: (1) federal insurance of deposits, (2) restrictions upon permissible activities for financial institutions, and (3) the unusually liquid condition of bank balance sheets and the "robust" condition of the financial system in general.

The Banking Crisis of 1931–33 was the most serious and widespread in the nation's history. As a result, sweeping changes in the financial system were introduced in the Banking Act of 1933. Perhaps the most significant change was the introduction of federal insurance of bank deposits, which did much to mitigate the severity of bank runs.

In addition, important restrictions were placed upon the activities of financial institutions. The payment of interest on demand deposits was prohibited, and ceiling interest rates were set on time deposits. Each type of financial institution was "compartmental-ized" and restricted to a specific type of lending, the mixing of banking and commerce was prohibited, and interstate banking was sharply proscribed. These regulations limited the activities of financial institutions, but also protected them from adversity and promoted stability.

The Depression also had a significant influence on attitudes concerning debt creation and risk. Financial market participants became more conservative and wary of conditions that could re-create the financial disaster of the Depression.

During the Depression there was a significant reduction of outstanding debt in the private sector, as firms went out of business, loan defaults were widespread, and economic activity was stagnant. Opportunities for private debt creation were limited during World War II because of the domination of the debt markets by government financing of the war effort.

As a result, the financial system at the end of World War II was unusually robust. Accompanying this stable financial system in the domestic economy was the stable international financial system set in place at Bretton Woods and based upon the dollar as a reserve currency.[4] These two together resulted in twenty years of relatively tranquil financial behavior in the period immediately following World War II.

THE EROSION OF THE POSTWAR INSTITUTIONAL STRUCTURE

However, the very success of the early postwar financial system began to undermine its stability. Conservative attitudes towards debt-creation and risk gradually began to change as memories of the Great Depression faded and time went by without any traumatic shocks to the financial system. With the growth of the system, more opportunities for private debt-creation developed, and the relative importance of government securities in bank portfolios began to decline.

With the decline in liquidity there arose more limitations on the banks' ability to manage their assets so as to accommodate loan demand and other needs for funds, especially in periods of tight money. So in February 1961 Citibank introduced the negotiable certificate of deposit (CD) and helped to create a secondary market for its resale. In doing do, it developed and rapidly expanded the practice of liability management, of "purchasing" liabilities in the market (rather than selling assets) to meet needs for funds.

The use of CDs and the rise of liability management was a response to the erosion of one of the important elements of the early postwar financial environment, the unusual liquidity of financial institutions. Yet this new innovation soon ran into trouble from another aspect of that environment — interest rate ceilings on time deposits. The first financial crisis of the postwar period, the Credit Crunch of 1966, was initiated when market interest rates rose above ceiling rates on large negotiable certificates of deposit.

In 1969, when ceiling interest rates again made the issuance of new CDs noncompetitive, the banks turned to the Eurodollar market to fill the gap. In the changing conditions of the late 1960s, an aspect of the postwar institutional structure — interest rate ceilings — put into place to protect financial institutions wound up inhibiting their growth. Partly in recognition of their limited usefulness, ceilings on CDs were phased out in the early 1970s. Ceiling rates on other types of deposits have been progressively removed since then.

The decline in profits in the business sector in the late 1960s led to a significant increase in the use of debt, much of it lent by the banks and other financial institutions. In fact, profits of the nonfinancial corporate sector have never in the recent period reached the peak that they attained in the mid-1960s, and the use of debt by corporations has continually increased in the past twenty years. The mid- to late-1960s, indeed, mark the transition point from a stable to an unstable financial environment.

With the continued growth and development of the financial system during the inflationary 1970s, other elements of the early postwar financial structure also changed from protective supports into barriers to further growth. An important example concerns the thrift institutions.

The early postwar structure, by its rigid compartmentalization of lending functions among financial institutions, was designed to provide stability and protection for those institutions. But the protective cushion for the thrifts, which had specialized in making long-term mortgages, disappeared with the rise in interest rates during the late 1970s and early 1980s. The thrifts, locked into low interest rates on their long-term mortgage assets, were nonetheless forced to pay market interest rates on their liabilities — due, ironically, to the easing of interest rate ceilings on their deposits. Earnings suffered, and the market value of their net worth turned negative in some cases.

The one element of the early postwar financial structure that has remained in something close to its original form is the federal insurance of deposits. Indeed, deposit insurance has played an important role in boosting confidence in the banking system and in reducing potential bank runs. Yet postwar developments have both limited and expanded the role that government supports like federal deposit insurance have played in containing financial instability. The scope of federal deposit insurance has been limited by the introduction of large denomination certificates of deposit and the reliance on other "purchased" funds for liability management. The growth of liability management has created an important class of bank liabilities that is not covered by deposit insurance. In fact, runs on CDs and on other uninsured liabilities by institutional investors have played a significant role in the recent financial crises.

This slippage in the ability of federal deposit insurance to contain bank runs has led to an expansion of the federal guarantee to a broader "safety net." The most significant components of this safety net include operations as a lender of last resort by the Federal Reserve; the "automatic stabilizers," whereby transfer payments automatically increase, and taxes decline, when aggregate income falls; and a conscious macroeconomic policy designed to limit the decline in output and employment that used to follow in the wake of financial crises.

This expanded role of the federal government in the economy has enabled the financial system to avoid the sharp crashes, panics, and banking crises that took place during the Depression and earlier. However, these macroeconomic policies, while successful in limiting the short-run consequences of financial instability, have encouraged the expansion of debt and have increased the long-run fragility of the financial system.

Each time that lender-of-last-resort operations have protected innovative debt instruments and markets (such as the CD, commercial paper, and Eurodollar interbank markets), the continued use of that and similar instruments for further debt creation are validated. Moreover, by putting a floor on the fall of asset values and the liquidation of debt, these macroeconomic policies have prevented the financial system from making the kinds of adjustments that in the past had led to the resumption of economic growth without excessive reliance on debt. There is also the problem of "moral hazard": the success of the federal safety net may be encouraging financial institutions to take more risk because they feel that public policy is oriented towards preventing significant adverse consequences.

In summary, out of the banking crises of the Great Depression a new, integrated financial institutional structure was created. This financial environment worked well to ensure stability during the early postwar period, but the growth of the system gradually eroded its foundations. The institutional structure that at an earlier time promoted stability later served as a barrier to the further growth and evolution of the financial system.

There are at least three important tasks that are suggested by this analysis. The first is to explore the connections between the creation and subsequent erosion of a stable institutional structure in the financial system with parallel developments in the nonfinancial system. The second is to understand how the dissolution of the old financial structure and the increase in financial fragility have changed the economy's current functioning, the alternatives of policymakers, and people's economic well-being. The third is to analyze current developments in the financial system, such as internationalization, innovation, and technological change, that will influence possibilities for a new financial structure.

ACKNOWLEDGEMENTS

Henry Martin is the pen name of the author, who is employed at a large financial institution. He would like to thank Gary Dymski, Michele Naples, Arthur MacEwan, and Jim Campen for helpful comments.

NOTES

1. For further background on the postwar crises, the reader can consult Hyman Minsky (1986), Albert M. Wojnilower (1980:277–326) and Martin H. Wolfson (1986).
2. The element of surprise plays an important role in initiating the financial crisis. Equally troublesome financial developments for which financial market participants have been prepared, e.g., the difficulties of Chrysler Corporation or the loan repayment problems of other Latin American countries since 1982, have not resulted in the same kind of shock to the financial system.
3. In addition, their impact on the financial system has been substantial because of the fragility that has existed.
4. The international financial system was an essential component of overall stability in the early postwar period, but its creation (and subsequent erosion) have been discussed elsewhere and will not be treated further here.

14

Structural Change and Increasing Fragility in the U.S. Financial System

ROBERT POLLIN

INTRODUCTION

Among the most significant manifestations of the long-term stagnation of the United States economy are the fundamental changes that have occurred in the economy's financial system since the mid-1960s. Accompanying these changes has been a sharp increase in the financial system's overall instability — the number of serious stress points in the system has grown, and its general structural integrity has deteriorated. Some of the most visible signs of change and increasing instability include the following:

— The dramatic rise in the bank failure rate since 1983 to a level unprecedented since the 1930s Depression;

— Rates of home and farm foreclosures and mortgage delinquencies experiencing similiar increases;

— Nominal interest rates, and later also real interest rates, rising to new highs as well;

— The spread of financial innovation, producing both the breakdown of traditional distinctions between various United States financial institutions, and the increasing integration of United States institutions into a single international financial system;

— The rising frequency and severity of financial crisis episodes — the 1984 Continental Illinois case being only the most dramatic of a number of such occurrences — and the increasing resort to government emergency bailouts to prevent these episodes from producing a full-scale debt deflation.

This paper attempts to provide a broad analysis of the forces generating long-term change and increasing instability in contemporary United States finance. It builds upon two sets of literature. One is the the post-Keynesian ''creditist'' literature on finance, discussed in Section 2, which stresses the high degree of flexibility in modern financial structures, and, more specifically, the endogeneity of the supply of credit. The other, considered in Section 3, is the contemporary Marxian discussions of economic crisis which recognize the observed declining rate of profit as a central feature of the economy's long-term stagnation.

Broadly speaking, this paper should be read as a companion to Henry Martin's contribution in this volume. Martin's article discusses both short and long-term elements contributing to financial instability and financial crises. This article concentrates on the long-term developments that have produced increasing financial instability over each succeeding business cycle since the mid-1960s. But of course, the real world economy does not make such fine distinctions between short and long-run factors: both need to be understood to make sense of today's increasingly crisis-prone financial system.

1. THE ANALYSIS OF DEBT FINANCING BEHAVIOR

The analytic focus of this paper is aggregate borrowing and lending activity in the United States, which determines the economy's overall rate of debt financing. By debt financing, I mean the financing of expenditures by nonfinancial economic units — businesses, households, and government — through borrowing rather than through "internal" sources such as corporate retained earnings, government tax revenues or household savings and disposable income. Corporations may also sell equity shares as a means of obtaining funds, the total of debt plus equity constituting the broader category, "external finance." However, because borrowing amounts to roughly 95 percent of total external financing activity for all sectors, it is legitimate for our purposes to concentrate on this portion of the total.

Focusing on the nonfinancial economy's debt financing behavior is an illuminating starting point for understanding the phenomena that have occurred in the sphere of finance since the mid-1960s. This is because the financing patterns for all nonfinancial sectors have undergone a fundamental change over this period. Through understanding the nature of this change, the entire range of problems that have emerged since the mid-1960s should then also become clarified.

What has occurred since the mid-1960s is that the proportion of the economy's total output (GNP) which is financed by borrowing has departed substantially from a long-term stable path, rising to an unprecedented level. To observe this, we may follow the classic investigation of this relationship by John Gurley and Edward Shaw (1956), who divided the years between 1897–1949 into three 17–18 year phases. Carrying their approach forward to the present, we see that the percentage of debt-financed GNP was remarkably stable up until the mid-1960s, ranging close to 9 percent over each long phase. Between 1967–86 however, the percentage of GNP that was debt financed rose to 14.4 percent — a 60 percent increase over the historical trend. Considering this same data somewhat differently, Gurley and Shaw also divided the 1897–1949 period into 13 shorter business cycles. Carrying this method to the present produces 20 business cycles. What emerges here is that prior to the mid-1960s, only during the cycles covering the two World Wars did the average proportion of debt financing ever rise above 10 percent. But over the three cycles since the mid-1960s, the proportion has increased from 12.0 to 16.4 percent.

Figure 1 shows debt financing behavior between 1950–86 for the aggregate United States nonfinancial economy, and for the three major nonfinancial sectors — households, nonfinancial corporations and the federal government. The figure shows that the aggregate nonfinancial economy as well as the three major sectors all experienced similiar upward trends in debt financing since the mid-1960s (though, on a cycle-to-cycle basis, the movements of the federal government's ratio tends to vary inversely with that of households and nonfinancial corporations). Clearly then, what needs to be explained — in terms of both the supply and demand side of financial markets — is why debt financing since the mid-1960s has so dramatically departed from its long-term path.

2. THE SUPPLY OF CREDIT

In neoclassical economics — Keynesian, monetarist and variants thereof — the prevailing view is that the supply of credit at any point in time is determined by two

Figure 1
Debt Financing Ratios for U.S.
NonFinancial Borrowers

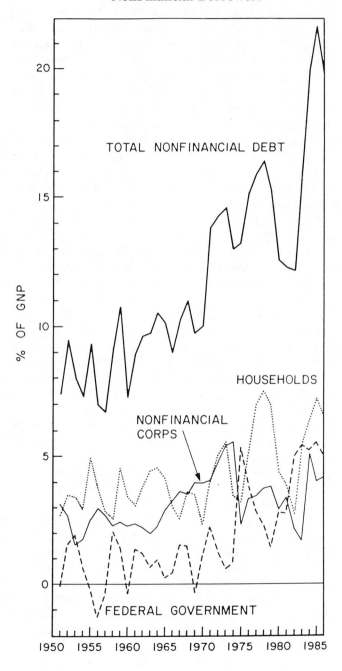

Source: Flow of Funds Accounts of Federal Reserve System.

factors: the rate of savings by households and businesses and Federal Reserve policy decisions in setting reserve requirements and the growth rate of the money supply (which here will be defined as M1, including cash, demand deposits, and effective equivalents of demand deposits such as NOW and ATS accounts). The story in any mainstream textbook proceeds as follows:[1] when financial intermediaries — banks, savings and loans, insurance companies, and credit unions — receive funds from net saving units, they are able to lend out a portion of the funds, while the rest must remain within the institution in the form of reserves. The amount they must keep in reserve is determined by the legal reserve requirement on each type of financial asset, as established by the Fed. Once the intermediaries have loaned all but the amount they are obliged to keep in reserve — having exhausted their "free reserves" — they cannot lend any more until their total reserves increase. Within this analytical framework, reserves can increase through three major mechanisms: by an increase in the flow of savings into the system; by a Federal Reserve decision to reduce reserve requirements; or by Fed action to increase the money supply growth rate. Most proponents of this view believe that the savings rate is generally believed to be basically stable over long periods of time (recent declines in personal savings rates notwithstanding). As a result, changes in the system's capacity to supply loanable funds almost always occurs as the result of the Fed acting to change reserve requirements or, more commonly, to change the growth rate of the money supply. This is the sense in which, in neoclassical analysis, the supply of loanable funds is said to be "exogenous": it is determined by the Fed's policy decisions, not by "endogenous" market forces.

The post-Keynesian creditist approach challenges the neoclassical view at its foundations. This approach contends that the supply of credit is a highly flexible magnitude, one that is responsive to profit opportunities in financial markets, and particularly to the forces of loan demand.[2] To develop this idea, one must focus on the behavior of financial intermediaries. Savings decisions and Fed policy remain as significant considerations in this approach. But to be properly evaluated, these factors must be seen within the larger framework of a highly developed system of intermediation.

Considering a single intermediary and its staff of loan officers at the micro level, it is now widely recognized that standard profit-seeking and career-advancing behavior entails first pursuing the maximum amount of loan commitments to solvent customers, then seeking the added reserves necessary to cover the legal requirements. The intermediaries, in other words, do not restrict their lending according to the supply of free reserves they hold at any given time. To assume that intermediaries should so restrict their lending — that they should passively allow their lending capacity to be constrained by savings decisions and Fed policy — is to deny them any profit-seeking motivation.

As long as one remains within a micro level of analysis, it is not difficult to acknowledge — even from an orthodox viewpoint — this flexibility of intermediary lending behavior. It is hardly controversial to recognize that intermediaries which have insufficient reserves for meeting their loan demand may borrow from those with free reserves. What is less apparent is how such micro level behavior is capable of expanding lending capacity for the system as a whole. Here is where the alternative view departs sharply from orthodoxy.

In fact, there are several ways in which intermediaries as a whole can expand aggregate lending capacity with a given supply of reserves. Taken together, these maneuvers of the intermediaries have been given the term "liability management" (though most current practices involve aggressive management of both assets and liabilities). First, as the market for free reserves grows and becomes increasingly sophisticated, the amount of unutilized reserves within the system diminishes. Funds can be moved with increasing speed from intermediaries with excess reserves to those with shortages. A given supply of reserves thus allows for a larger expansion of lending capacity. Another strategy is for nonfinancial businesses to extend trade credit (accounts receivables) in greater volume and over longer periods. By increasing trade credit in this way, credit market constraints can be bypassed completely: the amount of trade credit extended depends only on the ability of trading partners to come to terms. Intermediaries can also generate free reserves by convincing depositors to hold their assets in higher yielding instruments which carry lower reserve requirements. The creation of the Certificates of Deposit in the early 1960s is the best-known instance of this strategy. And finally, domestic intermediaries may also borrow from foreign sources, either their own offshore branches or other institutions. The increasing use of this practice was in fact a major impetus for the explosive growth of the Eurodollar market since the mid-1960s and it has since become a major source of United States loanable funds. Here, in short, is where the "globalization of finance" exerts a major influence on United States financial structures.

Thus far, considerable empirical research already exists supporting the view that the supply of credit is not strongly constrained by savings flows and Fed policy. Rather than summarizing this literature, I present here some basic evidence which strongly supports this contention. Figure 2 gives data for the postwar period on borrowing/lending flows, gross private savings flows, and the money supply, all relative to GNP. The data for borrowing flows is the same as in Figure 1, showing the strong upward movement of the trend beginning in the mid-1960s and continuing to the present. Now, contrast this movement with that of the other two series: gross savings remains relatively constant throughout the full period, and as a result, lending grows relative to saving throughout. Indeed, from 1983 onward, lending comes to exceed gross savings.

With the money supply data, we observe a steady downtrend over the postwar period relative to GNP, one which does not abate at all when borrowing growth begins its uptrend in the mid-1960s.[3] And, as with the savings data, lending exceeds the money supply by the end of the full period. These data, in short, clearly support the view that the supply of credit is highly independent of the behavior of savings flows and the money supply growth rate. Going a step further, these data are also consistent with the notion that the supply of credit is indeed a flexible, endogenously determined variable, one that is responsive to demand forces in financial markets.

3. THE DEMAND FOR CREDIT

Having recognized that financial intermediaries can increase the supply of credit independently of domestic savings rates and Federal Reserve policy, we must now also acknowledge that this capability becomes significant only when credit demand pressures are strong. In the absence of rising credit demand, the credit creating capacities of the intermediaries will remain dormant. Thus, to explain the observed 60 percent increase over the historical trend in the rate of debt financing since the mid-1960s, we must also

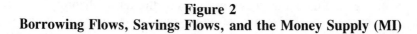

Figure 2
Borrowing Flows, Savings Flows, and the Money Supply (MI)

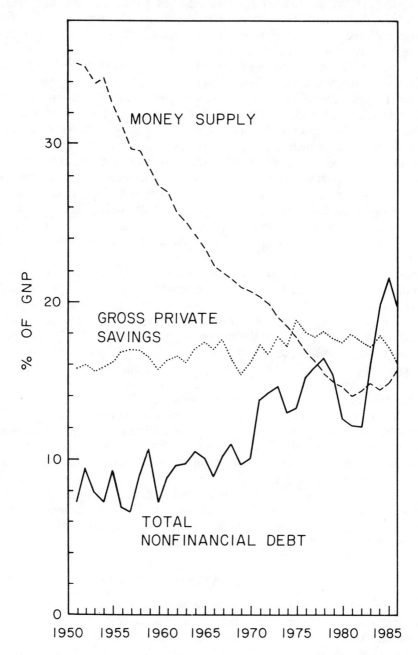

Sources: Flow of Funds Accounts; Economic Report of the President, 1987; Cambridge Planning Datadisk.

address the factors affecting credit demand over this period. We therefore consider here the borrowing trends of each of the three major nonfinancial sectors, nonfinancial corporations and households in addition to the federal government, as well as the interactive effects of borrowing by each of these sectors upon the other sectors' financial behavior. In addition, this investigation of demand forces will carry central importance for developing effective financial stabilization policies. Once one recognizes that credit supply is highly flexible and therefore difficult for policy to contain, it then follows that the only effective way to reduce the rate of debt financing will be through the demand side. Thus, understanding demand side pressures becomes the first prerequisite for formulating an effective set of financial stabilization policies.

Nonfinancial Corporations

The rise of corporate debt financing is the result of two closely related influences: a long-term trend that emerged in the late 1960s and continues to the present; and a more recent additional surge associated with the growth of mergers and acquisitions.

For explaining the long-term trend, the mainstream neoclassical view is that increasing corporate debt financing has been the product of sustained inflation.[4] Neoclassical economists point out correctly that both prices and interest rates rose in the high inflation years, but prices rose more rapidly. This lessened the real burden of interest payments, since debts could be repaid with cheaper dollars. In addition, because all interest payments were (until implementation of the 1986 tax reform act) tax deductible, deductions increased as interest rates rose. Finally, returns on equity ownership were doubly taxed, both through corporate and individual income taxes, thereby increasing further the attractiveness of debt relative to equity financing.

A second approach is advanced in the works of Hyman Minsky and other post-Keynesians. Minsky and the others contend that an inherent thrust towards increased debt financing always exists in mature capitalist economies. Indeed, Albert Wojnilower, a leading Wall Street economist and proponent of this approach refers to the "narcotic attraction of borrowing." With corporations in particular, the Minsky approach argues that positive expectations during business cycle upswings will induce firms to borrow more in an effort to expand their operations more rapidly and thereby capture a competitive edge. Minsky believes this tendency is generally controllable only through periodic financial crises in which the supply of funds collapses. In the absence of such crises, the tendency toward increased debt financing will strengthen with time.

Despite the distinctiveness of the neoclassical and Minskian approaches, there is an important common error in both arguments, rendering both inadequate for explaining the patterns since the mid-1960s. If corporations were motivated to increase debt financing either because of declining borrowing costs or as a result of a boom psychology, we would then also expect this increase in debt financing to be accompanied by an increase in corporate spending. In particular, pursuing the logic of either approach, we would expect increases in debt financing to be accompanied by increases in their fixed investment growth rate. But in fact what has accompanied the rise in corporate debt financing since the mid-1960s has been a *decline* in investment growth.

I therefore have developed a third explanation, one which tries to reconcile the rise in debt financing with the decline in real investment growth. This approach focuses on the effects on corporate behavior of stagnant real profit flows and declining profit rates, which has also occurred since the mid-1960s.[5] More specifically, because real profit levels were stagnating, this tended also to reduce the amount of internal funds corporations had available for investment. When internal funds fell, corporations were then faced with some combination of two alternatives: reduce expenditure levels to reflect the decline in internal funds, or increase borrowing to avoid having to cut back on spending.

Most firms in this situation will probably try to pursue both alternatives partially. However, we observe empirically that firms have tended first to borrow more rather than cut expenditure levels. For firms to opt first to cut expenditures would require that they also slow the rate at which they can innovate and lower production costs. Firms' competitive position would thus weaken by cutting back on expenditures; market dominance would be seized by those firms willing to make the requisite investments. Consistent with these competitive imperatives, we therefore observe that the rate of corporate debt financing has risen to fill the gap created by the decline in corporate internal funds. This is why the increase in debt financing has emerged in conjunction with declining, rather than increasing, rates of corporate investment growth.

The merger and takeover phenomena can also be directly linked to the decline in the average rate of corporate profitability, along with the extreme flexibility on the supply side of financial markets.[6] As average corporate profitability fell throughout the 1970s and early 1980s, corporate share prices declined as well, to a point substantially below the replacement cost of the corporations' physical assets. To measure the relationship between share prices and physical assets James Tobin devised his "Q ratio," which is precisely a ratio of firms' market value divided by their physical assets measured at replacement cost. The Q ratio was at a postwar low by the early 1980s, creating strong incentives for takeovers and, concomitantly, equal incentives for financial innovations such as "junk bonds" to finance takeover efforts. Once these financial innovations were put in place, takeover activity developed a momentum of its own (including the considerable push of illegal but enormously profitable insider trading). This momentum continued to encourage takeovers and mergers financed by borrowing even as share prices rose dramatically beginning in the fall of 1982. The Q ratio at present, moreover, even after years of rising share prices, remains considerably below its postwar peak levels of the 1960s. Objective (and even legal) incentives for further mergers and takeovers thus still exist. These activities should continue to exert upward pressure on corporations' rate of debt financing.

Households

To a considerable extent, the alternative arguments for the rise of household debt financing parallel those made for nonfinancial corporations.[7] Many economists have explained the phenomenon as largely a consequence of three factors: the maturation of the baby-boom generation into their heavy borrowing years; more sanguine attitudes by households towards incurring debt; and the impact of inflation.

The demographic argument has some initial plausibility since a household's demand for credit does vary with the age of its adult members. Households whose heads are between 25 and 45 years old are most heavily indebted because they are in the midst of major purchases of homes and expensive durable goods like cars and washing machines. The maturation of the baby boom generation has meant that a higher percentage of households are in these heavy borrowing years. However, the impact of the maturing baby boom generation has been largely offset by a sharp increase in the number of households over age 65, those carrying the least amount of debt. As a result, the demographic factor has had little, if any, influence on the increase in the households' aggregate debt financing ratio.

The argument about shifting attitudes is that this same large cohort of the baby boom generation, having had no direct experience of the 1930s depression or any economic contraction of comparable severity, feels much more economically secure than its elders. Consequently it is less willing to save and more eager to borrow. But this argument simply does not square with the evidence. Polls sponsored by the Federal Reserve Board on consumer attitudes towards debt show that, in the aggregate, attitudes have not shifted significantly over time. If anything, in fact, the polls indicate that households have become slightly more cautious in the 1980s relative to the 1970s.

There is additional evidence that demographic and attitudinal changes do not explain the rising rate of household debt financing. If more 25–45 year old householders were borrowing to purchase homes and consumer durables and otherwise spending in a free-wheeling manner, household spending should have increased at a faster rate than in previous years. However, the rise of household debt relative to income since the early 1970s has not been accompanied by faster increases in spending. In fact, the rate of growth in household spending slowed by about half over the period 1974–86 compared to the previous two decades.

Partially, the rise of household debt financing could be explained by inflation, which, until the early 1980s, lowered the real cost of borrowing for households as for corporations. But since the early 1980s, low real borrowing rates have been supplanted by extremely high real rates, and household debt financing has continued to rise. In addition, even though inflation made it cheaper for households to borrow money in the 1970s, we still must confront the fact that real spending growth did not increase along with the growth of debt. If households were increasingly lured to the credit markets, what did they do with the extra funds they obtained?

There are two separate answers to that question, one applicable to the small minority of wealthy families and the other to everyone else. The decline in borrowing costs enabled the wealthy to raise more funds to pursue speculative investments. Real estate and financial markets became especially attractive to wealthy investors because the costs of borrowing were falling while the returns on these investments were rising. The rich have also experienced sharply rising incomes since the early 1970s, so they have indeed become more "optimistic" — i.e. willing to borrow to finance luxury consumption.

But less wealthy households have also increased their rate of debt financing, especially those in the bottom 40 percent of the income distribution. What has motivated this majority of households to depend increasingly on debt, even though they have not increased their level of spending? To answer this we must consider what has happened to real wages, family incomes, and housing costs since the early 1970s. From their peak in 1972 until 1985, real wages fell by 14.1 percent. In response to this (as well as to changing social conditions), women entered the labor force in increasing numbers, to provide many families with a second income. This option was clearly preferable to a sharp cut in family living standards. But because average wages continued to fall, even the growth of two-wage households has failed to maintain family income levels: real median family incomes fell by 4.9 percent from their 1973 peak to 1985. At the same time, the median cost of a new home rose by 7.4 percent over these years (fueled to a large extent by the speculative activity of the wealthy) and overall housing costs increased by 8.6 percent over the general price level. Because housing is the least flexible item in the family budget and thus the first claim on its income, these relative increases in housing have been particulary burdensome.[8]

As a result of continued income declines and rising housing costs, average households have become threatened with a decline in their living standard. As such, they have become increasingly dependent on credit as a way of trying to maintain their living standard. In other words, the majority of households have taken on more debt not because they are trying to spend more, but because they are fighting to avoid losing what they have as incomes fall and housing costs rise.

The Federal Government

We have seen that corporations and households have increased their rates of debt financing both to avoid sharp reductions in their expenditure levels and to pursue speculative investment opportunities. To recognize this, however, does not itself explain why the aggregate rate of debt financing since the mid-1960s should have risen to its current historically unprecedented level. Certainly significant gaps between incomes and expenditure demands have existed in prior phases, as have waves of heavy financial speculation. Yet, as noted earlier, the aggregate debt financing ratio remained highly stable in these previous periods.

To explain this unique situation we have to bring federal government borrowing into the analysis. Federal government borrowing has contributed to the unprecedented rise in aggregate debt financing in two crucial ways. First, since peacetime government deficit spending is a relatively new phenomenon, becoming a conscious policy instrument only in the 1960s, its emergence has tended to increase total debt financing simply because it is a large additional component of the aggregate figure. Of course, this is especially the case since 1980, with the onset of the Reagan Administration's fiscal policy combining large tax cuts for the wealthy with a massive military buildup. Moreover, once we recognize that the total supply of credit is highly flexible, it becomes clear that large-scale government borrowing does not itself deprive the private sector of obtaining the funds it demands.

The second, and even more fundamental contribution of government deficit spending has been its counter-cyclical impact. In earlier historical phases, the rise of debt financing had been checked and reversed when credit bubbles were burst by severe debt deflations. These debt deflations would begin as a result of a sharp cyclical downturn in aggregate income. As a consequence of falling incomes, debtors' cash flow would become insufficient to meet their debt obligations. Widespread defaults would then occur, which in turn would set off a chain reaction of falling financial asset values, bank failures, and a contraction of available liquidity. Of course this process would force sharply downward the economy's aggregate rate of debt financing.[9]

In the contemporary period, government deficit financing counteracts the debt deflation process by increasing the level of aggregate income in the short-run. As a result of this intervention, defaults can and do still occur in a period of cyclical decline, but not as severely as would have resulted without the government intervention. When the wave of defaults is avoided, the incipient debt-deflation is thwarted.

Thus, large-scale government debt financing acts to circumscribe the private economy's contractionary tendencies. However, in accomplishing this task, government debt financing also necessarily acts to nullify the debt deflation process as a financial regulator. In the absense of debt deflations, no automatic mechanism exists for discouraging the sustained growth in private debt financing. This is why, as a result of large-scale federal government debt financing, we have experienced this unprecedented rise in the the economy's aggregate rate of debt financing during the contemporary period. To recognize this potency of the government's debt financing tool does not however imply that all government deficits — irrespective of size, circumstances, or the specific tax and spending policies they reflect — are equally capable of preventing sharp downturns and encouraging stability.[10] Clearly, some tax and expenditure policies will produce different effects on the private economy than others. In terms of financial effects specifically, some fiscal policies will be much more effective in reducing the gap between private sector incomes and expenditures, and thus in reducing private sector demand for credit. Some policies, in other words, may succeed not simply in avoiding debt deflations but also in preventing the worsening of problems associated with the persistent rise of private debt financing.

4. SUMMARY AND IMPLICATIONS

The basic points to extract from the foregoing discussion are as follows:

1. The fundamental measure of change in the United States financial structure since the mid-1960s has been the 60 percent increase in the rate of debt financing over its historical trend.

2. Profit-seeking activity of financial intermediaries, not individual savings decisions or Federal Reserve policy, is the final determinant of credit supply; the intermediaries possess considerable power in increasing total credit supply to meet a strong demand.

3. Declining real household incomes and corporate profitability as well as speculative pressures are the driving forces behind the rise of private sector debt financing. Corporations and households are choosing to borrow more rather than cut expenditures to levels commensurate with the declines in incomes and profits.

4. Increasing debt financing by the federal government has prevented the occurrence of severe debt deflations and depressions. But in so doing, it has also suppressed the debt deflation's constraining effect on financial activities. This has engendered a new set of financial problems, associated with the upward trend of aggregate debt financing.

Working from this perspective can provide a coherent basis for explaining the major features of the contemporary United States financial situation, including the persistent inflation, high real interest rates, and a fragile financial structure. To begin with, the basic phenomenon of debt financing rising faster than GNP is inherently inflationary, since it means that purchasing power is being injected into the economy at a rate faster than the growth of real output. Countering this inflationary pressure requires that strong deflationary forces — such as high levels of unemployment, falling real wages, or an overvalued dollar — also be present.

In addition, continuous financial market turbulence and pressures for innovation result through the scramble among intermediaries to meet, and profit from, the permanent strong credit demand. Naturally, such efforts become especially strenuous when the opportunities for profitable investment in the economy's nonfinancial sector have diminished.

Also, persistent upward interest rate pressure is exerted on one side from the nonfinancial economy's strong credit demand, and on the other from the intermediaries themselves, competing through liability management for the funds to meet demand. Through liability management, intermediaries must now pay market interest rates to obtain reserves, a dramatic change from only ten years ago when interest-free demand deposits and low interest time deposits were still the major source of reserves. This upward tendency of interest rates may also be countered, but only through monetary policies which fully accommodate the unprecedented demand-side pressures.

Finally, the combination of high rates of debt financing with high interest rates has created a heavy debt burden for borrowers. The weight of this burden is attenuated through inflation, since inflation lowers the real value of debt over time. But as inflation has fallen since 1982, repayment burdens have correspondingly worsened. This is a basic reason for the rise of bank failures and of home and farm foreclosures and mortgage delinquencies over the past two years.

5. POLICY DIRECTIONS

On the basis of these conditions, it is not difficult to identify what should be the major goals of financial stabilization policy in the contemporary United States economy: to reduce the nonfinancial sector's debt financing ratio to a figure approaching its historical level; to do so through means other than debt deflation and depression; and finally, to do so in a way which also addresses the real problems implied by the increasing gap between corporate and household incomes and expenditures.

These goals cannot be met using conventional tools of monetary and regulatory policy.[11] Through financial innovation and liability management, financial market participants have learned to successfully counteract the government's efforts at monetary and regulatory fine-tuning when such policies seriously inhibit the intermediaries' drive for profits. Within this present-day financial structure, monetary and regulatory policies are "effective" only when they are employed not with a fine-tuner but a sledge-hammer; that is, when the aims of policy can be achieved only through inflicting extreme pain in the process. The stringent monetary policies of 1980–82, a major factor in generating the most severe economic contraction since the 1930s, is the clearest example of this.

Several leftist economists have called for the "democratization" of the Federal Reserve as a strategy for promoting more effective and equitable financial market policies.[12] These democratization proposals include putting representatives of labor or community groups on the Board of Governors of the Fed, allowing the House of Representatives rather than the President to select Board Governors, shortening the term of office of the Governors from the current fourteen to four years, and having their terms run concurrent with that of the President. Such proposals may have some merit in terms of increasing the exposure of the Fed to political pressures, including those of an organized and assertive left. However, these proposals do not give adequate recognition to the powerful and deeply embedded destabilizing forces in the contemporary United States financial structure: they do not consider at all how a more democratic Fed could be more successful in counteracting financial innovation, liability management and demand-side pressures for increased debt financing. Indeed, the most likely outcome of attempts to promote financial stabilization by simply "democratizing the Fed" would be to erode the legitimacy of the democratization process itself, precisely because the more democratically chosen Governors would be equally limited in their capacity to neutralize the inherent destabilizing forces.

What is needed, instead, is a radical restructuring of financial market forces themselves, especially on the demand side. Such a restructuring should involve, for example, reducing corporate borrowing by instituting a public investment bank which directly subsidizes selected firms, thereby lowering their demand for debt financing while also establishing some democratic control over investment. A restructuring program should also aim to reduce household borrowing by promoting higher wages and lower housing costs and, through tax policy, circumscribing speculative investment in finance and real estate. In addition, the program should try to lower the federal government's credit demand. This could be achieved through sharp reductions in the military budget. Large military cuts would also allow budgetary space for the other initiatives.

How successful would such a restructuring program be in pulling the United States economy out of its long phase of stagnation? There is no computer model, crystal ball, astrological chart or other tool of the forecasting trade through which we can answer that question definitively. But it is clear that coordinated policies of this kind — emerging as the fruits of an ascendant left movement in the United States — could succeed in promoting the essential goals of democratic control over investment, better living standards for the majority, less militarism, and finally, an increasingly stable financial system.

ACKNOWLEDGEMENTS

I thank Cigdem Kurdas and Fred Moseley for useful comments on a previous draft, and the University of California-Riverside for financial support.

NOTES

1. See, for example, Goldfeld and Chandler (1986).
2. References to both the theoretical and empirical literature in this area are in Lavoie (1984) and Pollin (1987a).
3. This ratio is the inverse of what is a standard measure of the "velocity of money" — that is, the amount of money available to finance current expenditures. The figure thus shows velocity to be rising over the postwar period, contrary to monetarist assertions that velocity should either be stable or falling.
4. Pollin (1986) presents a much more extensive discussion of alternative explanations of the trend increase in corporate debt financing.
5. While this approach clearly derives from the Marxian falling-rate-of-profit discussions, it is not linked to any particular explanation as to why the profit rate has fallen (the alternative explanations are presented in this and the previous section of this volume). Rather, it begins from the *observation* of a trend decline in profitability for nonfinancial corporations and considers its implications for corporate finance. As such, it is consistent with all the competing Marxian explanations of the falling rate of profit, and should be regarded as an attempt to bring that discussion to a level of greater concreteness. Moreover, this analysis gains in robustness precisely because it does not stand or fall on the fate of any single theoretical approach to declining profitability.

6. Herman and Lowenstein (1986) is an insightful discussion of the merger and takeover phenomenon.

7. Detailed discussions of the growth of household debt financing are in Pollin (1988a) and (1988b).

8. Hartman (1983), especially the discussion by Stone, provides important background on this issue.

9. Wolfson (1986) and Minsky (1982) describe the process of debt deflation well.

10. The contributions of Michl and Miller in this volume clarify the range of possible effects of government expenditures and deficits.

11. This section is a highly abbreviated version of the discussion in Pollin (1985).

12. Bowles, Gordon and Weisskopf (1983), Carnoy, Shearer and Rumberger (1983), Collier (1985), and the Center for Popular Economics (1986) present proposals for democratizing the Federal Reserve. Sweezy and Magdoff (1984) offer an argument similiar to that presented here on the limitations of such a strategy.

15

Cyclical and Secular Productivity Slowdowns

MICHELE I. NAPLES

INTRODUCTION

The productivity slowdown of the 1970s and 1980s has proved to be a puzzle. It is not that periods of secularly slow productivity growth are so rare — three periods since 1913, including the late 1920s, have had productivity slowdowns comparable to the present one (Nordhaus 1980). The problem is that this slowdown has proved difficult for neoclassical models to explain. In the resultant vacuum, policy-makers have returned to the old-time medicine of cutting social spending and breaking unions to "strengthen the work ethic"; these policies too have failed to restore rapid long-term productivity growth.

Standard explanations fell short because the capital-labor ratio grew fairly rapidly in the 1970s, and the worst periods of the energy crisis were not the worst periods for productivity growth (see Baily 1981). In addition, the labor force's investment in education and training has increased steadily, which should have increased the contribution of "human capital." Even demographic-shift explanations resting on increased employment of "inherently less productive" women and youths imply that today's young inexplicably contribute half as much to the production process as their parents (Baily 1981).

Some radicals have debated whether the slowdown is an outcome or a cause of the crisis, or have seen it as artificial — resulting from the shift away from manufacturing towards lower-productivity service industries.[1] But secularly slower productivity growth is also evident in basic industry (see Table 1), calculated based on all employees' or production workers' hours.

Table 1
Cycle Averages of Annual Rates of
Production-Worker and All-Worker Productivity Growth

	1948–55	1955–59	1959–66	1966–73	1973–79	1979–86
Nonfarm Business						
All Employees	2.89	2.07	2.82	1.83	0.66	0.56
Production Workers	2.91	2.27	2.45	1.62	0.80	0.60*
Manufacturing						
All Employees	3.75	3.65	3.93	3.22	2.38	3.23
Production Workers	4.47	4.43	3.90	3.39	2.75	3.91

*Through 1985 only.

Sources: US Council of Economic Advisors, *Economic Report of the President 1987*, Washington, DC: US Government Printing Office (GPO), 1987; US Department of Commerce, *Survey of Current Business*, Washington, DC: US GPO, various months; US Department of Labor, Bureau of Labor Statistics, *Employment and Earnings*, Washington, DC: US GPO, various months.

Recent attention to productivity's secular or long-run behavior has overshadowed its cyclical slowdown from the early business-cycle expansion (when profits are rising and unemployment falling from its peak) into the late expansion (after profits peak, but before output and employment do; see Table 2). This end-of-expansion slowdown is also an anomaly for neoclassical theory (Gordon 1979), but is predicted by Marx's theory of the reserve army (see below). Interestingly, rapid productivity growth tends to slow inflation, holding other things constant. If radicals can explain the end-of-expansion productivity slowdown, they can also explain the Phillips Curve trade-off between unemployment and inflation.

Table 2
Annual Rates of Production-Worker Productivity Growth by Phase of the Business Cycle, US Manufacturing

Production-Worker Productivity Growth			Dates for Cycle Phases (Year:Quarter)		
A	B	C	A	B	C
5.88	3.61	2.61	1954:3-55:3	1955:4-56:4	1957:1-58:1
6.99	1.11	3.66	1958:2-59:1	1959:2-59:4	1960:1-61:1
4.28	3.66	3.94	1961:2-66:1	1966:2-68:4	1969:1-71:2
4.26	2.94	-0.28	1971:3-72:4	1973:1-73:3	1973:4-75:1
4.54	1.28	3.23	1975:2-77:2	1977:3-78:4	1979:1-80:2
4.43	3.48	3.06	1980:3-81:2	1981:3-81:3	1981:4-82:3
4.73	2.57		1982:4-85:4	1985:4-87:1	

Phase A: Maximum unemployment rate (U) to maximum real profit margin (P) (falling U).
Phase B: Maximum P to minimum U (falling profit rate, falling U).
Phase C: Minimum U to maximum U (rising U).

Sources: US Department of Commerce: *Business Statistics, 23rd Edition*, Washington, DC: US GPO, 1984; *Survey of Current Business*, various months. US Department of Labor, Bureau of Labor Statistics: *Employment, Hours, and Earnings, United States, 1909–84, Volume I*, Bulletin 1312–12, US GPO, 1985, and *Employment and Earnings*, various months.

It should be remembered that the long-wave and end-of-expansion productivity slowdowns are reduced rates of growth, not absolute declines. Only a few sectors, including construction and coal mining, have experienced lower productivity levels. The difficulty of measuring the quality of buildings calls into question the decline in construction (Magdoff and Sweezy 1980). Coal output can be measured in tons, and tonnage per miner-hour fell significantly from 1970 to 1977 (Naples 1987c).

This essay summarizes radical analyses of the determinants of productivity growth over the business cycle and the long run. Explanatory models which focus on the conflict-ridden nature of workplace relations under capitalism are examined in some detail. Empirical analyses of both cyclical and secular productivity slowdowns are then reviewed. A conclusion traces the implication of each productivity theory for future trends.

ALTERNATIVE THEORIES OF PRODUCTIVITY GROWTH

In an effort to distinguish radical contributions from neoclassical, this paper will not consider commonly agreed on determinants of productivity growth. Excluded from the discussion are increasingly capital-intensive production techniques, changes in the relative prices of inputs (e.g., rising energy prices), production bottlenecks, and generalized technological change.

Radicals have identified three main categories of cyclical and secular productivity determinants: effective demand, technological regimes, and the social relations of production (SRP). The first approach, known as Verdoorn's or Kaldor's Law, argues that the growth of output leads to increased productivity. Greater effective demand directly benefits productivity through extending the market and permitting greater specialization and more extensive division of labor. It also has indirect positive effects, through induced technical change and more rapid implementation of new techniques as old capital turns over more quickly.[2] Some advocates suggest that manufacturing is then the engine of growth: increases in its output reflect technical advances and generate demand for new capital equipment, further contributing to productivity growth. The slow growth of aggregate demand and output limit such opportunities for improving productivity.

However, the opposite lines of causation are also feasible. When the economy is growing quickly, firms earn tremendous profits simply by supplying the larger market, and have less incentive to look for ways to cut costs. It is when they face stagnant or shrinking markets that companies must streamline production if they are to increase their profit rates. If necessity is the mother of invention, it is slow economic growth which forces corporations to take advantage of the opportunity to specialize, etc.

The second literature draws on Aglietta's (1979) discussion of Fordism and the contradictions embedded in the technology of mass production.[3] In this view, the system of *regulation* (i.e., framework of rules and institutions) derives from technological imperatives. Thus the technology of mass production created both the pre-conditions and the necessity for the social contract and welfare system subsequently set in place in the postwar United States. Once the logic of mass production had played itself out, a lack of new techniques created the current productivity crisis and corresponding economic and social crisis.

This analysis begs the question of where technological revolutions come from, and particularly the role of class conflict in shaping firms' technical choices. It explains history by showing that developments were functional for the system as a whole, leaving open the question of how people knew to do what was functional. And there is no analysis of conflicting functions and purposes; the regulatory system works, it does not pull itself apart. Because the *regulation* analysis has rarely been subjected to econometric investigation, it will be left aside until the concluding section of the paper.

The third approach addresses productivity in terms of labor-management relations in the workplace. To extract maximum abstract labor from labor-power, and consequently maximize productivity (output per labor-hour), is not automatic. For capitalists, employees' work is the means to an end, the end being profits. But for employees, work is their experience, it is the way they spend a large part of their life. These conflicting perspectives mean that productivity has social as well as technical determinants. While capitalists' ownership of the means of production permits them to dominate workers, this domination is not absolute. Workers are active agents, not passive robots.

Because the class-relations approach to productivity analysis has proved particularly controversial, the next two sections develop the theory behind it in some detail and examine the criticisms which have been levied against it.

THE SOCIAL RELATIONS OF PRODUCTION

In the early 1970s, several radical economists suggested that conflict ridden production relations could have macroeconomic effects.[4] Low unemployment (a small reserve army of the unemployed, to use Marx's language) may permit workers to reduce the (growth of the) intensity and/or duration of their work each day. As job opportunities increase and quits rise, management finds it necessary to acquiesce to some employee demands and provide better working conditions if it is to retain good people. And workers have less fear of being fired, knowing other jobs are available and that management's hands are tied. They can challenge perceived abuses of authority, fight speed-up, take more frequent work breaks and trips to the bathroom, arrive late, or go home sick with fewer repercussions from supervisors.

When unemployment is low, such collective activity as strikes will cost labor less and hurt employers more; strikes can improve working conditions, obtain defensive work rules or staffing requirements, and constrain the growth of hourly effort. Workers no longer have to take as law a management order to reorganize the production process. Whether they directly challenge the order, or subvert it by working to rule (e.g., thoroughly checking the quality of each item), by minor sabotage (e.g., rejecting half the parts so produced), or by retaliating through other channels (e.g., reporting rats in the organic raw material bins to a health inspector), management's ability to increase output per labor-hour is constrained. Thus, despite capitalists' overall control, at this point in the business cycle or long-wave expansion, workers do have leverage and can act in their own interest, which can hurt productivity and profits.

The reserve-army analysis implies that high unemployment is sufficient to reestablish the conditions for accumulation. But David Gordon (1978) argued that secularly low profits and consequent intensified class conflict would lead to a break-down in mechanisms for channelling those conflicts, collectively called the Social Structure of Accumulation or SSA. As management attacks grew, workers would defend themselves, and in the process develop new consciousness of their legitimate concerns and power outside the bounds of historic practices. He believed this helped explain union workers' activism regarding the quality of worklife in the late sixties and early seventies, which in turn was particularly harmful for productivity growth (Gordon 1975).

From the SSA perspective, renewed accumulation requires that a new understanding about legitimate forms and objects of conflict be developed and institutionalized. Then emergence from long-wave crises is contingent, not structurally assured. It depends on accomodations among fractions of the capitalist class (e.g., vehemently anti-union firms and those in sectors with a highly unionized workforce) as well as between capital and the working class.

However, in this view workers' institutions only enter the analysis during the crisis phase, and the cause of the crisis lies elsewhere. I have suggested in other work that one component of the SSA, the industrial-relations system, unraveled because of its own contradictory logic even before profits began to fall. While collective-bargaining institutions enjoy their own resources, and institutionalized practices their own momentum, it is not possible for any set of rules to "handle" the class conflicts embedded in capitalism. When institutional mechanisms established to peacefully solve the irresolvable fail to meet both capital's and labor's demands, conflictive work relations will erupt, hurting productivity and profits.

The contradictory logic of the postwar truce between organized labor and capital had several aspects. While management agreed to grant union recognition, in exchange for relative industrial peace, this did not mean that after several strike-free decades they would still consider unions a necessary evil. Union leaders came to spend more time administering multi-year contracts than organizing strikes. If they proved readier to hear management's concerns than to fight for members', the stake of the rank-and-file in the truce would diminish. While union contracts typically acquiesced to managerial prerogatives in the workplace, workers would not indefinitely tolerate increasingly unsafe practices or unhealthy conditions.

Then the secular crisis of workplace relations which Gordon described can be seen as an endogenous outcome of the contradictions embodied in the postwar accomodation. This structuralist stance permits an understanding of the causes which underlay the increased strike activity, strikes over working conditions, wildcat strikes, rejections of negotiated contracts, and filing of grievances of the 1960s.[5] But it is necessary to examine the process whereby such changes took place as well as the outcomes. This means exploring workers' and capitalists' consciousness and choices; only then is it clear why the truce unraveled when it did, not ten years earlier or twenty years later.

DEBATES ON THE SOCIAL RELATIONS ANALYSIS

Critics of the social relations approach (or associated reserve-army and SSA analyses) have raised four main objections. First, it is said to use neoclassical rather than Marxian value categories, to study appearances rather than the essence of capitalism's dynamics, and therefore to seriously misinterpret the world (Shaikh 1978; Weeks 1979). Second, the focus on people's resistance to work effort implicitly treats work as undesirable, echoing neoclassical assumptions about the disutility of labor. To see humans as acting like mules seems at odds with the balance of Marx's analysis of the production process (Dorman 1987). Third, it is claimed that this approach amounts to blaming working people for the crisis, and only encourages conservative policies to smash organized labor and undermine working-class institutions to restore productivity growth (Sherman 1983). And fourth, while theoretically plausible, its empirical relevance is argued to be doubtful (Weisskopf 1978; Moseley 1986). The last objection will be answered in a separate section which reviews radical empirical studies of productivity. Responses to the other three follow.

The Productivity Slowdown and Value Analysis

The first criticism can be countered by showing that slow productivity growth contributes to declines in the value rate of profit. Marx argued that prices are determined by the abstract labor time required to produce goods, or values. The value of a good equals the value transferred from equipment and raw materials per unit (c) plus the living labor expended per unit (n). Productivity is $1/n$, the average units of output per current labor-hour.

Marx's theory of the profit rate rests on the recognition that firms cannot purchase labor-services directly, only rent out workers' labor-power or capacity to do work. Workers are paid a wage, and the value of wage-goods times the real wage gives the wage in value terms, called the value of labor-power (v). If workers were only productive enough each hour to pay their wage, there would be nothing left over for profits. But they are more productive, so each hour of value created minus the value they get (v) leaves the surplus value (s) they produce. Aggregate profits are simply hourly surplus values aggregated over all employee-hours.

When productivity increases, the value rate of profit rises for two reasons. Higher productivity causes lower values and prices. Thus wage-goods become cheaper, so v falls and hourly surplus value rises, and capital-goods become cheaper, which raises the rate of return on a less costly capital stock. In addition, an increase in productivity in one sector may mean that its workers perform more socially necessary abstract labor per hour than do their counterparts elsewhere (for instance, if work intensity rises). They therefore produce the equivalent of their wage in a shorter period of time, which increases hourly surplus value, the rate of exploitation (s/v), and therefore the profit rate.

So far it seems that as long as productivity rises, no matter how quickly, so will profits. But other factors may put downward pressures on the profit rate, such as rising real wages or other income claims (higher taxes, energy costs, import costs, etc.). In addition, the profit rate tends to fall because only workers can produce surplus value, and firms' efforts to increase productivity include replacing workers with machines.[6] Therefore, although the level of productivity typically rises, a sufficient pace of growth is necessary to counteract factors which depress the rate of profit (Christiansen 1976). Only if productivity growth is too slow can the struggle over the distribution of income or labor-saving technical change lead to a lower profit rate.

Labor Effort or Work Performance?

The second objection to the SRP approach is not completely unfounded. Many SRP investigations do speak of workers decreasing effort and thus harming productivity growth, seeming to echo conservative cries of a decline in the work ethic. However, such analyses are rarely limited to workers' resistance to alienated labor. People's concern with the quality of their worklives is also recognized, including the type of services they will perform and the physical and social conditions under which they will exert effort.

In fact, productivity growth depends on the growth of effort, not its level. Even if effort increases, a slower pace of increase will slow productivity growth. Furthermore, only one aspect of the extraction of labor from labor-power involves the expenditure of effort of a particular duration and intensity. Workers' effort simultaneously translates into the performance of concrete labor services. Productivity grows when either effort or services improve (see Christiansen and Naples 1986).

Case studies by radicals have demonstrated that under some conditions, workers value organizations of work which promote greater effort, belying the disutility of labor. People have been shown to prefer variety on the job to repetition, whether obtained through multi-task stations or through job rotation (Garson 1975). Yet job rotation often increases average effort, since at each new task workers initially exert more energy as a result of the change.

In addition, increased effort is neither a necessary nor a sufficient condition for greater productivity. First, even if effort falls, it is possible for productivity to remain stable if the quality of services is enhanced. For instance, with experience employees learn how to execute their given tasks with as little effort as possible. Second, increases in effort may be counterproductive if services suffer. Reorganizations of production which increase physical or mental stress or make conditions more dangerous may also reduce work quality, generating wasted materials or faulty products. Third, effort will be wasted if the services performed are not those required, whether due to poor managerial coordination or troubled industrial relations.

Labor-management conflict at the work site concerns how work is performed, not just the pace of the assembly line. Workers will resist new techniques which splinter informal work groups or eliminate jobs, even if the equipment introduced requires much less exertion on their part. Management's ability to learn about production problems from employees has less to do with effort and more to do with employees' willingness to share their knowledge with the boss.

Therefore the social-relations perspective does not just turn neoclassical theory on its head. Work may or may not generate "disutility." In any case, labor-services are not only due to workers' own efforts — the quality of performance depends on management and on the quality of workplace relations as well.

Blaming Labor?

The third objection to the SRP approach, that it "blames labor" for crises, interprets the approach from a purely voluntarist rather than structuralist perspective. The social relations analysis argues that under capitalism, rational behavior on the part of workers and capitalists pits them against each other. This does not blame workers (and exonerate capitalists). Rather the choice capitalism forces between jobs and reasonable working conditions is irrational, it is the economic system which must be held accountable.

The SRP analysis in fact shows why the conservative "old-time-medicine" may well not work. As Boddy and Crotty (1974) argued, stable high unemployment is inadequate for keeping labor costs stable. It tends to produce a pool of chronically unemployed who provide little competition to employed workers. If costs do fall, profits will induce accumulation, reducing unemployment cyclically, improving workers' leverage relatively, and ultimately productivity will suffer (consider the expansion of the mid-80s). Furthermore, workers' institutions and patterns of behavior act as real constraints on conservatives' efforts to smash labor. Anti-union policies will backfire if they return labor relations to the warfare of the 1930s.

Ironically, many who concur that the SRP analysis blames labor or who doubt its macroeconomic relevance look favorably on the labor-process and labor-market segmentation literatures. Yet these document the contingency of capitalist control in the workplace.[7] If workers' struggles in their own behalf matter, then productivity growth will suffer. If workers' willingness or ability to assert their priorities changes over time, then productivity will suffer more or less. The question is whether workers' efforts in fact hurt productivity growth in any systematic way.

RADICAL EMPIRICAL STUDIES OF PRODUCTIVITY GROWTH

This section explores the relative explanatory power of two approaches to productivity analysis — Verdoorn's Law and the social relations of production. While the first argues that increases in aggregate demand should lead to higher productivity growth, the latter argues that sustained high employment will reduce productivity growth, either cyclically or secularly.

Verdoorn's and Kaldor's Laws

For the analysis of Verdoorn and Kaldor effects, positive correlations between productivity growth and output growth, employment growth, or capacity utilization are interpreted as reflecting static and/or dynamic economies of scale. Researchers are concerned with long-term productivity growth, not cyclical productivity slowdowns, and typically rely on cross-country comparisons. In the mid-1970s one study found that Verdoorn's Law seemed to break down after 1965, and another suggested that even pre-1965 evidence was spurious, caused by including Japan in the data set.[8]

Other studies argued that these erred in using employment growth instead of output growth as the proxy for the growth of demand. Robert Boyer and Pascal Petit (1981) reported that correlations between sectoral productivity growth and sectoral output growth for 1960–1973 was stronger for manufacturing than for any other sector, and concluded that manufacturing was the engine of growth for productivity economy-wide. Tom Michl (1983) documented long-term Verdoorn effects, even controlling for the increasing capital-intensity of production. Tom Weisskopf (1986) concluded that the post-1973 productivity slowdown reflected the slow growth of output in manufacturing, even controlling for lower capacity utilization and the inefficiencies it generates.

Yet, like Cripps and Tarling (1973), Michl found a deterioration in the correlation between manufacturing productivity growth and output growth over the period 1950–1980. Rather than challenging Verdoorn's Law, he interpreted the anomaly as reflecting asymmetric effects of growth slowdowns and speed-ups.

Even strong positive correlations between aggregate demand and productivity growth have alternative interpretations. The proxy variables for economies of scale describe the level of economic activity. Productivity growth is known to rise from recessions into early expansions (see Table 2). So, significant proxies may be reflecting productivity growth's cyclical variability rather than explaining it. Furthermore, an increase in output growth and capacity utilization permit the spreading of overhead labor over more units of output, increasing the ratio of output to all labor-hours (total productivity) even if production-worker productivity does not change (see Naples 1987a). Then, strong cyclical or secular correlations may be due to increased utilization of overhead workers, not to induced technological change.

The Social Relations Approach

The Cyclical End-of-Expansion Slowdown. The foremost radical explanation for the end-of-expansion slowdown is the effect of a reduced reserve army of the unemployed on workers' leverage. Empirical studies have shown that productivity grows more slowly when layoffs and unemployment are low and/or quits are high, even controlling for such other cyclical influences as capacity utilization.[9] These prima facie confirmations of the reserve-army effect are based on annual and quarterly time-series data, for two-digit SIC industries, nonfarm business, mining and manufacturing.

There is evidence that the unemployment effect is mitigated by unions, or internal labor markets, and reduces absenteeism rather than increasing work intensity in union firms. One study also found no significant hoarding of redundant workers during recessions in more unionized industries, confirming an independent finding that unionized workers were more likely to be laid off than non-union.[10]

However, strike activity is reduced by unemployment, and in turn has been shown to negatively affect productivity growth in econometric studies.[11] Sean Flaherty (1987) recognized that higher productivity growth due to speed-up could generate more wildcat strikes, suggesting a positive relationship with productivity. But controlling for this, he found that increased wildcats in turn undermined productivity growth.

The Secular Productivity Slowdown. The perspective based on the social structure of accumulation provides several related but distinct empirical predictions. (1) Rapid accumulation and sustained low unemployment due to a stable SSA would be expected to increase workers' relative security in the workplace. Hence quits, absences and strike activity would rise secularly, and productivity growth would fall. (2) The welfare-state component of the national accord would itself be expected to reduce the impact of unemployment on workers' economic well-being. (3) Union members, disturbed by their leaders' accommodating stance towards management, would become increasingly willing to strike. (4) The truce's translation of concerns with working conditions to an income equivalent could not be expected to last given the tremendous increase in industrial accidents in the 1960s and 1970s. (5) Management's exploitation of their freedom of enterprise through intensified supervision of workers, while initially beneficial for productivity, could backfire as the legitimacy of their control decayed.

The first prediction of unemployment's negative effect on strike activity over the long run as well as the cycle has been empirically documented, as has the contribution of secularly high strikes and quits to the productivity slowdown (Naples 1986, 1987). This long-wave version of the reserve-army hypothesis stands in sharp contrast to the Verdoorn predictions of sustained high aggregate demand leading to higher productivity growth. It may explain the findings cited earlier that Verdoorn's Law broke down in the early 1970s if it was at that point dominated by reserve-army effects.

Second, a further refinement of this argument combines unemployment duration with the proportion of income foregone when workers lose their jobs. That ''cost of job loss'' declined through the 1960s due to low unemployment and increased social welfare spending, and rose in the 1970s (non-wage income includes federal health and education benefits as well as unemployment compensation, see Schor's article in this volume). Decreases in this variable led to higher strike activity and/or reduced productivity growth in the postwar United States, United Kingdom, Italy and France; but not in Sweden, Germany and Japan, and cannot explain much of the productivity slowdown *per se*.[12]

It has also been shown that the quality of industrial relations affects strike activity, independent of changing economic conditions. Jens Christiansen (1982) attributed different strike patterns in the United States and West German steel industries to greater labor-management accommodation in Germany, and more contention here. The large proportion of worktime lost to strikes in the United States accounted for its relatively slow productivity growth compared with West German steel. Leon Grunberg (1986) examined two auto plants with virtually identical technologies. In the mid-seventies the plant with numerous strikes had low productivity. The same plant's relatively high productivity in the mid-eighties was associated with a steep decline in strike activity due to greater resignation on workers' part.

I have suggested elsewhere that different kinds of strikes reflect different underlying workplace relations and consequently would have differential impacts on productivity growth. All strikes, strikes over working conditions, and wildcats did appear to play an important role in the initial productivity slowdown of the late sixties and early seventies, although defensive strikes also contributed to slower productivity growth thereafter.

The fourth hypothesis, that increasing workplace accidents would undermine workers' commitment to the truce, with negative consequences for productivity growth, has also been empirically supported. While higher accidents seem to help explain the rise in strike activity in mining and manufacturing in the 1960s and early 1970s, they also had a direct negative impact, even controlling for strikes' effects. Others have found that the high rate of growth of accidents was a critical cause of the productivity slowdown of the late sixties and early seventies; I found the level of accidents to have played an even more important role in explaining the late seventies slowdown.[13]

Because increased work intensity can itself lead to more industrial accidents, it is also possible that the relationship between accidents and productivity would be positive.[14] The consistent econometric finding of a negative correlation between accidents and productivity growth suggests that workplace-relation effects have dominated such a speed-up effect in recent United States experience.

Finally, the extraction of labor from labor-power depends on such mechanisms for supervising employees as bureaucratic control. One rough measure of the intensity of supervision — the ratio of non-production to production-worker hours — has been shown to benefit productivity growth in several studies, while others found it to be less effective in recent years, or to have no significant impact.[15] Such conflicting findings might have several causes. While 83 percent of non-production employees are managers and supervisors, many layers of such personnel play no direct role in production. And machine-monitored production systems, including closed-circuit televisions as well as direct monitoring by computerized production equipment, could substitute for such overhead labor.

Leon Grunberg (1986) found that from the mid-seventies to the mid-eighties the ratio of supervisors to production workers rose 40 percent in a militant French auto plant, and fell 28 percent in a comparable but more quiescent British plant. This suggests that there may also be problems of simultaneous determination: deteriorating workplace relations may hurt productivity and lead to increased supervision, creating a spurious negative correlation between supervisory intensity and productivity growth.

CONCLUSION

Much empirical research on productivity growth slowdowns remains to be done. Nevertheless, certain conclusions can be drawn. There is clear evidence that the end-of-expansion slowdown in productivity growth is due in part to workers' greater leverage in that part of business cycles, and increased willingness to quit and strike. The positive relationship between unemployment and productivity growth in cyclical expansions helps explain the Phillips trade-off between unemployment and inflation.

However, in contractions unemployment rises rapidly while productivity growth continues to fall or stagnate, implying an elliptical rather than positive relationship between unemployment and productivity growth, and therefore an elliptical rather than inverse Phillips relationship (see Figure 1). The prevailing image of a trade-off may be due to the fact that economic contractions are only one-third the length of expansions on average. Therefore the data available are mostly taken from expansions, and graphs of the data primarily plot expansions, not recessions.

Figure 1

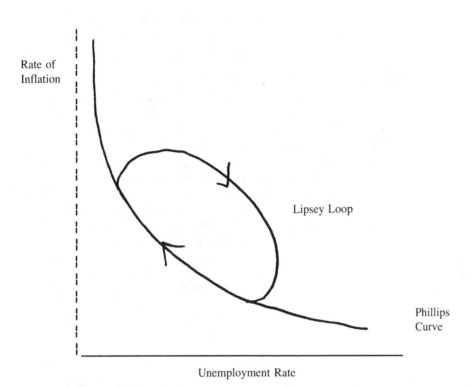

Unemployment Rate

Interestingly, empirical economists have observed what are called Lipsey loops (negatively sloped ellipses tangent to the Phillips Curve) during economic contractions. This empirical "oddity," the elliptical pattern, is precisely what the reserve-army theory predicts. That is, in contractions the economy moves off the Phillips Curve to the right, as unemployment rises while productivity growth stays low (and inflation high), and returns towards the Phillips Curve as productivity growth recovers during the contraction (and therefore inflation drops).

In terms of long-term trends, the *regulation* school sees a new technological paradigm as critical for securing renewed productivity growth. Michael Piore and Charles Sabel (1984) have argued that one source of the crisis of mass-production industries has been the inflexibility of that technology when faced with new foreign competition or demand fluctuations. They inferred that the next stage of technological advance may be based on small-batch production processes, tailored to respond quickly and directly to consumer demand. Such a structure would rely on craft workers with wide-ranging skills who could participate in production design as well as the provision of output. While such a strategy may be a rational response to current economic instability, it seems an unlikely basis for a new social structure and renewed growth.

The evidence from the econometric literature suggests that the productivity slowdown derives both from slow economic growth (via Verdoorn and Kaldor effects), and from a breakdown in the accommodation between capital and labor in the sphere of production.

The Verdoorn results do not, however, explain why the economy slowed in the first place. Moreover, they imply that policy-makers are irrational not to follow expansionary Keynesian policies to restore productivity growth. The social-relations studies suggest that a policy stance permitting long, deep recessions and slow growth may have been functional for profits, if replenishing the reserve army helped raise productivity, to labor's detriment.

However, the SSA aspect of the social relations analysis underlines the inadequacy of high or low aggregate demand for restoring productivity growth. The postwar mechanisms for managing inter- and intra-class conflict are now dysfunctional. The right claims that its efforts to deregulate represent a new worldview — is this the basis for the next SSA? I think not. It has attempted to dismantle OSHA and the welfare system, eliminate tax deductions and simplify the tax law, and deregulate finance, transportation systems and agriculture. While this may clear the slate, it does not provide a positive vision.

The management of conflict is being left to the anarchy of the market. The removal of structures which had insulated sectors or regions from economic dislocations assures that future shocks will spread that much more rapidly throughout the system. If, as the SSA analysis implies, the ''natural'' unregulated state of capitalism is crisis, the next economic downturn may prove to be more than monetary and fiscal policies can handle.

ACKNOWLEDGEMENTS

Thanks to Cigdem Kurdas, Fred Moseley and Bob Cherry for helpful comments on an earlier draft.

NOTES

1. Magdoff and Sweezy (1979, 1980); Perlo (1982); Szymanski (1984).
2. See the following: Boyer and Petit (1981); Cripps and Tarling (1973); Michl (1985); Weisskopf (1986).
3. See Marcuse, Book II of *The Imperiled Economy*; also Boyer (1986); Piore and Sabel (1984).
4. Boddy and Crotty (1974, 1975); Crotty and Rapping (1975); Gordon (1975).
5. Bowles, Gordon and Weisskopf (BGW) (1983); Gordon (1981); Naples (1981, 1982, 1986, 1987c); Reich, Edwards and Gordon (REG) (1982); Weisskopf, Bowles and Gordon (WBG) (1983).
6. Many mathematical equilibrium models have shown that even labor-saving technical change cannot cause the profit rate to fall. But Margaret Andrews (1987) proved that if the economy is out of equilibrium, an increase in the organic composition of capital can cause a fall in the average profit rate economy-wide.
7. For instance, see work by Burawoy (1979); Edwards (1979); Elbaum and Wilkinson (1979); Lazonick (1979); Marglin (1974); Stone (1974).
8. Cripps and Tarling (1973); Rowthorn (1975).
9. Gordon (1981); Naples (1986, 1987b); Oster (1980); Rebitzer (1986); Stern and Friedman (1980).
10. See respectively, Oster (1980), Rebitzer (1986), Burawoy (1979), and Medoff (1979).
11. Flaherty (1987a, 1987b); Naples (1986, 1987b, 1987c).
12. Schor and Bowles (1984); BGW (1983); Weisskopf (1986); WBG (1983).
13. Gordon (1981); BGW (1983); WBG (1983).
14. Grunberg (1983) found a positive relationship in a case study; see also Moseley (1986).
15. BGW (1983); Naples (1986, 1987b); WBG (1983).

16

Class Struggle and the Macroeconomy: The Cost of Job Loss

JULIET B. SCHOR

INTRODUCTION

Class struggle is a powerful, almost magnetic concept. After one hundred and fifty years, Marx and Engels's homage: "The history of all hitherto existing society is the history of class struggles" still fascinates. Despite endless funerals for the proletariat graciously staged by western social science, this pesky "world historic" actor refuses to disappear.

Yet for all its fascination, economists have failed to exploit the analytic potential of class. Abstract models have relied heavily on class differences but their scope has been limited. Class conflict has often been exogenous to economic models. Empirical applications are rare.

This paper reports on an ongoing attempt to quantify class struggle and assess its impact on the United States economy. It presents a novel measure of class power — workers' cost of job loss — and uses that measure to interpret macroeconomic performance. Before turning to the empirical evidence, I begin by setting the theoretical stage. I will look at the role that class struggle plays in the three major economic theories of our time by considering neoclassical, Keynesian, and Marxian growth models.

CLASS STRUGGLE IN MACROECONOMIC MODELS

The central variable of a neoclassical growth model is the rate of increase of the labor force.[1] Because it is assumed that full employment always prevails, the economy must grow at the rate required to support the growth of the labor force, which will be largely determined by the natural rate of population increase (see Figure 1).

Class struggle — or shifts in the distribution of income — plays a minor role in this model. If the distribution of income moves in favor of workers (i.e., the wage rate rises relative to the profit rate), consumption patterns over people's lifetimes will be altered, but the growth rate of the economy is unaffected. Labor income, received during years of employment, rises. Income from capital, received during retirement, falls. It should be noted, however, that recipients of labor income and capital income are not two distinct groups of people. All "agents" have access to both kinds of income.

Keynesian theory places distribution at the heart of its account of growth.[2] The economy is divided into two classes: workers, who consume their wages, and capitalists, who invest their profits. Capitalists own capital and organize production; workers sell their labor power. Growth is constrained by a dearth of investment.

To see the workings of the Keynesian model, assume the economy is proceeding with a constant rate of growth. Net output is divided between wages and profits. By assump-

Figure 1
Class Struggle and Macroeconomic Models

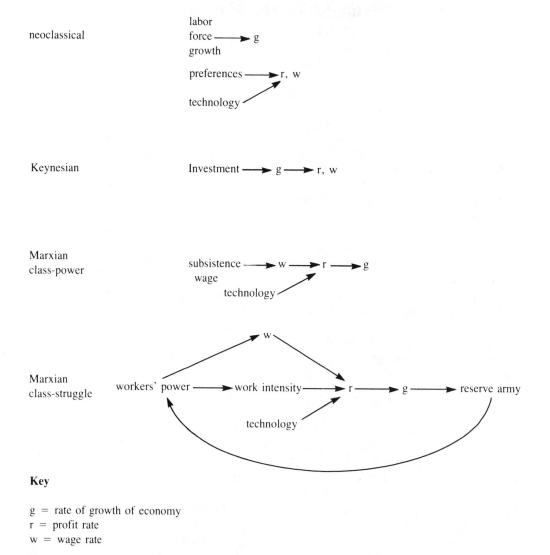

Key

g = rate of growth of economy
r = profit rate
w = wage rate

Preferences refer to agents' decisions with respect to present and future consumption, and the labor-leisure choice.

tion, capitalists invest all their profits. Now suppose that capitalists want to invest more. In a Keynesian world, added investment will raise the economy's growth rate. How does this occur?

To increase investment, capitalists must be able to spend more than their current level of profits. To do this, they borrow money, creating extra purchasing power which drives up output and thereby prices. It's the rise in prices which ultimately transfers added income to capitalists, and validates their desire to invest more. That's because when prices rise, workers' wages are assumed to stay constant. So the real wage falls and the profit rate rises. Less consumption by workers finances more investment by capitalists. The enhanced desire to invest raises the growth rate and the price level, lowers the real wage, and increases profits. Thus, the old maxim — capitalists get what they spend (and workers spend what they get).

In the Keynesian story the distribution of income plays an important role, but it is not a causal one. Business' willingness to invest is the exogenous variable which determines the rate of growth of the economy. The distribution of income is endogenous. So, while there are classes in this theory, their interaction does not determine many important outcomes of the macroeconomy, such as the rate of growth.

Indeed, workers and capitalists in the Keynesian model cannot be described as engaging in class struggle. Workers are essentially passive, accepting the reduction in their real wage which occurs whenever capitalists' desires to invest increase.

The Keynesian story reveals an important distinction among economic theories. I have already noted the difference between theories with and without *economic classes* (eg., Keynesian and Marxian versus neoclassical). Among class-based theories, we can distinguish between *class-power* and *class-struggle* theories. Keynesian theory has distinct classes with different structural positions. It has class power. (The capitalist class has the power to determine the real wage and the rate of growth of the economy.) But it does not have class struggle.

Despite the common characterization of Marxian economics as a — if not *the* — theory of class struggle, there is a class-power version of Marxian theory. Consider the account of capitalist industrialization contained in Volume I of *Capital*, which stresses above all else the power of the capitalist class and the inability of workers to withstand the onslaught of capitalism. The accumulation process progressively degrades the proletariat's material conditions of life, the intensity of labor is driven to the physical maximum, and the skills of the worker are destroyed with the advance of technology. Yet the work as a whole is ambivalent. Alongside this analysis we can find Marx's riveting description of the struggles concerning the Factory Acts.

In the class-power Marxian model, the wage rate is exogenous and set at subsistence. Once productivity is known, the profit rate is determined. Capitalists are assumed to invest all profits (no more, no less), which ensures the equality of the profit and growth rates. Economic crisis is ordinarily thought to be caused by a reduction in productivity, relative to the amount of capital stock which has been invested — the so-called falling rate of profit.

Like the Keynesian model, the class-power Marxian model has no role for class struggle. The real wage is fixed at subsistence. If class struggle raised the wage above subsistence, there would be a reduction in profits, growth, and employment. The "reserve army" would grow and the wage would fall once again to subsistence. The wage oscillates around subsistence.

The class struggle model is different. The balance of class power determines the real wage, with no anchor to subsistence. Class power also influences productivity through its effect on the intensity of work. When workers have more power, they are able to reduce the pace of work (Bowles 1985). The wage, work intensity, and the technology in use together determine the rate of profit and the rate of growth. (Again, capitalists invest all profits.) Class struggle has a strong effect in this model, because it determines the wage/work intensity combination.

Once the rate of growth is determined, there may be feedback effects which produce a cycle in the economy. (The feedback is represented by the dashed line in Figure 1.) Consider an initial rise in workers' power which raises wages and lowers work intensity, thereby reducing the profit and growth rates. The fall in the growth rate will reduce the demand for labor, and increase the reserve army of unemployed workers. This in turn reduces the class power which led to the initial rise in wages.

The strength of the feedback from growth to class power determines how much effect class struggle can have on the economy. At one extreme the reduction in growth perfectly offsets the original rise in workers' power. Wages, work intensity, and profits return to their original levels and there is no long-term effect of class struggle. The economy cycles around equilibrium values for the wage, work intensity, profits, and growth. This is perfectly analogous to oscillation around the subsistence wage in the class power model.

At the other extreme there are no feedback effects from growth to class power. Changes in class power are therefore capable of having strong, permanent effects on the economy. The former case is a pure class-power model; the latter a pure class-struggle model.

I have now briefly outlined four macroeconomic models.[3] In the pages which follow, I will consider further the class-struggle model, by looking at a new measure of class power.

THE COST OF JOB LOSS

Empirical evaluation of the class-struggle model requires a measure of the balance of power between workers and capitalists. For the most part, economists have relied upon one or two simple variables as proxies for class power. Usually, these have been the unemployment rate and the rate of unionization. A moment's reflection suggests that these measures are too limited in their scope. We begin by considering the nature of the class relation itself.

The basis of the Marxian distinction between workers and capitalists is an asymmetry of power.[4] This implies that we must conceptualize each side distinctly when we consider their bargains, exchanges, and arrangements.

The essential difference is revealed in the classical terminology. The worker is a *proletarian* — one who has nothing to sell but her labor.[5] Capitalists own assets which produce an income sufficient to live on. Proletarians own nothing of substance, and are therefore compelled to sell themselves.

This suggests that a worker's power vis-a-vis an employer will depend on alternatives to that employment.[6] If a worker is fired, or quits, what opportunities are available to her? What does it cost a worker to "opt out," or be forced out of current employment?

As in any bargaining situation, the costs to each party of terminating the relationship are a strong determinant of the outcome. I consider them to be sufficiently strong to base my measure of class power on the cost to the worker of an employment termination — or what I call the "cost of job loss." *The cost of job loss measures the difference between a worker's income in her current job, and what she will receive should she lose the job.* It is a more comprehensive account of the worker's situation than conventional measures such as the unemployment rate or the degree of unionization.[8]

When the cost of job loss is high, workers' bargaining power is low, because employment termination inflicts greater economic hardship. When the cost of job loss falls, workers are better able to resist the demands of management, and can bargain more effectively for higher wages or better working conditions. (Of course, costs to the employer will also be important, but in this essay considerations of space limit me to the worker's case.)

Although the concept is a universal one, the actual factors which enter into the cost of job loss will vary tremendously, according to the type of economy, time period, type of worker being considered, etc. In India, the cost of job loss might be the difference between the wage paid in a government textile factory and what would be available as subsistence if the worker returned to his village of origin to farm the land. A trip down a crowded street in Mexico City suggests a second measure: the difference between wages in capitalist industry and the proceeds from selling novelties on the street. (In economists' language: the difference between wages in the formal and the informal sector.) In poor countries, the cost of job loss is almost always very large, because the rate of unemployment for workers who want jobs in capitalist industry is extremely high.

In the rich countries there are far fewer alternatives to work in the capitalist sector. Agricultural employment has fallen dramatically in the last half-century. Opportunities for self-employment are limited. The only large sector of non-capitalist economic activity remaining is production in the home: for some women the cost of job loss is the difference between their wages in paid employment and the value of household production. However, this option is rapidly losing its desirability and/or feasibility, as increasing numbers of women enter paid employment.

These trends point to the following conclusion: for the average worker in a rich country, the relevant alternative to one's current job is another job in the capitalist sector. The cost of job loss measure should therefore pertain to conditions in the labor market.

Let us consider the case of an average worker. My aim is to calculate the difference between what she is currently earning, and the financial situation she will face once she is out of work. We assume that workers are aware of their own cost of job loss, and that this affects their willingness and ability to bargain in the workplace.[8]

The typical experience for a worker who is fired, laid-off, or quits, is to begin by spending a period of time unemployed.[9] Therefore, the first determinant of the cost of job loss will be the expected duration of unemployment.

Next we must consider the income available during the period of unemployment. This will primarily consist of social welfare benefits such as unemployment insurance, food stamps, and medical insurance.[10] These are income-replacing benefits.

After a period of unemployment the typical worker will be re-employed. We must therefore estimate earnings in the new job. Expected earnings will vary greatly by the type of job and sector of the economy. Where labor turnover is low and job tenure is long, a job change may be very costly, due to job ladders and steep wage paths within companies. In those jobs or sectors with high turnover and few possibilities for advancement, loss of a job may have small financial consequences. A fifteen-year worker at IBM may lose high wages, pension, and extended vacation benefits if she leaves her job. Chambermaids working at the Hilton Hotel for the minimum wage can walk across the street to the Hyatt with little loss in pay. Interestingly, many higher-paid workers with scarce skills can also change jobs without financial hardship.

These three factors — the duration of unemployment, the value of the social welfare benefit, and re-employment earnings — determine the income a worker can expect if she loses her job. The cost of job loss is just the difference between that income and current earnings.

AN ESTIMATE OF THE COST OF JOB LOSS FOR THE UNITED STATES

I have constructed an estimate of the cost of job loss for an average worker in the United States. To simplify matters, I have assumed there is no income loss after one year.[11] I have also expressed the cost of job loss as a percentage of the annual income, in order to provide perspective on the magnitude of the loss. The measure is defined as follows:[12]

$$w^* = \frac{w - [(u * b) + (1 - u) * wn]}{y}$$

where:

    w^* = annual cost of job loss, as percentage of total income
    w   = annual earnings in current job[13]
    u   = time spent unemployed[14]
    b   = annual income-replacing social welfare benefit[15]
    wn = annual earnings in next job[16]
    y   = total annual income[17]

Figure 2 shows the cost of job loss over the period it has been calculated. (Table 1 gives the numerical values as well as values for some of the components.) As Figure 2 shows, the cost of job loss varies from year to year. Longer term trends are visible as well, especially during the long expansion of the 1960s, when the cost of job loss fell continuously. For the next decade, the measure hovered between 20 and 24 percent. In 1980, it began to climb, with the advent of recession and Reaganism. By 1983, it was 32 percent, a 23 year high.

ECONOMIC DECLINE AND THE COST OF JOB LOSS

To investigate the relationship between the cost of job loss and the current economic crisis, let us return to the class-struggle model set out above. There I argued that the cost of job loss is a proxy for class power. Let us therefore trace through the model from changes in the cost of job loss to wages, work intensity, profits, and growth. Our aim will be to develop a rough account of the crisis of the United States economy from 1966 to the present.

We begin with some basic facts, which are set out in Table 2. From 1948–66, the economy grew 3.8 percent per year. Real income and labor productivity rose steadily as well. The rate of profit showed a steeply rising trend. This period was the Golden Age of Western capitalism.

In 1965 the profit rate reached its peak, and thereafter began a long-term fall. A large part of the initial drop was due to a reduction in the rate of growth of labor productivity, from 2.7 percent in the first period, to 1.8 percent from 1966–72. Firms got some relief from inflation, which kept the real wage from rising much after 1966.

Table 1
The Cost of Job Loss, 1948–1985

	Cost of Job Loss (w*)	Unemployment Duration (in weeks) (u)	Weekly Wage (1977 dollars) (w)	Weekly Social Welfare Benefit (1977 dollars) (b)
1948	.27	17	$113	$36
1949	.28	19	117	42
1950	.33	23	122	39
1951	.30	19	121	36
1952	.27	16	122	38
1953	.26	15	128	39
1954	.32	23	129	43
1955	.35	25	136	42
1956	.32	22	140	44
1957	.29	20	139	45
1958	.33	27	139	52
1959	.35	28	143	49
1960	.31	25	144	52
1961	.34	30	145	57
1962	.32	28	149	60
1963	.31	27	150	60
1964	.30	26	155	59
1965	.28	23	161	61
1966	.25	20	159	62
1967	.22	17	159	65
1968	.20	14	160	68
1969	.19	13	159	67
1970	.21	18	158	75
1971	.24	25	161	79
1972	.23	23	168	77
1973	.21	19	165	74
1974	.22	22	157	77
1975	.22	27	154	82
1976	.23	29	157	82
1977	.23	26	159	79
1978	.21	22	158	78
1979	.20	19	152	74
1980	.20	23	142	73
1981	.24	29	138	69
1982	.22	25	138	71
1983	.32	46	141	69
1984	.26	31	142	65
1985	.23	26	137	67

Note: See text for definitions of variables. w and b are in constant 1977 dollars.

Table 2
Macroeconomic Indicators, 1948–1985

	1948–65	1966–72	1973–79	1980–85	
g^1	3.8	3.2	3.0	2.0	
q^2	2.7	1.8	0.7	0.9	
w^{*3}	.31	.22	.22	.25	
wage^4	$136	$159	$157	$140	
	1951	**1966**	**1973**	**1979**	**1985**
r^5	7.6	11.5	7.5	6.7	8.8

Notes

1. g is the annual average rate of growth of Gross National Product, corrected for inflation (Source: Council of Economic Advisers, *Annual Report*).
2. q is the annual average rate of growth of labor productivity (Source: Council of Economic Advisers, *Annual Report*).
3. w* is the average cost of job loss, from Table 1.
4. Wage is the average weekly wage, in 1977 dollars from Table 1.
5. r is the after-tax net profit rate for the non-financial business sector (Source: Bowles, Gordon and Weisskopf, this volume).

During the first period of crisis (1966–72), the economy's underlying problems were not readily apparent. The fall in profitability was not matched by a significant slowdown in growth. Investment remained robust. Earnings showed little trend, but the growth in women's employment boosted family income. The government was spending heavily for the war in Vietnam. As a result of these factors, aggregate demand was maintained.

From 1973–79, the economy began to deteriorate. Productivity growth was especially poor, at 0.7 percent per year. The profit rate remained below 8 percent. (Profits were aided by inflation, and the resulting dollar depreciation, which boosted exports.) Growth slipped to 3 percent per year. An important event was the oil price increase of 1973, which considerably reduced the country's wealth. Workers and capitalists each tried to protect themselves from the oil shock, but the characteristic feature of this period was the failure of either group to place the burden decisively on the other. Neither profits nor wages fared well.

After 1979, economic decline accelerated. Productivity averaged 0.9 percent and weekly earnings fell 1.5 percent annually. The profit rate fell to 5.8 in 1980, although it has been rising steadily since 1982. The growth rate of the economy was 2 percent in this period.

How does the cost of job loss figure into these developments? Can its movements help explain the onset and deepening of economic decline?

During the Golden Age period, the cost of job loss was high, averaging 31 percent. The high cost of job loss kept wages low and productivity high. This led to the steady rise in the profit rate and high growth.[18]

The cost of job loss began falling in 1961, eventually losing one-third of its value. This had a powerful effect on productivity and subsequently profits. Weisskopf, Bowles and Gordon (1983) estimate that of the initial decline in productivity from 1966–73, all of it can be accounted for by a group of worker resistance variables which includes the cost of

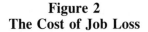

Figure 2
The Cost of Job Loss

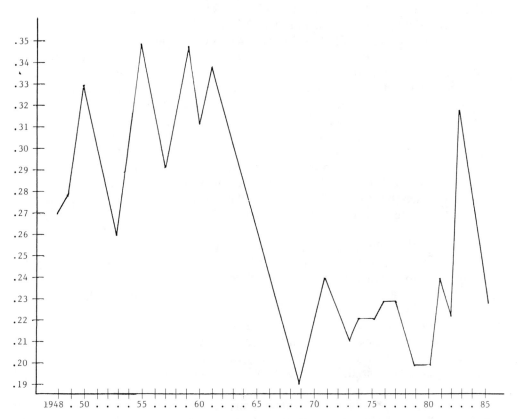

job loss. Apparently work intensity and shop floor discipline deteriorated, as workers' power grew.

A second measure of workers' power is explored by Schor and Bowles (1987). This research indicates that the cost of job loss is a major determinant of strike activity, and a far better predictor of strikes than any previous proxy for class struggle or bargaining power. During the period 1966–73, as the cost of job loss fell, strike activity accelerated.

Estimates of the relationship between profits and the cost of job loss indicate that the decline in the cost of job loss accounts for far more of the initial fall in the profit rate than any other variable (Bowles, Gordon, and Weisskopf 1986).

The evidence on productivity, labor militance, and profitability supports the hypothesis that the cost of job loss, through its effects on class conflict, was a strong precipitating factor in the onset of economic crisis after 1966.

After 1973, the story is more complicated. Between 1973 and 1979 the cost of job loss remained between 20 and 23 percent, considerably less than its average value during the Golden Age. The steady advance of labor's position during the 1960s was halted, but workers were able to maintain their earlier gains. The previous characterization of the period as one in which neither capital nor labor was able to decisively alter its position is supported by the movement of the cost of job loss.

This interpretation is consistent with the moderate decline in profitability, productivity, and growth during this period. The behavior of the wage is also congruent with the movement of the cost of job loss. After a large decline during the 1973 recession, the weekly wage showed little change until 1979.

In subsequent years the cost of job loss rose sharply, from less than 20 percent in 1979 to more than 32 percent in 1983. We can discern in this rise the feedback effect from low profits and slow growth to a rise in the cost of job loss. How did this feedback occur?

Both structural factors and deliberate economic policy led to an increase in the cost of job loss. The structural connection is through the reduction of profits and growth shown in Figure 1: aggregate demand fell and the reserve army grew. A larger reserve army lengthened the duration of unemployment, which increased the cost of job loss.

After 1979, the Federal Reserve further reduced aggregate demand through restrictive monetary policy (see Epstein in this volume). A study of Federal Reserve reactions to economic events sheds light on their behavior (Epstein and Schor 1986). Apparently, the Fed directly reacts to the cost of job loss. When the cost of job loss is low, the Fed raises interest rates and restricts demand. Conversely, a high cost of job loss leads the central bank to reduce interest rates and ease credit conditions.

This statistical evidence suggests a motive for the tight monetary policy of the early 1980s. The low cost of job loss during 1973–79 resulted in demands for wages and working conditions which were not compatible with high profits, given the oil price increases of 1973 and 1979, the growth of international competition, and accelerating inflation. In 1979, the Fed reacted to a 20 percent cost of job loss — the previous low in 1968 was 19 percent — by tightening credit.

The feedback effect can be seen in the link between the low cost of job loss and its eventual rise — through increased unemployment. But this process has a self-limiting property: unemployment also reduces the wage, which in turn reduces the cost of job loss.

The second policy change was a reduction in social welfare spending associated with the Reagan Administration. Eligibility for unemployment insurance declined 50 percent, and poverty programs shrunk. The average worker's expected benefits fell to the levels of the 1960s. Interestingly, the working poor — those who would be most affected by the cost of job loss — suffered the largest benefit cuts. This lends credence to the view that the conservative attack on the welfare state was aimed, at least in part, at raising the cost of job loss.

After 1983 the trends reversed. Profits rose dramatically and growth was high, which reduced unemployment. Wages stagnated. As a result, the cost of job loss declined in both 1984 and 1985.

It is difficult to know what path the cost of job loss will take. Which is the harbinger of the future: the rising values from 1980–83, or the falling values of 1984–85? If the last two years accurately picture the trend, it seems that the strength of the feedback effects have been weak, indicating that workers have consolidated long-term gains. It may be that class conflict has permanently reduced the cost of job loss, and profits and growth will remain low. If so, class struggle has had a powerful and long-lasting effect on the growth process.

CONCLUSION

I have now constructed an account of the relationship between class power and macroeconomic performance. Using the cost of job loss as a proxy for class power, I have argued that the Golden Age of United States capitalism was based on a high cost of job loss and high profits. During the long expansion of the 1960s workers gained power and the cost of job loss fell. Profits declined and growth began to slow. From 1973–79 the cost of job loss remained low and the economy deteriorated. Eventually, stagnation led to a rise in the cost of job loss, as unemployment rose and social welfare benefits were reduced. However, in the last two years for which we have data, the cost of job loss began to fall, so that its long-term trend cannot yet be discerned.

Whatever the future brings, this account of the last fifteen years reveals a painful feature of United States capitalism: workers' economic security and the macroeconomic performance of the economy appear to be inversely related. It suggests that full employment and successful capitalism may not be compatible, at least without far-reaching reforms of the investment, growth, and production processes.

ACKNOWLEDGEMENTS

Many of the ideas in this paper have been developed in collaboration with Sam Bowles. Research assistance was provided by Erik Beecroft and Dinah Leventhal. I am grateful to Fred Moseley for comments on an earlier draft. Financial support was provided by the Harvard Institute for Economic Research.

NOTES

1. For a complete account of the differences among neoclassical, Keynesian, and Marxian theory, see Stephen Marglin (1985).
2. It is important to distinguish between the long-run Keynesian models discussed here, and the short-run model of the standard macroeconomics textbook. See Marglin (1985).
3. Deciding which is the "correct" model of the economy is a difficult task. To a large extent, it depends on the particular economy in question and the period of time under consideration. It is to a great degree an empirical matter, and yet our ability to find the appropriate data and construct clear-cut tests is very limited. This suggests that purely theoretical and/or aesthetic considerations will come into play as well.
4. Class distinctions can be incorporated into economic models in either an individual or a collective manner. The first involves postulating two types of individuals whose structural characteristics differ. This is the approach adopted here, simply because the original theoretical models which use the cost of job loss concept have been formulated in this manner. Thus, we will discuss the behavior of individual workers. The second method involves modelling the economy as having only two agents — a working class and a capitalist class, and assuming that all members of the class act in concert.
5. Technically speaking, labor power — the ability to work — not labor, is sold.
6. Firing a worker is an employer's most severe sanction under today's labor laws, and is therefore the employer's most powerful threat in a bargaining situation.
7. See Schor and Bowles (1987) or Schor (1985), which discuss the cost of job loss.

8. We do not know the degree of precision with which workers estimate the cost of job loss. It is likely that their calculations are rough, and based on the actual experiences of other workers in similar situations.

9. The circumstances surrounding the employment termination may affect the cost of job loss. In this discussion I abstract from these differences. In the empirical estimates below I calculate the effects for workers who have lost their jobs involuntarily.

10. The unemployed may also receive other income, such as the earnings of a spouse. This income will not ordinarily enter into the calculation of the cost of job loss, because it does not change with employment status.

11. I have also calculated the cost of job loss for the worker's entire life. The lifetime measure is highly correlated with the one-year measure, and substitution between the two has little effect on the empirical results discussed below.

12. This is only a brief discussion of the actual methods and data used to calculate the cost of job loss. For a detailed discussion, the reader may consult Schor and Bowles (1987).

13. Current earnings are calculated as average spendable earnings multiplied by total annual hours. Spendable earnings are gross earnings minus taxes and social insurance contributions.

14. This is calculated as the duration of unemployment for job losers. Unemployment duration data is calculated in terms of numbers of weeks unemployed. I used that data to derive an estimate of the fraction of the year a worker would be out of work.

15. This estimate was derived by including five social welfare programs — Unemployment Insurance, Food Stamps, Aid to Families with Dependent Children, Medicaid, and General Assistance. Eligibility for benefits under each program was calculated according to data on the characteristics of the labor force. Eligibility for unemployment insurance, the largest of the five, was estimated econometrically.

16. No time series data exists for this measure, so I was forced to rely on one recent estimate for displaced workers.

17. Total income is defined as total earnings in employment plus the value of non-income-replacing social welfare spending.

18. The relationship between the cost of job loss and the profit rate has been econometrically estimated by Weisskopf, Bowles and Gordon (1986). Their research shows that the cost of job loss has a strong and statistically significant effect on the rate of profit.

17

The Welfare State and the Myth of the Social Wage

ANWAR SHAIKH
and ERTUGRUL AHMET TONAK

INTRODUCTION

This article deals with the relation between postwar fiscal policy and the standard of living of workers. Our aim is to analyze the growth of the so-called welfare state and its impact on the working class in the United States.[1] We will examine actual empirical patterns in the United States and use them to evaluate the radical literature on the workings of the welfare state and on the impact of transfer payments and socialized consumption on the economic crisis.

Conventional methodology makes it difficult to deal with many important issues concerning the social impact of state taxation and spending. To begin with, because conventional studies generally classify people according to the amount of income they receive, those whose income derives from labor are grouped together with those who derive their income from the ownership of property. This means that the distinction between workers and non-workers is obscured. Secondly, when analyzing the impact of state spending on these groups, *all* government spending is treated as a pure benefit. Within such a framework, the very notion of social benefit loses all meaning because a great expansion of military spending (as over the Vietnam War years) is treated as essentially equivalent to an expansion in social welfare spending. In these ways, the methodology underlying the research actually obscures the social costs and benefits of state intervention.

In recent years, some radical social scientists have attempted to correct for the above defects by focusing on the actual social welfare expenditures undertaken by government, and tracing their impact on workers. Here, the conclusion has been that there has been a dramatic rise in the benefits received by workers over the postwar period. These benefits are sometimes referred to as a ''social wage'' or ''citizen wage,'' and have been taken to imply that it is the state which subsidizes the working class. But a closer examination of such studies reveals that they have either ignored the taxes paid by the recipients of social welfare expenditures (Therborn 1984) or else seriously underestimated them (Bowles and Gintis 1982a). Once this important deficiency is recognized, it is no longer possible to conclude that the benefits received by workers constitutes a net addition to their wages, since part or even all of the observed benefit flows may be covered by the corresponding taxes paid by workers. Thus the major conclusions of these studies can no longer be accepted at face value.

In this article, we propose to re-examine the state's direct participation in the distribution process vis-a-vis the working class, and to identify its effect on the wages of workers. The above question requires an operational concept which measures the net impact of state activities in taxation and expenditures on the working class as a whole.

The concept proposed is that of the *net transfer,* namely, benefits and income received from the state *minus* taxes paid by workers to it. Estimating a net transfer series for the United States for the period of 1952–85 will enable us to examine the validity of the hypothesis that there exists a large social wage whose burden is borne by capital through a reduction in income available for profits. Since this latter hypothesis is a version of a "wage-induced profit squeeze" argument (Bowles and Gintis 1982a:53), our analysis also falls within the purview of the Marxist literature on crises.

In what follows, we will begin by pointing out some of the significant errors and omissions in the existing measures of the social wage. We will then construct an alternative definition, based on the concept of the net transfer from workers' income, and present our own estimates for the United States from 1952–1985. This will enable us to contrast our results with those of earlier studies, particularly the one by Bowles and Gintis (1982a).

THE RADICAL LITERATURE ON THE SOCIAL WAGE

The concept of some sort of net transfer appears fairly frequently in the literature on the welfare state (Shaikh 1978; Gough 1979; Bowles and Gintis 1982a, 1982b; Tonak 1984, 1987; Therborn 1984). But its definition varies considerably, and its use is sometimes quite misleading. In the interest of brevity, we will confine ourselves to discussing representative positions within the radical literature. Broadly speaking, we can distinguish two main positions. First, those, who tend to treat social expenditures as a kind of social wage, without regard to the taxes paid by workers; and those who deal with both expenditures and taxes, so as to estimate the net transfers involved.

The first position is represented by authors such as Therborn. He begins by noting that the rise of welfare state capitalism is attended by a rapid growth of "politically deter-mined and regulated income flows" and ends up concluding that "in advanced capitalist countries today, between one-fifth and one-third of all household income derives from public revenue and not from property or labor" (Therborn 1984:25-26). But his conclu-sion that a large proportion of household income derives from state expenditures is only valid if these expenditures represent a transfer which is the net of taxes paid. Obviously, if the taxes paid out of household income were equal to the sum of social welfare expenditures (including the wages of workers employed in administering these expendi-tures), then no matter how large or rapidly growing the state expenditures, households would experience no net gain at all. The state would have merely intervened to siphon off income in money-form (taxes) and then inject it back as a mixture of commodities and payments (social welfare expenditures). Whereas this might alter the distribution of income among households, it would leave the total income unchanged. Thus, a rising level of social expenditures would not in itself imply a rising burden for the system, since it could merely represent a rising amount of income re-circulated via the state. The line of argument represented by Therborn is therefore not adequate for an analysis of socialized consumption and its impact on accumulation and crises, because it improperly identifies the level of social welfare expenditures with that of the social wage.

This brings us to the second type of study, in which both social welfare expenditures and taxes are taken into account. Here, the debate turns on the direction and size of the net transfer between workers and the state. On the one hand, our earlier work on the United States (Shaikh 1978; Tonak 1984, 1987) found that over the postwar period there has been a net transfer from workers to the state: the so-called social wage is actually a social subsidy of the state. For the United Kingdom, Gough (1979) seems to get similar results in that his single estimate for 1975 yields a net transfer of 5.2 billion pounds from the overall household sector to the state (Gough 1979:109). However, because he adopts the conventional definition of an undifferentiated household sector, he fails to distinguish between workers and non-workers on either the side of taxes or expenditures. This severely limits the value of his results.

On the other hand, Bowles and Gintis (1982a) estimate that the net transfer in the United States goes the other way, from the state to workers. According to them, over the postwar period the state has induced a "substantial redistribution from capital to labor." The resulting "citizen wage" has grown so rapidly that by the 1970s it plays "a critical role in producing and prolonging" an economic crisis (Bowles and Gintis 1982a:69, 84-85). Bowles and Gintis's study adopts an empirical framework roughly similar to our previous studies (Shaikh 1978; Tonak 1984). It is therefore striking that the two sets of results should differ so dramatically. But the mystery is easily resolved because the Bowles and Gintis methodology contains major empirical deficiencies which serve to bias their results towards an egregiously inflated estimate of the social wage. The basic problem arises from their use of an official series on the gross and spendable income of an "average" production worker with three dependents. Bowles and Gintis treat this data *as if it is representative of the average working class family*. But in fact the published series merely refers to a hypothetical family with four people, only one of whom is assumed to work (Bowles and Gintis 1982a:73). In other words, this statistical series assumes a stereotypical family with one male worker, a *non-working wife*, and two children. By way of contrast, the actual average United States household in 1977 contained roughly three people, and 1.2 working members (which includes a significant proportion of working women).[2]

Since Bowles and Gintis overestimate the number of people per household by a third, they correspondingly overestimate the social welfare expenditures received by the average household.[3] At the same time, they underestimate the average household tax payment by two-thirds.[4] This occurs for two reasons. First, because they underestimate the numberof income earners per household (by implicitly leaving out working women) and thereby underestimate the federal income taxes paid. Second, because the published series they use leaves out all state, local, and other taxes paid.[5]

By definition, their "citizen wage" per household is the difference between social welfare benefits received and the total taxes paid. With the former overestimated and the latter underestimated, the measure of the social wage becomes greatly inflated. It is this set of mutually reinforcing errors which produces the apparently dramatic rise in their measure of the citizen wage. When one corrects for these sorts of errors, their conclusions are totally reversed. Instead of a social subsidy of workers in the United States, one finds a social subsidy of the state. And with this, their strained and artificial construction linking social welfare expenditures to the current crisis simply falls to the ground. In its place, as we shall see, emerges the possibility of a much simpler and more sensible explanation of the course of social welfare expenditures.

The above errors and lacunae in the works of authors such as Therborn, and Bowles and Gintis are symptomatic of a deeper problem. Namely, the absence of a consistent methodology and comprehensive framework in addressing these issues. Accordingly, in the next section of this paper we will attempt to construct just such a methodology and framework, rooted in a Marxian analysis of capitalist reproduction. We will then present the resulting empirical estimates and analyze their implications for the current crisis.

EMPIRICAL METHODOLOGY

In order to measure the net impact of state expenditures and taxes on the standard of living of the working class, we will focus on the net transfer in relation to workers' income. This is defined as wages and benefits received by workers minus taxes paid to the state. In what follows, we first briefly outline the methods of allocating both various government expenditures and taxes to labor and then report the estimates of the net transfer over the period 1952–1985. Because the net transfer is negative over most of this period, it actually represents a net tax on workers. Finally, this estimated net transfer is adjusted for inflation, changes in employment, etc. in order to capture certain significant trends within the context of cyclical capital accumulation. In determining the portion of state expenditures which are directed towards workers, we begin by classifying various state expenditure categories into three major groups. The first group consists of items such as Labor Training and Services, Housing and Community Services, and Income Support, Social Security and Welfare (except the small items called Military Disability and Military Retirement which we treat as a cost of war). These are assumed to be received entirely by workers either in money or in commodity form. The second group includes conventional categories such as Education, Health and Hospitals, Recreational and Cultural Activities, Energy, Natural Resources, Transportation, and Postal Services. These are treated as social consumption in general, and the workers' share in them is estimated by multiplying the group total by the share of total labor income in personal income.[6] The last group comprises two kinds of expenditures; those consisting of Central Executive, Legislative and Judicial Activities, International Affairs, Space, National Defense, Civilian Safety, Veteran Benefits, and Agriculture. These are the expenses of reproducing and maintaining the system itself (what Marx calls the *faux frais* [Marx 1977:446] of capitalist society). And those consisting of Economic Development, Regulation and Services, Net Interest, and Others and Unallocables. This last set represents expenditures directed mainly toward small businesses, related administrative activities, and interest payments to the highest income brackets. We therefore exclude both sets from labor income and consumption.

In analyzing the tax side, we begin with the primary category of Total Employee Compensation. This is the total cost incurred by capitalists for the purchase of labor power.[7] It comprises both wages and benefits including Employer Contributions for Social Insurance and Other Labor Income. We will identify two main groups of taxes which flow out of this total.[8] Employee Compensation is the cost to the capitalists of hiring workers. But the income received by workers is less than this because a certain portion labelled Employee and Employer "Contributions" is deducted for social security.[9] Accordingly, our first group of taxes consists of the portion of employee compensation which goes towards social security taxes. The second group of taxes consists of Personal Income Taxes, Motor Vehicle Licences, Property Taxes (primarily on homes) and Other Taxes and Non-Taxes (a very small category which includes passport fees, fines, etc.). Since these are levied on both earned and unearned incomes, the portion emanating from labor is estimated by using the share of total labor income in personal income.[10]

To summarize, *social welfare expenditures* directed towards workers are taken to comprise all of Labor Training and Services, Housing and Community Services, Income Support, Social Security and Welfare (except for Military Disability and Retirement), and the bulk of Education, Health and Hospitals, Recreational and Cultural Activities, Energy, Natural Resources, Transportation, and Postal Service expenditures. Similarly, *taxes levied directly on workers' compensation* are taken to include all Social Security Contributions, as well as the bulk of Personal Income Taxes, Motor Vehicle Licences, Property Taxes, and Other Taxes and Non-Taxes.[11] The *net transfer* is then the difference between social welfare expenditures directed towards the working class, and taxes taken out of the flow of employee compensation.[12] The Appendix illustrates derivation of the data for 1964 and presents our basic estimates for 1952-1985.[13]

Figure 1 shows the apparent real wage per worker (employee compensation) versus the true real wage (employee compensation plus net transfer). Figure 2 presents social welfare expenditures and taxes levied as proportions of employee compensation (which we call the benefit and tax rates, respectively). Finally, Figure 3 shows the net transfer as a proportion of employee compensation (the net transfer rate). The analysis of these trends and of their implications for the current crisis will be presented next.

Figure 1
Real Wages per Worker

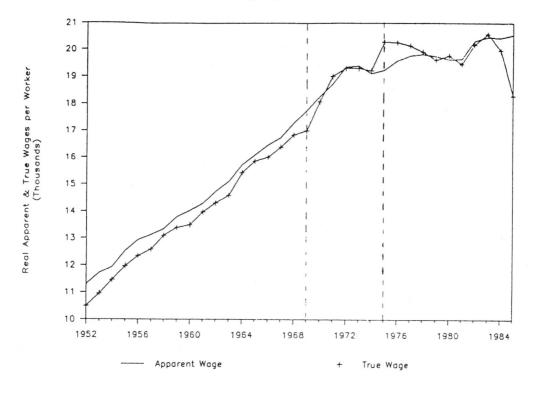

Figure 2
Benefit, Tax & Unemployment Rates

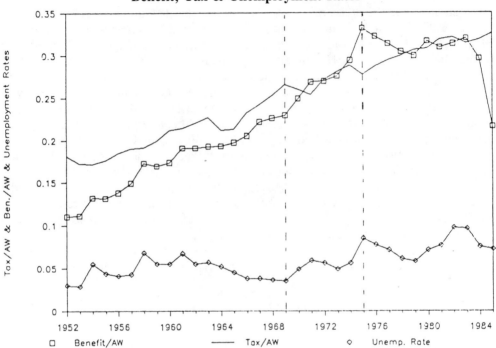

Figure 3
Net Transfer Rate

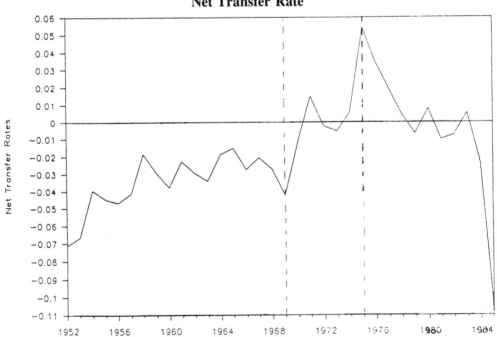

EMPIRICAL RESULTS AND THEIR IMPLICATIONS
FOR THE CURRENT CRISIS

We can draw several implications from the above trends. Figure 1 shows that the true wage of workers is almost always below their apparent wage. This means that it is the workers who generally end up transferring a net portion of their wages to the state. Arguments such as those of Bowles and Gintis, which claim that "there has been a substantial redistribution from capital to labor" over the postwar period, and which trace the current economic crisis back to a supposed increased social wage appear to be quite ill-founded.

A second implication of our results is that the intervention of the state has actually served to increase the rate of exploitation of workers (relative to its trend), since their true wage is below their apparent wage (Figure 1). [14] But this should not be taken to imply that the increased rate of surplus value has thereby raised the rate of profit (relative to its trend), because it does not follow that the net tax paid by workers was transferred over to capitalist enterprises. In all probability, this amount was absorbed by the state itself, in support of various activities ranging from general administration to the military. To analyze this further, one would have to extend our basic approach to encompass transfer to/from capitalist enterprises and the capitalist class itself. This is beyond the scope of the present paper.

The fact that a rising "social wage burden" cannot be blamed for the current crisis leads us back to the question of the causes of the crisis. Here we would argue in favor of the classical Marxian notion of a falling rate of profit in which a rising organic composition of capital lowers the rate of profit despite a generally rising rate of surplus value. The logical and empirical bases for this argument are spelled out in the paper by Shaikh (1987; in this volume). Within such a conception, the basic capitalist dynamic originates in the antagonistic process involving the production of capital itself, and is then modified by more concrete class struggles and by the intervention of the state. In the latter regard, it is important to realize that the state is not only subject to the general limits of the capitalist mode of production in its various stages, but also to the specific conjunctural limits arising from particular phases of accumulation. When accumulation is healthy and the economy is booming, the intervention of the state is least needed. Yet, paradoxically, this is precisely when the state has the greatest lattitude. Conversely, when the system enters a crisis phase, the capitalist state is at its most constrained even as the need for intervention is the greatest.

The preceeding point of view is nicely borne out by the history of the *net* transfer rate. This net transfer rate, it will be recalled, is the difference between benefits received and taxes paid expressed as a proportion of the apparent wage. Looking at the benefit and tax rates in Figure 2, and the net transfer rate in Figure 3, we can easily distinguish three broad historical phases (delineated on the graph). In the phase of normal accumulation, from 1952–1969, real taxes are higher than real benefits (Figure 2). But the security afforded by the boom, combined the strength of labor, serve to increase real benefits at a somewhat faster rate than real taxes. As a result, the net transfer rate becomes less negative, finally stabilizing around −3 percent (Figure 3).

The second phase, from 1969–1975, which is widely acknowledged as marking the onset of the economic crisis, is attended by soaring unemployment as the unemployment rate in Figure 2 jumps from 3.5 to 8.5. Because unemployment insurance and welfare payments accelerate with this jump in crisis-induced unemployment, benefits rise sharply relative to wage bill even though taxes paid per dollar of wages continue more or less on their long-run trend (in spite of erratic annual fluctuation). The sharp rise in the net transfer (from -4.2 percent to $+5.4$ percent, in Figure 3) is therefore a *consequence* of the crisis and its attendant unemployment, and not a cause.

The last phase from 1975–1985 is the one in which the state responds to the crisis by joining in the attack on labor, first through "benign neglect" and then through (Reagan's) direct attack. During this whole period, tax rates rise more or less steadily, so that the movements of the benefit rate dominate the trend of the net transfer rate. For instance, in the Ford–Carter years from 1975–1980, unemployment recedes somewhat from its previous high in 1975, benefit rates fall (Figure 2) which is then reflected in the net transfer rate (Figure 3). But in the first Reagan term from 1980-1983, although unemployment shoots up to an all time high, benefit rates fail to rise because Reagan's attack on labor has begun to be put into place. Then, as Reagan cutbacks accumulate, benefit rates drop sharply from 1983–1985 in the face of only moderate decline in unemployment rates. It is striking that by 1985 the social benefit rate had fallen to a *level below that of 1966,* while the tax rate continued to climb to an all time high (41 percent higher than in 1966, in Figure 3). The net transfer rate therefore falls dramatically from $+5.4$ percent in 1975 to -11.0 percent in 1985 (an all time low). All of this takes place in the context of true real wages per worker falling back to the levels of 1970, unemployment rates hovering at historically high levels, and ever larger numbers of people slipping into poverty. The benign welfare state, so long a favorite of social democratic theorists, has long since has begun to show its teeth.

APPENDIX

Table 1
The Estimation Procedure of Net Transfer

SOCIAL WELFARE EXPENDITURES[a]

GROUP I	Total	
		Labor
Income Support, Social Security and Welfare	31.01	29.7
Housing and Community Services	2.81	2.81
Labor Training and Services	.73	.73
GROUP II[b]		
Education	27.58	20.13
Health and Hospitals	6.42	4.69
Recreational and Cultural Activities	1.21	.88
Energy	1.03	.75
Natural Resources	1.96	1.43
Postal Service	.79	.58
Transportation	13.1	6.31
Total Benefits and Income Received by Labor		68.01

TAXES[c]

GROUP I	Total	Paid by Labor
Contributions for Social Insurance	28.66	28.66
Government — administered		
Lotteries and Parimutuels	.002	.002
GROUP II[d]		
Personal Income Taxes (Federal & State)	50.02	36.51
Other Taxes and Non-taxes	4.99	2.6
Motor Vehicle and Licenses	1.07	.78
Property Taxes	21.69	5.99
Total Taxes Paid by Labor		74.52
Net Transfer	$(68.01) - (74.52) = -6.51$	

a. The data for the Social Welfare Expenditures are directly available in BEA (1981:151, 159).

b. To obtain the portions of these expenditures directed towards labor, all of the items in this group are multiplied by the ''labor share'' (0.73 for 1964) except the item of Transportation which is also adjusted by the ''Gas Share of Passenger Cars'' (Tonak 1984:Chap.IV; Appendix II).

c. The data for the taxes are directly available in BEA (1981:121, 123, 129, 134). The item of Government-Administered Lotteries and Parimutuels is listed on the expenditure side and is also available in BEA (1981:170).

d. To obtain the portions of these taxes paid by labor, all of the items in this group are multiplied by the ''labor share'' (0.73 for 1964) except the item of Property Taxes. Regarding the latter, we consider only the part paid by home-owners which in turn is adjusted by using ''labor share'' (Tonak 1984:Chap. IV; Appendix I).

Table 2
Expenditures Received and Taxes Paid by Labor
Net Transfer, 1952–85

Years	Exp. & Benefits Received by Labor	Taxes Paid by Labor	Net Transfer
1952	21.01	34.58	-13.57
1953	22.73	36.31	-13.58
1954	26.85	34.89	- 8.04
1955	28.82	38.56	- 9.74
1956	32.69	43.68	-10.99
1957	37.08	47.68	-10.27
1958	43.29	47.84	- 4.55
1959	45.79	53.68	- 7.89
1960	49.21	59.96	-10.75
1961	55.67	62.27	- 6.60
1962	59.39	68.43	- 9.04
1963	63.14	74.28	-11.14
1964	68.01	74.52	- 6.51
1965	75.02	80.74	- 5.72
1966	85.84	97.21	-11.37
1967	99.36	108.52	- 9.16
1968	111.75	125.15	-13.40
1969	124.72	147.68	-22.96
1970	144.97	151.48	- 6.51
1971	166.21	157.06	9.15
1972	183.22	184.74	- 1.52
1973	207.39	211.25	- 3.86
1974	241.83	237.21	4.62
1975	289.12	241.70	47.42
1976	310.98	277.57	33.41
1977	336.39	315.86	20.53
1978	367.93	362.21	5.72
2979	404.81	413.94	- 9.13
1980	468.92	457.18	11.74
1981	504.37	520.44	-16.07
1982	548.14	561.18	-13.04
1983	591.40	581.09	10.31
1984	598.51	646.10	-47.59
1985	467.83	705.27	-237.44

ACKNOWLEDGEMENTS

We would like to thank Sungur Savran for his comradely criticisms.

NOTES

1. Our aim here is to determine the net impact of state redistributive activities on workers' living standards. We therefore focus on wages and net transfers. But neither the wage nor the adjusted wage ("social wage") should be taken to represent the overall standard of living of workers, since neither includes the critical component of production within the household. In a similar vein, we use the term "welfare state" as a convenient and widely used label for the redistributive activities of the state. This does not mean that we accept the notion that the capitalist state can be basically class neutral or structured around the welfare of the working class.

2. Bowles and Gintis even fail to notice that in order for the average worker to have three dependents the population would have to be 60–70 percent larger than it actually is! For instance, in 1977 there were 90.5 million employed workers, which implies a population of 362 million if each worker is assumed to have three dependents. But the actual population was only 217 million. Their implicit population estimate was therefore 67 percent larger than the actual figure.

3. Thus, in calculating the average family share of social welfare expenditures, they multiply the per capita social expenditure level by 4 (the hypothetical family size) as opposed to 3 (the actual household size): an overestimate of 33 percent in social expenditure per household.

4. For 1977, Bowles and Gintis estimate a direct tax per worker of $10 per week, in 1967 dollars. Since they assume one working member per household, this is also their estimate of the direct tax per household (Bowles and Gintis 1982a:73, Table 3, Col.2). On the other hand, Tonak (1984) shows that a more systematic accounting of direct taxes paid yields an estimate of $22.96 per worker (Tonak 1984:128, Chap. V, Table 5, Col.5), times 1.22 workers per household (Tonak 1984:123, Chap. V, Table 5, Col.5), for an overall estimate of $30.45 in direct taxes paid per household, per week. The Bowles and Gintis estimate is therefore two-thirds lower than Tonak's.

5. The BLS spendable earnings data are calculated by deducting only Federal income and social security taxes from gross earnings; all other taxes at the level of State and Local governments are left out.

6. For the rationale and procedures of "labor share method," see Tonak (1984: Chap. IV; 1987).

7. Within Marxian terminology this is the same as (nominal) variable capital if we ignore the distinction between productive and unproductive labor. When we do treat this distinction, variable capital becomes the total employee compensation of productive labor alone (Tonak 1984:Chap. IV).

8. We are interested here in tracing the taxes which flow directly out of employee compensation. This is quite distinct from the time honored question of tax shifting in which one attempts to estimate what workers' income *might have been* if some taxes (such as sales taxes) had been different. Our framework is similar to that of Bowles and Gintis (1982a). On the other hand, it is quite different from that of Miller (1986). First of all, his allocation of taxes between capital and labor is rooted in the tax shifting approach. Secondly, his treatment of expenditures is rooted in the debate around productive and unproductive expenditure rather than the present around the social wage.

9. An additional very small category was added here. It consists of net government receipts from lotteries, etc., which we treat as a kind of direct tax. It is actually listed as a net expenditure in government accounts, but since it is consistently negative we treat it as a positive net tax (Tonak 1987).

10. For further details, see Tonak (1984:Chap. IV; 1987).

11. We leave out the group of taxes comprising Corporate Profit Taxes, Indirect Business Taxes, Estate and Gift Taxes (which only apply to the highest income levels), because they are not levied on workers.

12. The preceeding concept of net transfer includes public assistance (i.e. welfare payments) on the benefit side. This is appropriate if we are interested in the issue of the overall effect of state

taxes and social expenditures on the standard of living of workers, since public assistance is a benefit to the working class as a whole. But if we are interested in the rate of exploitation of labor, we are concerned with employed workers alone. Public assistance is then not an appropriate item on the benefit side, since (unlike social security or unemployment insurance) it is not based upon the present or past employment of the individuals who receive it. For this reason, we leave out public assistance payments when adjusting the apparent rate of exploitation for the effects of state taxes and expenditures (Tonak 1984:Chap. IV).

13. A more detailed description of sources and methods is available in Tonak (1984:Chap. IV, Appendix I, II; 1987).

14. In calculating the effect on the rate of exploitation, we must leave out public assistance from the benefit side (see note 12). This means that the true wage of *employed* workers is even lower than that shown in Figure 2.

PART FOUR

INTERNATIONAL DIMENSIONS

18

Causes of the Debt Crisis

CHERYL PAYER

Most people think the Third World debt problem began with the OPEC "oil shock" of 1973–74. According to this interpretation, the OPEC countries, off in some sandy place in the Middle East, suddenly had billions of dollars they couldn't spend, so they put them in American banks and in the Eurodollar market. Meanwhile, the impoverished Third World, dependent on imported oil, faced depression for their economies and starvation for their people if they couldn't borrow enough money to pay for their imported oil.

Then, in an act that was considered statesmanlike by some and foolhardy by others, the American and Eurodollar banks agreed to "recycle petrodollars" to the impoverished Third World. The poor countries survived, and some even prospered, until the debt crisis in 1982 showed that recycling may have been statesmanlike in the short run but foolhardy in the long run.

The world is still trying, unsuccessfully, to "solve" the Third World debt crisis. But the seeds of the debt crisis were planted decades before the "oil shock" and have their roots in a fundamental contradiction of United States economic policy toward the Third World. We will not be able to solve this crisis, or prevent the next one, until we understand this.

The contradiction arises from two cherished concepts of United States foreign policy: (1) that the Third World must naturally import capital; and (2) that private capital can and should handle the major part of capital flows to the Third World. These two goals cannot both be satisfied over the long run; the history of the 1980s has given proof that the contradiction cannot be escaped in the real world.

Conventional economic theory holds that the so-called developing countries are poor in capital, and that because capital is scarce, returns to capital investment are higher in Third World countries than in the capital-surplus developed countries. According to this theory, private capital should *naturally* flow from developed to underdeveloped countries.

After the Second World War, however, private capital — especially bank capital — stayed away from the Third World, largely because bankers remembered the widespread defaults on Latin American bonds in the 1930s. Even worse for the theory, those Latin Americans who did have capital often preferred to hold it in bank accounts in Europe or New York (Latin America was a major *source* of Eurodollar deposits in the 1960s!).

"Indeed," a respected Latin American specialist wrote in 1971, "the problem is not to attract foreign savings but to prevent the region's savings from leaking abroad.... [ECLA's] estimate of the total net outflow of private domestic capital from Latin America is $5,000 million over the period 1946–62" (Griffin 1971:242–243).

The "foreign aid" programs of the United States government began in the 1950s as a means of supporting anti-Communist governments in the Middle East and in Asia. As developed countries began to "tie" foreign aid disbursements to purchases from their own countries' respective businesses, the distinction between aid and export promotion became blurred.

Capital flows from rich to (so-called) poor countries included private direct investment and loans made by government programs or guaranteed by government agencies. The official capital flows had two important benefits for the capital-*exporting* countries: they financed an export surplus for the developed countries (an import surplus for the poor ones) which contributed to domestic profits and employment; and they allowed the capital-exporting governments to purchase compliant behavior from the aid-recipient governments. This desired behavior included keeping communists out of a coalition government, voting on "our" side in international organizations, and accepting IMF and World Bank conditionality.

Because these capital flows were so useful for acquiring and controlling client states in the Third World, as well as for invading markets in which the United States companies were not otherwise able to compete, the idea that such flows were "natural" gained firm adherence, despite the clear evidence that even private investment would stay out of the Third World if it were not promoted and protected by United States bribery, backed up by military force and covert action where necessary.

There was a simple but fatal flaw in this policy toward the Third World. Corporations invested in Third World countries because they wanted to make profits there — and take the profits out of the country. But if loans — even "soft" loans — were the major vehicle of capital flows, they also required reverse flows of interest and amortization. With either loans or investment, the result would at some point be the reversal of the flow of capital. Any normal loan contract requires the repayment of capital plus interest after a certain initial period in which the borrower receives the loaned funds. But, once that point is reached, the *legal* flow of capital is from debtor to creditor.

In the jargon of international finance, the "net transfer" is the difference between the gross flow of new lending and the debt service (the principal repayments and interest paid from the debtor country). If new loans made to a country in a given year totalled $2 billion, repayments of capital totalled $500 million and interest another $500 million, the net transfer — the money available to finance an import surplus — would have been $1 billion. As debt service mounts, the net transfer shrinks rapidly and eventually becomes negative unless new loans rise even faster than debt service.

Since most countries were borrowing from several different creditor countries, and from a multiplicity of government agencies and, later, private creditors within each country, repayments could be made, for a while, out of the income received from new borrowing. One creditor's old debts could be serviced with the funds disbursed by this year's creditors. But this has nothing to do with real investment or growth; it is a "Ponzi scheme," a chain letter-type con game in which there are bound to be losers at the point where new suckers cannot be found to participate in the game. On Main Street, a scheme like this could land its promoter in prison.

Ultimately, payments have to come out of the foreign exchange earnings stream of the borrowing country. Conventional economic theory holds that capital inflows will produce growth from which the debt could be serviced. But there are two basic kinds of growth: domestic-led and export-led, and both posed problems for repayment. Domestically-led growth, the kind that puts more money in the hands of residents, tends to *worsen* the balance of trade because it increases the demand for imports in an open economy and depresses the export potential because wages and other costs rise.

Export-led growth, if successful, does produce foreign exchange earnings. But in order to service and repay debts, countries must be able to find markets which will accept import surpluses of the necessary magnitude and must moderate their own import demand to a level well below their export earnings. The most influential model of economic growth accelerated by capital imports did not even consider the problem of repayment, since it defined ''self-sustaining growth'' (the goal) as ''growth at a given rate with *capital inflow* limited to a specific ratio to GNP which *can be sustained* without concessional financing.'' (Chenery and Strout 1966:685n; my emphasis).

The conventional measure for gauging the ability of *nations* to repay their debts is the ''debt service ratio'': the ratio of debt service payments to export earnings, expressed as a percentage. But the debt service ratio had two severe defects as a guide to credit worthiness. The first was that no one could determine what a normal or safe debt service ratio might be. Was it 10 percent, or 20, or 30? Some countries with high ratios have serviced their debts faithfully, while others with much lower ratios have defaulted (Nowzad and Williams 1981:48).

The other problem was that the debt service ratio did not take account of new capital inflows. So long as new lending exceeded the total amount of debt service, no country had to dip into its own export earnings to pay debt service. It could all be paid with new borrowing, up to the ''break even'' point when the net transfer became negative. The widespread acceptance that it was ''natural'' for capital to flow from developed to underdeveloped countries meant that the presidents and finance ministers of Third World countries were led to believe that they should not have to spend their own export earnings for debt service.

There is no mechanism in international law to enforce the collection of cross-border debt. It is easy to understand that a borrower might be tempted to forget about repaying a loan. What must be remembered is that the United States administration, and most economists (mainstream or otherwise), as well as exporters based in developed countries who stand to profit directly, *did not want the debtors to reach the point of net payback of their loans,* any more than the debtors did.

If and when this should happen, exporters would lose markets. Industries producing for domestic consumption would find their markets invaded by imports — for the export of goods and services is the only way debtor countries can pay debt service. Workers in these industries would lose their jobs. And the United States government would lose its most powerful and effective tool for controlling the behavior of Third World governments.

Indeed, since developed country economies had been structured around running export surpluses to the Third World for nearly four decades, and Third World borrowers had structured their economies around the expectation of a net capital inflow for just as long, when the ''break-even'' point was actually reached in the early 1980s and the net transfer became negative first for Latin America, then for Africa and the Third World as a whole, it seemed as if the world had turned upside down, and water (money is suggestively called liquidity) were flowing uphill (from the Third World to the developed countries).

The creditor governments did not really want their money back. In the 1950s and 1960s, when debt crises were caused mainly by the accumulation of official and officially guaranteed debt, the standard procedure for handling a debt crisis was to convene the ''Paris Club'' consortium of creditor governments and reschedule the debt so that annual service payments would be lowered and positive net transfers could be resumed.

PRIVATE LENDERS ENTER THE PICTURE

Throughout the history of the foreign aid program, each United States administration had emphasized the belief that the chief purpose of government-to-government aid was priming the pump for private capital flows. Eventually, according to the official pieties, private capital should take over and make public capital flows unnecessary.

By the 1960s, a new generation of bankers who did not remember the lessons of the 1930s were taking over the reins of their corporations. Enticed by the official pump-priming and following their multinational customers who were expanding in the Third World (primarily Latin America) these banks rapidly developed a network of correspondent or branch banks in the foreign countries they considered most promising.

It seems ironic that the commercial banks became interested in Latin American lending at the same time that several of the most important countries were experiencing debt crises. A senior vice-president of Citibank in 1965 excoriated Argentina, Bolivia, Brazil, Chile, Uruguay, and Colombia as deadbeats which "year after year have had to come back to Washington for bail-out loans and foreign debt stretch-outs" (Costanzo 1965). Years later this executive was a prominent defender of Citibank's loans to these same countries. *Business Latin America* reported in 1968 that the average debt service ratio for Latin America was at least 14 percent in 1966 and quoted the Inter-American Development Bank's even higher estimate of 20 percent.

The Pearson Commission report, published in 1969, gave an even more alarming view. Already in the mid-1960s debt service was eating up 87 percent of new lending to Latin America (and 73 percent of new lending to Africa). The net transfer, or amount of new money left for the import of goods and services, was thus only 13 percent and 27 percent, respectively. These margins, slim as they were, could not be maintained in the 1970s even if gross lending increased by 8 percent each year. If gross flows of new lending remained unchanged, Latin America, Africa, and East Asia would all have been sending huge sums of capital back to the developed countries by 1977.

Why did the banks do it, if their senior executives knew very well that several of their new clients were already rescheduling debts? Anyone who read the newspapers must also realize that the prospect for increasing foreign aid (which had bailed out many private sector loans in the 1960s) was not good in the early 1970s.

Several partial answers can be given. First, attractive borrowers were scarce in the usual bank markets, as many of their prime corporate clients began to bypass the banks and raise funds by issuing their own paper. Second, the lenders made easy profits from loans for huge sums which carried high "spreads" and required relatively little executive time for appraisals and paperwork. Ironically, the spreads were high precisely because Third World borrowers, particularly sovereign borrowers, *were known to be bad risks*. The high profitability encouraged loan officers to forget the long-term risk; the short-term rewards were enormous and by the time troubles showed up everyone would have forgotten who was responsible. Third, the military coups (Brazil 1964, Chile 1973, Argentina 1966 and 1976, etc.), martial law declarations (Philippines 1972) and less obvious changes of economic policy by other governments, allowed the banks to believe that the old, bad policies had been changed and that borrowing governments were now on the right track. Some of these changes of policy (or governing teams) were provoked by cut-offs of external credit; many were supervised by the International Monetary Fund, which gave the banks a false sense that their loans were henceforth secure. Fourth, when the banks did try to do some serious analysis of the long-term risks involved in their new lending, the unsophisticated tool of the "debt service ratio" encouraged them to look mainly at the export prospects of the borrowing countries. And the export prospects looked excellent, especially in the critical two years before the oil price explosion. Commodity prices had risen to unprecedented highs and the Club of Rome produced a widely publicized report claiming that the world was running out of resources. Unless one had had long experience with the boom-and-bust volatility of raw materials prices (and the young lending officers seldom had such experience) it was plausible to imagine that the producers of such commodities were going to be creditworthy in the future — even if they demonstrably had not been in the past.

The last point is probably the most important one, the ace in the hole. The banks were assuming that bad debts could be made good just as they always had been in the recent past, with rescheduling and an infusion of new money from the interested governments of the creditor countries.

The banks did not fear rescheduling, as long as they could continue to collect market rates of interest; indeed, the first reschedulings of bank debt, in the late 1970s and early 1980s, made these loans even more profitable for the banks because they could increase the spreads and collect fat front-end fees for the rescheduling which were counted as instant profits. (The United States Congress ended this practice in 1983 as part of the law approving a capital increase for the IMF.)

It is clear that in case of default, the banks confidently expected a government bailout. This quotation from *Euromoney*, the trade publication of international banking, indicates their thinking:

> On the one hand, a purely technical analysis of the [non-oil developing countries'] current financial position would suggest that defaults are inevitable; yet on the other hand, many experts feel this is not likely to happen. The World Bank, the IMF, and the governments of major industrialized nations, they argue, would step in rather than watch any default seriously disrupt the entire Euromarket apparatus (Levine 1975:14).

THE ROLE OF THE "OIL SHOCK"

We are now in a position to reassess the role of the oil shock of 1973–74. Contrary to the assumptions spelled out in my opening paragraphs, many countries had heavy debts, and had experienced debt crises, before the oil shock; and many United States and international banks were deeply enmeshed in lending to them before 1973, despite (or because of?) their debt histories. The OPEC move was the culminating act of the commodity price boom which gave the banks an incentive to consider Third World countries good credit risks for the future. The most eager lending of the 1970s was to *oil-exporting* countries, many of which were heavily populated and had high import demand (Venezuela, Nigeria, Indonesia, Mexico).

Other borrowing countries, especially Brazil and South Korea, really did have to borrow to cover their oil import bills. The banks' confidence that there was an invisible United States umbrella guaranteeing their loans to these countries could only have been strengthened by the official encouragement given to the "recycling" of petrodollar surpluses by commercial banks. The placement of "petrodollars" owned by Saudi Arabians and Kuwaitis did contribute to the funds available for lending, but experts estimate petrodollars contributed only about 15 percent of total funds in the Eurodollar markets (Williams 1981:64). The oil price crisis was simply fuel added to an already blazing fire.

What the banks did not realize was that, (1) they were themselves bailing out (temporarily) the crisis of debts owed to *governments,* and (2) by lending tens of billions of dollars more to these already indebted countries on "hard" terms (high interest rates and short maturities) they were ensuring that the next crisis could not be "solved" in the traditional way — by restoring, via rescheduling and new lending, the net transfer of capital to Third World borrowers.

When Mexico and Brazil, the two largest Third World borrowers, defaulted in 1982, the traditional "solution" was put to the test. If the "marketplace" had been left to find a solution, the world would have plunged quickly into financial chaos, for the instinct of each bank creditor was to stop lending and try to retrieve what it could of its assets. This, the United States leadership (primarily the Treasury Department and the Federal Reserve Board) and the IMF realized, would leave all banks with nothing. The banks expected the United States and other governments, and the IMF to bail them out. The IMF and World Bank did devote billions of dollars to rescue packages, and the United States and the Bank for International Settlements (acting as intermediary for the central banks of OECD countries) provided some "bridge" finance, but it was by far not enough to bail out the banks.

Instead, the managing director of the IMF told the banks that they would have to bail themselves in, just as official creditors, acting through the Paris Club, had been doing for a quarter century. Each bank was required to put up a percentage of its existing total exposure to each country (7 percent in the cases of Mexico and Brazil) as new lending. This would enable the countries to pay their interest on schedule, *if the countries added a portion of their export earnings to the new lending.*

But this was exactly what most Third World borrowers were unprepared to accept. In a very short time, these countries were expected to make the wrenching change from a huge gross inflow of capital financing import surpluses (living above their means) to devoting a sizable chunk of their own earnings to debt service: "living below our means" in the words of Argentinian Aldo Ferrer (Ferrer 1985). The legal requirements of loan contracts had caused water to flow uphill: the Third World was again sending money to the industrial countries, this time as debt service *as well as* capital flight.

The net transfer had become negative, as it had to do sometime, barring an infinitely expanding financial universe. Just as bank lending had soared when inflation boosted export earnings in the 1970s (thus postponing the breakeven point predicted by the Pearson Commission for the mid-1970s) so it declined in tandem with the downturn in export earnings in the early 1980s, precipitating the crisis. Between 1981 and 1982, the seven largest debtors of Latin America (Argentina, Brazil, Chile, Colombia, Mexico, Peru, and Venezuela) experienced a collective rise in interest costs of $5 billion (17 percent), a fall in export earnings of $7 billion (9 percent), and a drop in new lending of $10 billion (16 percent). Mexico, however, inaugurated the debt crisis with its 1982 default despite the fact that its export earnings had *risen by 138 percent* in only three years, as its oil production came onstream just as oil prices reached their height (Inter-American Development Bank 1984:19, 34–35).

In the years after 1982 the "creditors cartel," which included the United States administration, the creditor banks (particularly the large ones represented on the steering committees for each errant debtor country), the IMF and the World Bank, tried to manage the debt crisis. They pretended that it was merely a "liquidity problem" which could be overcome if the creditors kept new loans flowing and required the debtor to accept IMF-designed austerity programs. (Among other conditions, the IMF insisted on trade liberalization, thus forbidding debtors to plan the most desirable use of their scarce foreign exchange.)

The plan did not work. Debtor countries would sign standby agreements with the IMF in order to get new money from their other creditors, only to break the agreements because the economic and social costs were unbearable. Creditors and debtors rescheduled debt service payments almost continually, in a process that resembled nothing so much as a poker game with the creditors hoping to recoup more in interest payments than they had to lay out in new money, and the debtors gambling on the opposite.

The patent failure of the strategy impelled the United States government to propose the "Baker Plan" in 1985, which was merely the old strategy with a few cosmetic changes. These changes included a newly exalted role for the World Bank (but with no abandonment of the requirement of IMF austerity programs) and a rhetorical emphasis on "growth," although no one could explain how countries were to grow at the same time they were shipping their wealth out in debt service payments.

One paradoxical effect of the creditors' strategy was the weakening of IMF discipline. This was inevitable when an agreement with the IMF was made the sine qua non for each rescheduling. Since everyone knew the only alternative to rescheduling was default, which the creditors feared even more than the debtors, the debtors gradually grew emboldened enough to write their own IMF agreements and lobby the United States government to force acceptance by the IMF (as Argentina did in 1984 and Mexico in 1986).

But a more basic reason for the decline of the IMF's authority was that the debtor countries were now sending funds to the North, rather than vice versa. Many governments (if not their citizens) found it attractive to accept IMF advice when this was rewarded by a generous inflow of foreign funds; but the reversal of this flow made the rewards much less attractive. Indeed, Brazil's President threatened, in 1986, to impose conditions on the United States — the acceptance of Brazilian exports in the United States market — in exchange for the timely servicing of the debt.

The real resources counterpart of the "negative net transfer" of funds from Latin America, the export surplus Latin America required in order to make any payments at all on its debt, was having its predictable painful effect on United States based manufacturers and workers. Just as the Latin economies had experienced a sudden wrenching reversal of their import surpluses, so the United States economy was suddenly forced to accept an import surplus from the Third World after decades of enjoying an export surplus with them. The loss of factories and jobs led inevitably to the political isolation of the big banks, as it was gradually realized that every dollar paid in debt service to the banks was a dollar that was not available to pay for imports. The debt solution proposed by Bill Bradley of the United States Senate in 1986 was a response to the pain of the United States economy at losing its unrequited markets in Latin America.

The Bradley plan challenged the myths of the Baker plan and for the first time brought into mainstream discourse the fact that solving the debt crisis must involve a *reduction* of debt and a recognition of losses. It was, however, just as imperialistic as the Baker plan in assuming that the United States had the right to impose conditions, chiefly trade concessions opening the debtors' markets to United States exports, in exchange for limited and case-by-case debt forgiveness.

The spring of 1987 brought two developments which mark a turning-point in the debt crisis. The largest Third World debtor, Brazil, stopped paying interest on the commercial bank portion of its $108 billion debt. Several smaller debtors; Ecuador, Peru, and Bolivia had previously suspended interest payments.

In response to this blow, Citicorp, the largest United States commercial bank and the perennial leader in lending to the Third World, announced it was setting aside $3 billion dollars as a reserve against dubious Third World debt. Citicorp thus completely reversed its previous position, abandoned the creditors' cartel it had so fiercely shepherded, and demolished what credibility was left in the Baker plan, leaving the United States government without a policy on Third World debt. Other American and British banks quickly followed suit.

CONCLUSION

What is the likely future of Third World debt? Leaders in both the developed countries and the debtor countries are still clinging to the hope that the "natural" order of capital flows from North to South can be restored. Elementary arithmetic indicates that this can only be achieved if gross inflows increase by stupendous amounts, or interest payments are drastically reduced. The first option is highly unlikely. The events of early 1987 make the second the probable outcome.

The seventies' credit boom led inexorably into the eighties' bust. The poor people of many debtor countries are worse off than they were before the borrowing spree began (McCoy 1987). The banks have received with ill grace the news that they must bear part of the costs of the party. The heart of the crisis of the 1980s is that no one can be found to join the Ponzi scheme at this point with large enough capital to restore the net transfer to the debtors. The debtor countries, for their part, are unwilling to deliver a net transfer to the North in perpetuity, which they would be doing if they kept paying interest in full. Therefore defaults, repudiation, write-offs and forgiveness, in some mixture, are the way in which this debt crisis will have to be "solved."

The debt crisis can never be solved as long as United States policy-makers insist that countries like Brazil and Korea must continue servicing their debts but must also restrict their exports to the United States. Such a contradictory stance illustrates a lack of comprehension of the very intimate connections between trade and finance, and perpetuates the very contradictions which led us inexorably into the present crisis.

The only way to prevent future debt crises is to drastically limit unbalanced international capital flows, which means abandoning the dangerous myth that Third World countries need to import foreign capital. The current crisis has practically wiped out "market" flows to problem debtors. Much damage could be averted if the lenders accepted their losses, the debtors repudiated their old debts (this would give them access to huge amounts of their own capital) and renounced hopes of future borrowing. The world could then be reconstructed on a pay-as-you-go basis, and international trade could resume growth on a slower but healthier basis. The most positive by-product of such a course would be enhanced autonomy for the previous debtor countries, in place of the slavish, but insincere, subjection to finance capital which still rules the Third World.

19

Imperial Decline and International Disorder: An Illustration from the Debt Crisis[1]

ARTHUR MacEWAN

I

Throughout the 1980s, the "debt crisis" has been a continuing difficulty of the international economy. The lives of millions of people in the Third World have been disrupted, as debt related problems and programs have forced down living standards. In the rich countries, the impacts have been less dramatic and visible, but they have nonetheless been real. International financial institutions have been under continuous strain, and the ever present danger of financial collapse has limited the flexibility of policy in the advanced capitalist countries. Moreover, it is widely recognized that, as much damage as the debt crisis has already caused, the situation could become much more serious, and many "worst case" scenarios envision the debt crisis leading the world economy into a severe depression.

The debt crisis, however, is a derivative crisis. Its origins lie in a more general crisis that has beset the international relations of capitalist countries during the last two decades. To be sure, the debt crisis has its own particular causes and its own dynamic. These are interesting and important. Yet if we focus on the debt crisis as a phenomenon unto itself, we miss a larger and more significant occurrence.

The purpose of this paper is to describe the way the debt crisis has evolved out of a larger crisis and thereby to illustrate the way in which that larger and more fundamental crisis has its particular manifestations. That larger crisis is best defined as the breakdown of the basic arrangements by which stability was maintained in the international economic affairs of capitalist nations during, roughly, the quarter century following World War II. A principal feature of those arrangements was the essentially unchallenged imperial dominance that was exercised jointly by the United States government and business.

This larger crisis, a crisis of imperial decline, is important because it is the central feature of international affairs in the current period. Moreover, it is a crisis that has existed for several years and is likely to continue for some time. In this paper, I do not intend to demonstrate the overwhelming importance of this general crisis, but simply to illustrate its operation through an examination of certain aspects of the debt crisis. If, however, we want to understand the evolution of international affairs, we had better recognize the crisis of imperial decline and figure out how it is evolving in the current period.

In the remainder of Part I of this essay, I want to describe briefly and in general terms the nature of United States imperial power in the post-World War II era and then point out ways in which the situation has changed. That will set the stage for a discussion of the debt crisis, and in Part II, I will argue that the origins of the debt crisis lie in the emergence of the crisis of imperial decline. In Part III, I will continue the story by describing how international investment processes were affected by the disorder and disarray that characterized imperial weakness in the 1970s (that is, imperial weakness relative to the imperial strength of the earlier period). The full blown appearance of the debt crisis in the 1980s has been the outcome. In Part IV, I will conclude by noting that, as a derivative crisis, the debt crisis is unlikely to be effectively overcome while the larger crisis continues. It will continue to produce instability and change in international affairs.

To avoid misunderstanding, I should note that I have no intention of providing a comprehensive discussion of the debt crisis. Emanating in part from events in the advanced capitalist countries and in part from events in the Third World, the debt crisis has a dual set of causes. I will deal only with the events that have developed in the center. (A similar argument regarding the connection of the debt crisis to the more general crisis can be developed by focusing on events in the Third World; see MacEwan [1985].)

Not so very long ago, the United States government and business based in the United States held a joint position of unchallenged dominance within the capitalist world. In that era, roughly the 25 years following World War II, the government established military alliances around the world, organized central institutions of economic affairs (most particularly, the Bretton Woods monetary agreement and the General Agreement on Tariffs and Trade), and pressured governments far and near to adopt "correct" policies and to be hospitable to United States business. Businesses based in the United States greatly expanded their international operations, extending their control of mineral resources in the Third World and setting up production operations in Europe and elsewhere in order to penetrate and control growing markets. United States international dominance was, of course, limited in the political realm by the Soviet Union, and socialist and nationalist movements throughout the world did not readily accept the economic power of United States business. Yet within the wide realm of capitalism — what the United States authorities have dubbed the "Free World" — there was no appreciable challenge. Other governments accepted their subordinate position, and businesses based in other nations found ways to fit in to an economic milieu organized by United States firms.

The period is often referred to as the era of United States hegemony. In modern times, it found its parallel in the degree of dominance exercised by Britain during the middle of the nineteenth century. That had been the era of Pax Britanica, and the mid-twentieth century became the era of Pax Americana. In each of these periods, a central power generally set the rules for international affairs. Direct political control in the form of colonies was not the central method of organization in either era. Instead, power flowed from unrivaled economic strength and was backed by seemingly unchallenged military superiority. In a world of formally independent nations, imperial power nonetheless was the principal organizing instrument of international affairs.

There is a good deal of dispute about whether the imperial power of Pax Americana was a beneficient or malevolent force in international affairs. There is, however, no dispute over the existence of that power or over its importance as the organizing foundation for international economic affairs. Everyone seems to agree that the great strength of the United States government and of business in international affairs provided one of the central pillars of the very rapid economic advance in capitalist nations during the quarter century following World War II. Stable financial arrangements and a relatively open organization of trade resulted in a rapid growth of international commerce, a more thorough international integration of capitalist economies. The flow of goods, capital and technology across international boundaries proved to be a strong stimulus to economic growth.

As it turned out, however, United States hegemony was an ephemeral phenomenon. The very success of the era meant the restrengthening of the economies of Japan and European nations. Businesses based in these nations came to challenge United States firms in every corner of the globe, including, of course, in the United States itself. Also, attempting to play international policeman for the operations of international capitalism, the United States government found itself extended beyond its capabilities. The war in Indochina was not only lost but also created a myriad of political and economic problems affecting both the domestic and international operations of the United States government. In the early 1970s, when the Bretton Woods monetary arrangements were abandoned, it was widely recognized that the international organization of power had changed.

No one doubts that the United States remains the leading power among capitalist nations, but the joint capability of United States government and business to set the rules of international affairs no longer exists. The United States government cannot readily impose economic policies upon its allies. United States business is no longer unchallenged — quite the contrary. It has been necessary to accommodate to challenges from Japan and Europe, and even from rising economic powers such as South Korea and Brazil — and there are also the OPEC nations. Only in the realm of conflict with the Soviet Union is the United States able to set the terms among its allies, and even there dissension arises.

The new situation is reflected in the poorer economic performance of capitalist nations during the period since the early 1970s. It is also reflected in a higher degree of instability in international economic affairs. Ironically, the very success of United States hegemony in integrating capitalist economies with one another created a world more susceptible to the instability that has arisen in the post-hegemony period. We have come to live in an era of international crises: the oil crisis; the dollar crisis; the debt crisis; the trade crisis; and so on. Each of these particular crises is, as I have said about the debt crisis, a derivative crisis. It is part of the larger crisis of imperial decline. Let me proceed to illustrate the point by examining the debt crisis.

II

As United States power began to ebb in the 1960s and as hegemony came to a marked termination in the early 1970s with the demise of the Bretton Woods monetary arrangements, a set of events were set in motion that led to a new role for banking and debt in the international economy. An almost defining feature of United States hegemony had been the central role of the dollar in international commerce. With dollars used for trade among other nations and held as reserves by other governments, large holdings of dollars were built up overseas. These growing holdings of dollars outside the United States reflected the fact that United States businesses, the government and private individuals were purchasing more abroad than foreign interests were purchasing from the United

States. (It was analogous to a private individual being able to write checks on her or his bank account and to operate as though many of those checks would never be cashed in.)

In the short run, at least, this was a very advantageous arrangement for the United States. In the longer run, however, the situation presented a problem for both the United States and the general stability of the international economy. As the holdings of dollars overseas grew — and they did grow at a rate of roughly $2 billion per year during the 1960s — the structure of the monetary system became increasingly unstable (Magdoff and Sweezy 1971:8).[2] The dollar's role had been secure while foreign interests maintained confidence that the United States government could redeem their dollar holdings, but, as those dollar holdings grew, it became evident that the United States government could not back the whole system with gold.

It was not at all clear how far the system could be pushed, but considerable concern developed in the late 1960s among international investors. Their fear, of course, was that as the supply of dollars continued to rise as a result of growing United States spending abroad, the demand for dollars would continue to lag behind, and ultimately the value of the dollar would have to fall relative to other currencies. Those holding dollars would then suffer losses. Moreover, the very existence of such a concern could cause the value of the dollar to fall, as speculators would shift their holdings to other currencies. If this process were to commence, the whole international economy could be disrupted and all players in the game would suffer.

In the late 1960s, the United States government took advantage of the dollar-dependent international financial system as domestic and international conflicts placed severe fiscal strains on the government and threatened to disrupt the United States economy. In order to finance, simultaneously, the war in Indochina and efforts to buy racial and social harmony in urban centers, the government followed a deficit spending program financed through an expansion of the supply of dollars.

While one might expect the expansion of the money supply to have led to considerable inflation, in fact, price increases were relatively mild in the United States during the late 1960s. The structure of international monetary arrangements allowed United States inflation to be exported. As the United States government ran deficits and increased the money supply, more and more dollars found their way overseas; in fact, the normal spending of funds, which would have spread the dollars abroad, was enhanced in this period by the growth of military spending. In these circumstances, central banks in other nations were faced with a dilemma. They could, on the one hand, refuse to increase the supply of their own currencies to the extent necessary to buy up the extra dollars. Such action, however, would tend to exacerbate the already existing downward pressure on the value of the dollar and threaten to disrupt the functioning of the international economy. On the other hand, they could expand the supplies of their own currencies to buy up the dollars. This latter course of action, however, would increase inflation in their own economies. In general, foreign central bankers accepted their secondary role, accepted the dollars, and imported the United States government-created inflation to their own economies.[3] Of course, it was a process that could not last. In 1970 and especially in 1971, investors began selling off their holdings of dollars in favor of other currencies. By mid-1971, it was clear that the situation could no longer be sustained. The United States government then eliminated the convertability of dollars for gold and placed a 10 percent surcharge on imports, effectively devaluing the dollar and drastically altering international monetary arrangements. Thoroughly crippled by these events, the Bretton Woods system, which had been the foundation of the international monetary system since the end of World War II, was formally terminated in 1973.

Nonetheless, the United States government's efforts to preserve empire and prolong domestic economic expansion had already worked to initiate a surge in the international supply of money, a wave of growth in international liquidity. This general growth in the supply of funds and, in particular, the growth in the supply of dollars held abroad were the foundation for the growth of international lending that would occur in the subsequent decade.

The dollars held abroad by commercial banks came to be called "Eurodollars," and the whole new wave of lending associated with the growth of international liquidity came to be called the "Eurocurrency Market." The essential feature that accounts for the rising role of the Eurocurrency Market is its relative lack of regulation. Within the United States, for example, the government can and does control the amount of new loans that a bank can finance with a new dollar of deposits; by requiring that banks hold a certain percentage of all deposits in reserve, the government both places a limit on the expansion of loan activity and protects the banking system from putting itself in a position where it cannot meet the demands of depositors for their funds. Moreover, government regulators establish restrictions that limit the degree of risk that can be undertaken by banks in extending new loans.

In the absence of such regulation, competition among banks could push them into riskier and riskier loans and lead them to hold a smaller and smaller percentage of deposits as reserves. In the Eurocurrency Market such regulation is, in fact, virtually absent. Furthermore, without regulation, governments have much less control over the supply of their currencies. When, for example, banks holding dollars abroad loan out those dollars they create new dollars; that is, new claims on goods and services in the United States. A dollar can be lent, and then, when the borrower deposits the new funds back in the banking system, they can be re-lent, and so on and so on, the process being limited only by each bank's willingness to take on risks.[4]

While the Eurocurrency Market came into being during the 1960s as a consequence of the structure of the international monetary system and of the particular policies followed by the United States government, during the 1970s it expanded much further. Again, United States government policies were the prime factor (though the unregulated international banking system, operating as noted above, also played a major role). As the general crisis emerged and slow growth beset the international economy, the government chose to deal with the problems by running large deficits financed through an expansion of the money supply. This policy commenced sharply in 1971 and 1972, and continued to one degree or another throughout the decade.[5]

In spite of the changes that took place in the international monetary system in the early 1970s, the growing supply of dollars continued to move overseas. United States hegemony had come to an end, but the great political and economic power of the United States continued to be reflected in a central, though altered, role for the dollar in international affairs. The Eurodollar Market, now fully operative, proved an attractive home for surplus dollars. Between the end of 1969 and 1972, foreign dollar claims on the United States government and on foreign branches of United States banks doubled, and then doubled again by the end of 1977. Similarly, international dollar reserves quadrupled between the end of 1969 and the end of 1972, and then more than doubled again by the end of 1977 (Triffin 1978–79:270).

Part of the growth in international dollar reserves — most of which was, of course, a growth in Eurodollars — was the arrival of "Petrodollars." The rise of oil revenues accruing to OPEC member governments after 1973 was so rapid and so large that in many countries the funds were not spent as rapidly as they were obtained (in spite of the huge growth of luxury consumption by elites and the surge in armaments spending). Surplus funds were usually invested in the international financial markets, the Eurocurrency Market, where they served to enhance once more the already expanding credit foundation. The data noted above, however, make it clear that the expansion of international liquidity was well established prior to the "energy crisis" of 1973. Indeed, during the 1970s as the international supply of money grew, two great surges of growth can be identified, one during the 1971–72 period and one during 1977–78. Each came just before, rather than after, a major rise in oil prices (McKinnon 1982:320, 322; and Triffin 1978–79). Thus, while many commentators have attributed the development of international financial instability to the Petrodollar phenomenon, it is clear that the origin of the great expansion of international liquidity does not lie with the expansion of OPEC revenues. Moreover, in so far as OPEC surpluses were important in generating the debt crisis — and surely they did play an important exacerbating if not originating role — they, like the original emergence of Eurodollars, are best explained as a symptom of the decline and breakup of United States hegemony. What clearer sign of the ebb of United States power than the ability of a group of peripheral states to alter the organization of international energy markets?

Thus we can trace the expansion of international liquidity to the emergence of general crisis in two senses. First, the emergence of the Eurocurrency Market, in both its Eurodollar and Petrodollar components, and the initiation of liquidity expansion were tied to the crisis as consequences of the nature of United States hegemony, of its decline, and of its dissolution. Second, as the crisis evolved and relative stagnation set in, United States government deficits and monetary expansion continued to fuel the fires of international inflation and liquidity expansion.

III

The developments of the 1970s, as indicated above, led to great changes in the practices of United States banks. United States banks had not participated as much as one might expect in the early post-World War II expansion of United States business abroad. Until the mid-1960s, their foreign operations grew relatively slowly. The growth of the United States economy and the more rapid growth of United States-based multinationals, which the banks could service from their domestic base, seem to have provided sufficient outlets for the banks' funds. In the 1960s, however, United States banks began to go abroad to join in the profits to be made from unregulated Eurocurrency operations. Moreover, the banks were forced to go abroad simply to protect themselves. The general reemergence of the competitive strength of the Japanese and European economies was given extra impetus in the banking industry by the emergence of the Eurocurrency system. Without well established foreign operations, United States banks would lose some of the foreign business of their United States-based customers to foreign rivals; this in turn might give foreign banks an inroad to the United States banking market (Koszul 1970).[6]

Various sets of data show the impressive growth of United States-based international banking, beginning in the late 1960s and continuing on through the 1970s and into the 1980s. In 1960, for example, domestic assets accounted for 98.6 percent of United States commercial bank assets; by 1967, the figure had fallen, but only to 96.5 percent; in 1980, however, domestic assets had dropped to 74.1 percent(Brimmer and Dahl 1975:345; and *Federal Reserve Bulletin* 1981:A17 & A54; also, see Pecchioli 1983). Or, in the Commerce Department's summary of "U.S. International Transactions," consider the category "Receipts of income on U.S. assets abroad" other than income from direct investments and United States government receipts; this category is mostly made up of banks' interest receipts on their foreign loans. In 1960 the figure stood at $646 million and had grown to $2.7 billion in 1970. The figure leaped to $32.8 billion in 1980 and to $59.5 billion in 1984 (see Table 1).

During the 1970s, Citibank's especially aggressive international operations played a major role in making it the largest of United States banks by the end of the decade. In one year, 1977, 82.2 percent of Citibank's earnings came from international operations. While that figure is an extreme one, composite figures for the ten largest United States banks in the years leading up to the recognition of the debt crisis reveal a striking reliance on foreign source earnings: in the six years, 1977 through 1982, those banks obtained on average 48 percent of their earnings from international operations (Salomon Brothers 1983:7).

This growth of United States-based international banking during the late 1960s and 1970s involved a major shift in the way United States capital was involved in the international economy, for it was accompanied by a decline in the rate of growth of United States direct foreign investments. During the 1950s and early 1960s, the total value of United States foreign direct investments, measured in real terms, increased at a rate of 7 percent to 8 percent a year. During the late 1960s and throughout the 1970s, the rate of increase was about 4 percent to 5 percent, and then in the early 1980s the real value of the stock of United States foreign direct investments declined somewhat (MacEwan 1982:16 and Howenstine 1984).[7] The dramatic change in the relative importance of foreign direct investments and loans shows up in Table 1, where "Receipts of Income on U.S. Assets Abroad" are shown.

While receipts from "other investments" (mainly loans) amounted to only 17.8 percent of receipts from direct investments in 1960 and 25.8 percent in 1965, the figure had jumped to 46.1 percent in 1975 before shooting up to the point where receipts from "other investments" greatly exceeded receipts from foreign direct investments in the early 1980s.[8]

The growth of United States-based international banking and the expansion of the Eurocurrency Market generated a new era of competition among banks. With the greatly increased base from which to make loans and without regulation, banks began to scramble to find new customers who would borrow these funds. Describing his bank's operating procedures during its rapid growth of the 1970s, Citibank's vice-chairman, Thomas Theobald, told *Business Week* (1983), "... if there [is] an opportunity, take advantage. Don't analyze it to death... Anytime you can get a license, take it; almost anytime you can get a customer relationship with a desired customer, take it."

At a much lower level in the banking hierarchy, Gwynne (1983) describes his role as loan officer in a "medium-sized Midwestern bank with $5 billion in assets." According to Gwynne, who in the late 1970s was "selling money door to door" in the Third World:

Table 1
Receipts of Income on U.S. Assets Abroad, 1960–1986
(millions of dollars)

| | **Receipts from:** | | |
	Direct Investments (1)	**Other Investments*** (2)	**(2) as a percent of (1)**
1960	3,621	646	17.8
1965	5,506	1,421	25.8
1970	8,169	2,671	32.7
1975	16,595	7,644	46.1
1980	37,146	32,798	88.3
1981	32,549	50,182	154.2
1982	21,381	58,050	271.5
1983	20,499	51,920	253.3
1984	21,217	59,464	280.3
1985	32,665	50,131	153.5
1986	36,697	45,191	123.1

*Includes primarily interest on bank loans, but also includes returns on other investments, e.g., on foreign bonds held by private individuals.

N.B. Receipts from direct investments are profits, while receipts from other sources is a gross interest figure.

Source: U.S. Department of Commerce, *Survey of Current Business*, June 1987, pp. 54–55.

''As a domestic credit analyst, I was taught to develop reasonable asset security for all loans. . . . As an international loan officer, I was taught to forget about that, and instead to develop a set of rationales that would make the home office feel good about the loan, even though, technically, it was 'unsecured.' ''

It should be stressed that the banking competition of the 1970s was not the consequence of some new ''style'' in the industry, some shift in psychology away from that of the stodgy, conservative and cautious banker. The competition was the direct consequence of two objective factors. One of these was the lack of regulation in international finance. Whatever else it accomplishes, regulation of the banking industry, when it functions, serves to limit competition. One bank cannot challenge others by extending its loans on a lesser and more risky reserve base, nor can it take on loans without proper security or extend credit to inherently risky customers. Thus regulation protects banks from combat with one another and from the risks that come with overextension. Yet these constraints did not apply in the Eurocurrency Market.

The second factor that encouraged competition among the banks was the impact of the general economic crisis itself on the demand for funds. With a decline in the growth rates of output and investment within the economies of the advanced capitalist nations, the rate of expansion of profitable and secure loan opportunities also declined. In the United States the annual growth rate of gross investment fell from 5.3 percent in the 1960s to 2.8 percent in the 1970s; in Japan, the fall was from 15.3 percent to 3 percent and in West Germany, from 3.9 percent to 1.2 percent (OECD 1979; OECD 1982; and *Economic Report of the President* 1984).[9] Thus, while, on the one hand, the onset of the general crisis was characterized by a great expansion in the supply of loanable funds, on the other hand, the crisis involved a relative decline in the growth of the demand for funds. The banks were forced to compete with one another in the search for new customers and new sorts of customers.

One set of evidence indicating this growing competition among the banks for Third World customers during the 1970s is the terms on which loans were made. Data on non-OPEC "LDCs" show that in the fourth quarter of 1975, the "spread" (the difference between the London Interbank Borrowing Rate and what banks charge their customers) averaged 1.65 percentage points and the average maturity of loans was about five and a half years. By the fourth quarter of 1979, the "spread" had fallen to 0.76 percentage points and the average maturity had risen to slightly over 10 years (Mills 1982, as cited by Darity 1984:12). Since there is little reason to think that this improvement in terms reflected an improvement in the economic outlook in the countries receiving the loans, these data are strong evidence of growing competition among the banks and of the "loan pushing" that resulted.

During the 1970s, then, as the general disarray and instability of the advanced capitalist economies began to be widely apparent, the factors that provided a basis for the debt crisis of the 1980s had been well established: the rising surge of liquidity, of a large supply of credit, in the international economy; the operation of a relatively unregulated international financial system; the full scale entrance of United States banks into international operations; rising competition in international banking; and slow economic growth in the advanced capitalist nations. These factors combined to "push" funds out of the central capitalist economies and into the periphery.

IV

The story of the "push" is certainly not the whole story of the debt crisis. There was also a "pull" emanating from events in the periphery. Moreover, the "push" and the "pull" only set the stage for crisis. Before the debt crisis itself could appear in full-form, it was necessary for a particular sequence of events to unfold in the international economy, yielding the high interest rates and then severe recession of the early 1980s. The story of the "push" is, however, an important part of the explanation of the debt crisis that became so important for international affairs in the early 1980s. It is a story, also, that illustrates the way in which a particular crisis is connected to the larger crisis of imperial decline.

The debt crisis emerged in the headlines of the financial pages in mid-1982, when the Mexican government found itself unable to meet its debt obligations. Since then, popular interest in the crisis has ebbed and flowed, but the crisis itself has been a continuing feature affecting the course of international financial affairs. In 1987, five years after the Mexican events brought attention to the crisis, it was still providing major financial news. Early in the year, Brazil suspended payments on its debt. In the late spring, Citibank announced that it was increasing its loan-loss reserve fund some $3 billion, effectively recognizing that many of its Third World loans would never be repaid. The Brazilian action and the Citibank action were part of a continuing struggle among the various interests involved in the debt crisis, a struggle to determine how and by whom the brunt of the crisis' costs will be born.

It is a struggle that is likely to continue for some time. As a derivative crisis, the debt crisis will not be fully resolved while the larger crisis of imperial decline continues. As to the larger crisis, there is no historical precedent to make us believe that it will quickly be resolved. In the debt crisis and in other realms, the crisis of imperial decline is likely to continue to generate major international and national struggles. There is no doubt that such struggles create severe dangers, but they also create some opportunities.

NOTES

1. A substantial portion of this essay originally appeared as part of my article "International Debt and Banking: Rising Instability within the General Crisis," *Science & Society,* Vol. L, No. 2, Summer 1986. I am grateful to *Science & Society* for permission to reprint that material.
2. From today's perspective, an increment of $2 billion per year to the foreign holdings of dollars seems like a paltry sum. However, at the end of the 1960s, foreign dollar and Eurodollar reserves were still only $20 billion, and an increase of $2 billion per year was considerable (Triffin 1978–79).
3. The acquiescence of European bankers was eased by the fact that inflation was not a paramount problem for them in the 1960s. Hawley (1979) provides a useful discussion of these issues.
4. Of course, even in the absence of regulation, banks will hold some reserves — i.e., keep some of their money available and not earning interest in order to meet the demands of creditors (depositors). However, since reserves do not earn interest, there is a cost in holding reserves, a cost that rises as interest rates go up as they did in the 1970s. By way of illustration, Pecchioli (1983:57) points out that if the actual reserve requirement is 10 percent, and a bank avoiding regulation can get by holding reserves of 8 percent, then this amounts to a cost advantage of 0.25 cents on the dollar if the interest rate is 10 percent. Were the interest rate to double, so too would the cost advantage of holding lower reserves.
5. In fiscal years 1971 and 1972 the federal budget deficits were $23.0 billion and $23.4 billion, respectively, which, with the exception of the $25.2 billion deficit at the peak of the Vietnam War in 1968, were by far the largest deficits of the post-World War II period. These deficits were to be dwarfed, however, by those of the second half of the 1970s; from 1975 through 1980, the deficit averaged over $60 billion. As to expansion of the money supply, M1 rose by 87 percent in the 1970s as compared to 53 percent in the 1960s, with 1977-78 being the two year period with most rapid growth (17.1 percent) followed by 1971–72 (16.4 percent). Data are from the *Economic Report of the President* (1985:303, 318).
6. In addition, early concern with emerging balance of payments problems in the late 1960s led the United States government to establish restrictions — albeit weak ones — on the export of capital. The U.S. banks would have had difficulty, therefore, continuing to service foreign business so predominantly from their domestic base.
7. The slowdown in the rate of expansion of United States foreign direct investments is often missed because the data are viewed without any correction for inflation. Then the rate of expansion appears quite stable over the entire 1950–1980 period. However, since inflation increased steadily after 1965, stable expansion in current dollars must mean slowing expansion in constant dollars.
8. Of course, part of the extreme change in the early 1980s was a result of the appreciation of the dollar. Direct investments yield returns in local currencies which must be transformed — either actually or for accounting purposes — to dollars, while loans are generally denominated in dollars. Conversely, the reversal of the trend in 1985 and 1986 is partly explained by the depreciation of the dollar.
9. These data are trend rates of growth for real private gross domestic investment.

20

The Promise and Pitfalls of Protectionist Politics

JOHN WILLOUGHBY

INTRODUCTION: THE INTERNATIONAL EXPANSION AND NATIONAL MANUFACTURING DECLINE OF THE AMERICAN ECONOMY

It is no secret that United States trade competitiveness has deteriorated over the past forty years. The late 1940s was the era of dollar shortage: when Western policy makers feared that United States economic might would throttle any European or Japanese drive to rebuild their war-torn national economies. In the late 1950s (1957–59), the Eisenhower Administration confronted a sharp two-year slump in net exports and worried about a coming dollar drain. The imperialist imperatives of the Vietnam War doomed any coherent approach to this problem, and the Johnson Administration's efforts to reverse its balance of payments difficulties resulted instead in a destabilizing Eurodollar explosion. Ten years and two steep dollar depreciations later, the Carter Administration presided over an unprecedented $30 billion trade deficit. And seven years after that (in 1986), merchandise imports into the United States outstripped corresponding exports by approximately $150 billion.

These nominal figures overstate the extent of the decline, since a generalized price inflation will increase the trade deficit's size even though export and import volumes and the relative values of currencies have not changed. Swings in the dollar's relative price also complicate any interpretation of trade balance figures. A cheaper dollar (holding trade volumes constant) will enlarge the United States merchandise deficit. It is possible for the same physical trade exchanges to produce a trade surplus in one year and a trade deficit in another. Despite these interpretative problems, Figure 1 clearly illustrates the deterioration in United States trade performance. Between 1946 and 1986, net exports as a percentage of GNP have declined from $+3.2$ percent to -3.5 percent.

This commercial decline has coincided with another forty-year secular trend: the international economy now plays a much more important role in the economic life of the United States. Richard Cooper has estimated, for example, that the share of international trade and investment in total American economic activity has doubled since the early 1960s, while global financial contacts have roughly tripled (Cooper 1987).

This expansion has had profound effects on particular sectors of the American labor force. Today about 50 percent of multinational corporate profits come from foreign operations (Cooper 1987), and it is no real surprise that this increasing international emphasis has combined with the global dispersion of industrial production to transform those cities which provide the financial, marketing and communication services for transnational corporate headquarters. New York, Los Angeles and Chicago are becoming less and less industrial, while a new army of professional, managerial, clerical and

Figure 1
U.S. Merchandise Trade Balance as Percentage of GNP

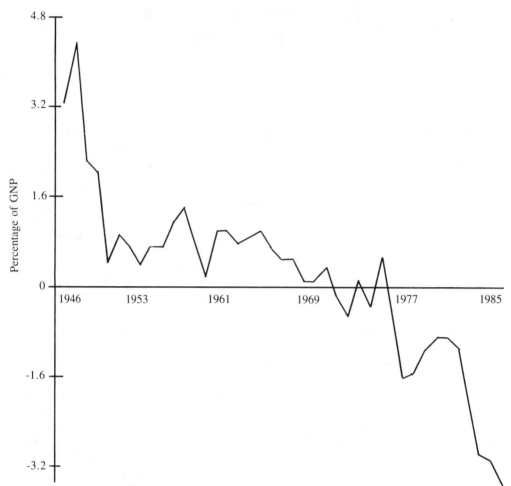

Source: Department of Commerce.

service workers has emerged to respond to the needs of multinational corporate headquarters.[1] These new workers are not necessarily well paid; clerical and service workers, in particular, suffer from poor wages and insecure working conditions. Nevertheless, the economic expansion of this sector contrasts starkly with the employment crisis facing the older industrial regions of the United States. The industrial Midwest — bounded by Pittsburgh and Buffalo in the East and Chicago and Milwaukee in the West — boasted the highest living standards and lowest unemployment rates in the nation only twenty years ago. Today, this area is popularly known as the Rust Bowl; unemployment rates are consistently higher than the national average, and the population base is stagnating.

Polarities of expansion and decline always characterize capitalist growth, and the last forty years has been no exception. The international dimension of this process, however, is unique in twentieth century United States economic history. Before World War II, most United States historians would have juxtaposed the rise of domestically oriented industrialism and urbanism to the decline of agrarian life. Now, the impressive expansion of American multinational enterprise is linked to the relative decline of domestic manufacturing industry.[2]

THE DECLINE OF TRADE UNION POWER AND ITS POLITICAL IMPLICATIONS

This regional and industrial transformation has considerably weakened the workplace and national political power of American trade unions. Before the sharp decline in their membership during the late 1970s and 1980s, the major industrial unions had the ability to limit some aspects of corporate power. Union officials were able to negotiate over work classification systems and promotion procedures as well as to bargain for higher pay. And local wildcat strikes — even when they were opposed by the trade union leadership — often effectively limited the pace and intensity of factory labor. Today, unions find themselves promoting forms of corporate-union cooperation that give managers much greater power to assign and promote workers to a multitude of tasks. This reassertion of capitalist prerogatives is possible because of legitimate grassroots fears of job loss. Union officials are struggling to maintain and attract new industrial enterprises, and shopfloor workers are much less likely to strike than they were twenty years ago. As a result of this new environment in manufacturing, the wages of union workers have risen more slowly than non-union workers since 1983 (Lacombe and Borum 1987:10–16).

This sapping of rank and file power has had effects that go well beyond the workplace. In the late 1940s and early 1950s, the AFL's and CIO's enthusiastic support of Cold War politics helped construct the capitalist world economy that is today so threatening to many United States workers. Nevertheless, the industrial trade unions, in particular, never completely acquiesced to this political economic order. As long as unions seemed strong, it was necessary for liberal capitalist politicians to propose social programs — such as Medicare, federal spending for education, and higher minimum wages — that occasionally became law. Moreover, the United Auto Workers granted significant moral and financial support to one of the most important popular movements of the postwar era: the struggle for Afro-American civil rights.

It is no coincidence that the collapse of postwar trade unionism in the late 1970s and early 1980s is contemporaneous with a steady retreat from the significant, but modest, liberal capitalist reforms implemented by Congress during the 1960s and early 1970s. The competitive pressures of the international economy have created a much more reactionary political climate within the United States. The question facing us is not whether, but how, to change the impact of these international economic processes. A successful response to international competition is necessary if the economic and political power of the majority of United States workers is to be strengthened.

THE CAUSES OF AMERICAN TRADE DECLINE

Appropriate pro-worker policies, however, require some understanding of the general causes of postwar trade decline. It would have been surprising if the United States trade sector had retained the overwhelming commercial superiority it enjoyed in the immediate postwar period. It took some time for the Western European and Japanese national economies to become reintegrated effectively into global capitalism after the devastation of World War II, and the relative slippage of the United States economy was not especially disruptive as long as global production continued to grow impressively. Even United States trade unions supported unrestricted trade during the 1950s and 1960s.

This catch-up process was completed more than a decade ago (Branson 1980:183– 257). The United States is still a leader in some of the more advanced computer, electronic, biotechnical and armaments technologies, but the know-how behind the production of most traded commodities has been shared by all of the advanced capitalist economies for some time now. Moreover, the East Asian "Newly Industrializing Countries" have demonstrated considerable skill in producing and marketing consumer durable and capital goods once considered beyond the ability of any less developed country.

This diffusion of knowledge and skill is a long-term tendency which threatens all less technologically sophisticated, high-wage industries in the United States. Nevertheless, this cause of sectoral competitive erosion can neither explain the erratic performance of United States trade during the 1970s nor account for the overwhelming deterioration of the trade balance during the Reagan era. Fluctuating exchange rates have also played a major role in regulating international competitive relations for the past fifteen years.

The late Nixon and early Carter Administrations, for example, were able to engineer a modest improvement in the trade balance by promoting the depreciation of the dollar. On the other hand, high interest rate policies in the mid-seventies and during the early 1980s reversed this process. Footloose foreign money capital flowed into the United States, appreciated the dollar, cheapened non-domestic goods and crowded out significant portions of the United States tradeable sector. The volume of 1986 United States exports was lower than it was in 1980; the real value of imports, on the other hand, rose by 55 percent.

The conclusion that a persistently overvalued dollar is responsible for much of the contemporary trade deficit, however, begs an important question: Why should the United States persistently pursue programs that weaken the competitive stance of United States industry? There are, of course, domestic roots to recent American monetary policies. In the late 1960s, the Johnson Administration did not wish to raise the price of imports (by cheapening the dollar) at a time when inflationary pressure was building. Similarly, the Volcker-Carter interst rate, exchange rate shock of late 1979 was partly designed to cheapen imports and thereby relieve serious upward price and wage pressures.

But there is another motive behind this defense of the dollar. United States imperial obligations have often led United States administrations to keep the value of the national currency relatively high. There are four reasons for this policy stance. First, there is the straightforward need to limit the budgetary costs of United States militarism. An appreciating dollar cheapens the dollar costs of maintaining the foreign presence of American might. Second, a high dollar value encourages the foreign expansion of United States capital through direct foreign investment. Since the early 1950s, the business establishment has placed a high priority on this form of global accumulation, and the internationally diversified industrial base that has resulted from the establishment of foreign manufacturing subsidiaries has limited the harm that an overvalued dollar can cause United States-based multinational corporate interests. Even if United States competitiveness slackens, American business is now well placed to export from other countries. Over the 1970s, in fact, the share of exports (in global total) from branches owned by United States capitalists did not decline at all, even though the share of domestic exports fell considerably (Lipsey and Kravis 1987).

The third reason for keeping the value of the dollar high also flows from the international expansion of United States capital. High levels of direct foreign investment have led to a large expansion in the international role of the dollar. United States corporations now hold huge dollar balances overseas as well as at "home." No financial manager wishes to see his or her financial assets devalued. Whenever the dollar begins to slump, the business press in American dutifully warns of the harmful consequences of a currency "free fall." Wall Street pundits who fear the complete evaporation of dollar balances seem to live in a paranoid fantasy world. Nevertheless, the real material interests in a stable dollar fuel these nightmares and place heavy pressure on any United States administration concerned about its relations with banking capital. The dollar may still, in November 1987, be overvalued by as much as 30 percent — despite the sharp devaluation in the currency over the past year (Dornbusch 1987). Exchange rates undoubtedly will continue to gyrate, but it is difficult for any United States government to lower the dollar's relative value so that the current account is brought into rough balance.

Finally, the United States government has important multilateral obligations. The present "free enterprise" structure of the world economy has benefitted American multinational capital enormously, but it has also allowed other national enterprises to prosper and advance — often at a faster pace than United States business itself. The United States nation-state, as the possessor of the largest domestic economy and the most powerful military apparatus, has consistently attempted to support the global economic system it has created. Dollar instability can enormously complicate inter-capitalist understandings about how the world ought to work.

The major capitalist governments have not been able to maintain stable currency relations, but one of the costs of United States hegemony has been the implicit acceptance of an overvalued dollar. As Blecker notes (in this volume), this expensive money policy provides real material advantages to American and foreign firms whose manufacturing plants are located in cheap currency countries. As a result, auto workers in Detroit, steel workers in Cleveland, and textile laborers in South Carolina will continue to bear a disproportionate share of the costs of United States hegemony's maintenance.

IS PROTECTIONISM HARMFUL?

The continued deterioration in American trade performance and the structural inability of United States administrations to rectify this problem through appropriate economic policy have forced many American trade unions to advocate import restrictions. Protectionist policies are not necessarily anti-corporate, since specific firms nearly always benefit from policies that guarantee a more secure market. On the other hand, subsidizing faltering business may be a price worth paying if, in the process, workers' economic security and political power are strengthened.

Many analysts contend, however, that protectionism is still too costly a policy. High tariffs or quantitative import restrictions may benefit a small subset of workers and capitalists, while proving harmful to the rest of society. There are three major arguments for this negative evaluation: the standard neoclassical perspective in favor of free trade, the economic-historical analysis which suggests that economic nationalism dangerously intensifies inter-capitalist rivalry, and the developmentalist concern that rising trade barriers harm those workers least able to protect themselves — the new industrial proletariat of the Third World.

The free trade position need not detain us for long. The static argument that unrestricted competition improves resource allocation depends on the full utilization of resources, the ability of governments to force firms to internalize all of their costs and the existence of competitive market structures. None of these conditions apply to the global economy. And given these "deviations" from the world of perfect competition, a good case can be made for some form of state intervention into the trading system.

What of the second argument? That trade control measures will usher in a dangerous period of economic rivalry, stagnation and political economic breakdown? The Depression experience and the successes of postwar reconstruction are responsible for the popularity of this historical dogma. In suggesting that protectionism was responsible for the 1930s breakdown, American leaders — with the assistance of pliant academics — have conveniently mistaken cause for effect. Keynes (1933) pointed out at the time that the collapse of stable currency relations and the raising of tariffs represented a pragmatic response to the misguided 1920s efforts to maintain unsustainable global economic commitments. And Alan Milward (1984) notes that, in the immediate postwar era, European governments (except for Italy) consistently sacrificed free trade policies in order to limit imports from the United States and promote growth.

If extensive tariffs and/or quantitative trade restrictions were implemented today, this would also be symptomatic of deeper structural imbalances. Nevertheless, it would be much more difficult for such measures to deconstruct the world economy into rival national blocs. The centralization of military power under the Pentagon's aegis and the concommitant consolidation of transnational corporate power have created powerful barriers to the complete disintegration of the present global economy. Import restrictions, for example, would probably stimulate intensified direct foreign investment and more integrated financial relations. Economic measures which are limited to regulating international trade are simply not that severe a threat to the world economy (Willoughby 1982).

The previous two arguments focus inwardly on the United States and the advanced capitalist world. There is no good reason, however, to limit this consideration of protectionism's possible negative effects to the globe's richer territories. The most effective advanced capitalist trade barriers are presently directed against Third World imports. It is still difficult for a raw material supplying country to develop industries that process these primary goods for sale to the West. Tariffs on raw materials are free, while those on processed goods often are not. More extensive protectionist measures would certainly attempt to slow consumer durable exports from East Asian and Latin American "Newly Industrializing Countries." Any proponent of trade regulation must frankly acknowledge the possibility that these measures could seriously disrupt export-led development efforts in the Third World.

Any response to this objection must focus on the contradictory effects of extroverted growth on much of the Third World. On the one hand, the shift of workers into higher wage sectors can benefit a significant portion of an impoverished population as well as promote more progressive trade unionism (Lim 1986). On the other hand, any less developed country wishing to promote manufacturing exports to the West must attract advanced technologies by promising a "stable" political climate for multinational capital. This pledge carries clear repressive and imperialist implications (Fernandez-Kelly 1983). Third World state managers often attempt to form reactionary alliances with Western capital and the repressive apparatus of the American state, and this process can, to say the least, frustrate popular movements' efforts to assert more democratic control over the economy and polity.

Thus, trade control measures in the West can conceivably disrupt both the livelihoods of workers and the imperial arrangements that help sustain authoritarian capitalist regimes that repress workers in the periphery. This contradictory conclusion suggests that means should be found to mitigate the negative employment effects while deepening the potential anti-capitalist implications of trade control. The United States government could, for example, connect import restrictions to anti-corporate, high employment policies that restricted the mobility of multinational capital. In this case, it might be possible to sustain or even raise the absolute level of Third World imports even as imports as a proportion of output declined (Cripps and Godley 1978).

FROM TRADE PROTECTION TO CAPITAL CONTROLS

Any measure which redirects trade will benefit some firms and some groups of workers — at least in the short term. The ambiguous class nature of protectionism should warn us against the abstract support of all competitive restrictions. Rather, it is important to analyze the political and economic effects of any specific trade policy.

It is useful, for this reason, to distinguish between two types of trade control measures: ad hoc efforts to restrict competition in one particular industry and more systematic macroeconomic and regulatory policies that allow the government to acquire broader control over the national economy's interaction with the rest of the world. The first response is in the realm of "practical politics," while the implementation of the second would require the building of a radical political movement.

Appeals for competitive relief often come with corporate support. It is important to recognize that United States labor is often unable to mobilize enough political power to persuade Congress or the President to intervene without some capitalist backing. This corporatist alliance, however, comes at a price. Labor may face government and business demands for the rationalization of production, or foreign producers may force the reorganization of the labor process by establishing advanced manufacturing subsidiaries within the United States. A protected output market will tend to expand employment, but the introduction of new technologies and management systems will contract labor utilization. It is not possible to predict the overall employment effects of protection, although it is probable that import restrictions will at least prevent a smaller medium-term employment loss than unrestricted trade.

Unfortunately, United States trade unions face more certain political problems from ad hoc protectionism. Given the weakness of labor, unionists often attempt to mobilize broader support for import relief by raising the spectre of "unfair competition." This conceptual framework accepts the legitimacy of an economic system organized by anarchic struggle. The price system — as it is presently constituted — is seen as providing an appropriate framework for evaluating the economic viability of a firm's activities. This acquiescence to capitalist rationality means that trade union leaders can produce few coherent objections to job destroying automation; they can evoke few serious protests against the relocation of productive enterprises within the nation.

This collaborative rhetoric is often linked closely to an intensified collaborative politics which, as I noted in the second section of this essay, focuses on developing new corporate-union mechanisms to regulate shopfloor conflict and increase output per work-day. Most unions have always policed contracts in the United States, but the establishment of corporate-labor quality work circles and production teams suggests a far more pervasive intervention into work relations. It is true that heightened international competition will normally push shopfloor politics in a pro-capitalist direction; the tragedy is that many union-sponsored measures also limit the ability of shopfloor workers to regulate production for their own benefit. Collaboration makes it very difficult for trade unions to resist the levelling-down logic of wage competition (Parker 1986; Slaughter 1985). Needless to say, this form of ad hoc protectionism also does not threaten the capitalist structure of the world economy. Third World workers will be harmed by specific trade regulations, but the likely result is the further international integration of production — as multinationals diversify their production facilities further in an effort to escape specific trade regulations.

This conclusion is disturbing. It is not difficult to understand why trade unions resort to collaborative and protectionist appeals, but the logic of this practical response to international competition is not progressive. Rather, such a politics more often legitimates and intensifies labor's subordination to corporate prerogatives. This does not imply that free trade is the best option available. Instead, a more extensive capital control program would better serve the long-term interests of labor.

Such a program would require trade and foreign exchange controls and the more direct regulation of transnational corporations in order to stabilize employment. Ultimately, a well-working international system would also entail a new system of multilateral trade and investment arrangements and the socialization of foreign manufacturing subsidiaries inside and outside of the United States. Countries on the periphery of the world economy might face serious adjustment costs, but these reforms are very similar to those long proposed by the Third World left.

Unfortunately, it is easy to construct ideal systems that are not likely to be tested in the real world. Sometimes, the pristine beauty of an alternative economic program is even politically enervating. How can we possibly get from here to there? A general articulation of a new policy vision is only useful if it suggests a framework which can guide political interventions today. In this case, there are two principles embedded in an alternative economic strategy which are important: the need to connect import regulation schemes to restrictions on capital movements and a related emphasis on rights to employment and income rather than on establishing a mythical world of "fair" competition.

In today's political context, there are at least six possible reforms that, in combination with trade control measures, could build a more progressive international economic policy.

1. The establishment of a broad network of income, educational and training supports for displaced workers.

2. The passage of local content laws in order to stabilize national production.

3. The adoption of trade legislation that links favorable import treatment to the respect for trade union rights.

4. The preservation of the economic viability of industrial communities through the adoption of plant closing legislation.

5. The required reimbursement of local governments and workers for any disruptions caused by shifts in production location.

6. The establishment of regional democratic planning mechanisms.

The first three proposals have received the support of much of the trade union hierarchy. Nevertheless, there are limits to these policies' effectiveness. Training programs and legislation which requires that a certain proportion of production take place within the nation cannot guarantee union employment or regional stability, since no restrictions are placed on the movement of enterprises within the country. The trade legislation referred to in point 3 also does not necessarily promote employment security, since even if there were full labor rights in South Korea and Taiwan, a goal which all of the left must obviously support, these lower-wage countries will still be able to compete effectively with American workers.[3] This is why the latter three policies are also crucial.

We should not be under any illusion, however, that the demands for controls over capital represented by points 4, 5, and 6 are an alternative to import controls. Plant closing legislation and measures which force firms to internalize the costs of industrial relocation cannot function effectively if enterprises must compete with low wage foreign or domestic competition. Similarly, programs to use domestic steel to rebuild the infrastructure of a particular area are only feasible if authorities can limit competition.

Grassroots efforts to control capital are superior to the narrow trade control politics more often practiced by trade unions. The sometimes desperate efforts to save jobs by combining trade restrictions with corporatist collaboration carry heavy long-term political economic costs. On the other hand, the linkage of trade controls to popular sectoral campaigns for a more secure and stable economy both have a chance of winning, and can take us far beyond the present conservative framework of United States politics and international economic policy. Effective campaigns for the control of capital also highlight a political truth of enormous importance: the unregulated movement of economic resources is incompatible with any sustained popular effort to construct an economy and society responsive to the public interest.

NOTES

1. The late Stephen Hymer (1972) first expressed this insight fifteen years ago. The Bureau of Labor Statistics reports that Los Angeles-Long Beach is the most industrial of the country's three major metropolises. The proportion of Chicago workers employed in manufacturing has declined from 25 percent to 19 percent over the past six years. The analogous 1986 proportion in New York is only 12 percent, while it is 23 percent in the Los Angeles area.

2. The relative decline in manufacturing employment is occurring in all of the major advanced capitalist countries. Indeed, the share of manufacturing in total employment has declined less in the United States than in much of Europe.

3. The trade union rights legislation can also be weakened by arbitrary executive branch enforcement. The Reagan Administration, for example, has used the present law to attack Nicaragua's labor policies, while lauding South Korea and Taiwan for "granting" workers more rights.

21

International Competition, Economic Growth, and the Political Economy of the U.S. Trade Deficit

ROBERT A. BLECKER

Some of the greatest controversy in political economy in the 1980s has concerned the relationship between international competition and economic growth. A widely held popular view asserts that some countries, such as Japan, have been able to sustain more rapid growth and lower unemployment with an export-led strategy. Implicit in this view is the notion that a nation can achieve an overall competitive advantage over its trading partners, resulting in chronic balance of trade surpluses at home and corresponding deficits abroad. Some United States corporations and unions attribute these competitive advantages solely to "unfair trade practices" on the part of foreign governments, practices which allegedly prevent a "level playing field" for American businesses.

I shall argue in this article that there is a connection between international competitiveness and economic growth, but that it is not simply a problem of "unfair" government intervention. Rather, competitive conflicts are inherent in the capitalist organization of international exchange. Although governments certainly can influence the competitive struggle, the "playing field" of international trade would not be "level" even if governments left the field alone. The world market is characterized by a continuous conflict between firms located in different countries over shares in the world market for their products.[1] Countries whose firms are more successful in this conflict can achieve sustained trade surpluses, and thereby maintain faster economic growth and lower rates of unemployment than they could otherwise achieve. This article will explain how such competitive advantages are obtained, as well as how they can be lost, and how they influence the uneven development of the world economy.

Before proceeding with my argument, we must acknowledge that the mainstream of the economics profession vigorously denies that trade surpluses and deficits reflect genuine competitive advantages and disadvantages. Standard international trade theory teaches that trade relations are determined only by "comparative advantages," not absolute competitive advantages. If all countries specialize according to their comparative advantages, it is claimed, all will gain from free trade. Of course, the theory of comparative advantages *assumes* that trade is balanced and that there is full employment in all countries.[2] But the problems of maintaining balanced trade and full employment are deemed to lie strictly in the domain of macroeconomic policy. That is, balanced trade and full employment can be ensured simply by adopting the right fiscal and monetary policies, either with a flexible exchange rate or a "realistically" pegged exchange rate. In this view, there is no underlying problem of competitiveness which could foster a chronic tendency for trade surpluses and deficits to persist.[3]

This controversy has become particularly acute in recent years in the United States, where trade deficits have risen dramatically.[4] By 1986, the United States had a merchandise trade deficit of $147.7 billion, and a current account deficit of $141.4 billion, amounting to a record 3.5 percent of GNP. The mainstream argument which focuses on macroeconomic policies is important for understanding these extraordinary trade and current account deficits of the mid-1980s. The contractionary monetary policies of the Federal Reserve System in 1979–84, together with the enormous federal government budget deficits under Reagan starting in 1983 (caused by his tax cuts and increased military spending), are indeed responsible for pushing the trade deficit to unprecedented heights by the mid-1980s. I shall discuss why this was the case later in this article.

But the problem of the United States, trade deficit began before Paul Volcker took over the Fed in 1979 and Ronald Reagan occupied the White House in 1981. In 1977 and 1978, the merchandise trade deficits were already over $30 billion, which at the time represented about 1.5 percent of GNP. I shall argue that there was an underlying problem of a loss of competitiveness in the 1970s, which was only exacerbated by the macro policies of Volcker and Reagan in the early 1980s. Even if those policies are reversed (and the tight monetary policy was already reversed in 1985–86), the trade problem will not be permanently solved as long as the United States tends to fall behind in the competitiveness of its industries.

To understand the links between international competition and economic growth, we have to understand first how competition affects the trade balance, and then how the trade balance is connected to the accumulation of capital. I shall define international competitiveness as the relative price of imports compared to exports, measured in a common currency (e.g., U.S. dollars). If imports become relatively more expensive, then domestic products become more competitive with foreign products. A country will sell more to the rest of the world, and buy less from it, when domestic products are relatively cheaper, and conversely.

Price competitiveness, as defined here, clearly depends on the exchange rate which is used to convert foreign currency prices into domestic currency prices. If e is the "price of foreign exchange" (domestic currency/foreign currency), P_m* is the foreign currency price of imports, and P_x is the domestic currency price of exports, then the relative price of imports is eP_m*$/P_x$. Now most international economic models take the prices as given in the seller's currency, and focus entirely on changes in the exchange rate (e).[5] While changes in the exchange rate are certainly important, we also must investigate what determines the prices in each country's own currency.

Numerous studies have shown that the prices of industrial commodities can best be explained by the hypothesis that firms charge a fixed profit markup on unit labor costs.[6] This hypothesis can be represented by the pricing equation,

$$P = (1 + m)\, a\, w\,, \tag{1}$$

where m is the markup rate, a is the labor coefficient (hours per unit of output), and w is the money wage rate (per hour). Note that this is really a *gross* profit markup, which has to cover certain costs (materials, interest, salaries of managers, and other overheads) as well as to provide a net profit for the firm (which is divided between dividends paid to the stockholders, corporate income taxes, and corporate savings). To understand international competition, then, we have to understand what determines the variables a, w, and m.

The labor coefficient (a) is determined mainly by the technology which the firms have installed, but also depends on the social relations between labor and management which affect how hard workers are willing to (or can be made to) work. The money wage rate (w) is set in labor contracts and depends fundamentally on the relative bargaining power of workers and firms. This relative bargaining power in turn depends on such factors as the strength of unions, the intervention of governments, and general economic conditions (especially the unemployment rate and the alternative incomes available to unemployed workers). In addition, in less developed countries, wages can be depressed by the presence of a precapitalist sector which supplies labor to the capitalist sector that is willing to work for a very low income.

The markup rate (m) is the most difficult (and controversial) variable to explain. The studies referred to above show that m tends to be fairly constant in the short run, but varies in the long run. Kalecki (1971) took m as an index of the "degree of monopoly" in an industry, i.e., a reflection of the degree of concentration, barriers to entry, etc. Kalecki's interpretation can be made more meaningful if we remember that firms compete internationally, and that the "degree of monopoly" must be understood to reflect the openness of the national market to foreign competitors.

If we take the markup rate (m) as a variable which can vary in the long run, but not in the short run, then industrial prices are proportional to unit labor costs (aw) in the short run. This means that the price (P) will tend to increase at the same percentage rate as unit labor costs (aw) in equation (1). Now the labor coefficient (a) tends to *fall* over time as the *productivity* of labor (output per hour, 1/a) *increases*. Suppose, for example, that productivity grows at the rate of 2 percent per year, while money wages increase at the rate of 5 percent. Then unit labor costs will rise at the rate of 3 percent per year, determined by *subtracting* the 2 percent growth of productivity from the 5 percent increase in money wages. If the markup rate (m) remains constant, then the price (P) will also increase at the rate of 3 percent per year.

Let us assume for the moment that the country's exchange rate (e) remains fixed. Then the country's products will become more competitive if foreign prices rise by more than 3 percent per year, and less competitive if foreign prices rise by less than 3 percent. Assuming that the foreign profit markup rate is also constant, the foreign rate of price increase depends on the difference between the rate of increase of money wages and the growth rate of productivity abroad. For example, if foreign money wages increase by 6 percent, while foreign productivity grows by 4 percent, then foreign unit labor costs (and prices) will increase by only 2 percent, and foreign products will become relatively more competitive. But if foreign productivity grows by only 2 percent, then foreign prices will increase by 4 percent, and domestic products become more competitive. Thus the home country's products will become more competitive, and its trade balance will tend to improve, if its productivity increases faster, *relative* to money wages, *compared* to the rest of the world, and conversely.[7]

At this point, the reader may wonder whether this conclusion will hold up if we allow the exchange rate (e) to vary. Since the United States has had a "floating" or "flexible" (market-determined) exchange rate since 1973, this is an important question. It might seem that a flexible exchange rate system would provide an automatic adjustment mechanism that would offset changes in relative prices of imports and exports, thus eliminating any competitive advantages. The mechanism would work as follows: in a country with a trade deficit, the currency would tend to depreciate, thus making its products more competitive (relatively cheaper), and eliminating the deficit. In a surplus country, the currency would tend to appreciate in value, thus making its products less competitive (relatively more expensive), and eliminating the trade surplus.

This simple view of flexible exchange rates providing an automatic adjustment mechanism for the trade balance is no longer tenable. To understand why, it is essential to realize that the balance of trade is only part of the whole balance of payments of a country. The narrowest definition of the trade balance is the "merchandise trade balance," which equals exports minus imports of physical commodities. If we add in net exports of services, net "factor" income from abroad (wages, interest, and profits repatriated), and net transfers received (foreign aid and private gifts), we obtain a broader measure of a country's trade position, called the current account balance.

If there is a current account surplus or deficit, it must be compensated by net flows of internationally traded assets, such as bank deposits, bonds, and monetary reserves. A current account surplus implies that a country is a net lender ("capital exporter") to the rest of the world; a current account deficit implies that it is a net borrower ("capital importer"). To see this relationship, we can use the following identity:

$$\text{Current Account} = \text{Net Capital Outflow} = (S - I) + (T - G) . \qquad (2)$$

In this identity, S is private saving (which comes mostly out of profits),[8] I is gross domestic investment (replacement of depreciated capital plus net accumulation), T is tax revenue, and G is government spending. Note that T - G is the government budget surplus, which is negative if the government is running a deficit. This identity tells us that the current account balance must be equal to the net excess of domestic savings over investment and the budget deficit, which is the same as the country's net lending to the rest of the world (capital outflow).

In the last few decades, financial capital has become extremely mobile, with capitalists able to move large amounts of funds around the globe at a dizzying pace in pursuit of higher interest rates or other perceived advantages. In the short run at least, exchange rates seem to be determined more by these flows of financial capital rather than by the trade balance.[9] In the United States, for example, in the period 1980–85, while the trade and current account deficits rose to unprecedented heights,[10] the dollar appreciated by over 40 percent! The movements of the dollar were driven mainly by a rising interest rate differential in favor of the United States and a speculative bubble of currency traders betting on continued appreciation. Only in March, 1985, after the announcement of intervention by the United States and other governments, did the dollar finally begin to depreciate, five years after the trade deficits began to worsen.

We conclude, then, that flexible exchange rates do not provide an automatic equilibrating mechanism that can be relied on to eliminate real competitive advantages and disadvantages. It follows that trade imbalances due to genuine competitive advantages and disadvantages may have a tendency to persist, as long as the underlying differences in relative rates of productivity growth and wage increases persist. And persistent competitive advantages and disadvantages will result in chronic trade surpluses and deficits, respectively. Now the question we must consider is how trade surpluses and deficits affect a nation's economic growth.

Suppose that a country obtains a balance of trade surplus through improved competitiveness (say, due to more rapid productivity growth). Standard Keynesian macroeconomics tells us that the trade surplus should have positive multiplier effects on national income and employment in the short run. The higher national income will cause an increase in import demand which will limit the rise in the trade balance, but it should rise nevertheless. As the trade surplus increases national income, demand for industrial products rises, and capitalist firms respond by increasing production. The result is not only more employment of labor, but also a higher rate of capacity utilization in industry. Higher utilization of capacity means that firms can make more profits with the capital equipment they already have. Therefore, the rate of profit on capital invested (r = profit/capital) rises.

The increase in the profit rate then has a two-sided effect on capital accumulation. On the side of savings (S), a higher profit rate means that corporations will have more funds available, i.e., business savings will be higher. Some of these funds will be used internally within an individual corporation; others will be lent from one corporation to another through the banking system or the bond market. On the side of investment (I), a higher profit rate stimulates capitalists to desire to invest more, since it makes them more optimistic about future returns. Moreover, the increased utilization rate also stimulates investment demand, since firms are more likely to invest more when their existing capacity is more intensively utilized.[11] As a result of this two-sided stimulus, we can expect more investment and a higher rate of capital accumulation[12] to occur when there is a trade surplus. The economy of a country thus grows faster when it has a trade surplus. By the same logic, a country grows slower when it has a trade deficit.

This analysis confirms that economic growth will tend to be higher in countries with trade surpluses, and lower in countries with trade deficits, compared to what it would be otherwise. This implies that even free international trade, in the absence of any government intervention, can be a mechanism for fostering uneven development between nations. A country will grow faster *at the expense of its trading partners* if its rate of productivity growth increases, or its money wage increases slow down, so that its unit labor costs fall relative to the rest of the world. Conversely, a country will grow more slowly (to the benefit of its trading partners) if its productivity growth slows down, or its money wages rise faster, so that its unit labor costs rise compared to the rest of the world.

Note that this result does not necessarily imply that international competition always favors the rich or more advanced countries over the poor or less developed countries. Countries in either category may benefit or lose from international competition, depending on historical circumstances. In the present context, the main beneficiaries of this mechanism seem to be newly industrializing countries such as South Korea and Taiwan, which have been able to achieve very high rates of productivity growth by playing technological "catch-up," while holding down their money wage increases through repression of the labor movement (here, the governments do indeed play a role). The main losers are countries such as the United States and United Kingdom, which were once winners in the same game. Even Japan, which still has very large trade surpluses with the United States, is starting to feel the threat of stiff competition from the newly industrializing countries.

The preceding analysis has profound implications for international political economy. Capitalist firms located in different countries (regardless of their ownership) must compete with each other for shares of the world market. In order to compete successfully, firms must hold down their unit labor costs relative to their rivals. This means that the workers in the various nations are pitted against each other in a battle for jobs and incomes. In this sense, we can say that international trade relations establish *internation-al relations of production* between workers in different countries.

This aspect of international competition does not necessarily result from any conspiracy by the capitalists, or by any "unfair" intervention on the part of foreign governments (although governments may certainly aid capital in repressing workers' wage demands). The logic of the ("free") marketplace fosters this conflict between workers in different countries regardless of the degree or nature of state intervention. If workers in one country try to increase their wages more rapidly, without an offsetting increase in productivity growth, they will only succeed in making their products less competitive, and thus will reduce national income, employment, utilization, profitability, and growth.[13]

At this point, however, we must reconsider our assumption of a constant profit markup rate (m in equation 1). After all, the capitalists in a country do not have to accept reduced competitiveness if their unit labor costs rise relative to other countries'; the capitalists have the option of reducing their profit markups in order to hold prices down. Indeed, strong international competitive pressures could well force firms to lower their markups under certain circumstances. In this case, however, profits will constitute a smaller share of national income, and the rate of profit (r = profit/capital) will be lower for any given rate of capacity utilization.[14]

There is considerable evidence that this in fact occurred in the United States in the 1970s. A number of economists (e.g., Bruno and Sachs 1985; Wolff 1986) have identified a squeeze on corporate profits which resulted from a drop in the rate of productivity growth in the late 1960s and early 1970s, while money wage increases did not fall as much, at the same time as United States firms were facing intensified competition from other countries (Japan, the newly industrializing countries of Asia and Latin America, etc.). The result was that United States firms were forced to accept lower profit markup rates, as documented by Nordhaus (1974). As we would expect, the profit share of national income and the profit rate (r) both fell. With profitability thus reduced, domestic investment demand fell off (or shifted abroad), and the economy entered a period of sluggish growth. At the same time, rapidly rising unit labor costs, combined with the oil price increases of 1973–74 and 1979–80, led to worsening inflation. The resulting combination of rising prices with stagnant growth became known as "stagflation."

This brings us to the point where we must bring macroeconomic policy into the story. Let us return to the late 1970s. In response to the rising trade deficits of the period 1977–78 (discussed above), the Carter administration pursued an expansionary monetary policy deliberately designed to depreciate the dollar in 1978–79. The trade deficit did fall somewhat, from about 1.5 percent of GNP in 1977–78 to about 0.9 percent in 1979–80. But rising import prices (due to the depreciation itself), coupled with a new oil price increase by OPEC, only added fuel to the inflationary fires. The inflation counteracted the positive effects of the depreciation on competitiveness, while destroying confidence in the dollar in financial markets. This in turn led to a major policy reversal, as Carter appointed Volcker to head the Federal Reserve System in October, 1979, with a mandate to contract the money supply in order to suppress inflation and restore the value of the dollar. The effort to eliminate the trade deficit through depreciation was thus abandoned.

Volcker's tight money policies halted the decline of the dollar of the Carter years, but at the expense of very high interest rates that crushed investment demand and produced a recession in 1980. In fact, the policy-induced recession of 1980 was a factor in Carter's defeat at the polls that November, as Reagan promised to "put America back to work." After Reagan took office, Volcker maintained generally contractionary monetary policies through early 1982. While the dollar began to appreciate in 1981–82, the economy soon plunged into the deepest recession of the postwar period. When the unemployment rate hit a forty-year high of 10.7 percent in November–December, 1982, even many mainstream economists began to call the downturn a "depression." Reagan's campaign talk of "putting America back to work" sounded like a cruel joke.

The United States economy began to recover from this depression in 1983. Two factors were primarily responsible. First, the Fed temporarily eased up on the money supply in the second half of 1982 and the first half of 1983, in a deliberate effort to prevent a financial collapse. And second, Reagan's infamous tax cuts began to take effect in 1982–83 and increased the following year. Although he did make massive cuts in social spending, he did not get all the spending cuts he wanted through Congress, and the cuts that took place were more than outweighed by the rapid increases in military spending. The result was a federal government budget deficit that soared from $64 billion in 1981 to $198 billion in 1985.

What were the effects of this sharply increased deficit? In the short run, the rising deficit certainly acted as a demand stimulus which helped to pull the economy out of the 1982 recession, as predicted by standard Keynesian macro theory.[15] But this expansionary impact of the budget deficit was restrained by a return to tight monetary policy by the Fed in the second half of 1983. In fact, M1 growth slowed down to 6 percent in 1984, the lowest rate since 1975 (when the economy plunged into a recession), while the budget deficit already stood at $170 billion. With the supply of funds thus artificially restrained by the Fed, the government's need to borrow to cover its rising deficit pushed up United States real interest rates even further, relative to foreign real interest rates. The result was an enormous net inflow of financial capital into the United States (part of which was a return of American funds from abroad) in pursuit of the higher interest rates. This in turn increased global demand for dollars relative to other currencies, and thus pushed up the value of the dollar even further. By early 1985, the dollar had appreciated over 40 percent compared to 1980.[16]

The appreciation of the dollar (fall in e) made United States products much less competitive than they had already become, and thus contributed to the record trade deficits of the mid-1980s. In addition, the growth of income in the recovery increased United States demand for imports, while contractionary macro policies abroad (especially in Japan and West Germany) held down demand for United States exports, thus further worsening the trade balance.

We can use identity (2) to gain more insights into the connections between the government budget deficit and the international trade deficit. An increase in the budget deficit is equivalent to a lower budget surplus, T - G. The reduction in T - G must be balanced either by a reduction in investment relative to saving (rise in S - I) or by a reduction in the current account. Since capital flows into the United States were relatively elastic, the pressure on domestic investment was relieved by large capital inflows, reflected in the current account deficit. In fact, by 1986, the total government (federal, state and local) budget deficit of $143.1 billion[17] was almost exactly matched by a current account deficit of $141.4 billion, with no appreciable difference between domestic savings and investment.

What this means is that, by 1986, the trade (current account) deficit completely cancelled out the stimulating effects of the budget deficit on aggregate demand.[18] This result points to a fundamental difference between domestic and foreign sources of demand in their ability to promote economic growth. We saw previously that an autonomous improvement in the trade balance, due to increased competitiveness, has lasting positive effects on profitability and growth. In this sense, growth can be "export-led." But a domestic demand stimulus, such as Reagan's tax cut, has only a temporary positive effect on profits and output in an open economy. Once the resulting current account deficit grows sufficiently to offset the government budget deficit, the stimulus to aggregate demand is blunted; there is no stimulus to long-run growth.

The contradictions of "Reaganomics" thus leave the United States perched on an economic precipice in the late 1980s. Starting in 1985, the Fed completely reversed its policy and began the most rapid expansion of the money supply in postwar history; M1 grew by 16.6 percent in 1986. This expansionary policy achieved its immediate objective of reducing interest rates and driving the value of the dollar back down, at least against the major European currencies and the Japanese yen. But the trade and current account deficits continued to set new records in 1986, and the United States rapidly surpassed Brazil as the world's largest net debtor country.

Why has the falling dollar not produced the hoped for improvement in the trade balance? For one thing, trade flows typically respond to changes in exchange rates with a lag, as it takes consumers and producers time to change their buying patterns to take advantage of the relatively cheaper domestic products. This is known as the "J-curve" effect: the trade balance typically gets worse before it gets better after a depreciation. But there are other factors at work. The dollar actually continued to rise in 1985–86 against the currencies of most newly industrializing countries (e.g., South Korea and Mexico), while these countries accounted for a rising share of United States imports. Furthermore, many United States firms had relocated their productive facilities in less developed countries in order to take advantage of their lower wages. Since the dollar has not depreciated against the currencies of those countries anyway, the firms that have invested in those countries have no incentives to abandon their new investments and restore production in the United States. And finally, there has been no significant change in fiscal policy. As long as the budget deficits continue to necessitate net foreign borrowing in excess of $100 billion per year, the United States will have to continue to run a large current account deficit.

A serious reduction in the federal government budget deficit would certainly help to improve the trade balance in the late 1980s or early 1990s. But the tax increases and/or spending cuts required to accomplish this would also have a depressing effect on the economy in the short run. And even if the United States were to endure such a recession or depression, it would not emerge with a permanent solution to its trade problems. To be sure, sufficient sacrifices of national income would reduce import demand, and thus could improve the trade and current account balances for a few years. But these sacrifices would not help to restore United States industrial competitiveness. On the contrary, a period of depressed demand would probably reduce precisely the kind of investment in

new productive capacity which could raise productivity growth and improve competitiveness in the long run. Thus, far from reversing the long-term loss of competitiveness,
the after-effects of Reaganomics are likely to accelerate that trend.

If the long-term loss of competitiveness of United States industries continues, any
improvement in the trade balance due to cuts in the budget deficit will prove to be
temporary, and trade deficits will continue to be a chronic problem for the United States
economy. This sobering conclusion raises the question of what can be done. Clearly, we
cannot expect free trade to solve a problem which we have seen to be endemic in
capitalist competition. Trying to convince other countries to abandon their "unfair trade
practices" is also unlikely to be very effective, and only begs the question of why the
United States should not imitate foreign practices which have allegedly been so successful in promoting exports. The only progressive alternative is to manage international
trade relations (along with macro policies) in such a way as to prevent international
conflicts over growth and employment opportunities. The prospects for such a progressive alternative are explored in the article by John Willoughby in this volume.

NOTES

1. Note that in this article we are concerned mainly with the location of the production process,
rather than with the national ownership of the firms. The competitiveness of a country's domestic
products in this sense may depend on the role of foreign capital in the country. By the same token,
"foreign" competition may actually take the form of the overseas products of a country's own
multinational corporations.
2. The assumption of full employment is implicit in models of trade where each country always
produces on its "production possibility frontier." The assumption of balanced trade appears in
the treatment of trade relations as the direct barter of one commodity for another commodity (e.g.,
wheat for cloth) in "pure" trade models. Without money or financial assets in the models, trade
surpluses and deficits cannot arise.
3. For a typical argument in favor of this view see McCulloch (1986).
4. See Figure 1 in the article by John Willoughby in this volume.
5. This is the practice in the derivation of the Marshall–Lerner condition in the "elasticities
approach" to the balance of payments.
6. These studies include Nordhaus (1974) and Coutts, Godley and Nordhaus (1978). More
complex versions of this hypothesis include materials costs together with the wages of production
workers as the base on which the markup is calculated. For our purposes, the simpler version is
sufficient.
7. This point was first made by Robinson (1946–47).
8. In the United States in 1986, gross private domestic savings totaled $680.5 billion, of which
only $116.3 billion (about 17 percent) were personal savings; the remaining $564.2 billion (or 83
percent) were business savings (including depreciation allowances).
9. This shift is recognized in the new "asset markets" and "portfolio balance" models of the
exchange rate which have come to dominate international monetary economics in recent years.
10. In 1980, the United States had a merchandise trade deficit of $25.5 billion and a current
account surplus of $13.0 billion. By 1985, the trade deficit was $124.4 billion and the current
account registered a deficit of $115.2 billion.
11. This theory of investment is based on Steindl (1952) and supported by the empirical evidence
of Fazzari and Mott (1986–87).

12. The rate of capital accumulation in the present context may be defined as (I-dK)/K, where K is the existing capital stock, d is the depreciation rate, and therefore dK is replacement investment and (I-dK) is net investment.

13. Of course, if workers in all countries simultaneously increase their wages faster, the anti-competitive effects will cancel out, and none of these negative results need occur. Marx's admonition, ''Workers of all countries unite!'' is thus seen to have a logical foundation in terms of the workers' self-interest.

14. The formula for the rate of profit is $r = \pi u / k$, where $\pi = m/(1+m)$ is the profit share of national income, u is the rate of capacity utilization, and k is the capital-capacity output ratio.

15. This is ironic, since Reagan campaigned as an anti-Keynesian ''supply sider,'' who believed that tax cuts would have magical effects in stimulating savings, investment, and productivity. In fact, the personal savings rate decreased under Reagan, while investment rates and productivity growth did not show any long-term improvement (after the cyclical recovery of 1983–84).

16. For two views of how monetary and fiscal policy affected the value of the dollar and the trade balance in the early 1980s see Epstein (1985) and Dornbusch (1987).

17. A federal deficit of $204.0 billion was partly offset by state and local government surpluses of $60.8 billion.

18. For further discussion of this point see the article by Tom Michl in this volume.

PART FIVE

MACROECONOMIC POLICY

22

Accumulation and State Intervention in the 1980s: A Crisis of Reproduction

JOHN A. MILLER

INTRODUCTION

In the United States, a lingering crisis of accumulation and the fiscal crisis of the state are two of the hallmarks of the 1980s. In the last eight years we have lived through the worst economic conditions since the Great Depression — a severe contraction followed by a hollow recovery (led by military spending and consumption, not investment), the deindustrialization of our economy and the decline of the international competitiveness of its basic industry, financial exhiliration mixed with financial crises, a widening gulf between rich and poor, and a dramatic increase in the incidence of poverty. At the same time, the growth of federal government expenditures, the fuel for the remilitarizing of the economy, has continuously outstripped the growth of federal government revenues, drastically reduced by a pro-rich cut in taxes on individual income and corporate profits. The result has been unprecedented peacetime deficits that have more than doubled the total public debt in less than a decade.

The relationship between these two crises of the 1980s — the crisis of accumulation and the fiscal crisis of the state — and the effect of each on the other is the subject matter of this essay. It addresses two questions: (1) how has the crisis of accumulation shaped the fiscal crisis of the state and the enormous budget deficits of the 1980s? and, (2) what role has the large state sector and the state spending and taxing policies in the 1980s played in the accumulation process? — has the state been a ''prop'' or a ''burden'' for accumulation in the 1980s?

The answers to these two questions developed in detail here argue that the crisis of the accumulation process and the fiscal crisis of the state in the 1980s combine to define a more general crisis of reproduction for the United States economy. United States policies of the 1980s — a massive military buildup, the slashing of social spending, and the pardoning of capital from taxation — promote short-term profitability (the production of surplus value) at the expense of the reproduction of the productive capacity of the economy, the reproduction of the conditions of everyday life for the working class, and even the reproduction of the state itself (a fiscal crisis of the state).

ACCUMULATION AND THE FISCAL CRISIS OF THE STATE

Traditional Macroeconomics

For traditional macroeconomics it is a matter of sharp debate whether the instability of the macroeconomy and the poor economic performance of the 1980s has caused the fiscal crisis of the state and its large deficit; or, if the state, its interventionist policies, and large deficits have caused the instability and poor economic performance in the 1980s.

For those macroeconomists who rely on a supply-side analysis the source of the economic instability of the 1980s is government intervention: either through the size of government and its incentive-stifling taxes and regulations (Reagan 1982); or monetary-fiscal policies (or shocks) which propel the economy along the ups and downs of an equilibrium business cycle (Friedman and Schwartz 1969; Lucas 1977).[1] The cure for the economic instability of the 1980s, of course, is to dislodge the impediment to economic growth, i.e. government. Reduce incentive-stifling taxes, slow the growth of federal spending and regulations (Reagan 1982); eliminate government stabilization policies that confound rational actors by making it impossible for them to distinguish between general changes and relative changes in prices (Lucas 1977); or, restrict active government stabilization policies by nailing monetary and fiscal policy to a cross of rules (Friedman 1971). Still the practice of conservative economics in the 1980s has been just the opposite, increasing the relative size of government, and incurring unprecedented peacetime deficits.

For other macroeconomists, those who rely on a demand-side analysis, the Walrasian auctioneer is a great myth (Tobin 1980:34) and any capitalist economy "needs to be stabilized, can be stabilized, and therefore should be stabilized by the appropriate monetary and fiscal policy" (Modigliani 1977:17). The poor economic performance of the 1980s has necessitated active government stabilization policies which have forced the government to incur deficits (Eckstein 1979). On the other hand, the structural deficit — the portion of the deficit that would persist even if the economy was at full employment — is a matter of concern, for when combined with restrictive monetary policy (like that of the early 1980s) it drives up real interest rates and restricts private investment (Rivlin 1984; Aaron et al. 1986). Nonetheless, for these Keynesians, government stabilization policies are not the source of the economic instability of the last fifteen years. In fact, if anything, government stabilization policies have been insufficiently expansionary over this period (Eisner 1986).

The Marxist Tradition
For Marxist political economy there is no question that the private economy itself is inherently unstable — dynamic but unstable — and no Marxist crisis theory identifies the state as the cause of the economic crisis of the 1980s. Here, a lack of profitability for private investment is both the immediate cause of the crisis of accumulation in the 1980s and the ultimate cause of the fiscal crisis of the state: "the tendency of government revenues to outrace revenues" (O'Connor 1973: 2). In fact, the fiscal crisis of the state and large deficits are but a sympton of the crisis of private profitability (Magdoff and Sweezy 1987:107). The crisis management policies of the state — expenditures to prop up failing business and pro-rich tax cuts — transform a crisis of profitability of the private sector into fiscal crisis of the public sector.

THE EFFECT OF STATE INTERVENTION ON ACCUMULATION

Points of Agreements in Marxist Theory
While Marxist political economy endorses the Keynesian depiction of the deficit as a by-product of the state's crisis management policies and not the cause of the crisis, a Marxist analysis of the effect on government intervention on economic crises and the

accumulation process is fundamentally different from the Keynesian analysis. Specifically, every Marxist political economist rejects, at least in part, two of the central premises of Keynesian theory: (1) "that a government will maintain full employment in a capitalist economy if it only knows how to do it" (Kalecki 1971:140); and, (2) "that the form of state expenditures [e.g. military spending, social welfare, or domestic government services] are unimportant to their impact on income and employment" (Mosley 1982:27).

Both of these Keynesian propositions are based on the assumption of a harmony of interests between the working class and the capitalist class. In a Marxist analysis, class conflict, not harmony, is the key to understanding the making of macroeconomic policy. This makes a difference.

For instance, in Keynesian theory the goal of macroeconomic policy is full employment through the promotion of profitable investment (Stein 1969:464). In Marxist theory, the goal of the macroeconomic policy of the capitalist state is the promotion of capitalist profits; a goal which is incompatible with the permanent full employment of workers (Boddy and Crotty 1975). A regime of continuous full employment would bring with it rising wages, increasing costs of production, and decreasing profits. Even more importantly, with continuous full employment, the social position of the boss would be undermined as the threat of unemployment was removed. To maximize corporate profits and maintain capitalist control over the production process, output must vary. The monetary and fiscal policy of the capitalist state ensures that that variation occurs by managing periodic downturns which suppress wages and discipline workers by turning workers out of their jobs. Stabilization policies in the postwar period, which in peacetime have never been sufficiently expansionary to promote full employment, exhibit this pattern, called the political business cycle (Boddy and Crotty 1975; Bowles, Gordon and Weisskopf 1984).

This remains true in the 1980s. Even after a credit crunch enforced a sharp recession (which induced wage constraint and tamed labor militancy) and was followed by now almost five years of expansion, the economy has not approached full employment.

For Keynes, it mattered not on what the state expended its monies — a railroad from London to York, building pyramids, or even digging up bottles filled with old bank notes — but that compensatory government spending with its multiplier effect took place (Keynes 1964). In the class analysis of political economy, the content of the state budget — the use values the state purchases or creates — is a matter of vital importance. Every government budget is a "class-budget" and the spending it commissions must be evaluated in light of its effect on the standard of living of the working class and its effect on the profitability of capitalist investment. The content of the state budget has a profound effect on the ability of state intervention to restructure the conditions for profitable investment by the capitalist class and on the impact of state spending on the everyday life of the working class. In the 1980s, the form of state expenditures is especially crucial because the Reagan budgets, while not reducing the relative size of government, have instituted a "class-war" intent on abolishing working class gains secured through the growth of the welfare state (e.g. expenditures on social insurance, housing, education) and remilitarizing the economy (Piven and Cloward 1982).

Just as the form of government expenditures and the content of the expenditure side of the government budget are important in a Marxist analysis of the effect of state intervention on the accumulation process, so too is the form of government finances and the content of the revenue side of the government budget. As opposed to Keynesian theory that focuses on the volume of taxes, in Marxist crisis theory the most crucial question is the class incidence of taxation; who bears the burden of financing the state — capital or labor? The answer to this question determines both the degree of tax exploitation of the working class and, the potential for state intervention to effect profitability and accumulation — both of which have been dramatically altered by the tax changes of the 1980s that shifted more and more of the tax burden onto labor and away from capital.

Differences in Marxist Theory Based on the Cause of Economic Crises

Like traditional macroeconomics, Marxist political economy has supply-side theories and demand-side theories (Foster 1982). While neither side identifies the state as the cause of economic crises, their emphasis on supply-side or demand-side factors as the cause of economic crisis shapes their quite different assessments of the ability of the state to promote accumulation. The more a theory emphasizes supply factors as the cause of crisis, the more limited the ability it assigns to the state to promote accumulation; and, the more a theory emphasizes demand factors as the cause of crisis, the greater the ability it assigns to the state to promote accumulation. For instance, the orthodox falling rate of profit theory, a supply-side theory of economic crises, assigns only a limited ability for the state to promote accumulation. On the other hand, the neo-Marxist underconsumption theories of the Monthly Review School, a demand-side theory of economic crises, assigns the state a powerful if historically circumscribed ability to promote accumulation. A brief discussion of these two cases, the dominant traditions in Marxist political economy in the postwar period, reveals the theoretical basis for different Marxist analyses of state intervention in the 1980s.

The Orthodox Falling Rate of Profit Theory. The orthodox writers' view of the ineffectiveness of state action originates in their analysis of economic crisis.[2] Using Marx's value categories they argue that the cause of crises is a relative lack of profitability or surplus value at the point of production, the supply-side of the economy. Capital costs (or the organic composition of capital; the ratio of constant capital to variable capital) increase more quickly than the exploitation of labor, the source of profits, causing a lack of profitability (surplus value) relative to total capital advanced, which in turn means the aggregate rate of profit falls and retards the accumulation process. Here, a lack of effective demand is only a reflection of a lack of profitability (surplus value) at the point of production. As a result, Keynesian demand management policies cannot resolve the crisis for they are incapable of addressing its cause. From this perspective, state expenditures are unproductive of profits and incapable of promoting accumulation in a "double sense" (Wright 1979:154).

The value rate of profit $(s/c+v)$, a measure of the aggregate profitability of private investment, illustrates the orthodox position. First, state revenues, principally taxes, come directly or indirectly from the profits (surplus value) already created by productive labor in the private economy. All taxes are profit (or surplus value) absorbing. This holds if taxes fall on capital or labor. In the former case, taxes directly take profits (surplus value) from capital, and, in the latter case, taxes indirectly take profits (surplus value) that capital would have expropriated from labor in the absence of the tax. Second, for these theorists, state expenditures cannot add to profits (surplus value). Here, while state expenditures might redistribute already produced profits (surplus value) from one industry to another, they can do nothing to augment the total profitability of the system.

Most simply, state revenues reduce the numerator of the profit equation and state expenditures are incapable of increasing that numerator. Hence, the state cannot increase the value rate of profit, the aggregate profitability of private investment, and cannot resolve the crisis. The state is an unquestionable, albeit a necessary, drag on the accumulation of capital.

In this supply-side theory, the best the state can hope to do is to move the locus of crisis from a crisis of profitability in the private sector to a fiscal crisis of the public sector. In fact, for these writers, the expansion of the not-for-profit state represents the erosion of the long-term profitability of private capital and is every bit as much a sign of a deepening crises as the short-term deflationary crises it might postpone (Yaffe 1973:217).

Neo-Marxist Underconsumption Theories. The neo-Marxist underconsumption theory, developed by the Monthly Review School, emphasizes the importance of demand factors and state policies in the monopoly economy of the postwar period.[3] They maintain that the increased concentration of the modern economy and the accompanying oligopolistic price mechanisms increase the relative share of output going to capital and decrease the share going to labor. As a result, "monopoly capitalism" suffers from a chronic lack of consumption demand, for which investment demand provides insufficient compensation, and has an overwhelming long-run tendency toward stagnation (high unemployment and excessive capacity).

In their model the portion of the product that labor receives is approximately equal to "essential consumption" while the remainder of the product is the "economic surplus" and represents potential profits (Baran and Sweezy 1966:9). These writers posit a tendency for the economic surplus of investable funds to rise absolutely and relatively under monopoly capitalism. The most crucial problem faced by the system is absorbing this rising surplus of investable funds in order to realize potential profits and counteract its tendency toward stagnation.

Government spending is the most important mechanism that monopoly capitalism has for absorbing surplus (or investable funds) for "it can create income by bringing idle capital and labor into production" (Baran and Sweezy 1966:175). The state can do this because taxes necessarily sop up the rising surplus of investable funds; if income can be taxed away by the state it must have been beyond essential consumption. In addition, state expenditures don't add to the rising surplus, but rather counteract stagnation by augmenting a private demand that is insufficient to absorb a rising surplus of investable funds.

While these writers see government spending as massive enough to counteract the tendency of monopoly capitalism toward stagnation as a logical possibility, they do not regard it as a real historical possibility for several reasons. First, government expenditures cannot be increased to the level necessary to counteract stagnation without coming into conflict with the private production of profit. Second, government expenditures over time become increasingly "irrational," "wasteful," and "destructive." Military spending is the chief example of this tendency. Third, the government spending (along with the expansion of credit) necessary to counteract the tendency toward stagnation engenders an accelerating inflation that has rendered Keynesian stabilization policies ineffective (Magdoff and Sweezy 1974). In short, for this demand-side theory, the state is a prop for the accumulation process, but a contradiction-laden one.

A MARXIST THEORY OF STATE INTERVENTION
AND ACCUMULATION

While the orthodox falling rate of profit theory and the neo-Marxist underconsumption theory establish the range of Marxist analyses of state intervention, neither theory, as traditionally presented, is adequate for analyzing the economic role of state expenditure and taxing policies in 1980s. Rather the analysis of economic crises and state intervention presented by both traditions need to be amended to recognize two propositions: (1) that both capital and labor finance the state; and, (2) that state expenditures have both demand-side and supply-side effects.

Capital and Labor Finance the State

In the real world the final burden of taxation is determined by the ebb and flow of class conflict, and will vary with the economic and political strength of the contending classes (Gough 1979:126). It is not true that the state is always financed out of profits (surplus value) regardless if taxes fall on capital and take profits (surplus value) directly or take "disguised profits" (surplus value) from labor (as argued by the orthodox falling rate of profit theory). Nor is the state always financed out of the economic surplus of investable funds (as the underconsumption theorists contend). In the first theory the state is always financed at the expense of capitalist profits and in the second theory the financing of the state always benefits capitalist profits. Both eliminate any class struggle over the burden of taxes.

To the extent that capital wins the struggle over taxes it forces the burden of financing the state onto labor. The more taxes fall on labor, the more taxes do not absorb profits and do not hinder potential accumulation. The remainder of the tax burden falls on capital and absorbs profits, reducing the amount of profits that capital has available to throw back into accumulation in the next round of production and, thus, impede the expansion of capital. Thus the outcome of these "tax struggles," determined by the balance of class forces, in turn, determines the potential of the state to promote accumulation.

State Expenditures Have Supply-Side and Demand-Side Effects

The analysis of economic crises and state intervention on both sides of the Marxist tradition is plagued by the failure of each to investigate the other side of the economy; the orthodox theorists neglect the realization of surplus value (on the demand-side), and the neo-Marxists neglect the production of the economic surplus (on the supply-side). This limits the analysis of the effect of the state on the accumulation process in each theory.

Theories of state intervention and accumulation must recognize both the supply-side effects (socializing the cost of reproducing capital and labor) and the demand-side effects (realizing profits or surplus value) of state expenditure. Thus, any examination of the effect of state expenditures on private profitability and the accumulation process needs to address two questions: (1) which expenditures are "productive" of surplus value (or profits): the demand-side effect; and (2) which expenditures are "reproductive" of capital, labor, and the economy: the supply-side effect (Gough 1979: Appendix B; Foster and Szlajfer 1984:325–349).

My answer to the first question, the demand-side question, is the following: state purchases from private capital (e.g. arms procurements) are "productive" of profits (surplus value) because they realize profits embodied in commodities produced by exploited labor under the control of private capital. State services and transfers, neither of which are under the direct control of capital, are unproductive of profits (surplus value) because they don't directly commission the private production for profit (Rose 1977).

The supply-side question, must be answered in a different way. State expenditures are "reproductive" if they provide services (use values) that reproduce, at least in part, capital and labor for the next round of production and thereby support the accumulation of capital by lowering private capital costs. For example, state spending on housing, education, and social security all socialize the cost of reproducing a well-trained and able-bodied work force, while state spending on research and development and on infrastructure (like highways or industrial parks) all socialize the capital costs of production. All other state expenditures are unreproductive and neither socialize the cost of reproducing the system nor reduce the cost of production for private capital.[4]

In sum, the state can promote accumulation and increase aggregate profitability by taking revenues from productive labor and either purchasing products from private capital (a demand-side effect) or providing reproductive services, especially for capital (a supply-side effect). The more state revenues come from labor, and the more state expenditures are purchases from private capital, the less there will be a drain on profits. In fact, the state acting as a collective consumer can guide profit generation into a new area, commissioning the expansion of productive capacity and guaranteeing a demand for output. The more revenues come from labor, and the more expenditures are reproductive services, especially for capital, the greater the state's ability to increase private profitability and promote accumulation in existing areas of production.

THE STATE AND THE ECONOMY IN THE 1980s:
A CRISIS OF REPRODUCTION

The outstanding features of state spending and taxing policies in the 1980s have been:
(1) a massive military buildup fueled by arms purchases;
(2) the slashing of the domestic budget;
(3) a dramatic shift of the tax burden away from capital and onto the working class;
(4) unprecedented peacetime structural deficits.

Using the theoretical categories developed above, we can see that each of these policies represents a political victory for capital that has worked to restore accumulation in the short term. At the same time, these policies provide "instant gratification" for capital only at the cost of (1) eroding the long-term conditions for the reproduction of capital, labor, and even the state and, (2) sustaining a hollow recovery lacking in fixed investment. For instance, from 1982 to 1985, the level of fixed domestic investment was anemic, about two-thirds of the postwar average (Aaron et al. 1986:23). In addition, fixed investment in producer durables was concentrated in just two sectors, high tech products and autos for business, sectors more closely associated with finance and sales than production (Magdoff and Sweezy 1987:70–74). This "Strange Recovery" is, at least in part, the unfortunate but logical result of the state policies of the 1980s. All four features of those policies, described above, have contributed to that result.

For example, the Reagan Administration accelerated the military build-up begun in 1978 under the Carter Administration, by increasing military spending 40 percent in real terms from FY 1981 to FY 1986 so that military-related spending now represents about one-third of federal outlays instead of one-fourth (Aaron et al. 1986:68). State purchases of military hardware, the special emphasis of the Reagan budget, are an example of state expenditures that are "productive" of profits (surplus value). Military purchases guide capital into new areas that counter stagnation by providing for the production and realization of (profits) surplus value through a guaranteed demand. These expenditures are not necessarily a drain on profits (surplus value). To the extent that they are financed by taxes on labor, which has largely been the case in the 1980s, they can support private profitability (surplus-value). As a result, the Reagan program of military spending, financed by the working class, and unprecedented peacetime deficits is a prop for accumulation, at least over the short term.

While military purchases are "productive" of profits (surplus value) for the individual capitalist, they are "unreproductive" of capital and labor for the economy. Military spending commissions the production of commodities (use values) that contributes to the reproduction of neither labor nor capital. Military purchases divert labor and capital away from the reproduction of the economic infrastructure; they dedicate more and more of the economy to the production of "unreproductive" articles — actually, destructive articles.

Hence, state expenditures on armaments present capital with the following dilemma: do the short-term demand-side benefits of military purchases (realizing surplus value) outweigh the long-term supply-side cost of the restructuring of the economy toward unreproductive production (Foster and Szlajfer 1984)? The remilitarizing of the economy makes clear the Reagan solution to this dilemma; a solution almost as dangerous as the arms it creates.

The slashing of the domestic budget, like the military build-up, is also in the interest of capital. But it too comes at the expense of reproducing the economy. This dismantling of the welfare state (cutting $30 billion from entitlement programs from FY 1981 to FY 1985) (Bluestone and Havens 1986:24) is an attack on working class gains that have increased the social cost of production (the sum of private and public costs of reproduction). These cuts (e.g. cuts in spending on education, housing, unemployment insurance, and even social security benefits) reduce the societal wage bill and don't increase private costs. In fact, they should limit one of the ways in which the state acts as a drain on profits (surplus value). Nonetheless, these policies do have a cost for capital. They jeopardize the reproduction of the working class, an able-bodied work force, and slow the growth of the productivity of labor.

The importance of tax policies in the state's effort to promote accumulation in the current period can not be overstated. By reducing the relative tax burden of capital, the tax policies of the postwar period have increased the profitability of private investment, have tried to provide capital with the funds to invest, and have granted state spending programs, like the Reagan program, the potential to promote accumulation. The Economic Recovery Act of 1981 and the Social Security Acts of 1977 and 1983 played a key role in this restructuring of the tax burden. The 1981 act dramatically reduced the taxation of corporate profits, through wildly accelerated depreciation allowances and an enlarged investment tax credit, and cut taxes on the income of the well-to-do by lowering the maximum tax rate for capital income. At the same time, however, the tax acts of 1977 and 1983 guaranteed that payroll taxes on wages continued to increase steadily in the 1980s. As a result, by 1986 the corporate income accounted for less than one-tenth of federal revenues (as opposed to one-fourth in 1960) and social security taxes provided over one-third of federal revenues (as opposed to one-sixth in 1960). The combined effect of these changes has been to shift a larger share of financing state expenditures onto labor and away from capital, or to grant those expenditures the potential to promote accumulation.

In this context, the tax "reform" of 1986 must be seen less as a reform of the discrepancy between the nominal and the effective rates of the federal income tax and more as the consolidation of the gains capital has enjoyed under the tax policies of the postwar period. The repeal of the investment tax credit is hardly just compensation for the dismantling of the corporate income tax. Nor is the modest increase of income that can be earned before taxing begins a fair return for the gutting of the hope of a progessive individual income tax.

Attempting to pardon capital from taxation, however, has an even greater cost; it robs the state of its ability to reproduce itself and saddles it with a large deficit. The Economic Recovery Act of 1981 has contributed more to the deficits of the 1980s than any other policy change (Rivlin 1984:31). In fact, the restoration of the corporate income tax to its effective rate in 1957, alone, would eliminate three-fourths of the deficit in the 1980s (Medlen 1984).

While the tendency of government expenditures to exceed government revenues is not new — federal government expenditures have exceeded federal government revenues in 19 of the last 20 years — the Reagan deficits are different. They have averaged about 2.7 percent of GNP as opposed to the 1 percent of GNP averaged by the 14 deficits of the 1960s and 1970s (Albelda 1987:13). In addition, for the first time in peacetime, the federal government has run large structural deficits. The need to abandon the hope of balancing the budget, even in the unlikely event of full employment, speaks to the depth of the economic crisis that government taxing and expenditure policies must counteract. Relying on the deficit to finance one-fifth of its outlays, testifies to the state's inability to reproduce itself in the 1980s.

Plans to balance the budget need to be considered in light of the expenditure and taxing policies that brought about large structural deficits; the military buildup and a pro-capital tax cut. For instance, the Gramm-Rudman Balanced Budget and Emergency Deficit Control Act of 1985 must be seen less as a deficit reduction plan and more as an attempt to eliminate the possibility of redressing the tremendous change in the composition of federal government expenditures begun in 1978. While it is true that this act would cut in equal proportion social programs essential for the reproduction of everyday life and military expenditures that prop up accumulation, it nonetheless would consolidate the gains of capital in the struggle over the government budget. Even the wholesale exemption of some social programs (like social security, Medicaid and Medicare, and student aid) from the Gramm-Rudman cuts, does not make it otherwise. Of course, even the "fair-minded" reduction in government support of the accumulation process proposed by Gramm-Rudman is a threat to the continuation of the expansion of capital.

CONCLUSION

Will the Reagan program, which is capable of promoting recovery in the short term, bring about the sustained expansion of capital? The answer to that question is not clear. While military purchases, financed through Reagan's pro-capital tax policies and the deficit, are a prop for accumulation, they alone can not guarantee that the United States economy will escape the 1980s without suffering another major downturn — perhaps even worse than that of 1982. One thing is clear, however. Reagan has fashioned a program that requires us to sacrifice more and more of what is necessary to sustain everyday life at the altar of capital accumulation. Our task is to stand up against such a program and its disastrous consequences.

NOTES

1. For a fuller discussion of this issue see the articles by Francis Green and Tom Michl in this volume.
2. See Mattick (1969) and Yaffe (1973) for classic formulations of the orthodox analysis of economic crises and the state. DeBrunhoff (1979) offers a revision of this position that gives more recognition to the role of the state in managing the economy.
3. Baran and Sweezy (1966) contains the essence of what remains the neo-Marxist underconsumptionist position. Foster (1986) gives a theoretical update to this position. Magdoff and Sweezy (1987) provides an analysis of the economic crisis of the 1980s written from this perspective.
4. State expenditures that reproduce capital and state expenditures that reproduce labor should not be treated in the same manner. Every increase in state spending to reproduce capital will necessarily reduce the private cost of reproducing capital. But once we explicitly recognize the class struggle between capital and labor over the government budget and the social wage (government services primarily benefit labor) an increase in expenditures to reproduce labor does not necessarily reduce the private cost of reproducing labor. Instead, it may increase the total societal wage bill (Gough 1979; Bowles et al. 1984). Thus, only reproductive expenditures for capital unambiguously reduce the cost of private production and increase the private rate of profit.

23

Federal Reserve Behavior and the Limits of Monetary Policy in the Current Economic Crisis

GERALD EPSTEIN

INTRODUCTION

In August 1979, virtually everyone with wealth and in the know were trying to get out of dollars. They were buying land. They were buying gold. They were buying anything "real" they could get their hands on. The dollar was in a free fall. And after presiding over three years of rapid, but inflationary economic growth, so was Jimmy Carter.

Carter replaced the presiding Fed Chairman, G. William Miller, an industrialist, with Paul Volcker. Volcker, who had been an economist for the Chase Manhattan Bank and Undersecretary of State for Monetary Affairs under President Nixon, was seen as a "bankers' banker," someone who could restore confidence in the dollar and the United States financial system.

Over the next three years, Volcker and the Federal Reserve engineered the postwar's most contractionary monetary policy by driving up interest rates and the cost of credit into the double digits. By dramatically reducing spending, that policy precipitated the worst depression in the United States, and elsewhere, since the Great Depression of the 1930s.

By the summer of 1987, the Fed's monetary policy had helped to drive the rate of inflation down to a little over 1 percent a year. But unemployment was still well above 6 percent and the rate of profit had still not been restored to its lofty heights of the 1960s. Overall economic growth was, by all accounts, sluggish.

On June 2, 1987 Volcker, routinely described as the second most powerful man in Washington, announced he would not be continuing on as Fed chairman. As *The Wall Street Journal* reported: "The dollar plunged in foreign exchange dealing... as traders lamented the resignation of... Paul Volcker.... 'There was all out panic in the market,.... Traders couldn't sell dollars fast enough," reported one trader. " 'Volcker's international stature was unequaled and its going to be very difficult to reestablish or maintain confidence in the Fed's resolve to fight inflation' " said one banker (*Wall Street Journal*, June 3, 1987, p. 3).

Alan Greenspan, a conservative economic consultant and Volcker's appointed replacement, immediately announced that he would continue Volcker's policies. The dollar and bond markets rebounded the next day. Admitting they may have overreacted, one banker said, "There really isn't that much difference between Volcker and Greenspan" (*Wall Street Journal*, June 4, 1987, pp. 45, 51).

As this chronology suggests, the history of Federal Reserve policy in the current economic crisis is that of trying to deal with fundamental problems, first by attempting an expansionary solution, and then by attempting a policy of draconian contraction. Constraints facing macroeconomic policy have prevented the Federal Reserve from carrying either of these policies to their conclusion.

However, these policies have had important consequences. Because of the relative independence of the Federal Reserve from democratic control, monetary policy has been capital's weapon of choice against labor. And by engineering depression levels of unemployment, it has succeeded in taking income and power away from labor and toward different fractions of capital at different times. And not surprisingly, given the structure of the Fed, we can expect much the same from Alan Greenspan.

At the same time though, the problems of the economy have proven to be so fundamental that monetary policy's successes of redistributing income and power away from labor has yet to solve the fundamental problems underlying the current economic crisis.[1]

Can more democratic control over monetary policy shift the balance of power in macroeconomic policy back toward labor and progressive forces? To understand both the nature of United States monetary policy and the possibilities and limitations of democratizing monetary policy we have to learn why the Federal Reserve conducts monetary policy as it does. We have to understand how monetary policy affects accumulation and crisis in the United States economy. And we have to analyze the determinants and effects of Federal Reserve policy during the current economic crisis.

THE ROLE OF THE FEDERAL RESERVE
IN MACROECONOMIC POLICY MAKING

To understand the role of the Federal Reserve in the current economic crisis one needs to understand both the motivation of, and the limitations on, monetary policy. In this section I will discuss motivation: Why is monetary policy what it is?

Mainstream economics is not much help in answering this question. Its view is that the central bank takes society's goals as its own and tries to maximize social welfare. In the hey day of Keynesian economics, this implied that macropolicy makers would try to maintain full employment. If, as has been the dominant monetary policy more recently, it pursues contractionary policy, that is because "society" has an aversion to inflation. If the central bank makes poor policy, these result from policy errors rather than systematic biases.

Analyses inspired by Marx give much more useful answers to these questions. Michal Kalecki, in his article, "The Political Aspects of Full Employment" argued that there was a class basis to macroeconomic policy (Kalecki 1971). He argued that state macroeconomic policy fails to maintain full employment not because of policy errors, but because, among other reasons, full employment generates inflation. And, inflation is bad, not because it harms "the general public," as mainstream economics holds, but because it harms creditors — bond holders, wealthy investors and banks, or, as Keynes referred to them, "rentiers."[2]

Emphasizing a different class basis for counter-cyclical macroeconomic policy, James Crotty and Raford Boddy, argued that it's not the dragon of inflation that contractionary macropolicy tries to slay, as the conventional wisdom suggests (Boddy and Crotty 1975). Macropolicy is geared toward replenishing the reserve army of the unemployed to increase non-financial corporate profits.

Thus, far from making policy in the general interest, as mainstream theory suggests, Marxian inspired theory suggests that macroeconomic policy is made in the interests of financial capital (rentiers) or industrial capital, or both.

Yet these theories suggest an unresolved, indeed, a central question in Marxist and neo-Marxist theories of the state: under what conditions will the state be able to articulate and carry out policies in the long-run interests of the capitalist class as a whole? To do so the state must have political independence from labor. But it must also have the independence to develop and conduct coherent policies for an often highly competitive and deeply divided capitalist class. If industry and finance or important subsectors of these groups have different views concerning policy, how can the state hammer those views into a coherent policy?

The central bank would seem to be a primary candidate to make policy in the interests of the capitalist class as a whole. In some countries it has relative independence from the elected representatives. And representatives of labor groups are kept from the corridors of central bank power. As Alan Sproul, former president of the New York Federal Reserve put it in a confidential memo in 1952: "Labor members — what we don't want is members of the Board of Directors of (Federal Reserve) banks representing and acting as a pressure point for one segment of the community. Have no objection, in principle, to labor on boards, but their record as militant class interest advocates is bad" (see Epstein and Schor 1986:20).

This independence may give the central bank significant insulation from labor and other non-capitalist groups who may have some political power in the elected state bodies. But if political independence at least partially solves the problem of which class monetary policy will serve, it does determine which fraction of capital will be served. Will policy take the Boddy-Crotty road or the Kaleckian one? We need a richer theory of central bank policy to answer this question.[3]

A neo-Marxian theory of the central bank views the state, and therefore the central bank, as a terrain of class and intraclass struggle. In this view, central bank policy depends on three factors: first, the interests and relative power of workers, industrial capitalists and financial capitalists (Kalecki's rentiers); second, the connections between finance and industry;[4] and third, the degree of political independence of the central bank. Moreover, policy is constrained by the dynamics and contradictions of capital accumulation itself.

As applied to the United States Federal Reserve, because of space limitations I will discuss the second two factors: the nature of Federal Reserve independence and the connections between finance and industry.[5]

Federal Reserve Independence

The status of the Federal Reserve is one of *Contingent Independence* (Epstein 1982). The Federal Reserve has effective independence from the government subject to two constraints, one vis a vis the President, and the second vis a vis the legislature. The President has the power to appoint members to the Federal Reserve Board. Though the appointments are for a long term this does mean that over time, the President can influence the policies of the Federal Reserve.

The second constraint is that the Federal Reserve is a creature of Congress. In principle, the Congress can change its charter any time and bring the Fed under its direct control.

At the same time, the power of the President and the Congress are themselves subject to two major constraints: the political constituency of the Federal Reserve and the need to maintain the confidence of the financial markets. The Federal Reserve's strategy to preserve its political independence is to cultivate a constituency, which tends to be the commercial banking industry, both for historical and structural reasons. This constituency lobbies the President and Congress when the Federal Reserve's independence is threatened.

This financial constituency provides what I call the Federal Reserve's first line of defense from encroachment by the executive and legislature. There is ample historical evidence that the Federal Reserve has often made policy biased toward the interests of finance. For example, during the Second World War, the Federal Reserve agreed to peg interest rates at a given level so the Treasury could borrow money at a fixed rate to finance the war effort. There was a large controversy over what that rate would be. The Federal Reserve argued against the euthanasia of the rentier and won; as Alan Sproul put it in a memo: "(The rate) should be fair to the market in that, while we may have the power to finance the war at whatever rate we might want to dictate, it seemed desirable to help preserve our banking system and our institutional investors" (see Epstein and Schor 1986:37). As Samuelson later put it: "This war is a 2% war. It should have been a 1% war" (Samuelson 1945:26).[6]

The Federal Reserve's second line of defense against political encroachment is the need to preserve confidence in the financial markets to avoid capital flight or panic. Even if the President manages to appoint a Federal Reserve Board opposed to financially "sound" policies, eventually the second line of defense may help restore the Federal Reserve's independence. G. William Miller, an industrialist, who was seen by many within and outside the Federal Reserve System as being too closely tied to President Carter and insufficiently attuned to the needs of the financial sector, was replaced by Paul Volcker. As *The Wall Street Journal* later reported it, "Wall street shoved Volcker down Carter's throat."

Notice, however, and this is a key point, that just as the two lines of defense help preserve Federal Reserve independence, they also can constrain the policy prerogatives of the Fed itself. Arthur Burns and G. William Miller could pursue policies more oriented toward industry than finance, in the short term, but in the longer term, the confidence of the financial markets were severely impaired, thus forcing a change in policy and personnel.

Connections Between Finance and Industry

This brings us to the connections between finance and industry. According to Marx, finance and industry have bases both for unity and for conflict. They have a basis for unity vis a vis the working class, because financial and industrial profits both come from surplus value. The basis for conflict is that industry and finance must divide the surplus between them.

The degree of connection between financial sectors and industrial sectors vary greatly across countries and over time (Epstein and Schor 1986, and the references therein).

Credit market-based economies like Germany (on which Hilferding based his arguments for *Finance Capital*) and Japan have had close connections between finance and industry, whereas capital market-based economies, like the United Kingdom and the United States, have typically had less close connections.

But even within these countries, the degree and type of connections have changed over time. During the hey day of the American Century, in the 50s and 60s, large United States multinational corporations and banks had strong common interests in global expansion. Later, their interests diverged as the economic crisis became more severe (Ferguson and Rogers 1986).

Working hypotheses developed from this approach suggest that, the more independent the central bank, the less central bank policy will be made in the interests of labor. But independent central banks will not necessarily make policy in the interests of capital as a whole. If the connections between industry and finance are weak, the less likely will central bank policy be made in the interests of capital as a whole. This will be particularly true in times of economic decline or crisis. Indeed where finance and industry connections are weak, for structural and historical reasons, independent central banks tend to bias policy toward the interests of finance. By implication, for any given level of working class power, central bank policy is most likely to make policy in the interests of the capitalist class as a whole and, therefore, have a positive affect on the overall capital accumulation process where central banks are independent and connections between industry and finance are strong.

In the United States, where connections between finance and industry in the current context are relatively weak, and the central bank is relatively independent, policy is unlikely to be made in the best interests of capital as a whole. Rather, as we will see below, it will vacillate between policies oriented toward different fractions of capital, undermining the accumulation process even from the point of view of capital. The main loser, however, is labor.

LIMITATIONS ON CENTRAL BANK POLICY

Even if the central bank wants to make policy in the long-run interests of capital, it may not be able to do so if its policy instruments are not powerful enough to affect the economy in a way which can improve the conditions of capitalist profitability. There is little agreement among economists however about the ability of the central bank to affect profitability and accumulation. Economists' analysis of monetary policy's role has moved between two poles. One is that monetary policy is a potent force in affecting economic dynamics. The other is that monetary policy is itself caused by economic dynamics and therefore has little independent effect on them.[7]

A neo-Marxian view of monetary policy argues that the effectiveness of monetary policy is historically and institutionally specific (see Epstein and Schor 1986, and Epstein 1982). This neo-Marxian view argues that the central bank has the power to create institutional structures that will allow it to pursue contractionary policy, and under some conditions, accommodating policy. These conditions require the central bank to exert control over financial innovations, the world level of interest rates or capital mobility, the cost or availability of credit, and expectations. Many central banks have the economic power to control policy by implementing regulations. The main question is whether they have the political power to do so.

Vis a vis the economy, the Federal Reserve system is not powerful enough to solve the underlying problems facing the system. But it is not weak enough to be benign. It can strongly affect who bears the cost of these problems. And, it may be able to ameliorate them in the short run, if not the long run (see Michl in this volume).

OVERVIEW OF U.S. MONETARY POLICY IN THE CRISIS

In the 1970s and 1980s, the Federal Reserve faced two often conflicting tasks: one was to restore the international competitiveness and profitability of United States manufacturing; the second was to maintain the profitability and stability of United States financial institutions. The limits of Federal Reserve policy are painfully etched in the failures of these attempts.

Federal Reserve policy in the crisis zone, 1971–1987, can be divided into roughly three periods. In the first period, 1971–1979, the Federal Reserve policy was basically designed to take advantage of the breakdown of the Bretton Woods System of fixed exchange rates to increase industrial profitability and international competitiveness. The Federal Reserve pursued an accommodating monetary policy which would allow the dollar to depreciate relative to other currencies and make United States products more competitive. The policy was interrupted by the oil crises of 1973–74, but was resumed in 1975–76.

The policy was successful in certain respects. The dollar depreciated dramatically and the United States trade balance was stabilized after having been declining for years. Moreover, the profitability of non-financial corporations increased over the period (see Figure 1).

But these successes came at a heavy cost to other sectors of United States business and world financial stability. The problem was that accommodating monetary policy was highly inflationary in the context of the crisis ridden United States economy. With the rapid fall off in productivity growth, and large reduction in United States terms of trade, workers and capitalists were unable to maintain their traditional rates of growth of real wages and profits. Workers and capitalists attempted to raise wages and prices to recapture their previous levels of income. In this context, accommodating monetary

Table 1
Selected Macroeconomic Indicators
Percentage Rate of Growth
(1960–1986)

	60–70	71–79	80–86	80–82	83–86	86
Real Interest Rate	1.4	− .4	4.2	3.8	4.5	3.5
Unemployment Rate	4.8	6.3	8.0	8.1	7.8	7.0
Real Wages	2.3	1.0	0.0	− .7	.6	1.1
Productivity	2.2	1.2	.9	0.0	1.6	.7
Inflation	2.6	7.2	6.1	10.0	3.2	1.9

Sources: Real Interest Rate: Three month treasury bill-rate of growth of GNP deflator, *Economic Report of the President*, (ERP), 1987, Table B-68, p. 324, Table B-5, p. 251. Unemployment Rate: Civilian unemployment rate, *ERP*, Table B-35, p. 285. Real Wages: rate of growth of real hourly compensation, non-farm business sector, *ERP*, Table B-43, p. 294, and *Economic Indicators*, (*EI*), June, 1987, p. 16. Productivity: Rate of growth of output per worker, non-farm business sector, ibid. Inflation: Rate of Growth of Consumer Price Index, *ERP*, Table B-59, p. 312.

policy maintained the ability of firms to rapidly increase their prices, while the depreciating dollar allowed them to maintain their competitiveness even as their prices were rising (see Table 1).[8]

The resulting acceleration of inflation and the rapidly depreciating dollar undermined the profitability of financial institutions (see Figure 1).

Figure 1
Inflation — Adjusted Return on Equity

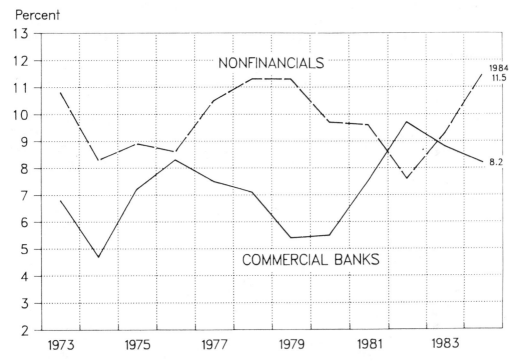

Source: Federal Reserve Bank of New York (1986), p. 105.

More significantly, given the central role of the dollar in the international economy, the rapid depreciation of the dollar threatened an overall flight away from the dollar and a full blown international monetary crisis. Hence, in the context of the crisis-ridden United States economy, expansionary attempts to solve industry's problems came at the expense not only of United States working people, but also at the expense of finance, a powerful sector of United States business. Moreover, by undermining the international role of the dollar, the expansionary policy threatened the overall stability of the world economy (Epstein 1985).

Paul Volcker's ascendence at the Federal Reserve marked the end of the expansionary/ depreciation approach to solving the United States crisis and the beginning of the second period, 1980–1982. It also marked a return to the historically more common dominance of the financial sector in the making of United States monetary policy. Starting in October of 1979, the Federal Reserve initiated a draconian, tight monetary policy that was to last at least until the summer of 1982. From 1980 to 1982, the unemployment rate shot up to an average of over 8 percent, as real interest rates increased five fold from the previous period (Table 1).[9] As a result of the high real interest rates and the depression, non-financial corporate profits fell dramatically (Figure 1). But in the process, inflation adjusted bank profits turned around, as the rate of return on bank equity rose just as dramatically (Figure 1).

The limits to such tight policies were reached on two fronts. The first was the outbreak of the Third World Debt Crisis with the announcement by Mexico in the summer of 1982 that it would no longer be able to service its debt. The high interest rates and the depression created by tight United States monetary policy threatened to drive Third World debtors into default. With nine United States banks holding debts equal to almost three times their capital, bank profits were thus severely threatened. As a result of these threats to finance, rather than from the devastation wrought on United States workers or even non-financial corporations by the tight monetary policies, the Federal Reserve loosened up.

On the second front, the high value of the dollar brought about by tight monetary policies in the face of large budget deficits, exacerbated the declining United States trade position. Tremendous pressure began to emerge from manufacturing for protection against foreign imports. The open trading system from which United States multinational corporations and banks benefitted so greatly in the postwar period was severely threatened.

In response to both these pressures, as well as new, Reagan appointed personnel on the Federal Reserve, the Federal Reserve pursued a much less contractionary policy from 1983–86, the third period of this chronology.

Partly as a result of this looser monetary policy, interest rates fell. As a result, the dollar fell by over 60 percent relative to the Japanese yen. The Federal Reserve was able to engineer the decline without a panic developing as in 1977–79, primarily because of two factors. Whereas in 1979, oil prices increased dramatically as the Federal Reserve was maintaining a relatively accommodative policy, this time world oil prices fell as the dollar fell in 1985–86. There was much less panic selling of dollars as a result. Second, Volcker was able to trade on some of his credibility in the financial markets which he had created by the previous four years of tight policies. Banks and investors believed that Volcker would have no qualms about generating double digit unemployment, once again to nip inflationary pressures in the bud.

The falling dollar has begun to help non-financial profits by facilitating manufacturing exports and industrial production. But the underlying problems of slow productivity growth and economic growth remain (see Center for Popular Economics 1985, and footnote 1, above).

CONCLUSION

What is the proper stance the left can take toward monetary policy? The issue of democratizing the Federal Reserve has become an important one in progressive circles. There are two common responses to this proposal.

One is that democratization will make no difference because the central bank cannot do other than what it is doing anyway. The second response is that democratization of the central bank will make for a substantial improvement in macroeconomic policy.

The results here suggest that the truth may lie in between. Federal Reserve independence does make a difference and it does reduce the ability of labor and the left to influence macroeconomic policy. But there is always the Federal Reserve's second line of defense. As long as the capital market is allowed to allocate resources in an unfettered way, maintaining the confidence of the financial markets will be a serious constraint on a democratized central bank.

ACKNOWLEDGEMENTS

This paper partly draws on joint work with Juliet B. Schor. Christine D'Onofrio provided very useful comments on an earlier draft. All remaining errors are mine.

NOTES

1. As some of the articles in this reader suggest, the issue of whether this redistribution of power has worked to shore up the system is still highly controversial. A full treatment of this question is beyond the scope of the present paper, but suffice it to say that I have very strong doubts that the strategy has worked from the point of view of capital, except for the very short run.
2. Kalecki also argues that industrial capital will oppose full employment policies, not because they reduce profits in the short run, but because they will reduce capital's control over the workforce in the long run. This concern over control, according to Kalecki, may create a coincidence of interest between finance and industrial capital against full employment policies in the long run. There may be important differences in the short run, however (see below).
3. The general theory of central banking described here is the product of joint work with Juliet Schor (see Epstein and Schor 1986).
4. By industry I mean capitals whose primary business is non-financial and by finance, I mean firms whose business is primarily financial. In particular circumstances other distinctions will be important, say between multinational and domestic capital or between small and large banks.
5. On capital/labor relationns in the United States see Epstein and Schor (1986).
6. See Epstein and Fergusonn (1984) for an example of finance biased policy during the Great Depression.
7. The arguments for the powerlessness of central bank policy take essentially three forms. The first is that the financial market will undo any policy the central bank tries to make, rendering the central bank impotent. The second kind of argument is that the central bank cannot affect the economy because the economy's problems are such that the central bank is boxed in. Anything it does cannot help, and may simply make things worse. Thus, according to this argument the central bank's hands are tied. Third, many Marxian analyses critique the ability of the central bank to affect the accumulation process at a deeper level; here the argument is that the contradictions of capitalism are so fundamental that no government policy can solve them. Neoclassical, post-Keynesian and Marxian economists share some of these positions, but, of course, for different reasons. And they certainly draw different conclusions from them (see Sargent and Wallace 1977; Kaldor 1981; Foley 1986; Magdoff and Sweezy 1987). As I argue below, there are important grains of truth to the post-Keynesian and Marxian arguments, but they should be seen as institutionally and historically conditioned and limited, not universal.
8. On a related discussion of this period see Bowles, Gordon and Weisskopf (1983).
9. If people who had given up searching for jobs (so-called "discouraged workers") are added to this official measures, the unemployment rate is actually much higher.

24

An Anatomy of the Reagan Recovery

THOMAS R. MICHL

INTRODUCTION

Macroeconomic policies in the 1980s have subjected the United States economy to extraordinary pressures. Large tax cuts in 1981, together with the continuation of a military buildup begun during the Carter Administration, drove budget deficits to unprecedented levels after 1982. Widespread union concessions on wages and benefits sharply redistributed income from labor to capital. And for the first time in recent history, the trade deficit of the United States economy reached alarming proportions. The current recovery is a rich source of information on how the economy responds to such stimuli.

This article interprets current policies in terms of the management of the long-run crisis tendencies of the capitalist economy. A long-run erosion of corporate profitability, it is asserted, underlies the economic stagnation of recent decades. From this perspective, the decline in the real wages of United States workers, which began in the 1970s but was accelerated by the concessions of the 1980s, represents what Marx once called a "countervailing tendency" to declining profitability: real wage reductions increase the potential long-run rate of profit. They also have contractionary demand effects which cannot be ignored in analyzing short-run episodes, but the stimulus of large budget deficits has essentially smoothed over these demand effects. The policy "mix" — large deficits plus wage cuts — has successfully contained the decline in before-tax profitability and actually increased the after-tax rate of profit to late 1960s levels.

While this account begins with the conventional Marxian focus on the long-run supply-side factors which regulate capital accumulation, it marshalls the insights of more "Keynesian" theorists like Michal Kalecki and Joseph Steindl in analyzing the short-run effects of both fiscal policy and the dramatic change in the respective bargaining power of labor and capital symbolized by union concessions in the 1980s.

THE BACKGROUND OF WAGE CONCESSIONS

The period of wage concessions was ushered in with the Reagan Administration's firing of over 11,000 striking professional air traffic controllers in 1981. But employer militancy, which was given the green light by Reagan's own example, could not itself have vanquished the trade union movement as swiftly and decisively as was done. Other policies contributed, especially the deregulation movement and the extremely tight monetary policy associated with the early reign of Paul Volker as head of the Federal Reserve Board. The fact that both these policies were initiated during the Carter Administration attests to the continuity between the two administrations over key aspects of policy.

From 1979, when Volker announced a new policy, to 1982, when monetary policy eased, restrictive central bank policy drove interest rates to historically high levels.

Financial capital from all over the world began to flow into United States financial markets, driving up the value of the dollar. A highly valued dollar in turn raised the price of United States exports, and intensified the competition faced by United States producers both on the world and domestic market.

In those internationally exposed industries like autos and steel, employers were emboldened by the atmosphere created by Reagan, and they demanded major concessions from trade unions. A similar pattern emerged in some deregulated industries like airlines. In 1981, about 8.0 percent of unionized workers who bargained that year accepted money wage freezes or cuts in the first year of their contract — the best single indicator of concessions.[1] As long as there is any consumer price inflation, such concessions obviously reduce real wages. The following year, concessions spread in epidemic fashion, afflicting nearly half the workers who bargained in 1982.

This epidemic of concessionary bargaining did not confine itself to the industries engaged in world trade, or to those subject to deregulation. It quickly fanned out to nearly all sectors of the United States economy, as is documented by Daniel Mitchell (1985), who estimates that from 1981 to 1984, between one-third and one-half of unionized workers experienced at least one such pay cut. Concessions, in other words, became a class-wide phenomenon. Perhaps even more significantly, pay cuts continued to run at unprecedented levels (with about 30 percent taking cuts on average), even during the employment recovery from 1982 to 1985. Must real wage restraint such as this necessarily increase profitability in the short run? To seek an answer we move the discussion to a more theoretical plane.

WAGE CUTS AND MACROECONOMIC POLICY

Marx qualified his famous law of the tendency of the rate of profit to fall with several well-known countertendencies or offsetting factors. Of these countertendencies, the "depression of wages below the value of labor power," meaning a reduction in real wages below their normal or customary levels, would seem to apply to economic conditions in the 1980s. The thesis being advanced here thus has some precedence in Marx's economic writings to the extent that the source of economic difficulty is low profitability. Of course, opinions are divided about the contribution of a declining rate of profit to the desultory performance of the United States economy in the last decade (see the selections in the first section of this volume). Let us accept as a beginning premise that declining profitability has indeed been an obstacle to the continued rapid growth of the economy. Can we accept Marx's implicit assumption that wage reductions must necessarily increase profits and stoke the fires of accumulation?

Profits represent a form of the surplus value which remains after the wages and other costs of annual production have been deducted from gross output. However, if effective demand is insufficient, the surplus value produced in a given year will fail to be realized (transformed into cash) and instead will take the form of an unplanned build-up of unsold goods. The volume of after-tax profits actually realized (assuming for simplicity that workers consume all their wages) is equal to the sum of (1) net investment spending, (2) capitalist consumption, (3) the budget deficit, and (4) the trade surplus.[2] This realization condition for profits will prove to be an important framework for organizing much of what follows.

The realization condition forms the basis for a long-standing critique by Kalecki and Steindl of Marx's belief that fluctuations in real wages automatically give rise to countermovements in profits. Steindl sums up his view as follows:

> . . . [an] increase in wages could never reduce profits as long as investment (and capitalists' consumption) remain high; a fall in wages could never increase profits, unless investment first increased. In Marxian terms, we should say that surplus value (profits) in order to be obtained, must not only be 'produced' but also 'realized' (Steindl 1968:256).

The crucial question Steindl has raised is whether a wage reduction will itself produce a stimulus to investment demand (abstracting from the other elements of the realization condition for the moment).

Rather than attempt to describe the behavior of the United States economy in all its complexity, the following discussion works through a thought experiment which builds the proper intuition about the behavior of a capitalist economy subject to a once-for-all decline in labor's bargaining power.[3] This thought experiment rests on two key propositions. First, investment spending is positively related to the rate of profit and the rate of capacity utilization, and inversely related to the real interest rate (the nominal interest rate minus the rate of inflation). Second, the rate of inflation is the outcome of a bargaining process between capital and labor over the real wage rate and the rate of profit.

The immediate effect of decreased bargaining power of labor is a decline in the rate of money wage growth, and since prices are in part based on marking-up unit labor costs, in the rate of inflation. Lower inflation in turn increases the real interest rate, retarding investment. Further, because wage inflation has declined more than price inflation, real wages are lower and the reduced demand for wage goods creates unused capacity, contributing further to the reduction in investment spending. Since realized profits depend on investment spending, the rate of profit will paradoxically fall as an immediate response to reduced labor strength.

At this point, firms are operating at rates of profit well below what they know to be normal, and they will raise prices by increasing their mark-up. As the resulting increase in inflation begins to lower the real interest rate, and stimulate investment spending, the economy enters a "virtuous cycle" in which higher investment realizes greater profitability and higher levels of capacity utilization, and these in turn drive investment spending still higher.

This process eventually reaches the limits on profitability imposed by the bargaining power of workers, but since labor is by assumption weaker, the new equilibrium rate of profit that is established will be higher than the old. This increase in the rate of profit is essentially what Marx assumed would happen instantaneously. Incorporating the realization condition into this thought experiment reveals that the short-term effect of a wage cut could well be to reduce profitability, until the economy adjusts to the new situation created by a weakened labor movement.

By combining budget deficits with reduced worker bargaining power, the current policy "mix" effectively overcomes the short-run demand-side difficulties described in the paragraphs above. Because budget deficits increase profits through the realization condition, they can smooth over the initial dip in profitability if they are of sufficient magnitude. By propping up profits and overall demand (both of which affect investment), budget deficits put an effective floor under investment and speed the economy's adjustment to the new, higher rate of profit made possible by the enhanced bargaining power of capital.

From the realization condition, it is also possible to appreciate the limitation imposed on the current policy mix by the growth of the trade deficit. The current recovery, by drawing in imports, generated a trade deficit sufficiently large by 1986 to neutralize completely the profit stimulus from budget deficits.

If this discussion has focused rather singlemindedly on profitability, it is because profitability is both a thermometer and a thermostat in relation to the accumulation of capital. A decline in the rate of profit makes economic crises possible because profitability regulates investment much like a thermostat regulates the temperature of a room, and a collapse of investment spending attends every capitalist economic crisis. Just as geologists can predict an impending volcano from the rumblings of the earth, so can we predict that an era of declining profitability will erupt into depression and stagnation. Many left economists, while disagreeing about the causes of declining profitability, have analyzed the disappointing macroeconomic performance of the 1970s in precisely these terms. By containing the decline in the rate of profit, even if only temporarily, Reaganomics has succeeded in papering over one of the outstanding contradictions of the system.

In this limited sense, current policy has succeeded in managing the crisis tendencies inherent in the United States economy. The success of the strategy, however, is in inverse proportion to the hardship it has inflicted on the working class. Unlike old-fashioned Keynesianism, which is sometimes described as a rising tide raising all boats, Reaganomics has succeeded in managing the crisis by serving the interests of capital and by transferring economic difficulties to the mass of workers, as evidenced by the continuation of mass unemployment, a rising poverty rate, the erosion of popular living standards, and a rising degree of income inequality.

The decline in the unemployment rate to about 6.0 percent as of this writing (the lowest level reached during the Carter years) has elicited warm praise in the press for the merits of current policy. How quickly commentators have forgotten that this still represents what can only be described as mass unemployment by historical standards. Compared to previous years of high employment, like 1953 (2.8 percent unemployment rate), 1969 (3.4 percent), or even 1973 (4.8 percent), it is clear the current policy has been a success only by virtue of the lower standards to which it is being held. But even those fortunate enough to have a job have not shared in the fruits of economic progress. Led by the wage concessions of organized workers, real wages have stagnated during the current recovery. By the standard of the welfare of the majority of United States citizens it is clear that Reaganomics has been an utter and miserable failure.

DID THE RATE OF PROFIT RISE?

Those few conventional economists who concern themselves with questions like this have concluded that in large measure the rate of profit has risen from the depths to which it had been depressed in the 1970s. Two important studies are Clark (1984), which shows that the cyclically adjusted nonfinancial corporate profit share has recovered in the 1980s, and Bosworth (1985), which shows that the cyclically adjusted profit rate has similarly recovered.[4]

Figure 1 displays the before and after-tax rate of profit for United States nonfinancial corporations. A strong pattern of decline is evident in the before-tax rate of profit, interrupted by a bulge during the 1960s — a sort of golden age of capital accumulation. This decline is consistent with the Marxian hypothesis mentioned above of a long-run tendency for the rate of profit to fall. The period of wage concessions appears to have arrested this tendency; by 1985, the before-tax rate of return was at about the same level it held during the late 1970s. This hardly represents a return to the golden age of capital accumulation in the 1960s, but it probably represents an improvement over the hypothetical rate of profit that would have obtained in the absence of wage concessions.

Figure 1
Rates of Profit in the Nonfinancial Corporate Sector of the U.S., 1948–1986

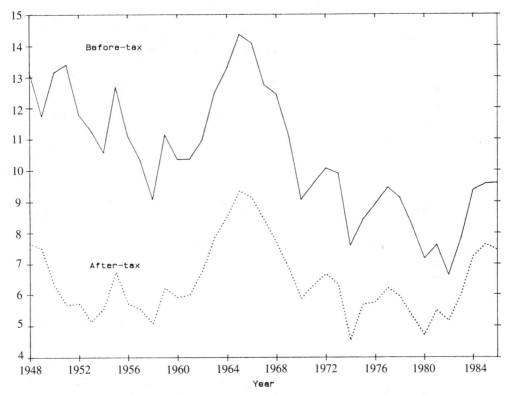

Sources: U.S. Department of Commerce, Board of Governors of the Federal Reserve System.

This long-run erosion of profitability is not evident in the after-tax rate of profit shown in Figure 1, owing to the trend over the postwar period toward lighter taxation of corporate income.[5] Again there is a noticeable bulge in the 1960s. In the 1980s, however, the after-tax rate of profit rises impressively, lending eloquent support to the hypothesis that current policies have materially and effectively benefitted corporate interests.

MACROECONOMIC PERFORMANCE IN THE REAGAN RECOVERY

In order to provide a statistical profile of the current recovery, Table 1 compares the behavior of key variables in the present recovery with previous postwar recoveries, using index numbers as a convenient way to represent growth. The first two columns of Table 1 show the growth of a variable from the cycle trough (1982.IV for the current recovery) to a date three years from the trough. The first column shows the average growth in previous cycle recoveries, while the second column shows the growth in the current recovery. Variables are transformed into index numbers, meaning they are set to 100 in the trough quarter and rise to the level shown in the table. An index number of say, 120, indicates 20 percent growth since the trough quarter three years ago. The third and fourth columns repeat this exercise for growth from the previous cycle peak rather than from the trough.

Table 1
Indexes of Cyclical Growth Comparing 1982–85
With Previous Postwar Recoveries

Variable	Trough = 100		Previous Peak = 100	
	Previous Cycle Average	1982.IV – 1985.IV	Previous Cycle Average[a]	1981.III – 1985.IV
Real[b] Average Hourly Compensation, Nonfarm	108	100	111	103
Real Corporate Profits After Tax with IVA and CCAdj	140	212	124	157
Civilian Employment	107	109	106	107
Real GNP	117	115	115	111
Real Disposable Personal Income	115	112	115	112
Real Personal Consumption	113	113	115	116
Real Nonresidential Fixed Investment	122	132	114	114

Notes: The postwar cycles are based on National Bureau of Economic Research dating. They are (trough-peak): 1949.IV-1953.II, 1954.II-1957.III, 1961.I-1969.IV, 1970.IV-1973.IV, and 1975.I-1980.I.

[a]These index numbers have been normalized to 17 quarters to be comparable to the current recovery.
[b]All real variables are in 1982 constant dollars.

Source: Citibase.

Care must obviously be taken in interpreting these comparisons between the current recovery and previous recoveries because the 1980 to 1982 recessions were so severe. Almost any kind of recovery would raise some of the variables in Table 1 by a large proportion over their depression-level lows in 1982, and displaying the data in this way is for that very reason a favorite trick of the trade among Reagan apologists. To illustrate the problem, it is sufficient to observe that the recovery of real gross investment spending from 1933 to 1936 would rank that among the greatest booms of the century, yet we know it was an extremely feeble recovery. Investment never even reached its 1929 level by 1936. To guard against such a base year effect, columns 3 and 4 show the behavior of the variables with respect to their previous peaks.[6]

The first thing to notice is the virtual absence of any growth in workers' hourly real wage rates coupled with the explosion in the volume of real after-tax corporate profits. As columns 4 and 5 show, the profit increase does not reflect the base year effect referred to above. To complete the picture of the behavior of real wages it should be added that in 1985 they were actually lower than in 1977 — a fact which is somewhat obscured by the method of presentation in Table 1.

The second general impression about the current recovery is that it is unremarkable in so many respects. Employment growth, for example, has been about average; as noted above, it has been inadequate from the point of view of the number of workers who need jobs. Real gross national product has not grown as much as it did in the average recovery, suggesting that the only supply-side miracle is that so much credence has been given to the ''supply-side'' theory which the Reagan Administration used to justify the 1981 tax cuts. While disposable income growth has been slightly below average, consumers have either reduced savings or gone into debt to attempt to maintain spending. Once again, this flatly contradicts a central tenet of supply-side theory, that tax cuts stimulate high levels of personal saving.

The effect on investment spending of an increase in profitability engineered by the state as described in the previous sections depends on the combined action of opposing influences. An improvement in profitability provides both the incentive and the finance for capital formation, but in the current recovery, high real interest rates and low levels of capacity utilization retard investment. Capacity utilization in manufacturing, for example, stood at 80.1 percent in 1985, compared to an average of 85.2 percent at similar points in previous postwar recoveries.

The evidence suggests that the retarding influence of low capacity utilization and high real interest rates has dominated the stimulating effects of increased profitability. Gross investment has indeed recovered from its trough values much more quickly in the current than in the average cycle. However, looking at columns 3 and 4, it is evident that this recovery has been largely a rebound effect rather than some kind of sea change in the rate of capital accumulation. Moreover, surveys of business investment by The Conference Board (1986) have found that an unusually large proportion of this investment has been directed toward modernizing existing facilities rather than expanding productive capacity. In a word, corporations are using the rewards of tax and wage cuts to improve their competitive position, not to lead the nation's economy to a new plateau of employment and productive capacity. This weakness of investment shows up even more clearly in the real volume of *net* nonresidential fixed investment (not included in Table 1), which equals gross investment minus depreciation. Even though net investment grew fairly substantially from 1982, by 1985 it had only recovered to its previous peak in 1979.[7]

THE CONTRADICTIONS OF CURRENT POLICY

It is useful to reflect on some of the limitations associated with several of the key aspects of the current recovery, especially those associated with large budget deficits, large trade deficits, and wage concessions.

Return to the realization condition for profits discussed above, and consider the interrelationships between two key determinants of the volume of profits: the budget deficit and the trade deficit. A large budget deficit contributes to profit realization, but to the extent that the demand it creates leaks out into imports, a budget deficit adds to the trade deficit, which has the opposite effect on profits. It is the net effect of these two offsetting forces which ultimately must be examined.

Table 2
The Budget Deficit and Trade Deficit, 1981–86.
(Billions of Dollars)

Year	Total Government Deficit (1)	Current Account Surplus (2)	Net Stimulus (1) + (2)
1981	29.7	+ 10.6	40.3
1982	110.8	− 1.0	109.8
1983	128.6	− 33.5	95.1
1984	101.5	− 90.7	10.8
1985	136.3	− 115.2	21.1
1986	143.1	− 143.7	− 0.6

Note: Current account surplus is derived from "net foreign investment" in the national income accounts.

Source: *Economic Report of the President, 1987,* Table B27.

At this point, an emendation of the realization condition as described above is in order. The relevant entry for applying the realization condition to the national income and product accounts is the current account surplus, which takes into account the role of net income from the foreign sector.[8] Table 2 assembles the relevant data for the budget deficit (column 1), the current account surplus (column 2), and the net stimulus to profits that results from these factors (column 3).

As the Reagan recovery advanced after 1982, the growth of demand in the United States acted like a huge pump, suctioning in large amounts of imported goods, and this effect was amplified by the high value of the dollar relative to other currencies. Other countries, however, did not reciprocate by buying United States exports, mainly because they have not experienced recoveries on the same scale as the United States.[9] Economists at the Organization for Economic Cooperation and Development (1985:76) estimate that in this recovery about 70 percent of world demand growth in industrial nations is accounted for by United States demand growth while in previous recoveries the United States typically contributed about 40 percent of world demand growth. The lopsided world recovery created a trade deficit of record proportions for the United States economy. From Table 2 it is evident that by 1986 the resulting rise in the current account deficit was sufficient to wipe out completely the profit-enhancing properties of large budget deficits.

In five years, the United States has gone from net creditor to net debtor status, implying that the rest of the world has claim to a share of the income originating in the United States. Some economists estimate that interest on foreign debt will consume as much as 1 percent of United States GNP over the next five years. How do countries eliminate a trade deficit? A tried and true method is to restrain the demand for imports by inducing recession. Both by increasing the need for a recession and by running up the foreign indebtedness of the United States economy, the increase in the trade deficit today threatens to reduce the income of United States residents tomorrow.

Similarly, a policy of restoring profitability by means of issuing government debt raises serious problems. First, interest must be paid on it, and the interest bill of the United States government now absorbs about 15 percent of its spending.[10] Second, large outstanding debt creates fears that the debt will be repudiated by the generation of inflation by the central bank, in turn creating political pressures to return to "fiscal responsibility." Moreover, it should be borne in mind that the political will to reduce the budget deficit may well materialize at an inopportune time, deflating the economy when the momentum from the current recovery has died and the economy is most in need of stimulus.

Wage concessions are also problematic as a solution to the underlying problem of profitability. Many of the wage concessions in the early 1980s took forms that are likely to arouse opposition such as the two-tiered wage system, whereby junior employees are paid less than senior employees for the same work. Already, workers in the airlines industry have rebelled against the obvious inequity of such a system. And even if the wage concessions already granted could be made to stick, should the rate of profit continue to decline it will be harder to repeat them a second time to the extent that workers are aware of their limited benefits in the first round of concessions.

PROSPECTS

The current recovery has reached its fifth year as of this writing, and one is inclined to ask whether we are witnessing a reversal in the trend toward economic stagnation in the United States. Several points militate against such a conclusion. First, past history suggests that the length of a recovery is a poor indicator of the underlying strength of the economy, as the four year recovery from 1933 to 1937 exemplifies (the longest recovery up to that time, yet it occurred in the midst of the Depression era). Second, it is clear from the evidence reviewed above that the redistribution of income from labor to capital has succeeded only in preventing further decline in the before-tax rate of profit, not in restoring it to the lofty heights of the 1950s and 1960s. Third, while this recovery has been driven by extraordinarily large levels of deficit spending which complemented the benefits to capital served up by a compliant working class, it has been attended by mounting foreign indebtedness, an enlarged public debt, and a growing imbalance of trade. The temporary nature of the stimuli and the much more permanent nature of these burdens will in all likelihood become evident in the aftermath of the Reagan era.

NOTES

1. These figures come from various issues of *Current Wage Developments* (U.S. Department of Labor). Specifically, they refer to workers in major settlements of over 1,000 workers taking money wage cuts or freezes.
2. Assuming for simplicity that only capitalists save, this equation follows from familiar macroeconomic identities. To give the reader the basic idea let,

$$Y = C_w + C_p + I + NX.$$

Output equals workers' consumption plus capitalists' consumption plus investment plus net exports. Workers' wages, W, equal their consumption by assumption. Profits are the excess of output over wages, or $P = Y - W$. Simple manipulation of these two equations gives,

$$P = C_p + I + NX.$$

Including government spending and taxation makes the algebra a little trickier and leads to the equation described in the text. For a seminal discussion of the realization condition, consult Kalecki (1971).

3. For the fully articulated macroeconomic model on which this thought experiment is loosely based, see Taylor (1985).

4. For the dissenting opinion that profitability barely increased in the 1980s, see Bowles, et al. (1986:155–157).

5. I am inclined to believe that lower profit taxes have not solved the problem of declining profitability, but by merely transferring the burden of taxation to workers, have caused the declining rate of profit to manifest itself as an increasingly contractionary fiscal stance rather than as a direct squeeze on investment. For a discussion of the role of the state and capital accumulation see the selection by John Miller, in this volume.

6. For real gross nonresidential fixed investment in the Great Depression, the 1933–36 index numbers would be 211 (trough to 1936) and 58 (previous peak to 1936). An index number below 100 obviously indicates negative growth. Data are from *The National Income and Product Accounts of the U.S., 1929–82* (U.S. Department of Commerce, Table 5.3).

7. The levels of net investment (in billions of 1982 dollars) for 1979, 1982, and 1985 are 124.3, 65.5, and 124.9. Data are from *Economic Report of the President, 1987,* Table B-16.

8. For further elaboration of open economy macroeconomic issues, consult the selection in this volume by Blecker.

9. Faced with the same problems of declining profitability, some of the other advanced industrial economies appear to be using protracted depression and stagnation as a policy tool to extract concessions from their own working classes. For discussion of policies in other countries in the 1980s, consult the selection in this volume by Green.

10. When the time comes to finance this interest burden by taxation rather than by continued borrowing, the effect under some conditions will be to reduce aggregate demand by redistributing income from taxpayers to bondholders. Since these latter represent the wealthiest households which typically have a lower propensity to consume, demand for consumer goods will decline. See Baldani and Michl (1987) for an analysis of the conditions which could bring this about.

25

On the Political Economy of Unemployment Policy

FRANCIS GREEN

INTRODUCTION

Macroeconomic policies across the globe are in a whirl. The 1980s have witnessed the open abandonment of the theory of Keynesianism both by politicians and by the core of the United States economics profession who have warmly embraced conservative economic theory; yet we can see the same old-fashioned Keynesian maneuver of managing aggregate demand upward or downward to suit the specific objectives of governments. United States taxation policy was erected on the naive basis of the Laffer curve, leaving the economics profession agape and unbelieving. Monetary and exchange rate policy in many countries has been hampered by the increasing fluidity of the international capital markets, and control has been further hindered by the simultaneous widespread deregulation of banks and money markets that has left the controllers sometimes not knowing what they were supposed to be controlling. If there is any theme to all these changes it is that Keynesianism, the dominant policy of the postwar boom era, has been replaced by policies of austerity. Across the world, governments have deliberately restricted demand in ways which would directly impose hardships on working people through wage cuts and unemployment. But the situation might equally be described as one of confusion and diversity. How can we make sense of this?

This paper aims to outline a Marxian framework for thinking about recent developments in macroeconomic policy which avoids the conventional dichotomy of Keynesian versus conservative economics, and attempts to show how this framework can be used to account for some of the diversity that we see in macroeconomic performance. One of the distinctive features of Marxian economics is that it conceives of capitalism in its entirety, rather than as a piecemeal set of independent units, each separate objects of study. Its approach is always interdisciplinary, since it weaves together a political and sociological theory with its analysis of economic relations. Its methodology is also powerfully historical. Economic events in specific conjunctures are seen as part of a contradictory process of accumulation which links each happening with the past and the future, and with other conjunctures in other parts of the world. Nothing is treated as though it were an isolated "exogenous shock," as is common in the method of neoclassical economics. And so, to understand the repressive macroeconomic policies we have witnessed in the 1980s, we have to think of them in a broad framework, and see their place in relation both to the economic crises of the previous decade and to the changes that are taking place in other spheres of capitalist life — in politics, in ideology and in social relations generally.

RESTRUCTURING

The "problems" of the 1970s and 1980s — unemployment, inflation, the developing Third World debt, energy imbalances, financial instability of banks, and so on — are linked in that they are symptoms of a crisis of capitalism which, in the Marxian view, is inherent to the system itself. Though no one of the manifestations of crisis is in itself necessary, the underlying periodic breakdown of capitalist relations is unavoidable. The current era is also, therefore, part of a prolonged period of continued attempts to "restructure" the system in ways which will allow renewed profitable capital accumulation: to re-establish conditions for the extraction of surplus value.

"Restructuring" is related to the Marxian idea of "expanded reproduction," in a similar way to the relation of "disequilibrium" and "balanced growth" in mainstream economics. ("Disequilibrium" reigns as the economy adjusts from one "balanced growth path" to another, through a process of market adjustments.) The Marxian term "expanded reproduction" incorporates the idea of quantitative growth, but is a wider and more useful concept as it draws attention to the way capitalist relationships have to be conserved from period to period: workers are reproduced as workers, for example, in that their energies are replenished, and they are again available as sellers of labor-power. The product, therefore, is not just a quantity of output, but a renewed set of relations. Many activities of the capitalist state fulfill part of this reproductive function — for example, the education system helps to produce the right qualities in the labor force.

"Restructuring," the Marxian counterpart of a disequilibrium process, means that after a crisis not only must there be a quantitative adjustment of economic variables — such as a fall in the wage level — there must also be a realignment of the institutions and relationships accepted prior to the crisis. For if a crisis becomes generalized to all spheres of the economy, and hence to most spheres of social life, it is impossible for the same qualitative relationships to hold. Unlike mainstream analysis of convergence to equilibrium, however, there is nothing automatic about the process of restructuring: it is essentially a continued process of political struggle.

Restructuring takes many forms. Very often crises have posed the impossibility of maintaining existing relations in the labor market, and so the institutions and expectations of labor have had to be transformed. The current era is such a time: the postwar consensus whereby acceptance of industrial peace and of the prerogatives of business is "traded" for a promise of steadily rising wages and near full employment was exposed as inherently contradictory from the 1960s onwards; now it has become necessary to limit those concessions and to reinforce consent through a more authoritarian approach to labor relations, and to limit (or even abolish) the role of organized labor. Another restructuring takes place between different sections of capital, for example between the more internationally oriented and the domestically oriented. Relations between the nation state and business are also altered, as the market becomes more international and as the size of businesses comes to rival that of the government. Meanwhile, the current era of restructuring has witnessed also a political realignment, both in the United States where establishment politicians, supported by big business, have shifted to the right, and in Europe where longstanding social democratic governments have given way to parties of the right. Finally, international relationships hanging over from the period of absolute United States hegemony are still in a process of realignment, following the defeat in Vietnam and the collapse of the Bretton Woods monetary system.

UNEMPLOYMENT POLICIES

Macroeconomic policies in the current era are part of the overall restructuring process.

They are also contradictory, in that they give rise to opposition and struggle, and they rarely fit into a consistent theoretical picture as painted by any of the schools of mainstream economics.

Employment and unemployment policy is a case in point. Mainstream economics texts will teach the mechanisms that create unemployment and how, using econometric techniques, to forecast it; but no purely technical methodology can substitute for an analysis of how unemployment is likely to be used to restructure relations in the labor market and inside the office and factory. From a Marxian standpoint, the "reserve army of the unemployed" is a necessary feature of how capitalism operates. It acts as a regulator of wages and as a discipline for the work force, without which workers' demands will lead inevitably to a crisis of profitability. And it is the periodic renewal of crises, together with labor-saving technical change, which continually replenishes the ranks of the "army." In the modern era, the state may consciously aid this process. As Michal Kalecki (1943) has shown, while full-employment policies are in the short-term interests of business since they raise profitability, the capitalists' "class instinct" is to oppose them because they know the long-term importance of "discipline in the factory" and "political stability"; in so far as the business class has control over what the government does, it tends therefore to favor conservative policies.

It is now widely agreed, even by many outside the Marxist tradition, that the mass unemployment created in the early 1980s across the capitalist world had the function of weakening trade unions and other working class institutions. How far this was a conscious policy varied from country to country and is, in any case, difficult to detect. Reagan's early policy of fiscal expansion accompanied by excessive monetary restraint may have been deliberate; or it may just have been a convenient outcome of the monetarist muddle that passed for an economic strategy at that time, which the White House saw little need to correct.

It would be wrong, however, to expect that just because unemployment is necessary it will be experienced uniformly across the capitalist world. What may be necessary after a crisis is a way of reorienting the structure of the economy so that businesses become more competitive in the changing international market; workers' skills and attitudes need to be changed along the way. How far this requires a more authoritarian and punitive labor market environment can depend on how antagonistic the institutions of labor relations are and how far the state can control the process of restructuring. That this does not necessarily involve mass unemployment, even in the dire circumstances of the 1970s and 1980s, is shown by an interesting recent analysis by the Swedish political economist Goran Therborn (1986).

Therborn's book draws attention to five countries that have survived the crisis and the subsequent restructuring without experiencing mass unemployment. Whatever other changes the working classes of Sweden, Japan, Norway, Austria and Switzerland have had to endure over this period, only comparatively small proportions have suffered the indignity and tragedy of being unable to find a job. The contrast between these and other countries is quite startling: Holland, to take one of the bad cases, went from a below average level of unemployment in pre-crisis days, about 2 percent, to levels of 12 percent to 14 percent in the present decade.

Table 1, which elaborates and updates Therborn's analysis, illustrates the divergency thesis, and shows how it occurred in two stages. In 1974/5, the first worldwide

Table 1
Unemployment in OECD Countries[a]

High (>10%)	1973	1979	1986
Belgium	2.7	8.2	11.4
France	2.6	5.9	10.5
Italy	6.2	7.6	10.9
Netherlands	2.2	5.4	13.3
Spain	2.5	8.5	21.5
UK	3.0	5.0	11.8
Medium (5–10%)			
Australia	2.3	6.2	8.0
Canada	5.5	7.4	9.6
Denmark[b]	1.1	6.8	7.8
Finland	2.3	5.9	5.5
Germany	0.8	3.2	8.0
USA	4.8	5.8	7.0
Low (<5%)			
Austria	1.1	2.1	3.4
Japan	1.3	2.1	2.8
Norway	1.5	2.0	1.9
Sweden	2.5	2.1	2.2
Switzerland	0.4[c]	0.3	0.8

[a]OECD standardized rates.
[b]non-standardized.
[c]1975.

Source: *OECD Economic Outlook*, June 1987.

simultaneous recession separated out the low unemployment countries from the rest of the pack; then with the recessions of the early 1980s another group of countries separated itself off and climbed to double-digit levels of unemployment. In Belgium, Holland, Britain and Spain these have been sustained for a number of years. A middle group comprising Australia, Finland, West Germany and the United States kept within a range of 5 percent to 10 percent. A few countries have switched between the middle and high unemployment groups. Comparison of these groups with the low unemployment countries seems to suggest that their tragedy may not have been necessarily so severe, even if the capitalist crisis was itself unavoidable.

Therborn rejects any simple economic explanation as to why the low unemployment countries did relatively so well. Taken as a group, they were not notably under less pressure from the crisis, as compared with the other countries. Even Japan, whose businesses had enjoyed such remarkable success in the 1950s and 1960s, was faced with the problem of 100 percent oil dependency after 1974. Switzerland's growth rate was lower than average during the crisis years. Nor did they, as a group, experience especially low rates of labor force growth. All these countries have gone through extensive restructuring of their industries in the past decade; and businesses have been able to restore their profitability after crises.

Their achievement in doing so without major unemployment is explained, instead, by the fact that all of these countries had an *institutionalized* commitment to full employment, established well before the onset of the crisis. In every case, either through strong trade union pressure, or through the commitment of bourgeois parties to the legitimation of the system, there was a widespread consensus that full employment should be a major priority of government and big business. Consequently, governments of any hue, whether social democratic or conservative, enacted whatever policies they considered necessary to ward off unemployment when the crisis struck. The strength of this commitment in Sweden, for example, is summed up in the following opening statement from the 1944 ''Post-War Program of the Labor Movement'': ''The whole people at work is the primary goal of our economic policy. Monetary system and public finance, price policy and wage policy, private and public enterprise — everything shall serve the provision of full employment to labor force and the material means of production.''

Two tools at the disposal of policymakers were the traditional methods of fiscal and monetary policy. The former was used to good effect. With the exception of Switzerland, all low-unemployment countries enacted sharply expansionary fiscal policies after the recessions of 1974 and the early 1980s. But Keynesianism was only a part of the story. In addition these countries used an array of labor market policies that operated on both the supply and the demand for labor. Through the crisis years the Swedish government, for example, devoted substantial effort to restructuring the labor force, both through vocational retraining and mobility policies, and through special public works schemes and subsidies to industry to manage the restructuring process while limiting the number of redundancies. Such subsidies were widely used, too, in Norway. In Switzerland, by contrast, the labor supply was managed in a particularly racist and sexist way, by securing the jobs of domestic male workers, and requiring foreign workers to leave. In Japan, much of the necessary restructuring was handled through the paternalistic strategies of the large corporations which could shift workers from one industry to another while keeping them still in the same company. This has meant numbers of workers being underemployed, and so the official unemployment figures need to be taken with caution. Yet the fact remains the companies have so far been able to restore profitability without mass unemployment. Appeals to loyalty, rather than the raw discipline of the unemployment threat, have been the traditional mechanism of gaining worker consent and eliciting sacrifices where necessary. (At the time of writing, September 1987, this system is under severe strain, faced with a near doubling in the yen's dollar value over the previous three years, and an unemployment rate of around 6 percent has been forecast. It may be that, for the first time, the corporation support system will be inadequate on its own and the Japanese state policies will be put to the test.)

The experience of other countries is put down by Therborn to their abandonment of the full-employment policy priority, as soon as the pressure of the crisis was upon them. West Germany is a case in point: never imbued with any wide institutional predilection towards full employment, it maintained through the 1970s a restrictive monetary policy sufficient to stifle an adequate growth of demand, and in 1981/2 the Social Democratic government even took a deflationary stance. In the United States, similarly, there has never been any substantial political pressure from organized labor for full employment policies, so it is not surprising that rises in unemployment even occasionally to double digit levels has been accepted. In Britain, despite a commitment in wartime to full employment in principle, subsequent policies to back it up at times of crisis have traditionally been subordinated to the interests of internationally-oriented financial capital: this was first shown most dramatically in the postwar era by the sacrifice of full employment to the goal of defending the pound in the 1960s. It happened again in 1976 when the Labour Government capitulated to the demands of the IMF. Later, Prime Minister Callaghan signalled his view that full employment was beyond the capacity of the government to aim at. And so the stage was set for Thatcherism before Margaret Thatcher actually came into power.

There is, however, a limit inherent in Therborn's kind of approach to unemployment: that is, that the restructuring of international economic relations itself undermines the theoretical relevance of looking at countries as appropriate units of analysis. International restructuring implies both that the centers of hegemonic power are shifting, primarily towards the Pacific rim, and that capital itself is becoming increasingly internationalized. Not only has trade continued to grow faster than the world's economies, also the world's money markets have in the 1980s become dramatically fluid, with vast sums of money changing hands in the major financial centers outside the control of any particular nation state. Production and direct investment, too, have ever increasingly tended to straddle country boundaries.

In the light of this internationalization, the significance of divergent national unemployment rates is reduced. If mass unemployment can be avoided in some areas of the global market, this may be to note nothing different from the regional diversity to be found within many countries: you can reduce unemployment in some regions, but not in all of them when a crisis occurs. Such a criticism is most obvious in the case of Switzerland, where, at least in part, the unemployment was exported with the foreign workers who had to leave the country. The successful restructuring of Japanese companies has been partly at the expense of businesses elsewhere. Furthermore, when the economy of a country becomes so internationally integrated, as for example it is in Britain, there is only a limited extent to which one can still talk of a specifically British capitalist class, and a functioning unit called the British economy (Radice 1984).

In other words, the success of a few countries achieving low unemployment during a time of restructuring does not repudiate the basic truth underlying the Marxian "reserve army" thesis.

REAGANOMICS AND THATCHERISM

In the framework suggested in this paper, Reaganomics and Thatcherism might be thought of as specific political forms for the restructuring of labor market relations, deriving from the particular conjunctures in the United States and Britain. Their similarities have often been noted. To take just one dimension, both leaders expanded military spending by substantial amounts, at the same time crashing the economy with deflationary policies within two years of taking office. Yet their subsequent fiscal and monetary policies have diverged. Let us briefly examine the political economic background to these macroeconomic strategies.

The recession generated in 1982 by the contractionary monetary and exchange rate policies of Volcker at the Federal Reserve Board (between 1979 and 1981 the real money supply fell by about 7 percent, while with deregulation of banks the demand for money rose) was enough, in the face of the already weak United States labor movement, to overcome much of workers' resistance to restructuring. Subsequently, the economy was expanded Keynesian style, with tax cuts and expanded military spending, providing the conditions for the realization of surplus value that had temporarily been removed in the recession. Profits improved from disastrously low levels, and unemployment came down to about 7 percent by 1986 (see the paper by Tom Michl in this volume). In Britain, by contrast, the trade union movement was still numerically strong, with over half the work force in 1980. There were no easy battles to be won, none comparable to Reagan's triumph over the air traffic controllers union, PATCO. The unemployment rate which soared in the first two years remained high even during the period of growth after 1982, held there by continuously restrictive fiscal and monetary policies. Only by 1984 did the government consider itself strong and well-prepared enough to challenge the strongest union's ideological grip: the miners' strike lasted a whole year, and there were gains in the support the miners mobilized in many sections of the working class, but the overall result was a split and defeat for the National Union of Miners. While other unions remain strong, however, and while labor relations remain potentially as antagonistic as they have been, a Keynesian policy to reduce unemployment through public spending or tax cuts would undermine the restructuring strategy.

Yet this view of Reaganomics and Thatcherism is too narrow to capture their full significance. Not only the old labor relations, also the old assumptions about consensus politics, based on the ideas of Keynesianism and social democracy, have been jettisoned in Britain. Traditional political processes and alignments were themselves being undermined in the 1970s, due in part to the recurring crises in the economy. Thatcherism is thus explained as rising from the phoenix of the ashes of social democracy. It is unreservedly a radical break from what had prevailed earlier, even though the macroeconomic policies were anticipated by the previous Labour Government. "Monetarism," interpreted as a strategy of targeting the growth of the money supply, began in the mid-1970s; interpreted, however, as a strategy of laissez-faire, as an attempt to reduce the state's role in the economy (especially the welfare state), it began with the Consevatives in 1979.

Thatcherism has been described as embracing a philosophy of "authoritarian populism" (see Hall 1985), a deliberately contradictory term. It refers to the way Thatcher reached out for her support directly to people, appealing to traditional family concerns via a highly professional and modern use of the media, while at the same time moving to strengthen the power of authority in many spheres of life: in law and order, by expanding the police and the military; in public sector employment by raising the relative pay and power of managers; in the workplace by removing some of the rights of workers; in politics by strengthening central government at the expense of local, and the cabinet at the expense of Parliament.

It is doubtful whether the appearance of Reaganomics was quite as radical in the environment of the United States. The tradition of laissez-faire and monetarism was lurking in the wings in the days of High Keynesianism, and never far from view. Social democracy and the welfare state consensus were never established there to the same extent in the first place. It is true that, with the rise to fame of Milton Friedman, the emergence of supply-side economics and the explicit rejection of Keynesianism, it appeared that a major break in the ways of doing macroeconomic policy was at hand.

Yet, in the post-1982 boom, Keynesianism in effect was re-asserted within the American economy. In the context of the world economy, too, the Keynesian spirit survives. Rather than leave the world market to adjust automatically, a continued effort has been made (especially by Treasury Secretary Baker) at summit meetings of the Group of Five or Group of Seven countries to overcome the international contradictions of Keynesianism and re-impose the doctrine on a global level, through coordinated macroeconomic policies.

Thatcherist policies and ideals have not been confined to Britain and the United States: similar policies, such as deflation, privatization of industry, contraction and privatization of health and welfare provisions, and so on have spread by example to Europe, where, for example in France, Prime Minister Chirac gained power. How far they provide a successful restructuring strategy for capital is, however, open to question especially as, contrary to mainstream textbook theory, successful capitalist regimes in the past tend to have been far distant from the free-market model. Most have enjoyed a modernizing and interventionist state sector.[1]

I conclude this section, however, with a note of caution over how far the framework of restructuring I have been using here is applicable to Thatcherism and the "authoritarian populist" strategies that appear in other small countries. The most widely accepted Marxist view, argued above, is that they constitute capitalist responses to the crisis. An alternative explanation is that they are simply the contradictory response to the increasing internationalization of capital, a tendency that has nothing directly to do with crisis as such. Thus, Atkins (1986) likens the politics of Thatcherism to similar tendencies in Latin America, where, even in the 1960s, authoritarian regimes arose with populist urges in the face of the disjunctures between national bourgeoisies and international capital. Nationalism, in this light, is in part an inter-capitalist struggle, rather than, as emerges from the "response to crisis" thesis, merely an ideological illusion which helps capital in the incorporation of the working class. This view, if correct, would suggest that Thatcherism and other manifestations of authoritarianism may be more than just a passing phenomenon in the evolution of capitalism.

CONCLUSION AND QUALIFICATIONS

It is common-place nowadays to argue that macroeconomic policy, particularly for small countries, is becoming almost completely determined by the global market. It is notable how similar policies come to be enacted by governments of diametrically opposite persuasions: compare for instance the monetarism of the later Socialist regime under President Mitterand with monetarism anywhere else. Conventional theory tells us that fiscal policy has limited effectiveness in a world with "perfect" capital mobility, since rises in government spending serve only to crowd out exports by pushing up the exchange rate. Interest rates are more or less completely tied to the world's money markets, differing only to the extent that there is an exchange rate risk to be discounted. Added to such economic mechanisms of conformity, there are the increased political efforts to coordinate macroeconomic policies across the countries.

Belying all this, however, is the fact that different countries do still follow different policies, and this is because of their differing institutional determinants. Moreover, the evolution of the economy in each country does still depend on these policies and the institutions. The divergence of unemployment rates across the sixteen major OECD countries is consistent with that. The conclusion is that while restructuring the economy is the major task of all modern governments in all countries, the methods whereby this is done, how far in collaboration with business, and how far it is pursued in a cooperative or antagonistic way, vary substantially from country to country.

NOTE

1. Some of the contradictions of the Reaganomics strategy are reviewed in the papers by Tom Michl and John Miller in this volume. See also Green and Sutcliffe (1987:Chap. 18).

26

The Perils of Economic Ramboism: The Next Recession Threatens Deflation and Depression

ANDRE GUNDER FRANK

Summary of the Causes of the Present Crisis 10. Official Optimism in the United States, when it would have been better to be pessimistic: which prolonged the crisis.
Maurice van Vollenhoven
Economic Crises (1933)

INTRODUCTION

The official economic optimism and claims of economic recovery by the Reagan Administration and its Western allies rest on the shakiest of foundations. In fact, the cyclical recovery since 1983 is now ending. Moreover, the recovery was largely based on speculation in and on the United States and its debt financed expansion. The recovery was very weak in Europe and Japan, bypassed much of the indebted Third World altogether, and even so used up most available orthodox monetary and fiscal policies to sustain it. The economic policies of the major powers are not coordinated, and the speculatively overladen and increasingly imbalanced world multilateral trading system cannot withstand the strain of another recession without major economic, social and political convulsions. For these and other reasons to be examined below, the next — that is the fifth — recession in the current world economic crisis threatens to become a major world wide deflationary depression with aggravated trade wars or even renewed economic bloc tendencies, reminiscent of the 1930s American "Good Neighbor" Policy in Latin America, the Japanese "Greater East Asia Co-Prosperity Sphere," and the German "Lebensraum" and economic bloc in Central and Eastern Europe.

The official economic optimism has already been belied by recent events. The 1986 *Economic Report of the President* predicted 4 percent growth of GNP in 1986, 1987 and 1988. Yet GNP grew only 2.5 percent in 1986, down from the 2.7 percent of the year before. Industrial output rose less than 1 percent, and industrial investment, factory orders and housing starts declined absolutely. Planned investment is flat, and real investment may decline additionally in response to the new tax law, which eliminates some tax concessions on business investment just when they may be most needed to combat the next recession. The dollar-yen/mark exchange rate fell, but the United States trade deficit continued to increase anyway, because United States industry is not competitive. The official growth forecasts for Japan and Western Europe were also wildly over-optimistic. Economic growth barely reached 2.5 percent in the industrial West in 1986, slowed down at the end of the year, and threatens to decline further.

DEEPENING WORLD ECONOMIC CRISIS FROM 1967 TO 1982

The developing fifth recession of the present world economic crisis must be seen in the context and as the continuation of the previous four recessions in 1967, 1969–70, 1973–75, and 1979–82. None of the intervening cyclical recoveries recovered previous highs; and each recession was deeper, longer lasting, and more widespread than the preceding one by several important measures. The Joint Economic Committee (JEC) of the U.S. Congress has charted this downward trend for the United States. In each consecutive recession, the growth rate of GNP declined more and the amount of production and income forgone was greater than in the preceding one. The increasing depth of the cyclical declines in business investment was even sharper. In none of the recoveries did the industrial capacity utilization rate recover its high point of the previous recovery, and in each recession the capacity utilization rate reached a new low point beneath that of the previous recession. The cyclical recession troughs and recovery peaks of the rate of productivity growth also declined from each recession to the next.

The rates and total amounts of unemployment rose in each recession relative to the preceding one, and the unemployment lows also rose from each recovery to the next. In Europe, Japan and the Third World, unemployment rose even more. In the industrial OECD countries as a whole, unemployment roughly doubled from each recession to the next — from 5 million in 1967, to 8 million in 1970, to 15 million in 1975, and 33 million in 1982. In the Third World, unemployment exploded with the 1979–82 world recession and the 1982 debt crisis; and it has continued to grow ever since. Real wages and salaries started to decline in the United States in the 1973–75 recession and later in Europe, and they have never reached their previous levels.

Economic and political policy acted far more in response to, than anticipation of, these short cyclical ups and downs. The exigencies of the economic crisis provoked the switch from Keynesian demand management to monetarist restraint and supply-side economic policy, first by the Callaghan Labour government in England in 1976, and then by the Carter Administration in the United States in 1977. Most other western and Third World governments did the same (for detailed analysis until 1980, see Frank 1980, 1981).

The negative developments in the real economy led to, and were more than matched by, growth in the financial sphere, particularly in speculation, which replaced real investment and production as these ceased to be profitable. Despite monetarist policies to restrict the supply of money, monetary reserves multiplied more than tenfold in a decade. Credit finance mushroomed. Debt balloons grew to bursting tensions. These financial and often speculative attempts to compensate for the decline of the real economy appeared somewhat successful — until what had seemed a solution became a source of new problems. The debt finance of the Third World reached crisis proportions by 1982, resulting in a drastic decline of real production, income and trade. The outcome was reduced growth rates during the recession and the succeeding recovery in Europe and Japan, which are more dependent than the United States on Third World markets; and defense and debt financed speculative growth in the United States (analyzing Third World debt has become a growth industry itself, witness Frank 1984a and others).

THE ILLUSIONS OF THE REAGAN RECOVERY SINCE 1983

The United States recovery since 1983 is based on a mountain of debt. The most discussed debt is the federal budget deficit of $200 billion, doubling the accumulated federal debt to $2 trillion by an administration pledged to eliminate the deficit. However, corporate and other debt has also increased spectacularly. In January 1986, financier Felix Rohatyn (1986) observed with alarm that corporate debt grew three times as fast in 1984 and 1985 as in the preceding eight years to exceed total corporate net worth by 12 percent. Much of the new corporate debt in the United States has gone into leveraged junk bond financed conglomerate mergers of already existing productive facilities or into junk bond debt financed buy-ups of one's own stock to avoid predatory takeovers by others. This has significantly increased the ratio of debt to equity in American business, despite the spectacular bull market. This rise of stock values on Wall Street is not warranted by earnings and threatens a stock market crash.

Corporate borrowing increased from 56 percent of external corporate finance in 1975 to 81 percent in 1985. Corporate debt service has risen from 27 percent of cash flow during the 1976–79 recovery to over 50 percent of cash flow in the present one (Rohatyn 1986). Other private debt has likewise piled up. Consumer debt, real estate and farm debt, which have placed the Bank of America in trouble, energy-related debt with the decline in the price of oil, which wiped out Continental Illinois, not to mention the bad debts of the savings and loans which disrupted Ohio and Maryland, have all grown spectacularly during the upside phase of the business cycle. The president of the New York Federal Reserve Bank, Gerald Corrigan (1985), the JEC (1987) and others have warned that as a result United States debt is growing 15 percent faster than GNP and that the proportion of debt to GNP rose from 140 to 160 percent between 1983 and 1985 alone and topped 170 percent in 1986. Therefore, interest payments on the federal, like the corporate, debt also eat up alarmingly growing shares (which in the 1980s more than doubled from 10 to over 20 percent) of revenues and expenditures.

Perhaps more significant still is the fact that the growing and persistent United States budget and trade deficits have had to be covered by United States borrowing abroad — of one-third of domestic savings and one-half of the United States budget deficit according to Corrigan. Thus, in the first half of the 1980s, the rich United States was converted from the world's largest creditor to the world's largest debtor. By the end of 1985, the United States replaced Brazil as foreign debt world champion with $100 billion; and by mid-1987 United States foreign debts are variously estimated between $340 and $420 billion (the latter according to a *Washington Post* editorial reprinted in the *International Herald Tribune,* June 27–28, 1987). This foreign debt is projected to reach $1 trillion by 1990; and the corresponding interest payments to foreigners represent an increasing burden on the balance of payments, whose deficit is thereby made to grow in a vicious spiral. Moreover, the formal United States debts to the rest of the world are dwarfed by informal but no less real IOU debt represented by a cumulative dollar overhang of an estimated $2.5 trillion in the Eurocurrency market and elsewhere. This sum is equal to nearly 8 months goods and services (GDP) produced in the United States or ten years of United States exports. It is the measure of goods and services the United States has consumed or owed without having produced them, thanks to being able to issue dollars.

In the United States itself, bank failures *have risen during each year of the recovery.* From the post-Depression high of 34 during the last recession year 1982, United States bank failures rose to 45 in the first Reagan recovery year, 1983, and to 78 in 1984, when the GNP growth rate reached its recovery maximum of 7 percent. In 1985 and 1986 the growth rate declined back to 2.5 percent, and the number of bank failures rose to 120 and 138 respectively. The number of banks said to be in trouble according to bank regulators exceeds 1,000. Beginning with Citibank's $3 billion, the major United States banks had to put billions of dollars into bad debt reserves in 1987 in order to enable them to write off uncollectable bad loans, especially to the Third World. The savings and loans (S&Ls) are in much worse shape still. The notorious failures of the Ohio and Maryland S&Ls were only the tip of the iceberg. About half of the 3,200 S&Ls have less than the regulatory 3 percent net worth (assets minus liabilities) and are only kept open by legal fictions, because the Federal Savings and Loans Insurance Corporation has only $6 billion of assets to cover over $80 billion of bad S&L loans. Delinquency rates of home mortgages rose from 1 percent to 6 percent of total mortgages annually during the 1980s. However, laxer government bank regulations, for instance relaxing the rules that require registration of losses after 90 days, are a temporary stopgap at best. In the next recession, government bailouts and de facto nationalization — all ideology to the contrary notwithstanding — are likely to become necessary on a massive scale. (These data were compiled by the author from several scattered sources. Similar data and analysis were recently published by Malabre 1987, also cited below.)

What makes these developments most alarming is the fact that they occurred *during the recovery* and that they were necessary to sustain this "recovery" as far as it has gone. What will happen when in the next recession revenues and cash flow decline, interest obligations become even more burdensome and junk bonds and other obligations are devalued and/or defaulted? What happens when much more deficit finance will be necessary to combat a recession, but — as evidenced by Gramm-Rudman — the necessary political capital and will has already been squandered on the previous "recovery"? Addressing American bankers, Corrigan (1985) warned:

> servicing even the existing levels of debt in a less favorable economic interest rate environment could prove very difficult. Taking account of where we are on the business cycle and it is still on the upswing, the already existing delinquency rates on home mortgages and non-performing loans in the banking system, the private sector might be in a false sense of security. Trends in the private sector may not justify the complacency.

Increasing cries of alarm are heard elsewhere as well. For instance, a *Fortune* (March 16, 1987) cover announced "The Coming Defaults in Junk Bonds." Financier Felix Rohatyn wrote in the June 11, 1987 *New York Review of Books*, "The United States today is headed for a financial and economic crisis . . . A probability five or six years ago became a probability more recently, and has now become a virtual certainty." The *Wall Street Journal* financial editor, Alfred Malabre, demonstrates even more assurance in his 1987 book *Beyond Our Means: How America's Long Years of Debt, Deficits and Reckless Borrowing Now Threaten to Overwhelm Us:* "The main message here is that the hurricane can't be stopped, that we can only try to make things less nasty when it hits, and the first step in that modest effort is to understand the nature of the trouble."

But the trouble is not only American but in the world economy, which we must try to understand as well. There is even less reason for complacency and more for alarm if we examine some of the ways in which these debts intersect internationally. Consider the relation between Third World and corporate debt. Once banks judged that loans to the Third World had ceased to be profitable or judicious after 1982, they expanded into United States corporate debt, increasing substantially the growth rate of their commercial loans. However, some of these new commercial loans to domestic United States corporations have proven even more speculative and less secure than the Third World loans, many of which are now acknowledged to have been unwise and to be uncollectable.

Connections between sectors and countries likewise conduct financial currents through the world economy. The decline in oil prices in early 1986 further reduced the capacity of exporters like Mexico to service their debts. The same is true of oil (and the entire energy sector) debt in the United States, which in turn affects real estate debt in domestic oil producing regions like Texas. Moreover, many of the takeovers have involved corporations with energy and particularly oil holdings. Similarly, agricultural prices affect Third World, as well as the United States and other industrial country, exporters who compete on the world market. Lower agricultural prices anywhere threaten farm sectors everywhere, and the banks that have lent to them. Latin American debt has generated import reductions and export surpluses, which spell massive losses of export markets and profits for American industry and agriculture.

In summary, the natural response to the decline in profits and investment opportunities in the real economy and the resultant slowdown of real growth, particularly during the 1973–75 recession, was to turn increasingly to financial speculation. In the 1970s much of this speculation was directed to Latin American, OPEC, socialist and other Third World economies, which was reflected in the growth of the Third World debt and OPEC surplus. The 1979–82 recession and the consequent decline in oil and other commodities prices, as well as the monetary and fiscal responses in the United States and elsewhere in the West, then generated the Third World debt crisis and the decline of OPEC. Therefore, further Western speculation in and on these economies became untenable. Accordingly, financial speculation, which became increasingly necessary as real growth continued to falter even in the "recovery" since 1983, had to look for greener pastures elsewhere. These were found first in the United States — in federal treasury certificates issued to finance the growing deficit, new and rising corporate equity stocks and junk bonds, etc. — and then also in Japan and some other markets. However, this newly directed 1980s increase in financial speculation is even less backed up by real growth than its immediate predecessor was in Latin America and OPEC in the 1970s. Therefore, the next recession threatens to make continuation of this speculation even more untenable in the West than the 1979–82 recession did in the Third World. Consequently, deflating, if not bursting, the new speculative balloon becomes ever more necessary and likely in the United States and more recently also in Japan, as the next recession renders continued reliance on financial speculation ever less possible. The apparent speculative solution threatens to turn into a real depressive problem with a vengence, now in the West as well.

AMERICAN POLITICAL ECONOMIC RAMBO-OPTIMISM AGGRAVATES THE CRISIS

The next recession therefore — whether it starts in the real economy and spreads to the financial sector or vice versa — is likely to aggravate the spread of the world economic crisis in all of these industrial and service sectors throughout the world's major economic regions. It will not only bankrupt Latin America and further undermine the development prospects of oil-exporting countries in the Middle East and Africa; it may also deprive the latter of foreign markets. It will also compromise export-led growth in East Asia. Singapore and Hong Kong already have experienced a severe growth crisis in 1985, due in part to financial over-speculation and reduced growth in electronics and petrochemical markets.

In particular, the next recession will aggravate the already growing imbalances between the United States, Japan and Western Europe, which may bring the existing international trade and financial system to or beyond a breaking point. The United States expansive military Keynesian fiscal policy, supply-side tax cuts, and restrictive monetary policy on the one hand, and West European and Japanese much more restrictive fiscal and more liberal monetary policies, including the liberalization of capital markets, contributed to the massive merchandise export surplus of Japan and trade deficit of the United States. The United States trade deficit is covered by, and can be sustained only through, corresponding capital inflows from Japan and to a lesser extent from Western Europe attracted by a higher rate of interest in the United States than elsewhere. This has generated the aforementioned growing American foreign debt.

The decline of American economic power, evidenced by the growing trade deficit and foreign debt, poses many problems and dangers. Not the least of these is the American refusal to acknowledge this changing reality of the world at both the official and popular levels. President Reagan's fondness for the ''Rambo'' film and the Rambo and Ollie North manias in the United States illustrate this refusal, as did their respective self-congratulations for invading tiny Grenada, bombing Libya, ''patrolling'' the Gulf, etc. The need to tie national pride to such symbolism is a measure of how far American power has really declined, and the American disregard of its allies in these incidents is a manifestation of American refusal to acknowledge the loss of any real basis for international leadership and cooperation.

With its present Rambo-like political economic policies, the United States seems to be repeating the mistakes of Britain, which tried to maintain a strong pound sterling as well as its imperial stance and consumption long after they had become unsustainable after World War I. The reality of world development produced a severe depression with deflation in Britain in the 1920s, and forced her to abandon unrealistic policies at even greater costs than if they had been modified in good time. Today, such policies in the United States threaten not only the American population, but the stability of the international economic and political system.

The growing imbalances between production and consumption among the world's major areas are stretching economic relations to a breaking point. Domestic financial speculation outpaces production of goods and non-financial services. International capital movements outvalue real trade by ten to one. Financial speculation and capital movements have become the monetary tail that wags the real economic dog, determining exchange rates, interest rates, demand and supply of money, prices, and through them production and employment. Exchange rate fluctuations respond almost entirely to speculative financial circumstances rather than to conditions of production and trade. They do not, therefore, correct trade imbalances but instead exacerbate them. Domestic fiscal policy has become largely powerless and monetary policy more adaptive than directive in even the strongest economies. For these and other reasons, the combination of the inevitability of the next recession, the financial bubble ready to burst, the exhaustion of readily available domestic monetary and fiscal policies, and the inability to coordinate even these inadequate domestic economic policies internationally threaten to turn the next recession into a major international deflationary depression, reminiscent of the 1930s.

THE NEXT RECESSION THREATENS WORLD DEFLATION
AND DEPRESSION

Coming economic events and policy could take three directions: deflation, inflation, or both. Contrary to the view of most observers, save Nobel Laureate James Tobin and lately UNCTAD (United Nations Commission of Trade and Development) there persists the danger of deflation. During the recovery, United States inflation declined largely due to the high dollar and low import prices. United States producer, and some consumer, prices declined by 1986, especially for raw material commodities, including petroleum and agriculture, and some real estate. Since 1981, the world commodity price deflation was about 40 percent — bringing commodity prices back to or below their depths during the 1930s depression — despite the cyclical "recovery." The reasons were low growth rates in the West; especially weak economic performance by European raw materials importers; savings in fuel, material weight and commodity use; investment slowdown and inventory control; moves to service industry and microelectronics/computerization, which use less materials; heavily subsidized agricultural exports by the EEC and others, which compete with Third World commodities; and the frantic pressure by many Third World countries and the United States, Canada and Australia to increase commodities production and exports so as to reduce their balance of payments deficits and service their foreign debts.

If the above happened during a *"recovery,"* the next *recession* threatens to generate another period of even more severe deflation, which could spread to many other credit supported and speculatively inflated values, which could deflate or collapse like an overinflated balloon. Then, declining profits, investment, production, and employment in the real economy can lead to bankruptcy and forced sales of real assets; and liquidity problems to forced sales of financial assets. As bankruptcy, write-down of assets, and demand constraint spread from one sector and area to another, so do deflation of values and depression of economic activity. In a highly interlinked world economy, a significant bankruptcy, financial scare, or political event anywhere can spark a global crisis.

Any significant deflation in the United States would by definition increase the value of the dollar relative to American goods and assets, but it is likely to devalue the dollar relative to foreign currencies and goods. Foreign holders of dollars — already over two trillion — would have an incentive to buy American assets and goods. The massive purchase of United States assets by foreigners could lead to nationalist objections. Preventive measures in the United States, such as new rules limiting foreign ownership of United States corporations, real estate, farm land, and perhaps of financial instruments as well could be enacted.

However, such measures would fuel a foreign capital flight from the United States, which could already be motivated by a decline in confidence in the United States economy in the face of bankruptcies, bank failures, and negative economic growth. This would drive the value of the dollar down instead of up, against other currencies. Any such decline in confidence in the banks, stocks, economy, or policy of the United States and a free fall of the dollar could have the most far-reaching and unforeseeable economic and political consequences. Exports from the United States could be stimulated, but American competition in European, Japanese, and other markets would not be welcomed and could generate pressures for anti-American protectionism or efforts to devalue other currencies or both. Interest rates in the United States could be forced up both by the demand for money in such a liquidity crisis and by the attempt to prevent the free fall of the dollar against other currencies. An increase in interest rates may be temporary as it would reinforce the depressive tendencies by further inhibiting borrowing and investment. Other countries would be loath to follow suit. These eventualities could generate increasing pressures towards protectionism and the formation of economic and political blocs.

The dangers of deflation could also induce governments to take an inflationary course. Small businesses and financial institutions may fail or submit to forced buyouts, thereby increasing monopoly concentration. For major economic enterprises and politically influential interests, however, central banks like the United States Federal Reserve could step in as the lender of the last resort. Other government intervention and industrial policy would be likely as well.

To come up with gargantuan funds, the central banks would have to create credit or print money, with the risk of generating inflation. In a deflationary and depressive context, however, money and credit creation need not be very inflationary if the velocity of circulation of this money declines as those who have cash prefer to hang on to it while prices decline. In 1985, the United States money supply increased by 13 percent (and GNP, 2 percent) while prices rose only 3 percent as the velocity of circulation fell appreciably.

As a debtor with huge obligations, the United States would benefit from reducing the value of its debt through inflation. Almost all of the large and growing government, corporate, consumer, and other private debt is denominated in United States dollars. To fulfill their debt obligations, other countries have to earn dollars; the United States government can print them. And if increasing the money supply stimulates inflation, so much the better, because inflation reduces the real value of foreign held United States dollars and debt. Indeed, if the United States could no longer service its debt, deliberate dollar inflation could reduce or wipe it out.

Inflation in the United States could have both inflationary and deflationary consequences elsewhere in the world. Prices of United States exports and other goods priced in dollars, such as petroleum, would rise in dollar terms. For countries with currencies pegged to the dollar or devalued against it, as in Latin America, the domestic consequences would be inflationary. But for countries with currencies revalued against the dollar the effects could be otherwise.

Monetary inflation in the United States would depress the dollar, and thereby stimulate United States exports to countries with stronger currencies, such as West Germany and Japan, reduce their exports, and exert recessive and perhaps deflationary pressures there. Indeed, any United States recession, whether accompanied by inflation or deflation, would have severe and deflationary consequences in Europe and Japan, whose industries are heavily dependent on the United States market, since their domestic markets have remained slack even during the past recovery. The loss or decline of the United States market during the next recession would depress Europe and Japan much more than the decline of the OPEC, Third World and socialist markets did in the last recession. Indeed, because these export markets did not revive during the recovery, the United States export market is all they have left. In Japan, slack domestic demand, export losses due to the declining dollar/rising yen, and therefore flat or declining real investment in 1986 and

1987 have already depressed the real economy and stimulated financial speculative "investments" following the recent American model. Any further loss of the vital American market could force Western Europe and Japan into a real depression — "Japan Is Heading Toward a Dangerous Depression" declares a five column headline on the opinion page of the July 30, 1987 *International Herald Tribune*. The possible response or alternative, foreshadowed in Japan by the 1986 Maekwa Commission and other recommendations and the more relationary 1987 budget, could be major domestic and/or regional expansive measures.

Another deflationary influence in Europe and Japan would be the loss of their dollar denominated assets through either bankruptcy or inflation in the United States. Deflation in the United States would involve the write down of some foreign-owned as well as United States-owned assets in the United States. Any rise in the domestic value of the dollar might be more than cancelled out for Europeans and Japanese, not to mention Arabs and others with assets in the United States, by bankruptcy, write-downs and forced sales. Inflation — perhaps deliberately — would also wipe out the real value of foreign-held dollar assets.

In short, a severe world deflation is not only very possible, but it is also compatible with national inflation in some countries and currencies. One way to see this apparent paradox is to consider what has already happened in the Latin American and some other Third World debtor countries. In terms of their national currencies, the effects of the debt crisis have been a severe depression — 10 percent decline in per capita national income in Latin America and Africa — accompanied by a severe inflation (exceeding 1,000 percent a year in Brazil and several times that in Bolivia). But in terms of foreign exchange (dollars and even more so, yen or European currencies) and the rampant "dollarization" (valuing everything in dollars) in their economies, not only commodity but also other product and asset prices, not to mention wages, in this part of the world have already suffered enormous deflationary declines. The new debt-for-equity swaps of Third World debts permits foreign purchases of Third World productive assets at bargain basement sale prices. However, with the 1980s world speculative shift from the Third World to the United States, the speculative bubble threatens to become un(main)tenable in the United States economy in the next recession as it did in the Third World and socialist debtor economies in the 1979–82 recession. Moreover, the same deflationary wave, which already engulfs the other debtor economies and sectors, including agriculture, mining and oil in the United States, now threatens to spread through much more of the United States and world economies. Moreover, the related domestic illusions in the United States, Europe and elsewhere that the great danger is inflation instead of deflation, cripples their potential reflationary monetary and fiscal policies — and thereby increases the pressure and likelihood of world deflation even more.

CONCLUSION: INTERNATIONAL ECONOMIC CONFLICT

These scenarios stand to sharpen economic and political conflicts of interest among the United States, Japan and Western Europe, as well as with the Third World. On debt, trade, exchange rates, fiscal, monetary, interest and other economic fronts, multilateral negotiations have lacked or come to naught. Negotiations for a New International Economic Order (NIEO) have come to a standstill, as have pleas for an agreement on Third World debt. Trade relations more and more resemble trade war. The United States, especially, has decried European and Japanese actions on steel, automobiles, agricultural products, military hardware, and East-West trade. The Group of Five agreement on exchange rates in September 1985 did serve to depress the value of the dollar, but during a period when it was already going down. Furthermore, the failure of the five participating industrial countries to reach an agreement to coordinate their domestic monetary and fiscal policies lends little foundation to their agreement on exchange rates. This failure is dramatized again and again at each Big Five meeting of finance ministers, who quarrel about their countries' budgets, interest rates, tariffs and trade policies, and the annual Big Seven "Economic" Summits at which the assembled heads of government manage to avoid the most pressing problems of economic coordination altogether by making political agreements about terrorism and the like.

American policymakers have sought to go it alone. Taking little account of the overseas effects of their domestic policies of high budget deficits, interest rates, and dollar exchange rates, they present their trade partners and allies with *faits accomplis* and then lord these over Europe and Japan, not to mention the Third World. This stance is based in part on arrogance and the delusion of United States economic superiority and invulnerability. But it is also based on the less than farsighted and principled use of valuable bargaining chips; the large American market, the dollar as the world reserve currency, the United States nuclear umbrella and military power, and the less tangible asset of foreign economic and political confidence in the United States.

The next recession, with an unfolding of the deflationary or inflationary scenarios or a combination of these, could erode some of these American advantages. American market demand would shrink, and increased protectionist pressure might restrict it still further, as the Hawley-Smoot tariff did in 1930. As the American trade deficit declines, and especially when it ceases to be covered by the massive voluntary inflow of Japanese and European capital now attracted to the United States, as well as by the less voluntary debt service from the Third World, the United States will lose the prerogative to live far beyond its productive means. Thus, living standards will be forced down in the United States as they already have been in Latin American and Africa.

The continued development of the world economic crisis and particularly the approach of its fifth recession then poses three main alternative scenarios. These may be summarized as; muddling through more of the same, star wars militarization of the economy, and political economic bloc formation. The first of these alternatives seems the least likely, as muddling through more of the same becomes increasingly difficult if not impossible because of the development of the crisis itself and its coming fifth recession, which would further aggravate, if not multiply, the unresolved problems already remaining from the previous ones.

A second alternative would be the attempt by the United States to press on even further with its unilateralist policy in the attempt to maintain its leadership against all odds — and the readiness of its Japanese and West European and other allies to continue to follow the American lead, particularly in its star wars program. This would involve an even more exaggerated militarization of the economy, in which the United States would seek to monopolize competitive technological/economic advantages and dominant political/ strategic power. In view of the American competitive disadvantages (which have not so far been enhanced by its military program), the feasibility of this scenario is uncertain, among other reasons because of its enormous costs. The civilian economy would have to be increasingly sacrificed to the military one, not only accompanied by more Rambo-Ollie mania in the United States itself, but among its allies as well. Therefore, the political costs of resistance and its repression would also be high to impose star wars on those whose interests would be sacrificed. It may be hoped that Democratic, Social Democratic, and Labour parties may still represent their constituents' domestic, foreign and East-West policy interests and play leading roles in preventing this star wars scenario from becoming dominant. Moreover, a United States-led star wars economy in the West would lead to analogous military programs, economic sacrifice, and political repression in a Soviet-led East.

A third alternative scenario (or set thereof) is the neo-mercantilist movement toward political economic blocs, in particular an American one in the Western hemisphere, a Japanese one in East Asia, or some combination of these in the Pacific Basin/Rim, and one of several possible West, East or East-West European arrangements with some ties to the Middle East and Africa (Frank 1984b). Of course, this scenario could also reenforce pressures for further militarization in some or all of these regions to close the vicious circle of increased United States ''defense'' expenditures. Japanese rearmament and a Franco-German military axis have already been proposed in influential circles. On the other hand a de-nuclearized Europe has also become a possible prospect. The continued development of the world economic crisis and the prospects of its coming fifth recession make this set of seemingly unthinkable scenario alternatives increasingly possible (for further analysis, see Frank 1986, 1987).

GENERAL BIBLIOGRAPHY

GENERAL BIBLIOGRAPHY

Aaron, Henry et al. 1986. *Economic Choices 1987*. Washington, D.C.: The Brookings Institution.

Aglietta, Michel. 1979. *A Theory of Capitalist Regulation: The U.S. Experience*. London: New Left Books.

Albelda, Randy. 1987. Coping With the New Federalism. *Dollars and Sense* 128:12–15.

Alcaly, Roger. 1978. An Introduction to Marxian Crisis Theory. In, *U.S. Capitalism in Crisis*, URPE/EEP. pp. 15–22. New York: URPE.

Armstrong, Philip, Andrew Glyn and John Harrison. 1984. *Capitalism Since World War II: The Making and Breakup of the Great Boom*. London: Fontana.

Atkins, Fiona. 1986. Thatcherism, Populist Authoritarianism and the Search for a New Left Political Strategy. *Capital and Class* 28:25–48.

Baily, Martin Neil. 1981. Productivity and the Services of Capital and Labor. *Brookings Papers on Economic Activity* 1:1–65.

Baldani, Jeffrey P. and Thomas R. Michl. 1987. A Balanced Budget Multiplier for Interest Payments. *Journal of Post Keynesian Economics* 9(3): 424–439.

Baran, Paul A. and Paul M. Sweezy. 1966. *Monopoly Capital*. New York: Monthly Review Press.

Bernstein, Peter. 1983. Capital Stock and Management Decisions. *Journal of Post Keynesian Economics* VI (1):21–38.

Blair, John. 1974. Market Power and Inflation: A Short-Run Target Return Model. *Journal of Economic Issues* 8(2):453–478.

Blaug, Mark. 1968. Technical Change and Marxian Economics. In, *Marx and Modern Economics,* David Horowitz (ed.). New York: Monthly Review Press.

Bluestone, Barry and Bennett Harrison. 1982. *The Deindustrialization of America*. New York: Basic Books.

_____ and John Havens. 1986. How to Cut the Deficit and Rebuild America. *Challenge* 29(2):22–29.

Boddy, Raford and James Crotty. 1974. Class Conflict, Keynesian Policies, and the Business Cycle. *Monthly Review* 26(5):1–17.

_____. 1975. Class Conflict and Macro-Policy: The Political Business Cycle. *Review of Radical Political Economics* 7:1–19.

Bosworth, B. 1982. Capital Formation and Economic Policy. *Brookings Papers on Economic Activity,* No. 1. Washington, D.C.

_____. 1985. Taxes and the Investment Recovery. *Brookings Papers on Economic Activity* 1:1–38.

Bowles, Samuel. 1985. The Production Process in a Competitive Economy: Walrasian, Neo-Hobbesian, and Marxian Models. *American Economic Review* 75(1):16–36.

_____ and H. Gintis. 1982a. The Crisis of Liberal Democratic Capitalism: The Case of the United States. *Politics and Society* 11(1):51–93.

_____. 1982b. The Welfare State and Long-Term Economic Growth: Marxian, Neoclassical, and Keynesian Approaches. *American Economic Review* 72(2).

_____, David Gordon and Thomas Weisskopf. 1983. *Beyond the Wasteland*. Garden City, NY: Doubleday.

_____. 1986. Power and Profits: The Social Structure of Accumulation and the Profitability of the Postwar U.S. Economy. *Review of Radical Political Economics* 18(1&2):132–167.

Boyer, Robert (ed.). 1986. *La Flexibilite du Travail en Europe*. Paris: La Decouverte.

Boyer, Robert and Pascal Petit. 1981. Employment and Productivity in the European Economic Community. *Cambridge Journal of Economics* 5(1):47–58.

Branson, William H. 1980. Trends in United States International Trade and Investment Since World War II. In, *The American Economy in Transition,* Martin Feldstein (ed.). pp. 183–257. Chicago: University of Chicago Press.

Braverman, Harry. 1974. *Labor and Monopoly Capital.* New York: Monthly Review Press.

Brenner, Robert. 1976. Agrarian Class Structure and Economic Development in Pre-Industrial Europe. *Past and Present* 70:30–70.

――――. 1986. The Deep Roots of U.S. Economic Decline. *Against the Current* 1(2):19–28.

Brimmer, A. F. and F. A. Dahl. 1975. Growth of International Banking: Implications for Public Policy. *The Journal of Finance* (May):341–363.

Bruno, Michael and Jeffrey D. Sachs. 1985. *Economics of Worldwide Stagflation.* Cambridge: Harvard University Press.

Burawoy, Michael. 1979. *Manufacturing Consent.* Chicago: University of Chicago Press.

BEA (Bureau of Economic Analysis). 1981. *The National Income and Product Accounts of the United States, 1929–76 Statistical Tables* (NIPA). Washington D.C.: U.S. Government Printing Office.

――――. 1984. *Survey of Current Business.* (July).

――――. 1986. *Survey of Current Business.* (July).

Business Week. 1983. Citibank's Pervasive Influence on International Lending. (May 16):124–126.

Carnoy, Martin, Derek Shearer and Russell Rumberger. 1983. *A New Social Contract: The Economy and Government After Reagan.* New York: Harper and Row.

Center for Popular Economics. 1986. *Economic Report of the People.* Boston: South End Press.

Chandler, Jr. A.D. 1977. *The Visible Hand.* Cambridge: Harvard University Press.

Chenery, H. B. and A. M. Strout. 1966. Foreign Assistance and Economic Development. *American Economic Review* 56(4):680–733.

Christensen, Laurits R. and Dale W. Jorgenson. 1969. The Measurement of U.S. Real Capital Input, 1929–1967. *Review of Income and Wealth* 15(4).

Christiansen, Jens. 1976. Marx and the Falling Rate of Profit. *American Economic Review, Papers and Proceedings* 66(2):20–26.

――――. 1982. Labor Productivity in the Steel Industry: A Comparative Study of the Federal Republic of Germany and the United States of America. Ph.D. dissertation, Stanford University.

―――― and Michele I. Naples. 1986. The Social Determinants of Productivity: Evidence from the U.S., U.K. and F.R.G. In, *The State, the Trade Unions and the Labour Market,* Vol. II, Gyorgy Sziraczki, (ed.). pp. 49–65, Budapest: Hungary Academy of Sciences, Institute of Economics.

Clark, Kim and Lawrence Summers. 1982. The Dynamics of Youth Unemployment. In, *The Youth Labor Market Problem*, Richard Freeman and David Medoff, (eds.). pp. 199–230. Chicago: University of Chicago Press.

Clark, Peter K. 1984. Productivity and Profits in the 1980s: Are They Really Improving? *Brookings Papers on Economic Activity* 1:133–163.

Cohen, Joshua and Joel Rogers. 1983. *On Democracy: Toward a Transformation of American Society.* New York: Penguin.

Cohen, Stephen S. and John Zysman. 1987. *Manufacturing Matters; The Myth of the Post-Industrial Economy.* New York: Basic Books.

Collier, Robert. 1985. Democratizing the Private Sector: Populism, Capitalism and Capital Strike. *Socialist Review* (March–April):41–63.

Conference Board. 1986. *Capital Appropriations and Capital Investment and Supply Conditions.* (January).

Coontz, S. 1966. *Productive Labor and Effective Demand.* New York: Augustus Kelly.

Cooper, Richard N. 1987. Arthur Okun Memorial Lecture. Yale University, (March 30).

Corrigan, Gerald. 1985. Address Before the American Bankers Association, New York, September 18.

Costanzo, G. A. 1965. Latin American Myths and Realities. *Barron's* (May 31).

Council of Economic Advisors. 1987. *Economic Report of the President.* Washington, D.C.: U.S. Government Printing Office.

———1987. *Economic Indicators.* Washington, D.C.: U.S. Government Printing Office.

Coutts, K., W.A.H. Godley and W.D. Nordhaus. 1978. *Industrial Pricing in the United Kingdom.* Cambridge: Cambridge University Press.

Cripps, F. and W. Godley. 1978. Control of Imports as a Means to Full Employment and the Expansion of World Trade. *Cambridge Journal of Economics* 2.

Cripps, T.F. and Roger Tarling. 1973. *Growth in Advanced Capitalist Countries, 1950–1970.* New York: Cambridge University Press.

Crotty, James. 1985. The Centrality of Money, Credit and Financial Intermediation in Marx's Crisis Theory. In, *Rethinking Marxism,* S. Resnick and R. Wolff, (eds.). pp. 45–82. New York: Autonomedia.

——— and Leonard A. Rapping. 1975. The 1975 Report of the President's Council of Economic Advisers: A Radical Critique. *American Economic Review* 65(5):791–811.

Darity, W. 1984. Loan Pushing: Doctrine and Theory. International Finance Discussion Papers, No. 247. Washington D.C.: Board of Governors of the Federal Reserve.

Davis, Mike. 1986. *Prisoners of the American Dream.* London: Verso.

de Brunhoff, Suzanne. 1967. *Marx on Money.* New York: Urizen Books.

———. 1978. *The State, Capital, and Economic Policy.* London: Pluto Press.

Denison, Edward F. 1969. Some Major Issues in Productivity Analysis: An Examination of Estimates by Jorgenson and Griliches. *Survey of Current Business* 49:1–27.

Department of Commerce. 1985. *The National Income and Product Accounts of the United States.* Washington, D.C.

Devine, James N. 1983. Underconsumption, Over-Investment and the Origins of the Great Depression. *Review of Radical Political Economics* 15(2):1–28.

———. 1986. Falling Profitability and Accelerating Inflation: A Conflict Theory Alternative to the Demographic Shift Theory of Full Employment. Loyola Marymount University, unpublished manuscript.

———. 1987. Cyclical Over-Investment and Crisis in a Labor–Scarce Economy. *Eastern Economic Journal.* (Forthcoming).

DeVroey, Michel. 1984. Inflation: A Nonmonetarist Monetary Interpretation. *Cambridge Journal of Economics* 8(4):381–399.

Diamond, S. 1979. *Towards a Marxist Anthropology.* The Hague: Mouton.

Doeringer, Peter B. and Michael J. Piore. 1971. *Internal Labor Markets and Manpower Analysis.* Lexington, MA: Heath.

Dorman, Peter. 1987. Micro-Models and Political Economy: The Case of Efficiency Wage Theory. Mimeo, University of California, Riverside.

Dornbusch, Rudiger. 1987. *Dollars, Debts, and Deficits.* Cambridge: MIT Press.

Dumenil, G., M. Glick and J. Rangel. 1984. The Tendency of the Rate of Profit to Fall in the United States, Part I. *Contemporary Marxism* 9:148–164.

———. 1985. The Tendency of the Rate of Profit to Fall in the United States, Part II: The Pattern of Irreversibility. *Contemporary Marxism* 11:138–152.

———. 1986. The Rate of Profit in the United States: From the Turn of the Century to the Nineteen Eighties. *Cambridge Journal of Economics* (Forthcoming).

———. 1987. Theories of the Great Depression: Why Did Profitability Matter? *Review of Radical Political Economics* 19(2).

Eckstein, Otto. 1981. *Core Inflation*. Englewood Cliffs, NJ: Prentice-Hall.

_____ and Allen Sinai. 1986. The Mechanisms of the Business Cycle in the Postwar Era. In, *The American Business Cycle: Continuity and Change*, Robert J. Gordon (ed.), pp. 39–105. NBER: University of Chicago Press.

Economic Report of the President. 1984. Washington, D.C.

_____. 1985. Washington, D.C.

Edwards, Richard C. 1979. *Contested Terrain*. New York: Basic Books, Inc.

_____, Michael Reich and Thomas Weisskopf (eds.). 1978. *The Capitalist System*. 2nd edition. Englewood Cliffs, NJ: Prentice-Hall.

_____, Michael Reich and Thomas E. Weisskopf. 1986. *The Capitalist System*. 3rd edition. Englewood Cliffs, NJ: Prentice-Hall.

Eisner, Robert. 1986. *How Real Is the Deficit?* Detroit, MI: The Free Press.

Elbaum, Bernard and Frank Wilkinson. 1979. Industrial Relations and Uneven Development: A Comparative Study of the American and British Steel Industries. *Cambridge Journal of Economics* 3(3):275–303.

Elliot, J. 1971. Funds Flow vs. Expectational Theories of Research and Development Expenditures in the Firm. *Southern Economic Journal* 37(4):409–422.

Epstein, Gerald. 1982. Federal Reserve Politics and Monetary Instability. In, *The Political Economy of Public Policy*, A. Stone and E. Harpham, (eds.). Beverly Hills: Sage Publications.

_____. 1985. The Triple Debt Crisis. *World Policy Journal* 2:625–657.

_____ and Thomas Ferguson. 1984. Monetary Policy, Loan Liquidation and Industrial Conflict: The Federal Reserve and the Open Market Operations of 1932. *Journal of Economic History* 64(4):957–983.

_____ and Juliet B. Schor. 1986. The Political Economy of Central Banking. Harvard Institute for Economic Research, Discussion Paper No. 1281.

Fairley, John. 1980. French Developments in the Theory of State Monopoly Capitalism. *Science & Society* XLIV(3):305–325.

Fazzari, Steven M. and Tracy L. Mott. 1986–87. The Investment Theories of Kalecki and Keynes: An Empirical Study of Firm Data, 1970–1982. *Journal of Post-Keynesian Economics* 9:171–187.

Federal Reserve Bank of New York. 1986. *Recent Trends in Commercial Bank Profitability*. New York: Federal Reserve Bank of New York.

Federal Reserve Bulletin. 1981. (August). Washington, D.C.

Feldstein, Martin. 1973. The Economics of the New Unemployment. *The Public Interest* 12:3–42.

_____ and Lawrence Summers. 1977. Is the Rate of Profit Falling? *Brookings Papers on Economic Activity* 1:211–228.

_____ and David Ellwood. 1982. Teenage Unemployment: What is the Problem? In, *The Youth Labor Market Problem*, Richard Freeman and David Wise, (eds.). pp. 17–34. Chicago: University of Chicago Press.

Ferguson, Thomas and Joel Rogers. 1986. *Right Turn; The Decline of the Democrats and the Future of American Politics*. New York: Hill and Wang.

Fernandez-Kelly, Patricia. 1983. *For We Are Sold, I and My People: Women and Industry on Mexico's Frontier*. New York: SUNY.

Ferrer, Aldo. 1985. *Living Within Our Means*. Boulder, CO: Westview Press.

Fine, Ben and Laurence Harris. 1979. *Rereading Capital*. New York: Columbia University Press.

Flaherty, Sean. 1987a. Strike Activity, Worker Militancy, and Productivity Change in Manufacturing, 1961–81. *Industrial and Labor Relations Review* (July).

_____. 1987b. Strike Activity and Productivity Change in the U.S. Auto Industry. *Industrial Relations* (July).

Foley, Duncan. 1982. The Value of Money, the Value of Labor Power and the Marxian Transformation Problem. *Review of Radical Political Economics* 14(2):37–47.

———. 1983. On Marx's Theory of Money. *Social Concept* 1(1):5–19.

———. 1986. *Money, Accumulation and Crisis*. New York: Harwood Academic Press.

Foss, M. 1984. *Changing Utilization of Fixed Capital: An Element in Long Term Growth.* Washington, D.C.: American Enterprise Institute.

Foster, John Bellamy. 1982. Marxian Economics and the State. *Science & Society* XLVI(3):251–283.

———. 1983. Understanding the Significance of the Great Depression. *Studies in Political Economy* 11:177–196.

———. 1984a. Investment and Capitalist Maturity. In, *The Faltering Economy*, J. B. Foster and H. Szlajfer (eds.). pp. 57–73. New York: Monthly Review Press.

———.1984b Marxian Economics and the State. In, *The Faltering Economy*, J. B. Foster and H. Szlaijfer (eds.). pp. 325–349. New York: Monthly Review Press.

———. 1984c. The Limits of U.S. Capitalism: Surplus Capacity and Capacity Surplus. In, *The Faltering Economy*, J. B. Foster and H. Szlajfer (eds.). pp. 198–213. New York: Monthly Review Press.

———. 1986. *The Theory of Monopoly Capitalism*. New York: Monthly Review Press.

——— and Henryk Szlajfer (eds.). 1984. *The Faltering Economy*. New York: Monthly Review Press.

Frank, Andre Gunder. 1980. *Crisis: In the World Economy*. New York: Holmes & Meier Publishers.

———. 1981. *Crisis: In the Third World*. New York: Holmes & Meier Publishers.

———. 1984a. Can the Debt Bomb Be Defused? *World Policy Journal* (Summer).

———. 1984b. *The European Challenge: From Atlantic Alliance to Pan-European Entente for Peace and Jobs*. Westport, CT: Lawrence Hill & Co. Publishers.

———. 1986. Is the Reagan Recovery Real or the Calm Before a Storm? *Economic and Political Weekly* XXI(21 & 22).

———. 1987. The World Economic Crisis Today: Retrospect and Prospect. Manuscript.

Freeman, Richard and James Medoff. 1982. Why Does the Rate of Youth Labor Force Activity Differ Across Surveys? In, *The Youth Labor Market Problem,* Richard Freeman and David Medoff, (eds.). pp. 75–114. Chicago: University of Chicago Press.

———. 1984. *What Do Unions Do?* New York: Basic Books Publishers, Inc.

Friedman, Milton. 1971. A Monetary Theory of Nominal Income. *Journal of Political Economy* 323–337.

——— and Anna Schwartz. 1969. *The Optimum Quantity of Money and Other Essays*. Chicago: Aldine.

Gans, Herbert. 1967. Income Grants and 'Dirty Work.' *The Public Interest* 6:110–113.

Garson, Barbara C. 1977. *All the Livelong Day: The Meaning and Demeaning of Routine Work*. New York: Penguin Books.

Gillman, Joseph M. 1958. *The Falling Rate of Profit: Marx's Law and Its Significance to Twentieth Century Capitalism*. New York: Cameron Associates.

Giussani, P. 1986. Profit Rate, Competition and the Choice of Technique. Unpublished paper.

Glick, M. 1987. Three Replies to the Okishio Theorem: An Industrial Organization View. University of Utah, mimeo.

Glyn, Andrew, and Bob Sutcliffe. 1972. *Capitalism in Crisis*. New York: Pantheon.

Gold, B. 1976. Tracing Gaps Between Expectations and Results of Technological Innovations: The Case of Iron and Steel. *Journal of Industrial Economics* XXV(1):1–28.

Goldfeld, Stephen M. and Lester V. Chandler. 1986. Ninth Edition. *The Economics of Money and Banking*. New York: Harper and Row.

Goldsmith, R. 1955. *A Study of Savings in the United States*. Princeton, NJ: Princeton University Press.

Goldstein, Jonathan P. 1985. The Cyclical Profit Squeeze: A Marxian Microfoundation. *Review of Radical Political Economics* 17(1&2):103–128.

Gordon, David M. 1975. Capital vs. Labor: The Current Crisis in the Sphere of Production. In, *The Economic Crisis Reader*, David Mermelstein, (ed.). pp. 392–406. New York: Vintage Books.

_____. 1978. Up and Down the Long Roller Coaster. In, *U.S. Capitalism in Crisis*, Union for Radical Political Economics (ed.). pp. 22–35. New York: Union for Radical Political Economics.

_____. 1980. Stages of Accumulation and Long Economic Cycles. In, *Processes of the World-System*, T. Hopkins and I. Wallerstein (eds.). pp. 9–45. Beverly Hills: Sage Publications.

_____. 1981. Labor-Capital Conflict and the Productivity Slowdown. *American Economic Review, Papers and Proceedings* 71(2):30–35.

_____ Richard Edwards and Michael Reich. 1981. *Segmented Work, Divided Workers*. New York: Cambridge University Press.

_____, Thomas E. Weisskopf and Samuel Bowles. 1986. A Conflict Model of Investment: The Determinants of U.S. Capital Accumulation in a Global Context. Mimeo, New School for Social Research.

Gordon, Robert J. 1979. The 'End-of-Expansion' Phenomenon in Short-Run Productivity Behavior. *Brookings Papers on Economic Activity* 2:447–461.

Gottheil, Fred M. 1966. *Marx's Economic Predictions*. Evanston: Northwestern University Press.

Gough, Ian. 1972. Marx's Theory of Productive and Unproductive Labor. *New Left Review* (November-December):47–72.

_____. 1979. *The Political Economy of the Welfare State*. London: Macmillan.

Grabowski, H. 1968. The Determinants of Industrial Research and Development: A Study of Chemical, Drug, and Petroleum Industries. *Journal of Political Economy* 76(2):292–306.

Green, Francis and Bob Sutcliffe. 1987. *The Profit System*. Harmondsworth and New York: Penguin.

Griffin, Keith. 1971. The Role of Foreign Capital. In, *Financing Development in Latin America*, Keith Griffin (ed). London: Macmillan.

Grunberg, Leon. 1983. The Effects of the Social Relations of Production on Productivity and Workers' Safety: An Ignored Set of Relationships. *International Journal of Health Services* 13(4):621–634.

_____. 1986. Workplace Relations in the Economic Crisis: A Comparison of a British and a French Automobile Plant. *Sociology* 20(4):503–529.

Gurley, John. 1971. State of Political Economy. *American Economics Review* 61:3–64.

_____ and Edward Shaw. 1956. Financial Intermediaries and the Saving-Investment Process. *Journal of Finance* (March):257–376.

Gwynne, S. C. 1983. Adventures in the Loan Trade. *Harpers* (September):22–26.

Hall, Stuart. 1985. Authoritarian Populism. *New Left Review* 151:115–124.

Hansen, Alvin H. 1938. *Full Recovery or Stagnation?* New York: W. W. Norton.

_____. 1955. The Stagnation Thesis. In, *Readings in Fiscal Policy*, American Economic Association (ed.). pp. 540–557. Homewood, IL: Richard D. Irwin, Inc.

Harrison, Bennett. 1972. Education and Underemployment in Urban Ghettos. *American Economics Review* 62:796–813.

Hartman, Chester (ed.). 1983. *America's Housing Crisis: What Is to Be Done?* Boston: Routledge & Kegan Paul.

Harvey, David. 1982. *The Limits to Capital*. Chicago: University of Chicago Press.

Hawley, J. 1979. The Internationalization of Capital: Banks, Eurocurrency and the Instability of the World Monetary System. *Review of Radical Political Economics* 11(4):78–90.

Heilbroner, Robert. 1980. *The Making of Economic Society*. Englewood Cliffs, NJ: Prentice Hall, Inc.

Herman, Edward S. and Louis Lowenstein. 1986. The Efficiency Effects of Hostile Takeovers. Working Paper #20, Center for Law and Economic Studies, Columbia University School of Law.

Hirschhorn, L. 1984. *Beyond Mechanization: Work and Technology in a Post-Industrial Age*. Cambridge: MIT Press.

Howenstine, N. G. 1984. U.S. Direct Investment Abroad in 1983. *Survey of Current Business* (August):18–40.

Hymer, Stephen. 1972. The Multinational Corporation and the Law of Uneven Development. In, *Economics and World Order from the 1970s to the 1990s*. J. H. Bhagwati (ed.). New York: Macmillan.

Inter-American Development Bank. 1984. *External Debt and Economic Development in Latin America*. Washington, D.C.: Inter-American Development Bank.

Itoh, Makoto. 1978. The Formation of Marx's Theory of Crisis. *Science & Society* XLII:129–155.

JEC. 1986. *The 1986 Joint Economic Report*. Washington, D.C.: Joint Economic Committee, Congress of the United Staes, March 11.

JEC. 1987. *The 1987 Joint Economic Report*. Washington, D.C.: Joint Economic Committee, Congress of the United States, March 5.

Jerome, H. 1934. *Mechanization of Industry*. New York: N.B.E.R.

Kalecki, Michal. 1939. *Essays in the Theory of Economic Fluctuations*. New York: Russell and Russell.

_____. 1943 (1971). Political Aspects of Full Employment. In, *Selected Essays on The Dynamics of the Capitalist Economy 1933–1970*, Michal Kalecki (ed.). pp. 138–145. Cambridge: Cambridge University Press.

_____. 1965. *Theory of Economic Dynamics*. New York: Augustus M. Kelley.

_____. 1971. *Selected Essays in the Dynamics of Capitalism*. New York: Cambridge University Press.

_____. 1984a (1967). The Problem of Effective Demand with Tugan-Baranovski and Rosa Luxemburg. In, *The Faltering Economy*, J. B. Foster and H. Szlajfer (eds.). pp. 151–158. New York: Monthly Review Press.

_____. 1984b. (1968). The Marxian Equations of Reproduction and Marxian Economics. In, *The Faltering Economy*, J. B. Foster and H. Szlajfer (eds.). pp. 159–166. New York: Monthly Review Press.

Kaldor, Nicholas. 1982. *The Scourge of Monetarism*. Oxford: Oxford University Press.

_____. 1986. *The Scourge of Monetarism*. New York: Oxford University Press.

Kamien, M. and N. Schwartz. 1975. Market Structure and Innovation: A Survey. *Journal of Economic Literature*.

Kaufman, Roger. 1978. Why Is the U.S. Unemployment Rate So High? *Challenge* 21:40–49.

Kenway, Peter. 1980. Marx, Keynes and the Possibility of Crisis. *Cambridge Journal of Economics* 4(1):23–36.

Keynes, John Maynard. 1933. National Self-Sufficiency. *The Yale Review* (June).

_____. 1964. *The General Theory of Employment, Interest and Money*. New York: Harcourt, Brace, and World, Inc.

Kindleberger, Charles. 1973. *The World in Depression: 1929–1939*. Berkeley and Los Angeles: University of California Press.

_____. 1978. *Manias, Panics and Crashes*. New York: Basic Books.

_____ and J. P. Laffargue. (eds.). 1982. *Financial Crisis: Theory, History and Policy*. Cambridge, England: Cambridge University Press.

Kolko, Gabriel. 1984. *Main Currents in Modern American History*. New York: Pantheon.

Kopcke, Richard W. 1982. Forecasting Investment Spending: The Performance of Statistical Models. *New England Economic Review* (Nov/Dec).

Koszul, J-P. 1970. American Banks in Europe. In, *The International Corporation*, C. P. Kindleberger (ed.). pp. 273–289. Cambridge: MIT Press.

Kotz, David M. 1982. Monopoly, Inflation, and Economic Crisis. *Review of Radical Political Economics* 14(4):1–17.

Krashevski, Richard S. 1986. What is Full Employment? *Challenge* 29(5):33–40.

Lacombe, John and Joan Borum. 1987. Major Labor Contracts in 1986 Provided Record Low Wage Adjustments. *Monthly Labor Review* (May):10–16.

Laibman, David. 1977. Toward a Marxian Model of Economic Growth. *American Economic Review* LXVII:387–392.

_____. 1981. Two-Sector Growth with Endogenous Technical Change: A Marxian Simulation Model. *Quarterly Journal of Economics* XCVI:47–75.

_____. 1982. Technical Change, the Real Wage and the Rate of Exploitation. *Review of Radical Political Economics* 14(2):95–105.

_____. 1983. Capitalism and Immanent Crisis: Broad Strokes for a Theoretical Foundation. *Social Research* 50(2):359–400.

_____. n.d. Technical Change, Profit and Growth: Immanent Crisis and Rigorous Theory. *Eastern Economic Journal*. (Forthcoming).

Lavoie, Marc. 1984. The Endogenous Flow of Credit and the Post-Keynesian Theory of Money. *Journal of Economic Issues* 18(3):771–797.

Lazonick, William. 1979. Industrial Relations and Technical Change: The Case of the Self-Acting Mule. *Cambridge Journal of Economics* 3(3):231–262.

Leadbeater, David. 1985. The Consistency of Marx's Categories of Productive Labor and Unproductive Labor. *History of Political Economy* 17:519–619.

Lefebvre, H. 1971. *Everyday Life in the Modern World*. New York: Harper and Row.

Leibenstein, H. 1966. Allocative Efficiency vs. X-Efficiency. *American Economic Review* LVI(3):392–415.

Leven, M., H. Moulton, and C. Warburton. 1934. *America's Capacity to Consume*. Washington, D.C.: Brookings Institution.

Levidow, Les and Bob Young (eds.). 1981. *Science, Technology and the Labour Process*. New York: Humanities Press.

Levine, David I. 1975. Developing Countries and the $150 Billion Euromarket Financing Problem. *Euromoney* (December).

Lim, Linda. 1986. The Progressive Effects of Foreign Investment on Third World Workers. Summer Conference, Union for Radical Political Economics.

Lipietz, Alain. 1985. *The Enchanted World: Inflation, Credit, and the World Crisis*. London: Verso.

_____. 1986. Behind the Crisis. *Review of Radical Political Economics* 18 (1&2):13–32.

_____. 1987. *Mirages and Miracles*. London: Verso.

Lipsey, Robert E. and Irving B. Kravis. 1987. Business Holds Its Own as America Slips. *The New York Times* (May 10).

Lloyd, Cynthia and Beth Neimi. 1979. *The Economics of Sex Differentials*. New York: Columbia University Press.

Lucas, Robert. 1977. Understanding Business Cycles. In, *Stabilization of the Domestic and International Economy*, K. Brunner and A. Meltzer (eds.). New York: North Holland.

_____ and Thomas J. Sargent. 1978. After Keynesian Macroeconomics. In, *After the Phillips Curve: Persistence of High Inflation and High Unemployment*. Federal Reserve Bank of Boston, Conference Series, No. 19.

Lutz, M. and K. Lux. 1979. *The Challenge of Humanistic Economics*. Menlo Park, CA: Benjamin Cummings.

MacEwan, Arthur. 1982. Slackers, Bankers and Marketers: Multinational Firms and the Pattern of U.S. Direct Foreign Investment — A Working Paper. Department of Economics, University of Massachusetts–Boston.

_____. 1985. The Current Crisis in Latin America. *Monthly Review* (February):1–18.

Magdoff, Harry. 1982. International Economic Distress and the Third World. *Monthly Review* 33 (11):1–13.

_____. 1971. The End of U.S. Hegemony. *Monthly Review* (October):1–15.

_____. 1974. Keynesian Chickens Come Home To Roose. *Monthly Review* 25(11):1–12.

_____. 1979. Productivity Slowdown: A False Alarm. *Monthly Review* 31(2):1–12.

_____. 1980. The Uses and Abuses of Measuring Productivity. *Monthly Review* 32(2):1–9.

_____ and Paul M. Sweezy. 1981. *The Deepening Crisis of U.S. Capitalism*. New York: Monthly Review Press.

_____. 1987. *Stagnation and the Financial Explosion*. New York: Monthly Review Press.

Mage, Shane. 1963. The "Law of the Falling Tendency of the Rate of Profit": Its Place in the Marxian Theoretical System and Relevance to the U.S. Economy. Ph.D. Dissertation, Columbia University.

Mandel, Ernest. 1975. *Late Capitalism*. London: New Left Books.

Malabre, Alfred L., Jr. 1987. *Beyond Our Means, How America's Long Years of Debt, Deficits and Reckless Borrowing Threaten to Overwhelm Us*. New York: Random House.

Marglin, Stephen A. 1974. What Do Bosses Do? The Origins and Functions of Hierarchy in Capitalist Production. *Review of Radical Political Economics* 6(2):33–60.

_____. 1985. *Growth, Distribution, and Prices*. Cambridge, MA: Harvard University Press.

_____ and Samuel Bowles. 1987. The Cost of Job Loss and the Incidence of Strikes. *Review of Economics and Statistics* 49(3):

Marx, Karl. 1935. *Wage-Labour and Capital/Value, Price and Profit*. New York: International Publishers.

_____. 1967. *Capital*. Three Volumes. New York: International Publishers.

_____. 1968. *Theories of Surplus Value*. Vol. 2. New York: International Publishers.

_____. 1970. *A Contribution to the Critique of Political Economy*. Moscow: Progress Publishers.

_____. 1973. *Grundrisse: Foundations of the Critique of Political Economy*. New York: Vintage.

_____. 1976. *Capital*, Volume I. New York: International Publishers.

_____. 1977. *Capital*, Volume 1. New York: Randon House.

_____. 1981. *Capital*, Volume 2. New York: Random House.

_____. 1982. *Capital*, Volume 3. New York: Random House.

Mattick, Paul. 1969. *Marx and Keynes: The Limits of a Mixed Economy*. Boston: Peter Sargent.

McCoy, Charles F. 1987. Beyond the Dollars: Debt Crisis Is Inflicting a Heavy Human Toll in the Dominican Republic. *Wall Street Journal*, August 20.

McCulloch, Rachel. 1986. Trade Deficits, Industrial Competitiveness, and the Japanese. In, *International Trade and Finance: Readings*, R.E. Baldwin and J.D. Richardson (eds). pp. 19–35. Boston: Little, Brown.

McKinnon, R. 1982. Currency Substitution and Instability in the World Dollars Standard. *American Economic Review* 72(3):320–333.

Medlen, Craig. 1984. Corporate Taxes and the Federal Deficit. *Monthly Review* 36(6):10–26.

Medoff, James. 1979. Layoffs and Alternatives under Trade Unions in US Manufacturing. *American Economic Review* 69(3):380–395.

Mensch, Gerhard. 1979. *Stalemate in Technology*. Cambridge, MA: Ballinger.

Michl, Thomas R. 1985. International Comparisons of Productivity Growth: Verdoorn's Law Revisited. *Journal of Post Keynesian Economics* 7(4):474–492.

Miller, John. 1986. The Fiscal Crisis of the State Reconsidered. *Review of Radical Political Economics* 18(1&2):236–260.

_____. 1987. Crisis Theory and the Expansion of the State. *Research in Political Economy,* Vol. 10. Greenwich, CT: JAI Press.

Mills, Rodney H. 1982. Spreads and Maturities on Eurocurrency Credits — Fourth Quarter 1981 and Two-Year Review. A memorandum. Washington: Board of Governors of the Federal Reserve.

Milward, Alan S. 1984. *The Reconstruction of Europe, 1945–51.* London: Methuen.

Minsky, Hyman. 1975. *John Maynard Keynes.* New York: Columbia University Press.

_____. 1982. *Can "It" Happen Again: Essays on Instability and Finance.* Armonk, NY: M. E. Sharpe.

_____. 1986. *Stabilizing an Unstable Economy.* New Haven: Yale University Press.

Mitchell, Daniel J. B. 1985. Shifting Norms in Wage Determination. *Brookings Papers on Economic Activity* 2:575–599.

Modigliani, Franco. 1977. The Monetarist Controversy or Should We Forsake Stabilization Policies. In, *Economic Review* (Spring, 1977). The Federal Reserve Bank of San Francisco.

Moseley, Fred. 1983. Marx's Concepts of Productive Labor and Unproductive Labor. *Eastern Economic Journal* 9:180–189.

_____. 1985a. The Rate of Surplus-Value in the Postwar U.S. Economy: A Critique of Weiss-kopf's Estimates. *Cambridge Journal of Economics* 9:180–189.

_____. 1985b. Estimates of the Composition of Capital in the Postwar U.S. Economy. Paper presented at the ASSA Annual Convention.

_____. 1986. Estimates of the Rate of Surplus-Value in the Postwar U.S. Economy. *Review of Radical Political Economics* 18(1&2):168–189.

Mosley, Hugh. 1982. Capital and the State. *Review of Radical Political Economics* 14(1):24–32.

Mueller, D. 1967. The Firm Decision Process: An Econometric Investigation. *Quarterly Journal of Economics* 81(1):58–87.

Musgrave, J. 1986. Fixed Reproducible Tangible Wealth in the United States: Revised Estimates. *Survey of Current Business* 66(1):51–75.

Nakatani, Takeshi. 1979. Price Competition and Technical Choice. *Kobe Unviersity Economic Review* 25.

Naples, Michele I. 1981. Industrial Conflict and Its Implications for Productivity Growth. *American Economic Review, Papers and Proceedings* 71(2):36–41.

_____. 1982. The Structure of Industrial Relations, Labor Militance and the Rate of Growth of Productivity: The Case of US Mining and Manufacturing, 1953–1977. Ph.D. dissertation, University of Massachusetts, Amherst.

_____. 1985. Dynamic Adjustment and Long-Run Inflation in a Marxian Model. *Journal of Post Keynesian Economics* 8(1):97–112.

_____. 1986. The Unraveling of the Union-Capital Truce and the U.S. Industrial Productivity Crisis. *Review of Radical Political Economics* 18(1&2):110–131.

_____. 1987a. Labor and Capital Utilization and the Productivity Slowdown. Mimeo, Rutgers University, New Brunswick, NJ.

_____. 1987b. Industrial Conflict, the Quality of Worklife, and the Productivity Slowdown in U.S. Manufacturing. *Eastern Economic Journal.* (Forthcoming).

_____. 1987c. Industrial Relations, Labor Costs and Long Waves in Postwar US Coal Mining. Mimeo, Rutgers University, New Brunswick, NJ.

Nell, E.J. n.d. *Prosperity and Public Spending.* London: Allen & Unwin. (Forthcoming).

Nordhaus, William. 1974. The Falling Share of Profits. *Brookings Papers on Economic Activity* 1:1974.

_____. 1980. Policy Responses to the Productivity Slowdown. In, *The Decline in Productivity Growth.* Conference Series No. 22. pp. 147–172. Boston: Federal Reserve Bank of Boston.

Nowzad, Bahram and Richard C. Williams. 1981. *External Indebtedness of Development Countries*. IMF Occasional Paper No. 3. Washington, D.C.: International Monetary Fund.

O'Connor, James. 1973. *The Fiscal Crisis of the State*. New York: St. Martin's Press.

Okishio, Nobuo. 1961. Technical Change and the Rate of Profit. *Kobe University Economic Review*.

Organization for Economic Cooperation and Development (OECD). 1979. *Main Economic Indicators, Historical Statistics*. Paris: OECD.

_____. 1982. Main Economic Indicators. Paris: OECD.

_____. 1985. *OECD Economic Outlook* 38.

Oster, Gerry. 1980. Labor Relations and Demand Relations: A Case Study of the "Unemployment Effect." *Cambridge Journal of Economics* 4(4):337–348.

Parboni, Riccardo. 1981. *The Dollar and Its Rivals: Recession. Inflation and International Finance*. London: Verso.

Parker, Mike. 1986. *Inside the Circle*. Detroit: Labor Notes Books.

Pasinetti, L. 1981. *Structural Change and Economic Growth*. Cambridge: Cambridge University Press.

Pecchioli, R. M. 1983. *The Internationalization of Banking: Policy Issues*. Paris: OECD.

Perlo, Victor. 1982. The False Claim of Declining Productivity Growth and Its Political Use. *Science and Society* 46(3):284–327.

Peterson, Wallace C. 1984. Economic Stabilization and Inflation. *Journal of Economic Issues* 18(1):69–100.

Pevzner, Ia. 1984. *State Monopoly Capitalism and the Labor Theory of Value*. Moscow: Progress Publishers.

Piore, Michael. 1978. Unemployment and Inflation: An Alternative View. *Challenge* 21:28–34.

_____ and Charles Sabel. 1984. *The Second Industrial Divide*. Chicago: University of Chicago Press.

Piven, Frances and Robert Cloward. 1971. *Regulating the Poor*. New York: Pantheon.

_____. 1982. *The New Class War: Reagan's Attack on the Welfare State and Its Consequences*. New York: Pantheon.

Pollin, Robert. 1985. Industrial Policy and Financial Stabilization: A Preliminary Outline. Unpublished manuscript, Department of Economics, University of California-Riverside.

_____. 1986. Alternative Perspectives on the Rise of Corporate Debt Dependency: The U.S. Postwar Experience. *Review of Radical Political Economics* 18:205–235.

_____. 1987. Two Theories of Money Supply Endogeneity: Some Empirical Evidence. Unpublished manuscript, Department of Economics, University of California-Riverside.

_____. 1988a. Deeper in Debt: The Changing Financial Conditions of U.S. Households. Joint Economic Committee of the U.S. Congress. (Forthcoming).

_____. 1988b. The Growth of U.S. Household Debt: Demand-Side Influences. *Journal of Macroeconomics*. (Forthcoming).

Porter, M. 1980. *Competitive Strategy*. New York: Free Press.

Pratten, C.F. 1971. *Economies of Scale in Manufacturing Industry*. Cambridge: Cambridge University Press.

Radice, Hugo. 1984. The National Economy — A Keynesian Myth. *Capital and Class* 22:111–140.

Rapping, Leonard A. 1979. The Domestic and International Aspects of Structural Inflation. In, *Essays in Post-Keynesian Inflation*, James H. Gapinski and Charles E. Rockwood (eds.). pp. 31–53. Cambridge, MA: Ballinger.

Reagan, Ronald. 1982. Introduction. In, *The Economic Report of the President*, The Council of Economic Advisors, (eds.). Washington, D.C.: U.S. Government Printing Office.

Rebitzer, James B. 1986. Unemployment, Long-Term Employment and Labor Productivity Growth. Ph.D. dissertation, University of Massachusetts, Amherst.

Reich, Michael, Richard C. Edwards and David M. Gordon. 1982. *Segmented Work, Divided Workers*. Cambridge: Cambridge University Press.

Rivlin, Alice. 1984. *Economic Choices 1984*. Washington, D.C.: The Brookings Institution.

Robinson, Joan. 1942. *An Essay on Marxian Economics*. New York: St. Martin's Press.

_____. 1946–47. The Pure Theory of International Trade. *Review of Economic Studies* 14:98–112.

_____. 1966. Introduction. In, *Studies in the Theory of Business Cycles, 1933–1939*, Michal Kalecki. New York: Augustus M. Kelley.

Roemer, John. 1978. Marxian Models of Reproduction and Accumulation. *Cambridge Journal of Economics* II:37–53.

_____. 1979. Continuing Controversy on the Falling Rate of Profit: Fixed Capital and Other Issues. *Cambridge Journal of Economics* (December).

Rohatyn, Felix. 1986. Address Before the Joint Economic Committee's 40th Anniversary Symposium. Washington, D.C., January 16.

_____. 1987. On the Brink. *New York Review of Books* 34(8):3–6.

Rosdolsky, Roman. 1977. *The Making of Marx's "Capital."* London: Pluto Press.

Rose, Stephan. 1977. On Classifying State Expenditures. *Review of Radical Political Economics* 9(4):31–42.

Rosenberg, Samuel and Thomas Weisskopf. 1981. A Conflict Theory Approach to Inflation in the Postwar U.S. Economy. *American Economic Review* 71(2):42–47.

Rost, Ronald F. 1983. New Federal Reserve Measures of Capacity and Capacity Utilization. *Federal Reserve Bulletin* (July).

Rowthorn, Robert E. 1975. What Remains of Kaldor's Law? *Economic Journal* 85:10–19.

_____. 1977. Conflict, Inflation, and Money. *Cambridge Journal of Economics* 1:215–239.

Rubin, I. I. 1972. *Essays on Marx's Theory of Value*. Detroit: Black and Red Press.

Salomon Brothers Inc., Bank Securities Department. 1983. *U.S. Multinational Banking Semi-annual Statistics*. December 22.

Samuelson, Paul. 1964. *Economics: An Introductory Analysis*. New York: McGraw Hill.

Schnader, Marjorie H. 1984. Capacity Utilization. In, *The Handbook of Economic And Financial Measures*, Frank J. Fabozzi and Harry I. Greenfield (eds.). pp. 74–104. Illinois: Dow-Jones Irwin.

Schor, Juliet B. 1985. Wage Flexibility, Social Wage Expenditures and Monetary Restrictiveness. In, *Money and Macro Policy*, Marc Jarsulic, (ed.). pp. 135–154. Boston: Kluwer-Nijhoff.

_____ and Samuel Bowles. 1984. Employment Rents and Class Conflict: An Empirical Investigation. Mimeo, University of Massachusetts, Amherst.

Schumpeter, Joseph. 1934. Depressions. In, *The Economics of the Recovery Program*, Douglass V. Brown, et. al. (ed.). pp. 3–21. New York: McGraw-Hill.

_____. 1939. *Business Cycles,* Vol. II. New York: McGraw-Hill.

_____. 1942. *Capitalism, Socialism and Democracy*. New York: Harper and Row.

_____. 1951. *Ten Great Economists*. New York: Oxford University Press.

Shaikh, A. 1978. *National Income Accounts and Marxian Categories*. Mimeo. The New School for Social Research.

_____. 1978a. An Introduction to the History of Crisis Theories. In, *U.S. Capitalism in Crisis*. New York: U.R.P.E.

_____. 1978b. Political Economy and Capitalism: Notes on Dobb's Theory of Crisis. *Cambridge Journal of Economics* 2:233–251.

_____. 1983. Marxist Theories of Crisis. In, *A Dictionary of Marxist Thought*, Tom Bottomore (ed.). London: Basil Blackwell.

_____. 1987. Organic Composition of Capital. In, *The New Palgrave: A Dictionary of Economic Theory and Doctrine*, John Eatwell, Murray Milgate and Peter Newman (eds.). London: Macmillan.

Shannon, Russell and Myles S. Wallace. 1985. Wages and Inflation: An Investigation into Causality. *Journal of Post Keynesian Economics* 8(2):182–191.

Shepherd, W.G. 1982. Causes of Increased Competition in the U.S. Economy, 1939–1980. *Review of Economics and Statistics* 64(4):613–626.

Sherman, Howard J. 1983. *Stagflation*. New York: Harper and Row, Publishers.

_____ and Gary Evans. 1984. *Macroeconomics: Keynesian, Monetarist, and Marxist Views*. New York: Harper and Row.

Slaughter, Jane. 1985. *Concessions and How to Beat Them*. Detroit: Labor Notes Books.

Solow, Robert. 1980. On Theories of Unemployment. *American Economics Review* 70:1–11.

Steedman, Ian. 1977. *Marx After Sraffa*. London: New Left Books.

_____, John Armstrong and Andrew Glyn. 1979. Comments on Political Economy and Capitalism: Notes on Dobb's Theory of Crisis. *Cambridge Journal of Economics* 4.

Stein, Herbert. 1969. *The Fiscal Revolution in America*. Chicago: University of Chicago Press.

Steindl, Josef. 1952. *Maturity and Stagnation in American Capitalism*. Oxford: Blackwell.

_____. 1968. Karl Marx and the Accumulation of Capital. In, *Marx and Modern Economics*, David Horowitz (ed.). pp. 244–269. New York: Modern Reader Paperbacks.

_____. 1976. *Maturity and Stagnation in American Capitalism*. New York: Monthly Review Press.

Stern, David and Daniel Friedman. 1980. Short-Run Behavior of Labor Productivity: Tests of the Motivation Hypothesis. *Journal of Behavioral Economics* 9(2):89–105.

Stone, Katherine. 1974. The Origins of Job Structures in the Steel Industry. *Review of Radical Political Economics* 6(2):61–97.

Stoneman, William E. 1979. *A History of the Economic Analysis of the Great Depression in America*. New York: Garland Publishing.

Summers, Lawrence H. 1986. Why Is the Unemployment Rate So Very High Near Full Employment? *Brookings Papers on Economic Activity* 2:339–383.

Sweezy, Paul M. 1942. *The Theory of Capitalist Development*. New York: Monthly Review Press.

_____. 1972. *Modern Capitalism*. New York: Monthly Review Press.

_____. 1981. *Four Lectures on Marxism*. New York: Monthly Review Press.

_____. 1987. Interview with Paul Sweezy. *Monthly Review* 38(11):1–28.

_____ and Harry Magdoff. 1975. Banks: Skating on Thin Ice. *Monthly Review* 26(9):1–21.

_____. 1984. Money Out of Control. *Monthly Review* (December):1–12.

Szymanski, Al. 1984. Productivity Growth and Capitalist Stagnation. *Science and Society* XLVIII (3):295–322.

Taylor, Lance. 1985. A Stagnationist Model of Economic Growth. *Cambridge Journal of Economics* 9(4): 383–404.

Therborn, G. 1984. The Prospects of Labour and the Transformation of Advanced Capitalism. *New Left Review* 145.

_____. 1986. *Why Some Peoples Are More Unemployed Than Others: The Strange Paradox of Growth and Unemployment*. London and New York: Verso.

Thurow, Lester. 1986. A Positive-Sum Strategy: A Review. *Scientific American* 255 (3):24–31.

Tobin, James. 1980. *Asset Accumulation and Economic Activity*. Chicago: University of Chicago Press.

Tonak, E. Ahmet. 1984. *A Conceptualization of State Revenues and Expenditures: The U.S., 1952–1980*. Unpublished Ph.D. dissertation. The New School for Social Research.

_____. 1987. The U.S. Welfare State and the Working Class; 1952–1980. *Review of Radical Political Economics* 19(1):47–72.

Triffin, R. 1978–79. The International Role and Fate of the Dollar. *Foreign Affairs* 57(2):269–286.

Tucker, Robert (ed.). 1978. *The Marx-Engels Reader.* 2nd edition. New York: W. W. Norton.

Tufte, Edward R. 1978. *Political Control of the Economy.* Princeton: Princeton University Press.

Turner, P. 1980. Import Competition and the Profitability of United Kingdom Manufacturing Industry. *The Journal of Industrial Economics* XXIX(2):155–166.

U.S. Department of Commerce. 1987. *Statistical Abstract of the United States.* (107th ed.) Washington, D.C.: U.S. Government Printing Office.

van Duijn, J.J. 1983. *The Long Wave in Economic Life.* London: George Allen and Unwin.

van Parijs, Phillippe. 1980. The Falling-Rate-of-Profit Theory of Crisis: A Rational Reconstruction by Way of Obituary. *Review of Radical Political Economics* 12(1)1–16.

Walker, John F. and Harold G. Vatter. 1986. Stagnation—Performance and Policy: A Comparison of the Depression Decade with 1973–1984. *Journal of Post Keynesian Economics* VIII (4):515–530.

Wallerstein, Immanuel. 1982. Crisis as Transition. In, *Dynamics of Global Crisis,* Samir Amin, Giovanni Arrighi, Andre Gunder Frank and Immanuel Wallerstein (eds.). pp. 11–54. New York: Monthly Review Press.

Wallich, Henry C. and Sidney Weintraub. 1971. A Tax-Based Incomes Policy. *Journal of Economic Issues* 5(2):1–19.

Weeks, John. 1979. The Process of Accumulation and the 'Profit-Squeeze' Hypothesis. *Science and Society* 43(3):259–280.

_____. 1982. *Capital and Exploitation.* Princeton, NJ: Princeton University Press.

Weintraub, Sidney. 1978. *Capitalism's Inflation and Unemployment Crisis.* Reading, MA: Addison-Wesley.

Weisskopf, Thomas E. 1978. Marxian Perspectives on Cyclical Crisis. In, *US Capitalism in Crisis,* Economics Education Project, Union for Radical Political Economics, (ed.). pp. 241–260. New York: URPE.

_____. 1979. Marxian Crisis Theory and the Rate of Profit in the Postwar U.S. Economy. *Cambridge Journal of Economics* 69:341–378.

_____. 1985. Sources of Profit Rate Decline in the Advanced Capitalist Economies: An Empirical Test of the High-Employment Profit Squeeze Theory. University of Michigan, mimeo.

_____. 1986. Class Conflict or Class Harmony?: A Study of the Effect of Worker Security on Productivity Growth in Eight Advanced Capitalist Economies. Working Paper, University of Michigan, Ann Arbor MI.

_____, Samuel Bowles and David M. Gordon. 1983. Hearts and Minds: A Social Model of U.S. Productivity Growth. *Brookings Papers on Economic Activity* (2):381–441.

_____, Samuel Bowles and David Gordon. 1985. Two Views of Capitalist Stagnation. *Science and Society* XLIX (3):259–286.

Weston, J. Fred and Eugene F. Brigham. 1982. *Essentials of Managerial Finance.* Sixth Edition. Chicago: Dryden Press.

Williams, R. C. et. al. 1981. *International Capital Markets, 1981.* IMF Occasional Paper No. 7. Washington: International Monetary Fund.

Willoughby, John. 1982. The Changing Role of Protection in the World Economy. *Cambridge Journal of Economics* 6:195–211.

Wojnilower, Albert M. 1980. The Central Role of Credit Crunches in Recent Financial History. *Brookings Papers on Economic Activity* 2:277–326.

Wolff, Edward N. 1986. The Productivity Slowdown and the Fall in the U.S. Rate of Profit, 1947–76. *Review of Radical Political Economics* 18:87–109.

_____. 1987. *Growth, Accumulation and Unproductive Activity: An Analysis of the Postwar U.S. Economy*. New York: Cambridge University Press.

Wolfson, Martin. 1986. *Financial Crises*. Armonk, NY: M. E. Sharpe.

Wright, Erik Olin. 1979. *Class, Crisis, and the State*. London: Verso.

Yaffe, David. 1973. The Marxian Theory of Crisis, Capital, and the State. *Economy and Society* 2(2):186–232.

Zeithaml, C. and L. Fry. 1984. Contextual and Strategic Differences Among Mature Businesses in Four Dynamic Performace Situations. *Academy of Management Journal* 28(4):841–860.

STATISTICAL APPENDIX

STATISTICAL APPENDIX

Compiled by Michele Naples, with Clara Graziano and
Bai-bai Chen for the Editorial Collective

These statistical tables are based on official government statistics, and are subject to the same qualifications as standard measures (e.g., the unemployment rate represents only those who meet the official criteria to qualify as unemployed). We have attempted to update most of those included in the previous URPE crisis reader (1978), as well as providing new series. However, the data are not always strictly comparable with those of the 1978 reader. The abbreviations used in headings and to identify sources are listed at the end, as are footnotes to particular series and sources.

	Gross National Product		**Corporate Sector**				
	1	**2**	**3** **After-tax** **corp** **profits**	**4** **After-tax** **profit** **rate,**	**5** **Corp** **debt/total**	**6** **Corp** **liquidity**	**7** **Bus** **failure**
Years	**B 1982 $**	**% C**	**B 1982 $**	**mfg[1]**	**debt, %**	**ratio[2]**	**rate[3]**
1947	1066.7	− 2.8	52.9	15.6		2.0	14.3
1948	1108.7	3.9	75.4	16.0		2.1	20.4
1949	1109.0	.0	75.7	11.6		2.2	34.4
1950	1203.7	8.5	71.1	15.4		2.0	34.3
1951	1328.2	10.3	68.9	12.1		1.9	30.7
1952	1380.0	3.9	71.0	10.3		1.9	28.7
1953	1435.3	4.0	67.2	10.5		1.9	33.2
1954	1416.2	− 1.3	72.2	9.9		2.0	42.0
1955	1494.9	5.6	92.3	12.6		1.9	41.6
1956	1525.6	2.1	84.7	12.3		1.8	48.0
1957	1551.1	1.7	81.8	10.9		1.8	51.7
1958	1539.2	− .8	72.1	8.6		1.9	55.9
1959	1629.1	5.8	91.4	10.4	22.75	1.9	51.8
1960	1665.3	2.2	86.7	9.2	22.65	1.8	57.0
1961	1708.7	2.6	88.5	8.9	22.81	1.8	64.4
1962	1799.4	5.3	107.5	9.8	16.49	2.0	60.8
1963	1873.3	4.1	115.4	10.3	16.95	2.0	56.3
1964	1973.3	5.3	129.8	11.6	16.99	2.0	53.2
1965	2087.6	5.8	149.1	13.0	18.05	1.9	53.3
1966	2208.3	5.8	151.1	13.4	18.84	1.8	51.6
1967	2271.4	2.9	143.2	11.7	18.62	1.8	49.0
1968	2365.6	4.1	136.3	12.1	19.84	1.7	38.6
1969	2423.3	2.4	119.8	11.5	21.80	1.6	37.3
1970	2416.2	− .3	96.0	9.3	21.61	1.6	43.8
1971	2484.8	2.8	111.0	9.7	21.11	1.6	41.7
1972	2608.5	5.0	126.5	10.6	22.09	1.6	38.3
1973	2744.1	5.2	129.5	12.8	23.86	1.5	36.4
1974	2729.3	− .5	92.4	14.9	21.98	1.6	38.4
1975	2695.0	− 1.3	112.5	11.6	20.11	1.7	42.6
1976	2826.7	4.9	128.4	13.9	19.92	1.7	34.8
1977	2958.6	4.7	151.3	14.2	19.90	1.6	28.4
1978	3115.2	5.3	157.5	15.0	21.10	1.6	23.9
1979	3192.4	2.5	142.6	16.4	22.70	1.5	27.8
1980	3187.1	− .2	107.8	13.9	22.81	1.5	42.1
1981	3248.8	1.9	113.6	13.6	22.67	1.5	61.3
1982	3166.0	− 2.5	86.9	9.2	20.95	1.5	89.0
1983	3279.1	3.6	131.4	10.6	20.02	1.5	110.0
1984	3489.9	6.4	156.9	12.5	18.68	1.5	107.0
1985	3585.2	2.7	169.4	10.1			114.0
1986	3676.5	2.5	172.0				
	Source: ERP	Source: ERP	Source: ERP	Source: ERP	Source: ERP	Source: ERP	Source: ERP

	Corporate Sector					Financial Sector	
	8	**9**	**10**	**11**	**12**	**13**	**14**
Years	**Inventories/ sales, US Bus**	**Mfg inventories/ Bus inventories**	**Profits top 500 corps/total US, %**	**Sales top 500 corps/total US, %**	**Assets top 500 corps/total US, %**	**Prime interest rate**	**Fedl Reserve's holdings of US govt securities B $**
1947	3.22	48.9					22.6
1948	3.35	48.6					
1949	3.09	47.0				2.00	
1950	3.41	47.0				2.07	
1951	3.40	51.0				2.56	23.8
1952	3.23	51.6				3.00	24.7
1953	3.18	52.5				3.17	25.9
1954	3.08	51.0	43.2	55.1		3.05	24.9
1955	3.14	51.0	44.6	57.9	54.6	3.16	24.8
1956	3.24	52.2	48.3	56.7	58.4	3.77	24.9
1957	3.18	51.3	49.0	58.8	60.8	4.20	24.2
1958	3.02	50.8	44.8	57.9	60.5	3.83	26.3
1959	3.03	50.4	43.1	58.4	60.8	4.48	26.6
1960	2.99	50.1	43.4	59.2	61.0	4.82	27.4
1961	2.87	50.4	42.1	58.7	73.3	4.50	28.9
1962	2.84	50.8	39.3	58.8	73.1	4.50	30.8
1963	2.78	50.2	39.7	59.4	72.4	4.50	33.6
1964	2.78	50.3	40.4	60.1	73.5	4.50	37.0
1965	2.70	50.1	39.7	60.6	74.9	4.54	40.8
1966	2.85	51.3	41.7	60.0	77.5	5.63	44.3
1967	2.88	51.6	41.6	67.1	82.1	5.61	49.1
1968	2.82	51.5	47.1	64.1	84.7	6.30	52.9
1969	2.91	51.5	51.7	64.0	84.8	7.96	57.2
1970	2.89	50.6	53.8	65.5	87.8	7.91	62.1
1971	2.82	48.2	47.5	67.0	85.0	5.72	70.2
1972	2.75	47.1	47.3	65.6	81.1	5.25	69.9
1973	2.97	47.4	60.3	65.6	79.6	8.03	78.5
1974	3.45	49.0	87.4	78.6	85.5	10.81	80.5
1975	3.11	48.8	56.7	81.2	88.1	7.86	89.8
1976	3.14	48.4	61.0	80.7	89.1	6.84	97.0
1977	3.10	47.2	51.7	81.8	88.1	6.83	102.8
1978	3.12	46.3	54.1	81.4	86.1	9.06	109.6
1979	3.24	47.3	69.8	83.0	85.2	12.67	117.5
1980	3.26	47.4	87.9	86.3	88.6	15.27	121.3
1981	3.25	46.7	78.8	82.7	90.4	18.87	131.0
1982	3.02	45.7	70.7	82.0	91.3	14.86	139.3
1983	2.87	44.6	50.4	79.8	86.9	10.79	151.9
1984	2.88	44.3	50.7	75.3	86.7	12.04	160.9
1985	2.73	43.0	36.8	77.5		9.93	181.3
1986	2.60	41.8	33.0			8.33	186.5
	Source: ERP	Source: ERP	Source: *Fortune,* ERP	Source: ib	Source: ib	Source: ERP	Source: FB

				Government Sector			
	Bank Failures[4]			**US Fedl Budget, B 1982 $[6]**			
	15	**16**	**17**	**18**	**19**	**20**	**21**
Years	**Number**	**Deposits held M $**	**US fedl govt spending B $[5]**	**Military**	**Net interest[7]**	**Transfers and social services[8]**	**Corp income taxes as % total fedl receipts**
1947	1.5	0.663	34.5	318.2	110.8	189.9	21.59
1948	1.5	0.663	29.8	278.0	123.7	187.2	23.39
1949	1.5	0.663	38.8	303.8	128.0	193.3	29.72
1950	1.5	0.663	42.6	311.1	139.0	203.5	28.69
1951	3.4	11.663	45.5	564.0	143.4	184.9	29.71
1952	3.4	11.663	67.7	1122.9	151.3	179.5	34.63
1953	3.4	11.663	76.1	1306.4	170.5	174.6	32.84
1954	3.4	11.663	70.9	1235.7	170.2	178.6	32.76
1955	3.4	11.663	68.4	1106.9	175.1	192.1	29.67
1956	3.8	8.214	70.6	1144.3	192.4	214.0	30.77
1957	3.8	8.214	76.6	1262.0	212.6	231.0	30.00
1958	3.8	8.214	82.4	1313.8	228.4	260.9	29.28
1959	3.8	8.214	92.1	1413.9	233.2	300.8	25.49
1960	3.8	8.214	92.2	1411.9	286.3	303.5	27.64
1961	5.6	19.773	97.7	1478.3	253.0	905.3	22.20
1962	5.6	19.773	106.8	1630.0	265.4	962.4	20.59
1963	5.6	19.773	111.3	1693.1	298.6	1086.2	20.25
1964	5.6	19.773	118.5	1763.1	322.7	1147.3	20.85
1965	5.6	19.7730	118.2	1675.7	350.1	1309.8	21.79
1966	2.5	8.842	134.5	1987.5	395.0	1536.0	22.98
1967	2.5	8.842	157.5	2515.9	451.9	1923.5	22.72
1968	2.5	8.842	178.1	3035.5	518.1	2299.4	18.65
1969	2.5	6.000	183.6	3233.0	628.5	2743.6	19.53
1970	1.0	15.000	195.6	3299.2	769.0	3602.7	16.94
1971	4.0	6.000	210.2	3365.9	870.3	4362.0	14.22
1972	2.0	57.000	230.7	3559.6	956.2	5286.2	15.42
1973	3.0	20.000	245.7	3689.8	1127.7	6336.8	15.57
1974	0.0	0.000	269.4	4200.2	1513.7	8446.3	14.58
1975	2.0	7.000	332.3	5073.2	1378.4	11120.4	14.55
1976	0.0	0.000	371.8	5655.0	1685.5	4455.9	13.89
1977	6.0	205.000	409.2	6544.3	2010.8	14923.4	15.44
1978	7.0	854.000	458.7	7544.5	2558.8	17548.4	15.00
1979	10.0	111.000	503.5	9144.5	3349.5	20988.3	14.18
1980	10.0	216.000	590.9	11483.4	4500.2	26754.4	12.43
1981	10.0	3826.000	678.2	14806.2	6461.0	33769.4	10.20
1982	42.0	9908.000	745.7	18530.8	8499.5	38868.0	7.97
1983	49.0	5459.000	808.3	21808.9	9327.5	44261.7	6.16
1984	80.0	2962.000	851.8	24537.9	11983.2	46617.2	8.54
1985	120.0	8059.000	946.3	28181.4	14431.5	52607.9	8.36
1986			989.8	31301.4	15568.5	55142.5	
	Source: SA	Source: SA	Source: ERP	Source: ERP	Source: ERP	Source: ERP	Source: ERP

	Government Sector			International Trade and Finance			
	22 Fedl surplus (+) or deficit (-) B 1982 $[9]	23 Fedl debt B 1982 $	24 Fedl debt/total debt nonfinancial sectors	25 Imports as % GNP	26 US direct investment abroad B 1982 $	27 Balance of payments on current account M $	28 % Fedl debt held by foreigners
Years							
1947	18.1	1163	63.38	3.7		8992	0.16
1948	50.0			4.2		2417	
1949	2.6			4.2		873	
1950	− 13.0			4.5		− 1,840	
1951	24.3	1034	51.10	4.3		884	
1952	− 5.9	1049	49.76	4.6		614	
1953	− 25.1	1063	48.44	4.9		− 1286	
1954	− 4.6	1060	47.16	4.8		219	
1955	− 11.0	1032	43.31	5.1		430	
1956	13.9	985	40.51	5.5		2730	
1957	11.7	945	38.48	5.7		4762	
1958	− 9.4	953	37.43	6.0		784	
1959	−42.1	957	43.22	6.3		− 1282	4.13
1960	1.0	940	41.01	6.1	103.2	2824	4.48
1961	− 10.6	950	39.51	6.0		3822	4.52
1962	− 22.3	953	37.87	6.4		3387	5.03
1963	− 14.8	957	36.12	6.2		4414	5.13
1964	− 17.9	969	34.58	6.2		6823	5.24
1965	− 4.1	951	32.44	6.5		5431	5.20
1966	− 10.6	942	31.17	6.9		3031	4.34
1967	− 24.0	960	30.38	7.1		2583	4.58
1968	− 66.8	950	29.10	7.8	172.4	611	3.99
1969	8.0	925	27.89	8.2	178.4	399	3.04
1970	− 6.7	927	27.59	8.6	186.2	2331	5.29
1971	− 51.8	955	27.46	8.8	194.1	− 1433	11.06
1972	− 50.3	966	26.42	9.4	202.8	− 5795	12.31
1973	− 30.1	949	24.87	10.0	216.8	7140	11.96
1974	− 11.3	912	23.89	9.8	204.1	1962	11.93
1975	− 89.7	972	25.68	8.9	209.4	18116	11.53
1976	− 116.8	1036	26.29	10.1	216.8	4207	11.95
1977	− 79.6	1068	25.67	10.7	222.6	− 14511	15.25
1978	− 82.0	1093	24.87	10.9	225.3	− 15427	17.46
1979	− 51.1	1075	23.76	11.1	239.1	− 991	14.72
1980	− 86.1	1085	23.86	10.4	251.3	1873	13.94
1981	− 83.9	1094	24.04	10.6	242.9	6339	13.28
1982	− 127.9	1197	25.68	10.6	221.5	− 9131	12.49
1983	− 200.0	1358	27.08	11.2	199.4	− 46604	11.79
1984	− 171.7	1541	27.95	13.0	197.4	− 106466	11.60
1985	− 190.4	1745	28.71	13.1	208.7	− 117677	11.03
1986	− 192.8			14.2			
	Source: ERP	Source: FB, ERP	Source: FB, ERP	Source: ERP	Source: ERP	Source: ERP	Source: FB

	International Trade and Finance	Exchange Rate of the $[10]		Employment, Unemployment, Underemployment			Civilian U Rates by Race and Sex
	29 Repatriated profits on US foreign investments M $	30 nominal	31 real [Mar 1973 = 100]	32 Civilian U rate	33 Ave duration (weeks) each spell of U[11]	34 % LF experiencing U	35 Whites
1947	1303.0						
1948	1553.0			3.8	8.6		3.5
1949	1615.0			5.9	10.0		5.6
1950	1839.0			5.3	12.1		4.9
1951	2154.0			3.3	9.7		3.1
1952	2120.0			3.0	8.4		2.8
1953	2215.0			2.9	8.0		2.7
1954	2555.0			5.5	11.8		5.0
1955	2817.0			4.4	13.0		3.9
1956	3100.0			4.1	11.3		3.6
1957	3263.0			4.3	10.5		3.8
1958	3287.0			6.8	13.9	17.9	6.1
1959	3586.0			5.5	14.4	15.3	4.8
1960	4616.0			5.5	12.8	17.2	4.9
1961	4998.0			6.7	15.6	18.4	6.0
1962	5619.0			5.5	14.7	18.2	4.9
1963	6157.0			5.7	14.0	16.7	5.0
1964	6823.0			5.2	13.3	16.2	4.6
1965	7436.0			4.5	11.8	14.1	4.1
1966	7526.0			3.8	10.4	13.0	3.3
1967	8021.0	120.0		3.8	8.7	12.9	3.4
1968	9368.0	122.1		3.6	8.4	12.4	3.2
1969	10912.0	122.4		3.5	7.8	12.5	3.1
1970	11746.0	121.1		4.9	8.6	15.3	4.5
1971	12706.0	117.8		5.9	11.3	16.3	5.4
1972	14764.0	109.1		5.6	12.0	15.5	5.0
1973	21808.0	99.1	98.8	4.9	10.0	14.3	4.3
1974	27587.0	101.4	99.2	5.6	9.8	17.9	5.0
1975	25351.0	98.5	93.9	8.5	14.2	20.2	7.8
1976	29286.0	105.6	97.3	7.7	15.8	19.1	7.0
1977	32587.0	103.3	93.1	7.1	14.3	17.9	6.2
1978	43465.0	92.4	84.2	6.1	11.9	15.9	5.2
1979	66700.0	88.1	83.2	5.8	10.8	15.8	5.1
1980	75936.0	87.4	84.8	7.1	11.9	18.1	6.3
1981	90056.0	102.9	100.8	7.6	13.7	19.5	6.7
1982		116.6	111.7	9.7	15.6	22.0	8.6
1983		125.3	117.3	9.6	20.0	19.6	8.4
1984		138.3	128.5	7.5	18.2	17.4	6.5
1985		143.2	132.0	7.2	15.6	16.7	6.2
1986		112.0	103.4	7.0	15.0		6.0
	Source: BS	Source: ERP	Source: ERP	Source: ERP	Source: HLS	Source: HLS, SA	Source: ETRP and MLR

Years	Civilian U Rates by Race and Sex			U Rates by Occupation [12]			
	36 Blacks	37 Women >=16	38 Men >=16	39 Professional, Technical	40 Sales, Clerical	41 Service workers	42 Crafts
1948	5.9	4.1	3.6				
1949	8.9	6.0	5.9				
1950	9.0	5.7	5.1				
1951	5.3	4.4	2.8				
1952	5.4	3.6	2.8				
1953	4.5	3.3	2.8				
1954	9.9	6.0	5.3				
1955	8.7	4.9	4.2				
1956	8.3	4.8	3.8				
1957	7.9	4.7	4.1				
1958	12.6	6.8	6.8	1.85	4.31	6.9	6.8
1959	10.7	5.9	5.2	1.15	3.73	6.1	5.3
1960	10.2	5.9	5.4	1.20	3.80	5.8	5.3
1961	12.4	7.2	6.4	1.48	4.69	7.2	6.3
1962	10.9	6.2	5.2	1.26	4.09	6.2	5.1
1963	10.8	6.5	5.2	1.30	4.09	6.1	4.8
1964	9.6	6.2	4.6	1.22	3.64	6.0	4.1
1965	8.1	5.5	4.0	1.02	3.33	5.3	3.6
1966	7.3	4.8	3.2	0.91	2.87	4.6	2.8
1967	7.4	5.2	3.1	0.89	3.13	4.5	2.5
1968	6.7	4.8	2.9	0.89	2.95	4.4	2.4
1969	6.4	4.7	2.8	0.91	2.97	4.2	2.2
1970	8.2	5.9	4.4	1.36	4.05	5.3	3.8
1971	9.9	6.9	5.3	1.86	4.67	6.3	4.8
1972	10.0	6.6	5.0	1.68	4.59	6.3	4.3
1973	8.9	6.0	4.2	1.46	4.06	5.8	3.7
1974	9.9	6.7	4.9	1.68	4.49	6.3	4.4
1975	13.9	9.3	7.9	2.48	6.39	8.6	8.3
1976	13.1	8.6	7.1	2.53	6.14	8.8	6.9
1977	13.1	8.2	6.3	2.34	5.74	8.2	5.7
1978	11.9	7.2	5.3	1.92	4.69	7.5	4.7
1979	11.3	6.8	5.1	1.83	4.49	7.2	4.5
1980	13.2	7.4	6.9	1.98	5.07	7.9	6.6
1981	15.6	7.9	7.4	2.24	5.42	8.9	7.5
1982	18.9	9.4	9.9	2.74	6.64	10.6	10.2
1983	19.5	9.2	9.9	2.68	5.44	9.6	8.4
1984	15.9	7.6	7.4	2.35	4.74	8.5	6.6
1985	15.1	7.4	7.0	2.12	4.36	8.9	7.2
1986	14.5	7.1	6.9	2.21	3.99	8.0	6.7
	Source: ib	Source: HLS, MLR, SA	Source: ib	Source: HLS, E&E	Source: ib	Source: ib	Source: ib

	U Rates by Occupation[12]			LF Participation Rates			
	43	44	45	46	47	48	49
Years	Operatives	Nonfarm laborers	Farmers, farmworkers	Layoffs /100 Employees	Civilian LF	Women	Married women husband present
1947				1.0	59350		
1948				1.3	60621	32.7	22.0
1949				2.4	61286	33.1	22.5
1950				1.1	62208	33.9	23.8
1951				1.2	62017	34.6	25.2
1952				1.1	62138	34.7	25.3
1953				1.3	63015	34.4	26.3
1954				1.9	63643	34.6	26.6
1955				1.2	65023	35.7	27.7
1956				1.5	66552	36.9	29.0
1957				1.7	66929	36.9	29.6
1958	11.0	15.1	3.2	2.3	67639	37.1	30.2
1959	7.6	12.6	2.6	1.6	68369	37.1	30.9
1960	8.0	12.6	2.7	2.4	69628	37.7	30.5
1961	9.6	14.7	2.8	2.2	70459	38.1	32.7
1962	7.5	12.5	2.3	2.0	70614	37.9	32.7
1963	7.5	12.4	3.0	1.8	71833	38.3	33.7
1964	6.6	10.8	3.1	1.7	73091	38.7	34.4
1965	5.5	8.6	2.6	1.4	74455	39.3	34.7
1966	4.4	7.4	2.2	1.2	75770	40.3	35.4
1967	5.0	7.6	2.3	1.4	77347	41.1	36.8
1968	4.5	7.2	2.1	1.2	78737	41.6	38.3
1969	4.4	6.7	1.9	1.2	80734	42.7	39.6
1970	7.1	9.5	2.6	1.8	82771	43.3	40.8
1971	8.3	10.8	2.6	1.6	84382	43.4	40.8
1972	7.0	10.3	2.7	1.1	87034	43.9	41.5
1973	5.7	8.5	2.6	0.9	89429	44.7	42.2
1974	7.5	10.1	2.6	1.5	91949	45.7	43.1
1975	13.2	15.6	3.6	2.1	93775	46.3	44.4
1976	10.1	13.7	4.5	1.3	96158	47.3	45.1
1977	8.9	12.1	4.7	1.1	99009	48.4	46.6
1978	7.5	10.8	3.9	0.9	102251	50.0	47.5
1979	7.8	10.9	3.9	1.1	104962	50.9	49.3
1980	11.4	14.6	4.6	1.7	106940	51.5	50.1
1981	11.4	14.7	5.3	1.6	108670	52.1	51.0
1982	16.2	18.5	6.5		110204	52.6	51.2
1983	11.9	15.8	12.0		111550	52.9	51.8
1984	10.3	15.3	11.8		113544	53.6	52.8
1985	9.9	12.8	9.4		115461	54.5	54.2
1986	9.7	13.7	9.1		117834	55.3	54.6
	Source: ib	Source: ib	Source: ib	Source: E&E	Source: ERP	Source: ERP	Source: HLS

Years	LF Participation Rates		The Price Level and Inflation				Productivity Output/ hour Nonfarm Bus
	50 Married women with children under 6	51 Women as % of N	52 GNP deflator	53 Consumer price index (CPI)	54 Energy price index	55 Rate of inflation (of CPI)	56 All Employees
1947		28.1	22.1	69.9		14.4	51.6
1948	10.8	28.5	23.6	72.1		7.8	53.1
1949	11.0	29.0	23.5	71.4		−1.0	54.3
1950	11.9	29.4	23.9	72.1		1.0	57.7
1951	14.0	30.3	25.1	77.8		7.9	59.6
1952	13.9	30.8	25.5	79.5		2.2	60.9
1953	15.5	30.6	25.9	80.1		0.8	62.3
1954	14.9	30.8	26.3	80.5		0.5	63.2
1955	16.2	31.4	27.2	80.2		−0.4	65.0
1956	15.9	32.0	28.1	81.4		1.5	64.9
1957	17.0	32.3	29.1	84.3	90.1	3.6	66.2
1958	18.2	32.7	29.7	86.6	90.3	2.7	67.9
1959	18.7	32.7	30.4	87.3	91.8	0.8	70.1
1960	18.6	33.3	30.9	88.7	94.2	1.6	70.9
1961	20.0	33.6	31.2	89.6	94.4	1.0	73.1
1962	21.3	33.8	31.9	90.6	94.7	1.1	75.5
1963	22.5	34.1	32.4	91.7	95.0	1.2	78.2
1964	22.7	34.4	32.9	92.9	94.6	1.3	81.3
1965	23.2	34.8	33.8	94.5	96.3	1.7	83.3
1966	24.2	35.6	35.0	97.2	97.8	2.9	85.1
1967	26.5	36.2	35.9	100.0	100.0	2.9	87.0
1968	27.6	36.6	37.7	104.2	101.5	4.2	89.3
1969	28.5	37.3	39.8	109.8	104.2	5.4	88.9
1970	30.3	37.7	42.0	116.3	107.0	5.9	89.1
1971	29.6	37.8	44.4	121.3	111.2	4.3	91.8
1972	30.1	38.0	46.5	125.3	114.3	3.3	94.7
1973	32.7	38.5	49.5	133.1	123.5	6.2	96.4
1974	34.4	38.9	54.0	147.7	159.7	11.0	94.3
1975	36.7	39.6	59.3	161.2	176.6	9.1	96.0
1976	37.5	40.1	63.1	170.5	189.3	5.8	98.5
1977	39.4	40.5	67.3	181.5	207.3	6.5	100.0
1978	41.7	41.2	72.2	195.4	220.4	7.7	100.8
1979	43.3	41.7	78.6	217.4	275.9	11.3	99.2
1980	45.1	42.4	85.7	246.8	361.1	13.5	98.8
1981	47.8	42.8	94.0	272.4	410.0	10.4	99.8
1982	48.7	43.5	100.0	289.1	416.1	6.1	99.2
1983	49.9	43.7	103.9	298.4	419.3	3.2	102.6
1984	51.8	43.7	107.9	311.1	423.6	4.3	104.3
1985	53.4	44.1	111.5	322.2	426.5	3.6	104.8
1986	53.8	44.4	114.5	328.4	370.3	1.9	105.5
	Source: HLS	Source: ERP	Source: ERP	Source: ERP	Source: ERP	Source: ERP	Source: ERP, BLS, BS, E&E, MLR, SCB

Productivity Output/hourNonfarm Bus

| Years | 57 Nonsupervisory employees | Output/hour Mfg | | Rate of Growth (C log) Nonfarm Bus | | Rate of Growth (C log) Mfg | |
		58 All employees	59 Production workers	60 All employees	61 Nonsupervisory employees	62 All employees	63 Production workers
1947	51.7	36.5	31.4				
1948	53.4	38.1	33.1	0.02866	0.03263	0.04330	0.05348
1949	55.3	39.5	35.0	0.02235	0.03539	0.03625	0.05517
1950	58.0	42.4	37.1	0.06073	0.04645	0.07097	0.05815
1951	59.2	42.5	37.4	0.03240	0.02146	0.00103	0.00808
1952	60.5	43.5	38.9	0.02158	0.02049	0.02500	0.03948
1953	62.0	45.1	40.4	0.02273	0.02538	0.03554	0.03935
1954	64.0	46.2	42.4	0.01434	0.03155	0.02430	0.04816
1955	65.3	49.3	44.9	0.02808	0.01974	0.06375	0.05606
1956	65.8	50.6	46.6	− 0.00154	0.00860	0.02615	0.03771
1957	67.4	51.9	48.7	0.01983	0.02382	0.02682	0.04472
1958	70.2	52.5	50.5	0.02536	0.04011	0.01163	0.03598
1959	71.7	55.5	52.7	0.03189	0.02121	0.05407	0.04269
1960	72.8	56.9	54.7	0.01135	0.01558	0.02511	0.03740
1961	75.3	58.5	57.0	0.03056	0.03376	0.02853	0.04035
1962	77.3	61.1	59.2	0.03230	0.02594	0.04276	0.03769
1963	79.5	64.0	62.2	0.03514	0.02777	0.04728	0.04965
1964	82.6	67.1	64.9	0.03888	0.03902	0.04627	0.04346
1965	84.2	70.4	67.6	0.02430	0.01827	0.04868	0.04045
1966	85.4	72.0	69.0	0.02138	0.01420	0.02192	0.02036
1967	87.2	73.6	71.7	0.02208	0.02135	0.02202	0.03801
1968	89.1	76.2	74.4	0.02609	0.02154	0.03576	0.03782
1969	88.4	78.2	76.6	− 0.00449	− 0.00770	0.02561	0.02828
1970	88.9	79.0	78.5	0.00225	0.00594	0.00934	0.02441
1971	91.9	83.2	82.4	0.02985	0.03270	0.05282	0.04921
1972	94.1	88.5	86.5	0.03110	0.02329	0.06081	0.04847
1973	95.8	91.1	88.7	0.01779	0.01825	0.02959	0.02473
1974	94.0	91.3	90.1	− 0.02203	− 0.01915	0.00162	0.01564
1975	96.2	90.9	92.2	0.01787	0.02276	− 0.00429	0.02331
1976	98.2	95.6	95.7	0.02571	0.02108	0.05020	0.03737
1977	100.0	100.0	100.0	0.01511	0.01817	0.04547	0.04370
1978	101.0	102.6	102.5	0.00797	0.01035	0.02584	0.02461
1979	99.5	104.5	104.9	− 0.01600	− 0.01581	0.01809	0.02281
1980	99.5	106.1	109.2	− 0.00404	0.00068	0.01534	0.04082
1981	100.5	108.8	112.8	0.01007	0.00974	0.02493	0.03226
1982	100.7	109.7	117.5	− 0.00603	0.00160	0.00862	0.04037
1983	104.1	118.1	124.9	0.03370	0.03381	0.07348	0.06176
1984	105.5	124.8	130.3	0.01643	0.01326	0.05525	0.04194
1985	105.4	128.8	135.8	0.00478	− 0.00135	0.03130	0.04142
1986		132.9	140.1	0.00666		0.03169	0.03137
	Source: ib	Source: ib	Source: ib	Source: ib	Source: ib	Source: ib	Source: ib

Years	Industrial accident rate[13]	Strikes			Income Distribution		Ave Gross Hourly Earnings, Private Non-farm	
	64	**65**	**66**	**67**	**68**	**69**	**70**
				Wages and salaries as % of national income	Spendable hourly earnings, nonsupervisory workers 1977 $[16]		
	Industrial accident rate[13]	Number of work stoppages[14]	Workers involved in strikes[15]			Current $	1977 $
1947	18.8	3693	2170	66.2		1.13	58.5
1948	17.2	3419	1960	64.2	2.83	1.22	58.9
1949	14.5	3606	3030	66.0	2.98	1.27	62.3
1950	14.7	4843	2410	64.8	3.07	1.33	64.0
1951	15.5	4737	2220	65.5	3.03	1.45	63.6
1952	14.3	5117	3540	67.3	3.07	1.52	65.5
1953	13.4	5091	2400	68.6	3.23	1.61	68.7
1954	11.9	3468	1530	68.4	3.30	1.65	70.5
1955	12.1	4320	2650	67.2	3.43	1.71	73.3
1956	12.0	3825	1900	68.7	3.55	1.80	75.9
1957	11.4	3673	1390	69.2	3.58	1.89	76.9
1958	11.4	3694	2060	69.3	3.60	1.95	78.0
1959	12.4	3708	1880	68.7	3.67	2.02	80.0
1960	12.0	3333	1320	69.8	3.72	2.09	81.4
1961	11.8	3367	1450	69.6	3.76	2.14	83.0
1962	11.9	3614	1230	69.2	3.85	2.22	85.0
1963	11.9	3362	941	69.1	3.87	2.28	86.3
1964	12.3	3655	1640	69.0	4.01	2.36	87.5
1965	12.8	3963	1550	68.3	4.14	2.46	89.0
1966	13.6	4405	1960	69.0	4.13	2.56	90.3
1967	14.0	4595	2870	70.2	4.18	2.68	92.2
1968	14.0	5045	2649	71.0	4.22	2.85	94.0
1969	14.8	5700	2481	72.5	4.22	3.04	95.0
1970	15.2	5716	3305	74.3	4.25	3.23	95.7
1971	15.5	5138	3280	73.4	4.37	3.45	98.3
1972	15.9	5010	1714	73.1	4.54	3.70	101.2
1973	17.0	5353	2251	72.4	4.48	3.94	101.1
1974	17.6	6074	2778	74.1	4.31	4.24	98.3
1975	17.0	5031	1746	73.6	4.26	4.53	97.6
1976	18.1	5648	2420	72.7	4.34	4.86	99.0
1977	19.3	5506	2040	72.7	4.43	5.25	100.0
1978	21.2	4230	1623	72.3	4.40	5.69	100.5
1979	22.3	4827	1727	72.8	4.26	6.16	97.4
1980	20.4	3885	1366	74.3	4.03	6.66	93.5
1981	19.2	2568	1081	74.0	3.93	7.25	92.6
1982	16.6	96	656	75.7	3.97	7.68	93.4
1983	16.2	81	909	74.3	4.03	8.02	94.9
1984	17.7	62	376	73.0	4.03	8.32	94.6
1985	17.3	54	324	73.5	3.92	8.57	94.1
1986		69	533	73.8		8.76	94.9
	Source: N&G, MLR	Source: HLS	Source: ib	Source: ERP	Source: BGW	Source: ERP	Source: ERP

Median Family Incomes by Race and by Marital and N Status

		All Married-couple Families				Unrelated Individuals	
	71	72	73	74	75	76	77
Years	All black families	All married-couple families	Wife in paid labor force	Wife not in paid labor force	All female-headed families	Males	Females
1947	1614.0	3109.0			2172.0	1349.0	792.0
1948	1768.0	3272.0			2064.0	1244.0	861.0
1949	1650.0	3195.0			2103.0	1437.0	856.0
1950	1869.0	3446.0			1922.0	1539.0	846.0
1951	2032.0	3837.0	4631.0	3634.0	2220.0	1909.0	917.0
1952	2338.0	4061.0	4900.0	3812.0	2235.0	2002.0	1019.0
1953	2461.0	4371.0	5405.0	4117.0	2455.0	2177.0	972.0
1954	2410.0	4333.0	5336.0	4051.0	2294.0	1696.0	966.0
1955	2549.0	4599.0	5622.0	4326.0	2471.0	1831.0	1054.0
1956	2628.0	4973.0	5957.0	4645.0	2754.0	1980.0	1160.0
1957	2764.0	5157.0	6141.0	4833.0	2763.0	2102.0	1264.0
1958	2711.0	5315.0	6214.0	4983.0	2741.0	2114.0	1268.0
1959	2917.0	5662.0	6705.0	5317.0	2764.0	2118.0	1318.0
1960	3233.0	5873.0	6900.0	5520.0	2968.0	2480.0	1377.0
1961	3191.0	6037.0	7188.0	5592.0	2993.0	2638.0	1407.0
1962	3330.0	6263.0	7461.0	5764.0	3131.0	2351.0	1461.0
1963	3465.0	6593.0	7789.0	6039.0	3211.0	2424.0	1476.0
1964	3839.0	6932.0	8170.0	6338.0	3458.0	2965.0	1555.0
1965	3994.0	7330.0	8633.0	6706.0	3535.0	3194.0	1767.0
1966	4691.0	7944.0	9279.0	7256.0	4074.0	3181.0	1908.0
1967	5094.0	8398.0	9917.0	7570.0	4269.0	3514.0	1917.0
1968	5590.0	9144.0	10686.0	8215.0	4477.0	4086.0	2239.0
1969	6190.0	10001.0	11629.0	8879.0	4822.0	4134.0	2397.0
1970	6279.0	10516.0	12276.0	9304.0	5093.0	4540.0	2483.0
1971	6440.0	10990.0	12853.0	9744.0	5114.0	4627.0	2688.0
1972	6864.0	11903.0	13897.0	10556.0	5342.0	5000.0	2858.0
1973	7269.0	13028.0	15237.0	11418.0	5797.0	5657.0	3300.0
1974	8006.0	13847.0	16461.0	12082.0	6413.0	5998.0	3493.0
1975	8779.0	14867.0	17237.0	12752.0	6844.0	6612.0	3978.0
1976*	9242.0	16203.0	18731.0	13931.0	7211.0	7217.0	4318.0
1977	9563.0	17616.0	20268.0	15063.0	7765.0	7831.0	4840.0
1978	10879.0	19300.0	22100.0	16200.0	8500.0	8900.0	5500.0
1979	11574.0	21500.0	25000.0	17800.0	9900.0	10200.0	6000.0
1980	12674.0	23141.0	26879.0	18972.0	10408.0	10939.0	6668.0
1981	13266.0	25065.0	29247.0	20325.0	10960.0	11848.0	7370.0
1982	13598.0	26019.0	30342.0	21299.0	11484.0	12470.0	8058.0
1983	14561.0	27286.0	32107.0	21890.0	11789.0	12888.0	8863.0
1984	15432.0	29612.0	34668.0	23582.0	12803.0	13566.0	9501.0
1985	16786.0						
	Source: HS, SA	Source: ERP, CPR, SA	Source: ib	Source: ib	Source: ib	Source: ERP, CPR, SA	Source: ib

	Income Distribution				Households Earning > $35,000 (1983 $) 1967 on [or Families > $35,711 (1983 $) before 1967]	
	78	**79**	**80**	**81**	**82**	**83**
Years	**% Persons below poverty level**	**% Blacks below poverty**	**% Hispanics below poverty**	**% Poor who are white**	**% All**[17]	**% Black**[18]
1951					4.6	0.5
1952					5.1	0.8
1953					6.3	1.1
1954					6.6	1.1
1955					7.2	0.9
1956					8.7	1.3
1957					8.2	1.2
1958					9.0	2.1
1959	22.4	55.1		72.15	10.8	2.1
1960	22.2			70.93	12.0	3.9
1961	21.9			70.38	13.1	4.3
1962	21.0			69.05	13.9	3.8
1963	19.5			69.27	15.1	4.3
1964	19.0			69.22	16.6	5.7
1965	17.3			67.79	18.0	5.9
1966	14.7	41.8		72.98	20.3	7.3
1967	14.2			68.36	17.0	5.9
1968	12.8			68.51	18.6	7.0
1969	12.1	32.2		69.29	20.0	7.5
1970	12.6	33.5		68.90	19.7	8.3
1971	12.5	32.5		69.56	19.6	7.5
1972	11.9	33.3		66.24	21.8	9.3
1973	11.1	31.4		65.91	22.6	9.5
1974	11.2	30.3		67.33	25.5	10.9
1975	12.3	31.3	26.9	68.73	23.8	10.6
1976	11.8	31.1	24.7	66.80	25.3	11.5
1977	11.6	31.3	22.4	66.40	25.9	11.6
1978	11.4	30.6	21.6	66.53	27.2	13.4
1979	11.7	31.0	21.8	65.90	26.8	12.7
1980	13.0	32.5	25.7	67.24	24.3	11.2
1981	14.0	34.2	26.5	67.92	23.3	10.1
1982	15.0	35.6	29.9	68.31	23.3	9.5
1983	15.2	35.7	28.0	67.99	24.3	11.1
1984	14.4	33.8	28.4	68.25		
1985	14.0	31.3	29.0	69.18		
	Source: CPR, SA	Source: ib	Source: ib	Source: ib	Source: CPR	Source: CPR

				Family Status			
	84 **% Women** **14 and** **over,** **never** **married**	**85** **% Women** **18 and** **over,** **never** **married**	**86** **% Women** **14 and** **over,** **married**	**87** **% Women** **18 and** **over,** **married**	**88** **% Women** **14 and** **over,** **divorced**	**89** **% Women** **18 and** **over,** **divorced**	**90** **% Families** **with 3** **or more** **children**
Years							
1950	19.6		66.1		2.2		14.1
1951	19.1		66.5		2.1		
1952	19.1		66.6		2.3		
1953	18.3		66.9		2.3		
1954	18.5		67.0		2.3		
1955	18.2		66.9		2.3		17.5
1956	18.2		66.7		2.4		
1957	18.6		66.6		2.3		19.1
1958	18.8		66.0		2.3		19.5
1959	18.7		66.3		2.4		20.0
1960	19.0	11.8	65.9	71.3	2.6	2.9	20.5
1961	19.4		65.3		2.8		20.8
1962	19.6		65.3		2.7		21.4
1963	20.0		64.9		2.8		22.2
1964	20.3		64.4		3.0		22.3
1965	20.7	12.4	63.7	70.5	3.1	3.3	21.9
1966	20.9		63.7		3.1		21.6
1967	20.9		63.2		3.2		21.3
1968	21.7		62.6		3.2		21.2
1969	21.8	13.5	62.3	68.9	3.3	3.7	20.7
1970		13.7		68.5		3.9	20.3
1971		14.1		68.1		4.0	19.7
1972		13.8		68.5		4.3	18.8
1973		13.9		68.1		4.5	17.6
1974	22.5	14.3	61.1	67.6	4.4	4.9	16.9
1975		11.0		66.7		5.3	16.2
1976		11.5		66.2		5.7	15.6
1977		12.2		65.3		6.2	14.7
1978		13.0		64.2		6.6	13.8
1979		13.6		63.5		6.6	13.0
1980		14.3		63.0		7.1	11.9
1981		14.8		62.4		7.6	11.5
1982		15.3		61.9		8.0	10.9
1983		16.0		61.4		7.9	10.6
1984		16.4		60.8		8.3	10.4
1985		16.4		60.4		8.7	10.2
	Source: SA	Source: ib	Source: ib	Source: ib	Source: ib	Source: ib	Source: ib

ABBREVIATIONS IN HEADINGS

Ave   average
B   billions
Bus   business
C   change from previous period
Corp corporations, corporate
Fedl federal
ib   *Ibid.*, same as previous column of data
LF   labor force
M   millions
Mfg   manufacturing
N   employment
O   output
Tr   trillions
U   unemployment
$ dollars
%   percent

NOTES

1. Profit rate is on stockholders' equity, mfg corps. The data series after 1973 is not strictly comparable with earlier data. The figure for the old series in the fourth quarter of 1973 was 13.4, for the new series 14.3.
2. This is current assets/current liabilities.
3. Rate is per 10,000 US corps.
4. The data for 1947–1969 are based on totals published for the periods 1947–50, 1951–55, 1956–60, 1961–65, 1966–68, which have been evenly divided among the respective years to give yearly estimates.
5. The figure for the transition quarter between 1976 and 1977 was $96.0 billion.
6. Price index used is GNP deflator.
7. Includes interest 1947–74, net interest 1974–86.
8. Includes education, veterans' benefits, health, labor and welfare. Income security included only from 1961 forward.
9. The figure for the transition quarter 1976–77 was -23.3
10. This is the multilateral trade-weighted value of the US dollar.
11. Since one person may have more than one spell of unemployment in any year, this understates the ave duration of unemployment experienced per person.
12. Data from 1983 on are not strictly comparable with earlier data.
13. Rate is lost-workday accidents per 500 full-time equivalent workers.
14. Data for 1982–86 only include strikes involving $> = 1000$ workers; in 1981 there were 145 such strikes.
15. Data for 1982–86 only include strikes involving $> = 1000$ workers; in 1981 there were 729 such strikers.
16. Hourly wage and/or salary income plus benefits (e.g., health insurance) minus personal income taxes and Social Security taxes.
17. The % all families over $35,722 (1983 $) in 1967 was 22.2.
18. The % black families over $35,722 (1983 $) in 1967 was 9.6.

ABBREVIATIONS AND SOURCES

BGW — Bowles, Samuel, Gordon, David, and Weisskopf, Thomas. 1982. A Continuous Series on 'Real Spendable Hourly Earnings.' New York: Economics Institute of the Center for Democratic Alternatives; and their unpublished data.

BLS — US Dept of Labor (DOL), Bureau of Labor Statistics (BLS). 1986. *Employment, Hours, and Earnings, United States, 1909–84,* Bulletin 1312–12. Washington, DC: US Government Printing Office (GPO).

BS — US Dept of Commerce (DOC). Various years. *Business Statistics.* Washington, DC: US GPO.

CPR — US DOC, Bureau of the Census (BOC). Various years. *Current Population Report.* Washington, DC: US GPO.

ERP — US Council of Economic Advisors. 1987. *Economic Report of the President.* Washington, DC: US GPO.

ETRP —US Office of the President. Various years. *Employment and Training Report of the President.* Washington, DC: US GPO.

E&E — US DOL, BLS. Various months. *Employment and Earnings.* Washington, DC: US GPO.

FB — US Federal Reserve Board. Various months. *Bulletin.* Washington, DC: US GPO.

HLS — US DOL, BLS. 1985. *Handbook of Labor Statistics.* Washington, DC: US GPO.

HS — US DOC, BOC. 1975. *Historical Statistics of the United States.* Washington, DC: US GPO.

MLR — US DOL, BLS. Various months. *Monthly Labor Review.* Washington, DC: US GPO.

N&G — Naples, Michele I. and Gordon, David M. 1981. The Industrial Accident Rate: Creating a Consistent Time Series. New York: Institute for Labor Education and Research.

SA — US DOC, BOC. Various years. *Statistical Abstract.* Washington, DC: US GPO.

SCB — US DOC, Bureau of Economic Analysis. Various months. *Survey of Current Business.* Washington, DC: GPO.

LIST OF CONTRIBUTORS

LIST OF CONTRIBUTORS

Robert A. Blecker is Assistant Professor of Economics at American University, Washington, D.C., where he teaches international economics and political economy. He received his B.A. at Yale and his Ph.D. at Stanford.

Samuel Bowles teaches economics at the University of Massachusetts, Amherst and with the Center for Popular Economics in Amherst, MA. Among many publications, he is co-author of *Beyond the Waste Land* and *Democracy and Capitalism*.

Robert Cherry is Associate Professor of Economics at Brooklyn College of the City University of New York. His main academic and political activities involve the struggle against discriminatory ideas and practices.

James Crotty is Professor of Economics at the University of Massachusetts, Amherst. His general interests are macroeconomics and Marxian theories of accumulation and crises. He is currently concerned with the role of financial markets in capitalist macrodynamics.

James Devine teaches economics at Loyola Marymount University, Los Angeles. His specialties are macroeconomics, labor economics, economic history, economic development, and political economy. He also does public speaking for progressive groups.

Christine D'Onofrio is a doctoral candidate at the New School for Social Research in New York and teaches urban economics.

Gerald Epstein is Assistant Professor of Economics at the University of Massachusetts, Amherst, specializing in domestic and international finance. He is also a staff economist for the Center for Popular Economics.

John Bellamy Foster teaches sociology and political economy at the University of Oregon. He is the author of *The Theory of Monopoly Capitalism* and co-editor (with Henryk Szlajfer) of *The Faltering Economy: The Problem of Accumulation Under Monopoly Capitalism*, both published by Monthly Review Press.

Andre Gunder Frank is Professor of Economics at the University of Amsterdam and the author of twenty books on the present world economic crisis, world system history, and Latin American development.

Mark Glick is Assistant Professor of Economics at the University of Utah with a specialty in Industrial Organization. He received his Ph.D. from the New School for Social Research.

David M. Gordon teaches economics in the Graduate Faculty of the New School for Social Research and directs the Center for Democratic Alternatives in New York City. Among many publications, he is co-author of *Beyond the Waste Land* and *Segmented Work, Divided Workers*.

Francis Green teaches economics at Leicester University (UK) and is co-author, with Bob Sutcliffe, of *The Profit System* (Penguin).

David Kotz is faculty member in the Economics Department at the University of Massachusetts at Amherst. He is also a staff economist at the Center for Popular Economics, Amherst, and writes a monthly economics column for *In These Times*. He works on macroeconomic theory and policy, industrial structure and economic concentration, and U.S. economic history.

Cigdem Kurdas teaches economics at New York University and the New School for Social Research. Her areas are the economics of growth and the history of economic thought.

David Laibman teaches economics at Brooklyn College of the City University of New York. He is also an editor of *Science and Society*.

Arthur MacEwan teaches economics at the University of Massachusetts — Boston. He is a member of the editorial collective of *Dollars & Sense* magazine.

Henry Martin is the pseudonym of the author who works in a large U.S. financial institution.

Thomas R. Michl teaches economics at Colgate University. He received his B.A. from Oberlin College, has been active in anti-war, anti-racism and trade union movements, and received his Ph.D. from the New School for Social Research.

John Miller teaches economics at Wheaton College and writes about the role of the state in economic crisis. He is a member of URPE and the *Dollars & Sense* collective.

Fred Moseley teaches economics at Colby College, Waterville, Maine. He is also the Book Review Editor of the *Review of Radical Political Economics*. His major field of research is Marxian crisis theory, especially empirical research related thereto.

Michele Naples is Assistant Professor of Economics and Women's Studies at Rutgers University. She has researched the postwar history of industrial conflict in the United States, and its empirical relationship to productivity growth. She has twiced served on the URPE steering committee.

Edward Nell is Professor of Economics in the Graduate Faculty of the New School for Social Research. His publications include *Rational Economic Man: Growth, Profits, and Property* and *Free Market Conservatism: A Critique of Theory and Practice*.

Cheryl Payer is the author of *The Debt Trap: The International Monetary Fund and the Third World* and *The World Bank: A Critical Analysis*. She holds a doctorate in political science from Harvard University and is preparing a book on the debt crisis.

Robert Pollin teaches economics at the University of California, Riverside. He specializes in money and banking, international trade, and macroeconomics. He is a member of the URPE national steering committee.

Juliet B. Schor is Assistant Professor of Economics at Harvard University, and Staff Economist at the Center for Popular Economics in Amherst, MA. She is also a researcher at the World Institute for Development Economics Research in Helsinki, Finland. She is co-author of the recently released *Tunnel Vision: Labor, the World Economy, and Central America*.

Anwar Shaikh teaches in the Graduate Faculty of the New School for Social Research. He is currently working on the Marxian theory of effective demand, growth, and cycles.

E. Ahmet Tonak teaches at Simon's Rock of Bard College, Great Barrington, MA. He has recently co-edited *Turkey in Transition: New Perspectives,* and is also currently working on profitability and taxation.

Thomas E. Weisskopf teaches economics at the University of Michigan. Among many publications, he is co-author of *Beyond the Waste Land* and co-editor of *The Capitalist System*.

John Willoughby teaches economics at American University, Washington, D.C. He has been a member of the URPE national steering committee and has served as an editorial board member of the *Review of Radical Political Economics*.

THE UNION FOR RADICAL POLITICAL ECONOMICS

The Union for Radical Political Economics (URPE) is an interdisciplinary association devoted to the study, development, and application of political economic analysis to social problems.

Founded in 1968, URPE has sought to present a continuing critique of the capitalist system and of all forms of exploitation and oppression while helping to construct a progressive social policy and create socialist alternatives.

Through its publications, conferences, informal study groups, and other projects, URPE provides a forum for education and debate in which divergent and often conflicting interpretations can be critically evaluated.

URPE's Members

URPE members, both in the United States and abroad, come from a wide range of academic disciplines, theoretical traditions, and political activities. We work and study in universities and other educational institutions, community organizations, trade unions, non-profit groups, and other progressive institutions. Many view URPE as a haven for careful, dispassionate, non-sectarian discussion of often charged or controversial theoretical and political issues.

Publications

URPE publishes an informal quarterly newsletter on its activities and the quarterly journal, *Review of Radical Political Economics (RRPE)*. The *RRPE* presents articles on radical political economic theory and applied analysis from a variety of theoretical traditions — including Marxism, institutionalism, post-Keynesianism, and feminism. Special issues of the *RRPE* have included five on women on the economy and single issues on energy, imperialism, regional economic development, and value theory.

Other educational materials published by URPE include *Reading Lists in the Radical Social Sciences,* jointly published with Monthly Review and MARHO and periodically updated; *U.S. Capitalism in Crisis,* and *Crisis in the Public Sector* (jointly with Monthly Review). URPE has also published a variety of shorter pamphlets for use in teaching and research.

Conferences

URPE holds two national conferences every year.

The summer conference is held at a low-cost camp and is intended to provide an informal setting in which URPE members and other interested friends and family can discuss academic and political work, join in organizational business, and socialize.

A second, more formal academic conference is held each winter as part of the annual meetings of the Allied Social Sciences Association, the umbrella gathering for professional economists, where we present critiques of mainstream economics and discuss radical alternatives.

Regional groups and special caucuses also occasionally sponsor other events, often in cooperation with allied groups. Some sample conference topics in recent years have been energy, the rise of the right, the political economy of the Third World, race and class, Rainbow Coalition politics in New York, and political economics for progressive journalists.

Other Activities

URPE members also occasionally organize around special academic and political interests or goals — working on conferences, through study groups, around curriculum development, or to develop special topics.

One important activity is the long-standing Women's Caucus, which publishes a newsletter for URPE women and those interested in Class and Gender studies.

The quarterly URPE newsletter provides information on various working groups and special activities within URPE and other similiar organizations.

How to Join

A new one-year membership with four-issue subscriptions to the *RRPE* and the URPE *Newsletter* as well as a discount on the summer conference is $20 (or $10 without the *RRPE*). We hope you'll complete and mail the attached form and join URPE today. For further information contact the URPE National Office at the address listed on the order form.

JOIN URPE:
Union For Radical Political Economics

Founded in 1968, URPE is an association of people devoted to the study, development, and application of radical political economics.

In our work we cooperate with other organizations and publish a journal — **THE REVIEW OF RADICAL POLITICAL ECONOMICS,** a **NEWS-LETTER,** and other educational materials. We hold forums for debate and discussion through our national and regional conferences. We also have active working groups for study and discussion, as well as an active women's caucus.

NEW MEMBERSHIP AND SUBSCRIPTION RATES

MEMBER and SUBSCRIBER [and NONMEMBER, please specify]

☐ $40 Membership and Subscription to RRPE [U.S. and Canada]; ☐ $45 Foreign
Members are entitled to the following:
- **Review of Radical Political Economics**
- **Newsletter**
- Voting Rights
- Be part of a national network — receive and communicate through URPE mailings.

NEW MEMBERS

☐ $20 for the first year

SUBSCRIBERS — NONMEMBERS

☐ $60 Libraries and Institutions [U.S. and Canada]; ☐ $65 Foreign

$40 PER MEMBER IS THE PROJECTED AVERAGE COST PER MEMBER TO RUN URPE'S ACTIVITIES.

We recognize that some members are unable to pay this much, but it does cost us this much per member to continue to operate. We ask that you pay as much as you can afford. The minimum rate for a low-income member is $25. We actively encourage those who can afford to pay more than $40 to do so since some other members must pay less.

CONTRIBUTOR

I wish to enclose a contribution of

☐ $5   ☐ $10   ☐ $25   ☐ $50   ☐ $100   ☐ More, if possible.

URPE is a nonprofit, tax exempt organization. Your donations are tax deductible.

Name _____

Address _____

City _____ State _____ Zip _____

Send to URPE, 122 West 27th St., 10th Floor, New York, New York 10001